Partisans and Progressives

Partisans and Progressives

*Private Interest and
Public Policy in Illinois, 1870-1922*

Thomas R. Pegram

University of Illinois Press
Urbana and Chicago

This book is printed on acid-free paper.

Library of Congress Cataloging-in-Publication Data

Pegram, Thomas R., 1955–
    Partisans and progressives : private interest and public policy in
Illinois, 1870–1922 / Thomas R. Pegram.
        p.   cm.
    Includes bibliographical references and index.
    ISBN 0-252-01847-8 (alk. paper)
    1. Pressure groups—Illinois—History.   2. Public interest—
Illinois—History.   3. Progressivism (United States politics)
4. Illinois—Politics and government—1865–1950.   5. Illinois—
Economic policy.   I. Title.
JK5774.5.P44   1992
322.4'3'09773—dc20   91-14298
                                                          CIP

Contents

Acknowledgments

I can never repay the financial, intellectual, and personal debts I have accumulated in the course of this project, but I can acknowledge them. An Irving and Rose Crown fellowship from Brandeis University sustained me in graduate school, provided travel funds, and lightened the burden of research. Librarians and archivists at the Illinois State Historical Library, the Illinois Historical Survey, the Illinois State Archives, the Chicago Historical Society, the State Historical Society of Wisconsin, the University of Chicago Library, the University of Illinois–Chicago Library, the Center for Research Libraries, the Boston Public Library, the State Library of Massachusetts, the Harvard University Libraries, the Ohio State University Libraries, and Brandeis University Library provided expert assistance, sometimes far beyond the call of duty. Michael Jackson of the Inter-Library Loan Office at Brandeis deserves special citation for his swift response to a mountain of loan requests. In Chicago, Felicia Sonn and Michael Baskin offered directions, warm hospitality, and the largest map of Illinois I have ever seen outside a government agency. Dean David Roswell of Loyola College generously provided material support in the concluding stages of this project.

Advisers, friends, and colleagues (and I suppose a few critics) read various portions of the manuscript and offered valuable advice. William Childs, Daniel A. Cohen, Daniel Dupre, Ruth Friedman, Wendy Gamber, Dallett Hemphill, John Hill, Mary Beth Klee, Tamara Miller, William Novak, David Sicilia, David Starr, and Susan Tanabaum read, listened to, or talked over sections of the manuscript. Craig H. Roell gave me the benefit of his willing ear, expert advice, and valued friendship as I worked to convert a dissertation into a book. Matthew Gallman provided a detailed critique of the entire manuscript that strengthened it in innumerable ways. Frank Freidel and James T. Kloppenberg expertly evaluated my argument, suggested ways to sharpen it, and generously furnished professional advice to a novice. Morton Keller brought remarkable patience and balanced judgment to his supervision of the dissertation on which this book is based. He teaches young scholars how to think as historians without controlling what they think as historians. Encouragement and sharp questions from two anonymous readers for the University of Illinois Press helped improve the final product. Richard Wentworth, Karen Hewitt, and Bruce Bethell of the University of Illinois Press did a superb job of crafting a book out of a manuscript. I thank each of these people for helping me and absolve them of any errors into which stubbornness drives me.

Portions of chapter 2 were originally published as "Public Health and Progressive Dairying in Illinois," *Agricultural History* 65 (Winter 1991). Portions of chapter 3 were originally published as "The Illinois Manufacturers' Association: A Case Study of Interest Group Politics in the Progressive Era," in *Transactions of the Illinois State Historical Society* (Springfield: Illinois State Historical Society, 1988). I thank the Agricultural History Society and the Illinois State Historical Society for permission to republish this material.

Finally, I would like to express my gratitude to those who share my life. Fellow graduate students, faculty, and staff in the History of American Civilization program at Brandeis University created a stimulating intellectual environment and personal network of support and friendship that I will always cherish. I had come to believe that no academic department could rival that atmosphere of hard work and good fellowship; then I arrived at Loyola College's history department. Chuck Cheape, Matt Gallman, Steve Hughes, Jack Breihan, Bill Donovan, Katherine Brennan, Nick Varga, and everyone else associated with Loyola's history program have made my first year on the job exciting and rewarding. My parents have supported my scholarly efforts far beyond the ties of family. Most of all, to my wife Patricia Ingram I gratefully offer love, devotion, and shared expectations for years to come.

Introduction

If you understand Illinois, you understand the nation.
—Senator Paul Simon, 1987

This book is not about progressivism so much as it is about the formation of public power in the Progressive Era and its influence on modern American politics and governance. It is intended as a contribution to the "new policy history" that is currently reconstructing and analyzing the legislative and organizational context of progressive political reform.[1] Although my lens is focused on a single state on the shadowy edge of modernity, neither local interest nor antiquarian curiosity has driven my labors. I believe that the essential nature of the modern American polity—the system that identifies and shapes public issues, allocates power, and transforms the private needs and desires of the population into public policy—is rooted in the experiences of the Progressive Era. The patterns that would come to define public life in twentieth-century America, especially its often tenuous link to reform aspirations, emerged with particular clarity in Illinois.

But this study also has something to say about progressives and progressivism. Progressivism was a complex and many-faceted phenomenon: a cultural milieu that sparked creative advances in the arts; a burst of innovative energy in the professions that transformed American education, philosophy, medicine, religion, and the social sciences; and a reform impulse combining the moral enthusiasm of American Protestantism with the social scientific techniques of investigation and expert analysis. My focus is on the political rather than the cultural or intellectual expression of these progressive themes. In the public realm, progressivism represented an optimistic attempt to master the altered conditions brought on by a half-century of unregulated expansion in American society. Progressive activists felt a responsibility to heal the ills associated with modernity, including unchecked industrial development and the ascending power of big business; the expansion of urban populations beyond the capacity of cities to house, employ, protect, and govern them; the arrival of new immigrants and the new structure of work that grew around them; and the venal system of politics that fed off disorder. Progressive political activists sought not only order but also harmony in a society that could overcome its differences and create a unified public life that would be both efficient and democratic.[2]

Whether inspired by the Social Gospel, informed by professional training and an environmental outlook, shocked by exposure to the material conditions of American life, or stung by awareness of their own marginality, progressive reformers declared their intention to translate ideas into action. Taking those intentions seriously, I have attempted to evaluate the influence of progressive concerns on the concrete political and bureaucratic institutions of a major industrial state. In a shrewd evaluation of progressive historiography, Daniel Rodgers suggests that more can be gained by careful investigation of "the world in which the progressives lived and the structure of social and political power shifting so rapidly over them" than by another tilt at the essence-of-progressivism windmill. The aim of this work is to assess the impact of an important progressive standard—that of the public interest—on those structures of power. Rodgers reminds us that most progressives were "users rather than shapers of ideas,"[3] so my attention here centers less on the construction of the notion of public interest and more on the ways in which Graham Taylor, Raymond Robins, Jane Addams, Charles Merriam, Ernst Freund, and like-minded associates in civic organizations, settlement work, and the professions attempted to make it the basis for practical politics. Their inability to do so exposes the self-interest and partisanship that many progressive activists could not shed and, more fundamentally, the formidable barriers that stand between ideas and their political realization.

Lastly, this study makes a case for the continuing importance of political organizations in the twentieth century. The best recent work in political history concludes that the early twentieth century marked the "end of the party period" in the United States. The continuing bureaucratization of power that accompanied the growth of government commissions, boards, and agencies stood in marked contrast to the relative loss of authority on the part of political parties. Simply put, as the state emerged, parties receded. Two measures reveal the decline of political parties. First, there were clear changes in electoral behavior. National voter turnout, which had run as high as 80 percent in the late nineteenth century, dipped below 70 percent in 1904, dropped below 60 percent in 1912, and never recovered. New ballot laws encouraged ticket splitting, while a more restrictive focus on education and advertising in political campaigns replaced the inclusive spectacle that had marked deeply partisan nineteenth-century elections. Political participation and party loyalty seemed less important to Americans in the twentieth century than they were to their predecessors in the nineteenth. Second, the cultural attachment to political parties that had been central to the self-identity of most Americans in the late nineteenth century weakened drastically. Instead of defining themselves in terms of parties, Americans increasingly turned to organized interest groups that directly bartered with government for goods and privileges, bypassing outdated party channels.[4]

It is clear that there was a critical change in voting behavior and popular attitudes toward political parties during the Progressive Era, but it is less clear that parties lost influence over public policy as the structure of modern American government took form.[5] As progressive reformers reshaped government administration so as to bypass the partisan concerns of politicians, new types of political organizations *within* political parties formed around officeholding leaders, usually mayors and governors. These powerful officeholders used streamlined electoral procedures and heightened executive authority to build loyal personal followings within the parties; they also used the new salience of public issues as a means to identify and appease powerful social or economic groups. The development of "partisan reform" retained the centrality of political concerns in the formation of American public policy and, together with the ad hoc scramble among competing interest groups that I term "marketplace pluralism," ensured that the public interest would remain an ideal of American statecraft, not a measure of reality.

◆

Progressive reformers at the turn of the century, confident in the unifying power of the public interest, took steps to create a system of government and public policy that would transcend barriers of locality, class, ethnicity, and self-interest and serve the deeper needs of the collective citizenry. They did not succeed. Twentieth-century American public life has been shaped not by a single design but rather by the accumulated settlement of endless conflicts between self-defined interest groups over such issues as public goods, services, privileges, and punishments. Some moderns argue that this system of pluralistic competition fosters diversity, guards against extremism, and, through endless complexity, approximates a national political consensus. Nevertheless, it seems increasingly clear that the contentious, fragmented character of the modern American polity inhibits thoroughgoing solutions to the problems of an advanced industrial society and fails to provide equal access to power and preferment. This study explores how the unifying, progressive conception of the public interest failed to take root in Illinois and the public-policy consequences of that failure.

No account of progressivism, public-policy formulation, or the changing nature of politics and government in the United States can safely ignore Illinois, the state at the center of the nation. Progressive innovations in politics and government appeared first and developed most fully at the municipal and state level. A rigid focus on Washington not only distorts the progression of political developments in the progressive period but also makes abstract a process that was quite real in the lives of many Americans. Breakneck industrial expansion, urban growth, and the paralyzing hold of party organizations on government—the motivating fears of progressive creativity—assumed especially menacing proportions in Illinois. Reformers of all stripes, from "new middle class" businessmen to social workers and radical teachers, organized in Illinois to create a more active and compassionate state. Nevertheless, Illinois, home to many of the most talented and dedicated progressives in the nation, failed to define or enact the public interest. The impact of organized interest groups, the persistence of local, ethnic, economic, and class loyalties, the strength and adaptability of political organizations, and the limitations of the progressives' own outlook in Illinois have much to teach us about the role of partisanship in American public life.

The Progressive Era saw the first extended, organized attempt to bring modern American government into line with the broadened expectations of its citizens. Because of the increasing fragmentation of identification and loyalty in American society (from party, nationality, and locality to a multitude of more narrowly defined interests that combined with the older, broader loyalties in a series of complex configurations), numerous and sometimes conflicting groups sought to mold politics, government, and social policy to fit their separate visions of American society. The recognition of this competition among differing interests lies behind recent assaults on the idea of a unified progressive movement.[6] But that there was a progressive *era*, during which thoughtful Americans took steps to control the problems of economic expansion, urban growth, and social dislocation, there can be no doubt.

The characteristic progressive standard of social utility was the public interest. In the following chapters I analyze the difficulties encountered in transferring progressive notions of the public interest into concrete public policy. The analysis is divided into three major sections: the progressive political agenda and the ways in which progressive-inspired regulation was reshaped by organized interest groups; institutional and democratic reform in Chicago; and progressive efforts to reform politics and sever the links between government and self-interested political leaders. Part 1 includes an analysis of progressive political ideals within the context of partisan public institutions, a history of the roots of agricultural organization in Illinois and its impact on public health concerns, and the story of how organized employers seized control of Illinois factory regulation from progressives and organized labor. Part 2 examines both the ethnic conflict that frustrated charter reform in Chicago and the city's failure to democratize or rationalize its public schools and streetcar system. Part 3 compares the progressive ideal of nonpartisan politics with the creation by Illinois governors of a new politics of executive leadership and partisan reform. Progressives developed administrative remedies to the abuses they saw in the political system, yet those efforts not only failed, they also damaged hopes for democracy and solidified the control of partisan leaders over the machinery of state.

Several important caveats are in order. Chief among them is one concerning the use of the term *progressive* in the context of this study. I have labeled as progressives those reformers who attempted to transform the partisan, selfish institutions of politics and government into compassionate, efficient agents of the public interest. Most of these men and women came from the professions, universities, settlement houses, churches, and urban reform organizations such as the City Club of Chicago or the Municipal Voters' League. They tended to cluster in the educated middle class. At times they formed alliances with working-class organizations or business groups, but they did not share the goals of either partner. Of course, these reformers were not the only progressives in Illinois, and their public actions did not represent the sole avenue of progressive ingenuity. Indeed, Illinois progressivism was most noted for the quality of its thought and social activity, not its political achievements. But my purpose is to find why the political actualization of progressive goals proved so elusive. Such standard topics of progressive historiography as the development of the Chicago school of philosophy and the full range of settlement house activities fall outside the scope of my inquiry, although both enterprises shared to some degree the peculiar progressive commitment to the practical application of the public interest. For my purposes, the activities of University of Chicago philosopher George Herbert Mead as president of the City Club, as an officer of the Chicago Bureau of Public Efficiency, and as a participant in the Chicago school controversies were more pivotal than his contributions to pragmatism. The struggle for women's suffrage and the purity crusade that produced the Chicago Vice Commission, both important elements of progressive concern in Illinois, make at best only incidental appearances in the pages that follow. Aside from brief passages, mention of black migration into Illinois and of issues concerning black citizens is absent as well. Each of these subjects has its able historians, but their exclusion should alert readers that this is by no means a comprehensive history of Illinois society between 1870 and 1922.[7] Rather, it is an examination of how public policy was molded by politics, clashing social groups, and the progressive devotion to the public interest. The foundations of modern American public life emerged from that mixture and deserve careful analysis.

PART ONE

Interest Groups and the Public Interest

The irresistible ground swell and tidal movement of the
present quarter century has been away from
individualism toward a new solidarity.

—Graham Taylor, 1913

1

Progressivism and Public Policy

As Sherlock Holmes remarked, sometimes the most curious incident involves not the dog that barked during the night but rather the dog that remained still. During the explosion of midwestern progressive political reform at the turn of the century, Illinois maintained a puzzling silence. In nearby Wisconsin progressive public policy triumphed through the collaboration of expertise and democracy. The celebrated Wisconsin Idea brought the resources of the University of Wisconsin to bear on the legislative agenda of Robert La Follette's political movement. Popular politics and expert guidance were bound together in the state legislature by a common devotion to the public interest, a "yardstick" created by reformers in the 1890s "that provided the thrust to Wisconsin progressivism as it united diverse groups against selfish and special interests in their communities."[1] Illinois reformers did not duplicate the achievements of their northern neighbors, however. A comprehensive survey of reform politics in the Midwest found Illinois "touched only lightly by progressivism."[2]

What is known of progressive politics implies that the opposite should have been the case. Illinois shared the historical antecedents of progressivism with Wisconsin: Granger agitation against railroads, distrust of corporations, and a venal political system dominated by the Republican party. By the 1890s Illinois appeared to be in the vanguard of a new reform consciousness. The Haymarket riot in 1886 and the Pullman strike in 1894 signaled a crisis in the relations between labor and capital, as well as between working-class frustration and middle-class opinion. Governor John Peter Altgeld's attempts to close the gap anticipated the urban liberalism of the Progressive Era. Altgeld's expansion of the University of Illinois and the opening of the University of Chicago, both in the 1890s, introduced academic professionals as a potent force in Illinois public life. After Jane Addams founded Hull House in 1889, Chicago became the center of a national settlement house movement that pioneered a new approach to democracy by integrating social, economic, and political reform. Under the inspiring leadership of Frances Willard, the Woman's Christian Temperance Union, headquartered in Evanston, linked the control of alcohol to a broad array of proposals intended to improve the lot of American women. Municipal reform organizations bent on civic improvement were alert and active in Illinois cities. By the measure of the late nineteenth century, Illinois surpassed Wisconsin—and much of the nation—in the peculiar intensity of its reform convictions.

If progressivism represented an attempt to confront and master the altered conditions of life in the twentieth century, then Illinois was perhaps its most exhilarating laboratory, for at the end of the nineteenth century the Prairie State contained within its borders the essence of the nation's past and the shadow of its future. A major producer of corn, hogs, and dairy products, Illinois also was commercially linked through its rail network and processing plants to western livestock and grain producers. Stretching from latitudes above New York City to below Richmond, Illinois was riven by the conflicting sectional loyalties of settlers from Kentucky and Tennessee to the south and the children of New England, Pennsylvania, and New York to the north. Nonetheless, in the 1890s Illinois was also becoming what its centennial historians called the industrial state: dotted with coal mines and factories; full of Germans and Swedes and growing fuller with Irish, Czechs, Poles, Italians, and blacks; and increasingly dominated by the polyglot city of Chicago, grown in fifty years' time from an insignificant town to the fourth largest city in the world.[3]

"If there is to-day anything living on the continent, it is Chicago," wrote an admiring journalist in 1910.[4] Its nearly 1,700,000 residents accounted for 35 percent of the state's population at the turn of the century. A decade later Chicago was home to almost 2,200,000. The extravagant was commonplace there, from its incongruous first-ward aldermen "Bathhouse John" Coughlin and Michael "Hinky Dink" Kenna to its stately skyscrapers watching over "breathless canyon streets" (the words of a perpetually awestruck long-term resident) clogged with monumental traffic jams. To observe the aspirations and the fears connected with industrial development, urban expansion, and immigration, one need only have come to Chicago; there dwelt eastern capital and western radicalism, prosperity and want, confidence and despair, tawdry corruption and civic virtue—the image of fallen or transfigured America.

Chicago became a magnet for those sharing the progressive outlook that ideas can take concrete shape. Louis Sullivan transcended marketplace demands for increased office space and created commercial buildings that were also monuments to the glory of the city. His onetime partner, Daniel Burnham, developed in his Chicago Plan an integrated system of parks and boulevards that gave coherence to the explosive expansion of the city. For another of Sullivan's associates, Frank Lloyd Wright, Chicago proved to be the inspirational classroom that helped shape his commitment to an organic architecture truly reflecting what he once called "Spirit America."[5] Chicago also attracted writers anxious to override the stale limitations of literary convention and turn art to the purposes of social investigation or political action. Theodore Dreiser explored life in the factories, boardrooms, and neighborhoods of Chicago to illustrate the dehumanizing consequences of an age built on anonymity and capital. Upton Sinclair prowled the stockyards in the hope that his fictionalized investigation would jolt Americans into recognizing the justice of socialism. *The Jungle* failed as a socialist tract, but, contrary to the expectations of its author, it shook public faith in the meat-packing industry and contributed to compensatory federal legislation aimed at easing the national dyspepsia. Sinclair unwillingly became the most celebrated representative of the new journalism of investigation and moral outrage to which Theodore Roosevelt gave the name *muckraking*.[6]

Surpassing the vitality of these artists, however, an extraordinary community of scholars and activists committed to the practical application of democratic ideals flourished in Chicago at the turn of the century. Its most profound intellectual spokesman was the philosopher and educational reformer John Dewey, who taught at the University of Chicago from 1893 to 1904. Dewey argued that truth can be discovered only through experience. Truth is a process, not a creed. Democracy, defined as a free system of inquiry and exploration within a shared communal purpose, reveals truth in concrete social relationships. In turn, the "social consciousness" and creative imagination vital to democracy depend on a new system of education that encourages children to think. Progress comes from an active participation in life.[7]

Dewey's relationship with Jane Addams and Hull House cemented the bond between ideals and activism. Dewey served on the Hull House board of trustees, modeled his laboratory school at the University of Chicago on the Hull House kindergarten, and named his youngest daughter after Jane Addams. For her part, Addams explained the purpose of Hull House in Deweyite terms. The settlement was "an attempt to express the meaning of life in terms of life itself, in forms of activity."[8] The establishment of the settlement on Halsted Street in the midst of Chicago's struggling Italian immigrant community was not an exercise in philanthropy to Addams, but an expression of "good citizenship." Hull House education programs, social evenings, and campaigns to improve neighborhood sanitation, eradicate sweated labor, and resist boss-dominated politics were part of "an effort to add the social function to democracy," that is, to restore the "social organism" that had "broken down through large districts of our great cities."[9]

Volunteers from Chicago's settlement houses, universities, and civic clubs followed the examples of Dewey and Addams. On the West Side, Chicago Theological Seminary professor Graham Taylor opened the Chicago Commons settlement in 1894. His protégé, capitalist and adventurer turned Congregationalist minister and "people's politician" Raymond Robins, moved from the Northwestern University settlement to municipal politics. In Packingtown, where Chicago's slaughterhouse workers lived beside the effluvia of their trade, Mary McDowell set up shop at the University of Chicago settlement in 1894 and embarked on a career devoted to the interests of working people. At Hull House, Florence Kelley, daughter of a protectionist Republican congressman, and Julia Lathrop worked to rescue children from the ravages of industrialism. Kelley and Margaret Dreier Robins, wife of Raymond, moved beyond Addams in their devotion to working-class concerns. University of Chicago professors spurned the ivory tower and entered public life: George Herbert Mead overcame his own extraordinarily diffident manner and acted forcefully to improve public education and working conditions in Chicago, Charles R. Henderson served on city and state investigatory commissions, Ernst Freund provided legal and constitutional expertise to a variety of causes, and Charles E. Merriam plunged headlong into reform politics on the Chicago Common Council, in races for the mayoralty, and as a leading figure in the Illinois Progressive party. Members of the City Club of Chicago, the Civic Federation, and other civic organizations entered public service; some of them, most notably Walter I. Fisher and Harold Ickes, achieved political prominence.[10]

The Power of Partisanship

If Illinois represented the direction in which the entire country was moving in the early twentieth century, if it was blessed with dedicated reformers, if its metropolis was a national center for the most advanced reform thinking, why did its reform effort fail to keep pace with Wisconsin's? What hampered the political success of progressive ideals in Illinois? What lessons do the Illinois experience hold for an understanding of progressivism? The answers to these questions can be found in the public side of progressivism in Illinois, the attempt to transfer private ideals into concrete public policy. Dewey's confidence in democracy rested on a sense of shared purpose, of community values originating in a system of education for citizenship. Progressive democracy was to be contingent on community. Mead recognized that "an authoritative public sentiment upon a public issue is very infrequent," yet "there cannot be self-government until there can be an intelligent will expressed in the community." Progressive activists were apostles of democratic ideals that, according to Mead, "we admit are not realized, but which *demand* realization."[11] In the absence of a unified community outlook, Illinois progressives seized the standard of the public interest as a means to rally and educate would-be citizens, but in the public world of politics and government, a rigid administrative structure and implacable sectional and ethnic tensions resisted public-spirited appeals. Unable to achieve democracy in public life, many progressives settled for efficiency. More and more, they counted on revised electoral procedures, increased executive authority and professional responsibility in government, and other administrative reforms to install the public interest as the guiding force of the Illinois polity.

Buoyant and vigorous in its intellectual expression, Illinois progressivism was muffled politically. Progressives grappled with Illinois politicians for the control of government, and the politicians won. Politicians learned to thrive on social diversity and to profit from the reorganization of government during the progressive years. Reformers working to construct an activist government devoted to the public interest cut themselves off from powerful voting blocs and came to trust the very mechanisms of government that the politicians had infiltrated. Even so, Illinois matched many of the political, social, and industrial reforms enacted in Wisconsin and other states. Still, progressivism faltered in Illinois on a more basic level: it could neither harmonize divergent social elements behind a common devotion to the "public interest" nor eliminate the influence of organized professional politicians over public affairs. Partisanship—economic, cultural, and geographic, as well as political—mixed with progressivism to shape public policy.

The inability of Illinois progressives to translate their ideal of a democratic community into political reality did not result from the inexperience or gullibility of reformers. Enormous obstacles stood between progressives and their goals. Appeals to citizenship and community made shallow imprints on neighborhoods such as those surrounding Hull House. "The streets are inexpressibly dirty," Jane Addams reported, "the number of schools inadequate, factory legislation unenforced, the street-lighting bad, the paving miserable and altogether lacking in the alleys and smaller streets, and the stables defy all laws of sanitation. Hundreds of houses are unconnected with the street sewer. The older and richer inhabitants seem anxious to move away as rapidly as they can afford it. They make room

for newly arrived immigrants who are densely ignorant of civic duties."
Existing social institutions did little to improve matters. "Our ward contains two hundred and fifty-five saloons," Addams continued. "There are
seven churches and two missions in the ward."[12]

Hull House attempts to gain better city services for the neighborhood
ran up against a sophisticated political machine. Between 1895 and 1898
settlement workers entered ward politics to eliminate the influence of
seventeenth-ward alderman John Powers. Powers, they complained, refused to pave the streets or collect the trash, resisted needed school
expansion, and connived with streetcar magnate Charles T. Yerkes to
extract maximum fares from the strapped working people of the neighborhood. Posters from the reform campaign depicted Powers as an ele-
gantly attired, champagne-sipping *bon vivant,* a marked contrast to the
Hull House candidate, an honest bricklayer who carried a dinner pail.

Powers drew on his resources as a powerful member of the city council
and Cook County Democratic committee, his understanding of the
people in his ward, and his prestige to quash the reformers and give Jane
Addams a lesson in politics that she never forgot. He doled out good city
jobs to buy off his reform opponents, including the bricklayer William
Gleeson. More importantly, he provided his constituents with personal
services that outshone the withheld city services. Powers secured jobs
as streetcar workers and telephone operators for ward residents; indeed,
2,600 of them, a third of ward voters, were on the city payroll. When
people got in trouble with the law he bailed them out of jail. He provided
food and free rail passes on holidays. He was on hand for weddings and
funerals and provided a friend in high places at a time when civil servants
and social workers were too often aloof and insensitive. Actions that re-
pelled reformers helped endear Powers to seventeenth-ward dwellers. He
blocked street repairs and thereby saved constituents from tax levies. He
stopped construction of a new public school but provided support and
charitable contributions for a neighborhood Catholic school. Most voters
did not despise Powers for his wealth and high living; on the contrary,
they expressed pride in a man who could "stand up with the best of
them."[13] "The alderman is really elected because he is a good friend and
neighbor," Jane Addams learned. "He is corrupt, of course, but he is not
elected because he is corrupt, but rather in spite of it."[14]

Powers's domination of the seventeenth ward was representative of
the feudal nature of municipal politics in Chicago. The city and Cook
County were not dominated by any one "boss" or unified machine.
The two political parties were splintered into numerous factions that
came together and split apart without ideological consistency. Beyond
the tightly controlled wards, power was decentralized. The mayor grew

stronger as the Progressive Era unfolded, but the executive was never sufficiently powerful to overcome the opposition of the Chicago Common Council. Shifting alliances between constantly feuding local power brokers, most of whom sat on the council, gave Chicago a deserved reputation as an ungovernable town.

If a political system based on personal service and decentralized authority within Chicago blunted progressive efforts to build a community fit for democracy, frosty relations between the Windy City and downstate Illinois created further barriers at the state level.[15] Rural Illinois, which still held the balance of power in the General Assembly at Springfield, utilized the resources of state government to deny Chicago the power to match its population. The state constitution placed limits on Chicago's ability to raise money or reorganize municipal government, and a variety of state overseers exercised authority over city parks, sewage facilities, and other public services.

At stake was the cultural and political future of Illinois. Chicago's size, ethnic composition, and history of industrial turmoil frightened the native Protestant farmers and small businessmen downstate. They read that German anarchists threw a bomb at Chicago police at Haymarket in 1886 and that striking Chicago workers blocked mail trains and brandished arms at federal troops in 1894; in disbelief they read that Governor Altgeld, a Chicago politician, pardoned the convicted anarchists and resisted President Grover Cleveland's use of troops against strikers. They knew that Chicago defied an Illinois law forbidding saloons to do business on Sunday, and they knew that the influence of Chicago's immigrant majority was the basis for that defiance. Unless Chicago was bridled by the state, its expanding population would soon give it the means to dictate law and social standards to the rest of Illinois. Consequently, downstate interests built a government structure that resisted change. Its foundations were partisan.

Illinois government at the turn of the century reflected a general American tendency to place public affairs in the custody of courts and political parties. On most important public questions in Illinois, the only authorities that really mattered were the Illinois Constitution of 1870 and the Republican party. The 1870 constitution restricted government activity, as did most state charters revised after the Civil War. Explicit in their numerous prohibitions, these documents "served more as codes than as charters."[16] Spurred by the General Assembly's concern with private acts to the exclusion of public legislation, Illinois's new constitution severely attenuated the range of government activity to prevent further abuses. Limitations on legislative authority were accompanied by a complicated amendment procedure that prevented wholesale revision of the docu-

ment. Restrictions written into the constitution, such as those that hamstrung Chicago, had to be unraveled strand by strand.

The power denied the legislature, cities, and executive administration
was exercised in Illinois by the Republican party. Following the Civil War
Illinois was essentially a one-party state. Democrats controlled the General Assembly for a total of only four years between 1880 and 1932, and
all but three governors between 1865 and 1932 were Republicans. Unre-
stricted by law and professionally organized, the Illinois GOP was better
equipped than state government to redress wrongs and furnish services to
citizens. As guardians and intrepreters of state constitutions, state judges
in much of the country possessed supreme authority over government
activity, but in Illinois the courts bolstered party rule. There the bench
was an elective office, and the courts became more an extension of party
organization than an independent force.[17]

Political reformers across the United States worked to break down the
rule of courts and parties. Beginning in the late nineteenth century, state
regulatory agencies expanded the realm of public responsibility as public
health and state charities boards, railroad commissions, and labor bureaus
cropped up around the country, with an especially high concentration in
the Midwest, mountainous West, and industrial Northeast. By the turn
of the century, according to some historians, a "new American state"
started to emerge. A wave of constitutional revisions reasserted governmental authority in the first two decades of the twentieth century. Progressive "state builders" constructed, on a national scale, effective bu-
reaucracies capable of wielding purposeful administrative power. Illinois
progressive activists, frustrated by administrative barriers to democratic
reform, joined the effort to expand public responsibility through governmental authority. Nonpartisan politics and governmental efficiency became increasingly important to Illinois reformers until a new state constitution was presented to the voters in 1922.[18]

Progressive ideals of harmonious community and responsible democracy lay behind the appeal of governmental efficiency. Citizens angered
by the degradation of working-class life and labor or frustrated by inadequate municipal services and corrupt city government blamed restrictive
courts and boss-dominated parties for the poor state of affairs. "Partisanship has become a real menace in the government of American cities,"
claimed settlement reformer Mary McDowell's 29th Ward Woman's Civic
League. "Republicanism cannot regenerate Chicago; neither can the
Democratic party save us. Partisanship with its many factions has not
raised the standard of the City Council personnel, but it has raised the
taxes, and given us inefficiency and waste."[19] Efforts to develop more
responsive institutions forced reformers to confront the barrier of the

1870 constitution. Unless Illinois government could be freed from its constitutional restraints, no unified and lasting solution to the problems stemming from urban and industrial expansion would be possible. Because the alternative was piecemeal reform that relied on the parties and the courts for its implementation, the creation of centralized, efficient state and municipal government became the *sine qua non* for progressive public policy in Illinois.

Thus, Illinois progressives were driven by necessity to advocate the restructuring of government. Time after time, voluntary reform committees from settlements, the City Club, or labor organizations would call on state or municipal government to respond to an intolerable situation, only to find government unwilling or unauthorized to act decisively. Reformers would then help sponsor advisory boards, regulatory commissions, or charter bodies that brought together private experts, contending interests, and government representatives to forge a workable compromise in the name of the public interest. Such mechanisms of incremental reform were vulnerable to political manipulation, however; only thorough revision of state and municipal administration could separate public service from partisan politics.

The concrete achievements resulting from this progressive public-policy activism fell short of the progressive ideal of democracy. Efficiency measures failed to dislodge the hold that courts and parties maintained on government, nor did structural reforms in the name of the public interest mold a unified community outlook.[20] In Illinois, the reform constitution of 1922 was stiffly rejected by the voters. The hard lesson of progressive-era Illinois was that "state building" on the basis of the public interest does not work. On the other hand, a state based on pluralism and the values of the free market must endure corruption, abuse of power, and deficient public services.[21] This dilemma requires an understanding of the impact interest groups made on the progressive public agenda, the difficulties encountered in reforming the city, and the triumph of politics and failure of administrative reform. But first it calls for a closer look at the progressive understanding of the public interest.

The Perils of the Public Interest

The focus on public interest was part of the progressives' attempt to assert control over a changed American economic and social environment. The categories of progressive concern were urban and industrial; its tools were expertise, organization, and compromise—ideals embodied in the government-sponsored industrial commission. Progressive innovations became necessary because the older governing institutions—courts and parties—were unable to solve problems generated by the careening expansion of the industrial economy and the cities that fueled it. The wave of state workmen's compensation acts after 1909 serves as a case in point. State courts and the common-law doctrines governing industrial accidents could not manage the "litigation crisis" brought on by rising on-the-job injuries, demands by organized labor for factory safety laws, and skyrocketing insurance rates. Erratic judgments by the courts convinced both business and labor that relying on the judicial process was the path of folly. Instead, in state after state, both sides participated in state-government-sponsored commissions to draw up workers' compensation laws that would protect workers and allow businesses to carry on their operations.[22]

A belief that the public interest required special advocates distinguished progressivism from an earlier outlook that presupposed a natural harmony of interests. The Illinois Industrial Commission of 1908 included not only union officials and business representatives but also Graham Taylor, a Congregational minister and director of the Chicago Commons settlement house. His seat on the commission represented neither of the interested parties, but rather the public. Between 1908 and 1917 Taylor participated in three such state commissions as a representative of the public interest.[23] "My life has swung like a pendulum, almost every twenty-four hours, between the privileged few and the struggling many," Taylor recalled in the twilight of his career, "between the crowded tenements of the day laborers and the homes and offices of captains of commerce; between industrial wage-earners and their employers; between trade unions and manufacturers' associations; between academic circles and the masses of the people; between the native-born and the foreign-born populations; and in politics and religion, between conservatives and progressives, reactionaries and radicals."[24] Somewhere between the extremes of interest and competition, Taylor believed, resides community, a higher good of social cooperation that he defined as the public interest. Thus, the role of the reformer should be to occupy that central ground and defend it from the disruptive force of conflict; "to restore the spirit and bond of neighborship is the need of the hour," Taylor wrote.[25] Jane Addams also was afflicted by a "passion of conciliation." It became the trademark of progressive political activism.[26]

Progressive stewardship of the public interest demanded not neutrality but positive action. Taylor's role as a reformer pursuing the public interest was indistinguishable from his role as a minister of the Gospel seeking the salvation of humankind. Organized Christianity provided the model for civil society. Taylor wrote in 1913 that the "function of the Church, the fulfillment of which is most essential to all social and civic organisations, is to generate that public spirit and self-sacrifice which serve the common interests at the cost of personal ease and gain, or of class and institutional aggrandisement."[27]

The settlement house and the industrial commission performed the same institutional function as did Taylor's ideal church: they identified tears in the social fabric that would expand if ignored and took care to knit them up. Taylor's relationship with Thomas Morgan, the leader of Chicago's working-class socialists, illustrates the ameliorative purpose of progressive institutions. As a young man in England, Morgan expressed his rage at class injustice through jarring but mute episodes of personal confrontation; he would stalk onto fashionable promenades and shoulder aside aristocratic strollers. Years later, on the free floor at Chicago Commons, Morgan regularly participated in public discussions intended to bridge the gap between antagonistic social philosophies, discussions that Taylor characterized as "settlement safety valves." Similar discussion groups flourished at Hull House and in the clubrooms of civic organizations.[28]

The notion of the public interest became a device through which progressives confronted the reality of social conflict while remaining loyal to an abstract notion of shared purpose, or "community." It also reflected the tension between the ideals of democracy and the practice of efficiency that beset progressives. American settlement workers found their commitment to "cooperative and consensual" social reform straining against "their corresponding conviction that the determination of what constituted the social good might best be made by experts: individuals specially prepared to undertake informed speculation on the course of public life." Even at Hull House, the assimilationist agenda of Jane Addams edged subtly but firmly away from the goals of her immigrant neighbors.[29] The public interest acted as an instrumentalist tool that allowed reformers and public officials to intervene in crippling social disputes when the irresponsible actions of the mighty or the downtrodden threatened social peace. Gross inequalities in private power—and the class identification they provoked—necessitated vigilance on the part of the public-spirited. Ernst Freund of the University of Chicago demanded that "those who have no direct interest either on the side of labor or on the side of capital should be willing to serve to mediate between the two parties so as to safeguard the interests of the great third party, the community."[30]

Nevertheless, the idea of the public interest also reflected the progressive belief in the underlying harmony of society. Social cooperation could be achieved only with effort, yet it remained the natural end of social organization. Progressives such as Taylor and Addams, who were motivated by a religious conception of community and service, and others such as Freund, who were drawn to reform by a desire for civil order, devotion to an abstract legal understanding of community interest, or a commitment to nonpartisan political reform, shared an essentially ideal conception of the public interest that attributed the values of the arche-typal citizen to the collective citizenry—the "community." The public interest, progressives seemed to say, demands justice, honesty, and effi-ciency in government, even when the public received specific reform pro-posals with indifference or hostility. "The only people who can stomach a pluralistic philosophy are those who in some way or another have grown strong enough to do without an absolute faith," wrote Walter Lipp-mann in 1914.[31] Despite their best efforts to break free from the formalist platitudes of nineteenth-century America, many Illinois progressives re-tained their faith in the unifying force of the public interest. Ironically, that faith caused them to exaggerate the efficacy of administrative re-form and prolonged the influence of political organizations over Illinois government.

◆

Tensions between private and public interest created one of the major barriers to the success of the progressive vision, for in the Progressive Era appeared a new political system geared toward the demands of organized interest groups. As the national transportation network developed in the late nineteenth century, the residents of self-contained "island commu-nities" were drawn out of their isolation into a denser web of relationships that challenged habitual notions of community and group identity. Quickening immigration, urban migration, and the emergence within the middle class of a careerist "culture of professionalism" contributed to a growing national consciousness of discrete, competitive interests in soci-ety. As the state became a permanent fixture in the everyday life of the new cosmopolitan order, interest-group demands for government assis-tance helped transform the dynamics of the political system. By the early twentieth century American politics had evolved from a system based on the distribution of goods and privileges to one based on regulation.[32] The political parties were the conduits and chief beneficiaries of the earlier, distributive politics. This politics of patronage appealed to broad constitu-encies and fostered loyalty to the parties. Industrial growth, partisan re-alignment, and the passing of the Civil War generation of party stalwarts introduced a new political system in which government acted as a broker between competing interests, thereby squeezing out the parties as the ma-jor link between citizens and the government. Progressive politics thus became a race for influence among "extra-party pressure groups of all sorts: manufacturers' organizations, labor lobbies, civic leagues, trade associations, women's clubs, professional associations, and issue-oriented lobbies, all trying directly to shape policy."[33]

Many progressives searched for an alternative to the corruption and waste of the party system, but an interest-group melee was not an attractive replacement. The progressive vision of social harmony, efficiency, and justice demanded a public sense of responsibility largely absent from the private goals of organized interests. Ideally, progressives expected government—municipal, state, and national—to promote the public interest and mediate between contending social factions, yet limitations in government authority, unresponsive officeholders, and the persuasive resources of organized private interests made it necessary to force the public interest on government. To that end, progressives not only organized private associations such as the National Consumers' League, the Women's Trade Union League, and the Chicago Civic Federation, they also lobbied for efficiency, justice, and social harmony. It was an ironic dilemma: the most effective way to promote the public interest was to mimic the pressure tactics of private associations and occasionally to ally with them. The mechanisms of interest-group lobbying—the sharply focused issue, intense publicity, and satisfaction with short-term gains—produced the kaleidoscopic pattern of shifting coalitions that characterized progressive reform.

A politics of reform built on choppy coalitions of private interests could not long sustain an outlook devoted to social harmony, efficiency, and the public good. Still less could it support a carefully wrought, systematic plan of reform intended to create a model society. How, then, were successful progressive political "movements" carried out on the state and municipal levels?

◆

The most thoughtful students of progressive politics identify the lowest common denominator of private interest—the unity all citizens shared as consumers and taxpayers—as the crucial feature in the creation of popular support for progressive campaigns. In Wisconsin this shared identity created a new notion of activist citizenship that allowed municipal reformers to translate their programs to the state level and maintain popular support for reform over a number of years.[34] There and elsewhere, however, it took shocking public revelations to galvanize citizens into united action. Across the United States examples of corporate arrogance and political malfeasance—what Richard L. McCormick calls the discovery that business corrupts politics—created a public mood and constituency for progressive reform. In the high rates and inefficient service of municipal traction companies corruptly allied with boodling city councils, in the startling tales of kickbacks and political favors in the heretofore respectable life insurance industry, and in case after case of an unholy alliance between those licensed to serve the public and those elected to govern it historians have found the intersection of private and public interest that gave the spark of life to progressive reform politics.[35]

Between the depression of 1893 and 1906, popular reform movements attacking corporations in league with corrupt political organizations appeared in every section of the country. During the hard times following the economic downturn of the 1890s, midwesterners rebelled against the power of the railroads and municipal utilities. Wisconsin citizens urgently reconsidered the relationship between utility companies and city governments after the depression spurred utility consolidations, price increases, and service cuts that struck at consumers. They found a moralizing champion in Robert La Follette, who refashioned his insurgency against the dominant faction of the state Republican party into a popular crusade to overthrow the state railroads, municipal utilities, and their political protectors. The depression transformed Detroit mayor Hazen Pingree from a conservative good-government Republican into a reformer determined to make the utility corporations servants and not masters of the people. In Ohio, Samuel Jones and Brand Whitlock took on the utilities in Toledo; Cleveland's Tom Johnson, who as a traction entrepreneur had scuffled with Pingree in Detroit, divested himself of his corporations and led a public fight against Mark Hanna for municipal ownership of utilities. In each instance these municipal campaigns widened into popular movements for statewide political reform. Pingree became governor of Michigan, and La Follette rose from governor to United States senator from Wisconsin.[36]

From 1903 until 1906, disquieting revelations by muckrakers of the inner workings of city politics, official investigations into fraud and corruption, and popular resentment of the influence railroads exercised over state governments launched political reform campaigns in the East, West, and South. After familiarizing himself with the process of urban government in America, Lincoln Steffens announced that he found business interests "buying boodlers in St. Louis, defending grafters in Minneapolis, originating corruption in Pittsburgh, sharing with bosses in Philadelphia, deploring reform in Chicago, and beating good government with corruption funds in New York."[37] Public outrage followed in the wake of each new disclosure. The 1905 Armstrong investigation of the great New York life insurance companies not only destroyed the trustworthy apolitical image of the industry and thrust commission chief counsel Charles Evans Hughes into the forefront of political reform in New York, it also spurred worried legislatures in several states to probe into the affairs of insurance companies, influenced twenty states to strengthen regulation of the industry, and prompted greater general attention to the political activities of corporations. Beginning in 1906, the spectacular San Francisco graft prosecution touched off a California rebellion against the political power of the Southern Pacific Railroad that led to the formation of the Lincoln-Roosevelt League and the rise of Hiram Johnson. Attacks on railroads and their Bourbon allies were decisive components of the southern variant of progressive political reform emerging in Alabama and Georgia.[38]

Citizens of Illinois were regularly reminded of the seamy union between business and politics. Illinois became a national symbol of retrogade politics from the 1890s through the end of the Progressive Era. The Chicago Common Council and the city's utility barons cheated each other and the public; charges of bribery and legislative logrolling concerning the Chicago streetcar system produced a chair-crashing fracas in the General Assembly worthy of an Old West saloon. Spurious and extravagant contracts handed out by municipal administrations and guardians of state institutions energized political organizations. William Lorimer, the "Blond Boss" of Chicago and the most powerful Republican in the state, protector of the packing houses and street railways, was expelled from the United States Senate in 1912 for bribing the electors in the Illinois General Assembly, and in 1921 it came to light that while serving as state treasurer three years earlier, Governor Len Small, a Lorimer confederate, had used state money under his care to fund a personal investment portfolio that netted him over one million dollars.

In each successive crisis, progressive reformers organized "citizens' movements" to restore honest government. Individual campaigns were capped with modest success, and reformers expressed confidence in the transforming power of the public interest. In 1903, midway through the Municipal Voters' League campaign to hound the peculating "gray wolves" off the Chicago city council, Lincoln Steffens pronounced Chicago "half free and fighting on."[39] "Out of the darkest hour of the night and under the shadow of Illinois' deepest shame," intoned Graham Taylor at the height of the Lorimer scandal, "the dawn of the brightest day and of the best order of things is already beginning to gild the future of Lincoln's state."[40] The luminous center of Taylor's confident vision was a civil service platform devised by a gathering of self-described "progressive conservatives" at the Peoria Conference, a clear sign that public-interest activism had begun to stray from the democratic ideal envisioned by Dewey and Jane Addams. Progressives began to believe that the soul of democracy would revive when the machinery of politics was repaired.

The progressives intended to transform government by making it responsive to the public interest, but their underlying belief that selfish political organizations and restrictive laws exaggerated social conflict caused them increasingly to put their confidence in administrative reforms: extended civil service, new electoral procedures, consolidation of state administrative functions under the governor, and a new constitution. On the one hand, such a reliance on procedural reforms assumed a social consensus that did not exist; on the other, it misjudged the deeply partisan nature of politics. When progressives attempted to implement a "nonpartisan" public policy they discovered it was impossible.[41] Chicago and the downstate region divided over social policy and political representation. Even the most cooperative public officials practiced "partisan reform," using popular reforms to build personal political organizations. Reform sentiment split between advocates of efficiency and of popular democratic control of policy. Private organized interests often shunned the counsel of disinterested progressives, and among reformers, the pull of partisan loyalties (especially Republican) were greater than expected.[42]

The rigidity of Illinois's constitutional structure, the durability of its political organizations, and the complexity of its organized interests foretold the fate of progressivism elsewhere. David Thelen finds that after 1913 consumer-taxpayer unions began to give way to a new orientation based on occupational "producer groups" and that this interest-group identification fueled a drive on many separate fronts for prosperity and efficiency. This occupational emphasis created divisions between the contending "producer groups" and transformed the original democratic impulse of insurgent progressivism into a campaign for expert control, thereby unleashing divisive ethnocultural loyalties that had been curbed by the consumer-taxpayer union.[43] Loyalty to particularist interests dissolved the public spirit of progressive reform.

The inability of progressive reformers to control the centrifugal tendencies of private interests entailed a great irony. As a new generation of realist social observers, progressives rejected the old orthodoxy of the community of interests and insisted on the necessity of recognizing clashing interests and acting to repair their disabling impact on government. "Men are bound together to-day by common interests far more than by living in the same place," declared Walter Lippmann in a blunt appraisal of the prevailing social order. "It is the union, the trade association, the grange, the club and the party that command allegiance rather than the county or the state."[44] Progressive public policy initiatives derived from the explicit understanding that traditional community bonds had been sundered and that only a new public activism could restore social tranquility.

The progressives faltered not because they misunderstood the social forces at work in the early twentieth century—for they understood them well—but because they largely failed to recognize their own place in the constellation of interests. Progressives tended to view themselves as immune from the pull of private advantage, as representatives of a greater social consciousness that could regulate partisan disputes without being stained by selfishness. Motivated to reform society by profound personal feelings of urgency or anger, progressives nevertheless portrayed their public-policy goals in terms of the public interest, the common good. Robert Crunden characterizes the progressive temperament as one of "innovative nostalgia."[45] This combination of iconoclastic originality and romantic attachment to the past formed the basis of the progressive notion of the public interest. Progressives discarded the nineteenth-century community of interests as an outmoded conception but retained in their hearts the hope that common citizenship could forge new bonds of community. Underneath the "scientific" language of the public interest, progressive politics were emotional, intensely personal, and laced with the dogmatism that faith imparts.

That picture contrasts with the image of a triumphant "new middle class" drawn by some historians of progressivism. In their view, the forces of industrialism that broke down traditional American identities based on locality, religion, and party allowed organized middle-class professionals and businesspeople to assert new values of efficiency, centralization of authority, and expertise as the guiding principles of national life. City planners, educational theorists, and social scientists valued order over community, stability over democracy. Businesspeople helped establish regulatory agencies to control dangerous competition and head off consumer demands for more stringent oversight. To a certain extent, these generalizations match the reality of progressive-era Illinois: "administrative progressives" on the Chicago Board of Education did favor rationality over democracy in running public schools; businesspeople in the Illinois Manufacturers' Association did try to control regulation when they failed to choke it off altogether. Nonetheless, the majority of Illinois progressives are not best understood as "new middle class" elitists.[46]

The organizational component of Illinois progressivism entailed more than a self-conscious attempt to deflect popular assaults on capitalism and its power structure. Professionals fitting the profile of the "new middle class" were genuinely dedicated to the improvement of social and political conditions in Illinois. Steven J. Diner has isolated a core group of 215 reformers in Chicago who utilized their expertise as lawyers, doctors, social workers, and university professors, as well as their social connections in reform organizations such as the City Club of Chicago, to press for better immigrant housing, pure milk for Chicago's children, protective labor legislation in Springfield, and administrative home rule for Chicago.[47]

One such reforming professional, University of Chicago political science and law professor Ernst Freund, was an unsung giant of progressivism. Himself an immigrant, Freund worked with the Immigrants Protective League, the Illinois Association for Labor Legislation, the Committee on Social Legislation, and the Short Ballot Association. Most importantly, he contributed his legal expertise as the state's principal consultant for labor legislation, untangling constitutional knots and explaining comparative labor law to reformers and elected officials. Freund also was much sought after as a legislative draftsman, serving both the Illinois Industrial Commission and the Chicago Charter Convention in that capacity.[48] "The way in which a law is framed," Freund noted, "may make the difference between success and failure, between hardship and injustice and beneficient operation."[49] Improving the lives of all citizens of Illinois, not simply securing themselves from turmoil, was the goal of the reforming "new professional class" in the Prairie State.

Many progressives, contrary to the image of the "new middle class," also refused to abandon the localistic, religious, and even political values by which they were raised. Old loyalties did not disappear in the organizational society but rather commingled with other bonds arrayed along economic or occupational lines. Walter Lippmann, a symbol of the progressive generation's willingness to march off in new directions, nevertheless retained from his Republican boyhood home "a subtle prejudice against Democrats that goes deeper than what we call political conviction."[50] Illinois reformers Jane Addams and Raymond Robins, an indefatigable battler for social and political reforms, shared with Graham Taylor a commitment "to fraternise the conditions of life and labour, to Christianise the framework and spirit of the community, and to humanise religion for the promotion of these ends."[51] Taylor and Robins pursued the Men and Religion Forward movement, a campaign to revive masculine Christianity, as diligently as they worked for improved factory safety or responsible political representation. "This word 'brotherhood' is really the key word of civilization," Robins confided to his wife.[52] Even Charles E. Merriam, the scholar in politics from the University of Chicago, grounded his political activism in the community verities he learned growing up in a small Iowa town.[53]

◆

Progressive sentiment in Illinois combined a belief in constructive intervention in the social process with a lingering commitment to the older American tradition of voluntarism. "Every thinking man nowadays admits that the state has a duty to interfere when it is a question of the

protection of women and children," declared Freund.[54] The "natural processes" of unregulated social and economic development led no longer to
social harmony, but to discord and strife. Dedicated reformers effectively
organized into voluntary associations could restore some sense of community to a broken society by isolating social ills and treating them by
cooperative action.[55] If women and children were exploited in unregulated sweatshops, then citizens should investigate working conditions and
force the state government to eradicate unwholesome work environ-
ments. If factory workers were endangered by unshielded machinery and
made to bear the medical expenses should they be injured on the job,
then reformers should push for government-sponsored investigative commissions to create safety legislation and establish a compensation system
agreeable to both capital and labor. If the previous thirty years of Illinois
labor strife, punctuated by explosions and gunfire at Chicago's Haymarket
and the use of federal troops to overwhelm the strike at Pullman, threatened to create a sullen, bitter laboring class permanently divorced from
middle-class sensibilities and hostile to middle-class society, then positive
steps to restore social stability were warranted—all in the name of the
public interest.

Effective interventionism required an active state, controlled by honest and efficient public officials. Progressive activists worked to eliminate
political organizations from influence over public policy, and to centralize
administrative power in municipal and state government. Centralized
governmental authority was not an end in itself to most Illinois reformers
but an effective instrument to counteract the evils of social dislocation
and irresponsible machine politics. Nevertheless, the active state in Illinois took the form of a partnership between public authority and private
interests, with private associations of citizens serving as the catalyst for
each successive reform.

The progressive invocation of the public interest was the ironic cen-
terpiece of unresolved tension in progressive-era Illinois. The reformer
saw a clear public—that is, community—interest in preventing class conflict, providing a more rational tax structure for Chicago, or even removing the scourge of saloon life from society. But the "new middle class" was
not itself united behind a particular reform agenda, nor was it the only
influence on public policy; historians increasingly recognize the participation of working-class and immigrant groups in progressive reforms.[56]
Powerful working-class and immigrant associations joined organized professional and business interests to influence the direction of public policy
in Illinois. The political organizations the reformers sought to uproot still
attracted widespread popular allegiance. With so many different viewpoints, the public interest became a highly subjective measure.

The protean quality of the public interest can be traced in the progressive-era career of the *Chicago Tribune*. According to one persuasive study, the large city dailies were instrumental in creating a "new politics" of urban reform in the late 1890s, a politics grounded in the detailed consideration of specific local issues (most notably that of city traction franchises) by reform groups supported with the force of united public opinion. Newspapers carried the messages of the reformers, educated the public in the intricacies of franchise law and city taxation, and, through constant repetition of these issues, helped create a broader civic consciousness among their readers. [57]

The *Tribune* did provide a detailed public record, but it was a poor judge of the popular mood and catered to the partisan concerns of its management and the moderate reform wing of the Illinois Republican party. In the 1890s, the *Tribune* hysterically denounced Governor John Peter Altgeld. Twenty years later, it led the effort to purge William Lorimer from control of the state GOP. Between these two incidents, the newspaper played the role of the arrogant corporation in an extended battle with the Chicago Board of Education over the *Tribune*'s profitable downtown leases on property owned by the city schools. Which stance reflected the public interest: the conservative assault on Altgeld, the good government attack against Lorimer, or the newspaper's defiance of the school board?

◆

The crosscutting loyalties that determined the shape of public policy in progressive-era Illinois were another dimension of the tension between stubbornly resistant patterns of localism and the force of more uniform centralized control that characterized American public life through the late nineteenth century. [58] During the Progressive Era efforts to resolve that tension took on a special urgency, as dedicated reformers worked to square their vision of the good society with the grimy realities of political, social, and economic life in the Prairie State. What follows is neither a comprehensive history of Illinois during the progressive period nor an exhaustive examination of the motivations, aspirations, and behavior of progressive reformers and their opponents. It is a study of the junction of progressivism and partisanship in Illinois public policy from the late nineteenth century to the final collapse of progressive administrative reform in 1922. During those years of challenge and resourcefulness, progressives and partisans carved out a path of public responsibility somewhere between the poles of drift and mastery. Most twentieth-century Americans passed down that road. The legacy of the Progressive Era for American public policy, as sketched out in the case of Illinois, is the discovery that neither democracy nor a rational consideration of the public interest directs the American state. The state, like the people it governs, is partisan and responds to the partisan expression of power.

"Why should not the state be the Efficiency Expert?" asked Charles McCarthy of Wisconsin in 1912.[59] In the absence of social cohesion, or without exceptional political leadership to organize a ruthless "reform machine" as La Follette did in Wisconsin, American democracy could not support such a disinterested monolith. Nor could democracy fulfill the hopes invested in it by Dewey and Addams. The progressive-era experience of industrial, heterogeneous, quarrelsome Illinois more closely approximated the reform struggles in twentieth-century America than did the Wisconsin success story.[60] What emerges as the basis of public policy is not harmony but dissonance. Illinois society was driven by a complex series of alliances and antagonisms between urban and rural interests, working-class organizations and employers, radical democratic reformers and good government efficiency enthusiasts, immigrants and native Protestant churchgoers, reformers and politicians. In that pluralistic scramble for influence, the competitive values of the marketplace overwhelmed the moral calculus of the public interest. Progressive-era Illinois was not silent after all; the reformers simply were drowned out by the tumultuous voices of the distinctive twentieth-century American polity.

2

Agricultural Organization and Progressive Reform

The transformation of the United States into an "organizational society" at the dawn of the twentieth century found its most arresting symbol in the metamorphosis of farmers from the disinherited outcasts of the Populist movement to the businesslike lobbyists of agricultural pressure groups that later coalesced into the powerful "farm bloc" of the 1920s. Historians intent on exploring the modernizing influences of industrial expansion and urban growth have relished the neatness of the farmers' conversion from anachronistically whiskered hayseeds hanging their battered hopes on an outdated "producer mentality" and the wreck of third-party politics into sharp-eyed traders committed to the nonpartisan market orientation of the American Farm Bureau Federation. It was, in the words of Richard Hofstadter, a transformation "from pathos to parity," as farmers discovered in the city markets that demanded their produce and drained off their excess population the economic abundance and political power that had eluded them during the "farmers' age."[1]

Nowhere was the bond between prosperous commercial agriculture and urban growth as obvious as in Illinois. Chicago was the greatest of the midwestern cities that provided machinery, transportation, and markets for the specialized agriculture of the prairies. In Illinois, as elsewhere, permanent, nonpartisan, market-oriented agricultural trade associations assumed positions of substantial influence after the turn of the century, and in 1916, with the creation of the Illinois Agricultural Association, Prairie State farmers profited from one of the first and most powerful of the umbrella agricultural associations affiliated with the American Farm Bureau Federation. The social and political context of these developments has not been brought into clear focus, however. The agricultural modernization thesis makes little attempt to analyze the impact of agricultural trade associations on progressive reform in general. Instead, supporters center their attention on the shared prosperity of city and countryside wrought by economic interdependence; detractors, on either the submersion of authentic rural democracy by the commercial demands of elite-dominated agricultural pressure groups or the destruction of a "preindustrial" rural way of life by urban reformers intent on lowering food prices.[2]

None of these drastic scenarios captures the public-policy consequences of agricultural organization. The development of progressive farming produced neither a triumph for science or democracy nor a shared vision of the public interest. Competition between the Illinois State Dairymen's Association and Chicago public-health authorities to regulate milk shows that the symbiotic economic relationship between modernizing agriculture and city markets did not foster a parallel comity of interests on the vital progressive concern of public health. On the other hand, the Dairymen's Association did not play the role of an organizational colossus crushing out the egalitarian spirit of small farmers. Instead, stubborn small dairymen resisted the association's attempts to improve the industry's sagging sanitary practices and then defeated its effort to force state regulation over them. Illinois's small farmers displayed less public spirit, and the large operators of the Dairymen's Association possessed less power, than historians have ascribed to them. Most importantly, conflicts among city health reformers, large dairymen, and small farmers denied consumers a guaranteed supply of clean, safe milk.

Understanding the relationship between progressive efforts in agriculture, small farmers, and urban public policy concerns requires examining the roots of agricultural organization. Recent scholarship exploring the depths of partisan loyalty in the late nineteenth century and the widespread dissatisfaction with the governing system of courts and parties casts a revealing light on the familiar outlines of the Granger agitation, the Alliance movement, and the Populist campaign in Illinois. Seen from this perspective, late nineteenth-century Illinois farmers acted much like their twentieth-century fellows. Reluctant to abandon their party loyalties, farmers relied on pressure tactics to redress their grievances against the railroads, tax inequities, and other financial burdens. Behind the imagery of producers battling monopolists, a rural hierarchy of substantial farmers in league with bankers, lawyers, and businesspeople interested in agricultural prosperity generated very effective agricultural pressure groups for brief periods.

The Farmer in Illinois Politics, 1870–1900

The independent political campaign was the residue rather than the basic stuff of the Illinois farmers' movements of the late nineteenth century.

Not yet able to sustain pressure with permanent trade associations, farmer organizations such as the Illinois State Farmers' Association (1873–77) hastily flared up around specific issues and quickly burned out thereafter. The absorption of farmer organizations into the Greenback and Populist parties was largely the work of professional third-party agitators who stirred the ashes of these organizations after the farmers ceased tending them. Farmer support for the Alliance political campaign and especially the Populist crusade was notably cool. The failure of the governing system of courts and parties represented by the Illinois Supreme Court's 1873 *McClean County* decision created the one major exception to organized agriculture's pattern of avoiding independent political gambits. In that case, a feeling of betrayal rather than independent political tendencies sparked the actions of the Farmers' Association. Significantly, the effective work of the association concluded with the onset of the independent electoral campaign.

Farmers seldom grouped together—as farmers—for political purposes in the late nineteenth century or during the progressive "age of organization." Melvyn Hammarberg's study of voting behavior in Indiana during the 1870s concludes that farmers were not a cohesive political group. Physical separation and social isolation bred in farmers a psychological individualism that set them apart from one another as much as from other social groups. Strong partisans of neither party, Indiana farmers failed to act as a bloc except under "highly pervasive" economic pressures that transcended the barriers of markets, crop specialization, and individual circumstances. On such occasions, Hammarberg concludes, "the farm community has responded to pervasive economic events en masse, with an explosive quality that has been unique among categories of voters—a response with great force but with little duration."[3]

The political activity of Illinois farmers in the late nineteenth century amply displayed this explosive but evanescent quality. The most thorough study of midwestern legislative politics notes that "policy fragmentation, rather than a coherent politics of agriculture, characterized midwestern farmers of the late nineteenth century."[4] Rural Illinois would not support a farmers' party or a single "farmers' lobby." Crop diversification in the latter half of the nineteenth century delivered most Prairie State farmers from the disastrous reliance on grain production that bankrupted and radicalized the northern Plains wheat producers. The more prosperous northern Illinois farmers either grew corn or raised cattle and produced dairy products on large farms; central Illinois farmers raised hogs, corn, and wheat; and in the southern part of the state farmers on smaller plots of land with less productive forest soil continued to rely on wheat and a small amount of fruit cultivation. Tenants operated nearly 40 percent of Illinois farms by 1900, but these were concentrated in the more prosperous northern and central regions of the state. Southern Illinois, particularly toward the end of the century, was the area of greatest agricultural distress and the most radical farm protest. This mixture of prosperous and struggling farmers, owner-operators and tenants, and different crops on soil of varying quality ensured that unified agrarian action in Illinois would be rare and short-lived.[5]

But certain types of economic distress—burdensome transportation costs, land taxes, or falling prices—that affected broad classes of Illinois farmers led the rural hierarchy of large farmers, country bankers, and town merchants to sponsor associations that focused agricultural concern onto specific legislative proposals. If neither the courts nor the dominant parties provided relief, rural notables might use their influence and the farmers' numbers to force constructive action out of the General Assembly. Based on an immediate demand for action, these coalition pressure organizations possessed impressive drawing power but little staying power.

The Granger Movement

The Illinois Granger movement of the early 1870s, inappropriately named for the politically timid Patrons of Husbandry, capped ten years of agrarian agitation for railroad regulation.[6] Growing faster than the free market could control them, railroads represented the power of an unchecked monopoly to farmers whose attempts to market their crops suffered from rate discrimination that favored commercial centers over rural spur lines. Nonetheless, the "Granger laws" that introduced state regulation of railroad shipping charges were not the fruits of mass farmer protest so much as the products of a coalition of forces, including the rural hierarchy, intent on amending the rule of courts and parties. The Illinois State Farmers' Association, an agricultural pressure group, steered by a respected corps of prominent farmers, received the support of the regulatory coalition for a time and thereby exerted influence at Springfield.

Rural agitation began on the local level. Frustrated groups of farmers, unable to accept the disparity between long-haul and short-haul shipping rates and the profits of intermediaries handling their goods, gathered in farmers' clubs throughout Illinois in the late 1860s to discuss the railroad issue. These clubs were patterned after the organization of the Grange, even though the Grange itself forbade political discussions at its local meetings.[7]

Substantial farmers quickly stepped in to add the controlling hand of organization to this grassroots agitation. Henry C. Wheeler, a prominent Du Page County farmer, called for a Producers' Convention that would allow "the farmers of the great North-west [to] concentrate their efforts, power, and means, as the great transportation companies have done theirs, and accomplish something, instead of frittering away their efforts in doing nothing."[8] The convention, which met in Bloomington during April 1870, attracted "a considerable number of leading Illinois farmers" and drew a sympathetic statement from Illinois Governor John M. Palmer.[9] Concern over farmers' expenses and the unchecked strength of the railroads led the convention to endorse the need for "an efficient organization on the well-known principles that give the great corporations such tremendous power."[10] Milling crowds of farmers and the harsh antimonopoly spirit of the convention should not shroud the fact that this was a gathering of prosperous agriculturalists who resolved not to outlaw but rather to mimic the political tactics of their industrial nemesis. Amid the inflamed passions of the antimonopoly campaign rural notables displayed the roots of an organizational sensibility that the agricultural associations of the more sedate Progressive Era supposedly acquired from secure markets and a more sophisticated understanding of politics.

◆

But in 1870 Illinois farmers were not the primary actors in the drama surrounding railroad regulation. Other interests across the state— especially shippers and the Chicago Board of Trade—were also enmeshed in the transportation question. The issue of railroad regulation received its most important treatment not at the Producers' Convention but at the Illinois Constitutional Convention of 1869–70, a conclave of lawyers (fifty-six of the eighty-five delegates) at which the agricultural lobby did not display a powerful presence. Reuben Benjamin of Bloomington, a future ally of the farmers' movement, persuaded his fellow delegates on legal grounds that the legislature possessed the right to regulate railroad rates. In fact, both railroad and warehouse charges came under state regulation, but the Chicago Board of Trade influenced the warehouse provisions far more than farm groups affected the railroad article.[11]

Armed with this constitutional *imprimatur*, the 1871 General Assembly passed laws preventing railroads from discriminating against short freight hauls in favor of longer hauls, establishing maximum rate schedules for passenger travel on various lines, and creating a three-member state Railroad and Warehouse Commission to oversee the new laws. The 1871 session also witnessed the formation of the Legislative Farmers' Club, which was composed of sixty-five members of the General Assembly from both parties. The club's purposes were to discuss agricultural topics and support legislation beneficial to farmers. Some House members accused the Legislative Farmers' Club of joining Senator Allen Fuller in an attempt to force more stringent passenger and freight rate bills through the House, but Fuller apparently failed to build any formal alliance with the club. Members from some western and southern Illinois counties desired further railroad construction in their localities and opposed uniform passenger rates that would hinder the extension of smaller lines. Fuller and the advocates of strong uniform regulation concentrated their efforts on breaking the power of the large trunk lines. The resulting friction between the weak-road and strong-road forces most likely prevented the club from taking a firm stand on either side of the matter, and so the legislative club devoted to the interests of Illinois farmers played no significant role in the resolution of the single most dominant agricultural concern of the period.[12]

◆

To this point, the organized activity of farmers had been neither decisive nor even especially significant in the development of state railroad regulation, but the situation changed dramatically in 1872–73. As several test cases of the 1871 railroad laws made their way through the Illinois courts in 1872, impatient farmers took it on themselves to determine the degree of railroad compliance with the maximum passenger fare law. Rustic passengers tendered the newly authorized but contested fare and then resisted the attempts of railroad personnel to eject them from the train; on one unpleasant occasion, farmers defended their seats by producing guns and knives.[13]

Before local militants got out of hand, the rural hierarchy channeled angry sentiment into an effective agricultural pressure group. Encouraged by the secretary of the State Board of Agriculture, delegates from the various farmers' clubs in Illinois met in October of 1872 at Kewanee to consolidate the growing farmers' movement. The meeting created a structure of committees to serve as a foundation for further organization and at least partially assuaged the animosity between the Patrons of Husbandry and the competing independent clubs by welcoming local Granges into the movement. In mid-January 1873 the consolidation movement came to fruition with the formation of the Illinois State Farmers' Association at a convention of agrarian clubs in Bloomington. The opening address advised the 800 delegates that "this is an age and an era of organization," in which "nearly every profession, calling, and pursuit, except our own, associate, organize, and combine to promote their interests."[14] Convention speakers denounced the judicial conservatism that hampered railroad regulation in Illinois and called on farmers to assert their power to curb the transportation monopolies. The new Farmers' Association demanded strict enforcement of the 1871 railroad laws and the inclusion of a representative farmer satisfactory to the organization on the Railroad and Warehouse Commission and pledged "that the power of this, and all local organizations, should be wielded at the ballot-box by the election to all offices . . . of such . . . persons as sympathize with us in this movement."[15]

Prominent, respected leaders and broad public support characterized the Farmers' Association at its founding. Association president Willard C. Flagg owned an 11,000-acre farm in Alton, had served as secretary of the State Horticultural Society for nine years, was a leading figure in the state movement for agricultural education, and pursued a political career that included terms as a member of the Republican State Central Committee, an eight-year stint as U.S. collector for the Twelfth Illinois District, and membership in the state Senate from 1869 to 1872. Temporary chairman of the Bloomington Convention L. D. Whiting also was a state senator and sat in the 1870 constitutional convention. S. T. K. Prime, a noted agricultural expert and officer at the Bloomington Convention, was still buying land from bankrupts, improving it, and renting it out to farm tenants twenty years later. Prominent attorneys Reuben Benjamin, late of the constitutional convention, and J. H. Rowell, who with Benjamin was a volunteer counsel in the *McClean County* test case, spoke before the convention. Other notable Farmers' Association personalities included the brothers of Illinois Supreme Court chief justice Charles Lawrence and of the poet William Cullen Bryant. This was a movement of prosperous farmers, a reality punctuated by the convention's refusal to include mechanics in the name (and presumably the ranks) of the association.[16]

Strong popular support for effective railroad regulation widened the influence of the Farmers' Association. Favorable coverage from the *Chicago Tribune* and other newspapers arrayed public opinion behind the farmers' movement. Commercial groups also provided encouragement. As the *Tribune* put it, in Bloomington the Wholesale Dealers' Association and the area's "ablest lawyers and most influential business men . . . expressed their determination to go hand in hand with the farmers."[17] As county farmer meetings across the state gathered to endorse the proposals of the Bloomington Convention, observant state legislators followed the example of Will County assemblyman Amos Savage by attending these local meetings and adding their voices to the call for further legislative action to restrain the railroads. A vibrant public issue, respected leadership, and influential backing rapidly established the Illinois State Farmers' Association as a forceful pressure group.[18]

The organized farmers' movement had an immediate impact on the 1873 legislative session. Attorneys Rowell and Benjamin had been appointed by the Bloomington Convention to lobby for legislation against those railroads that ignored the 1871 statutes, but after the Illinois Supreme Court struck down the Railroad Act of 1871 in February, the Farmers' Association decided on more direct action. On April 2 another great convention gathered in Springfield to impress the General Assembly with its resolve. This time both Governor John L. Beveridge and former governor Palmer addressed the association and seconded its call for strengthened railroad regulation. "Members of the Legislature are becoming exceedingly sensitive to the sentiment against the railroads which inspires the farmers," observed the *Tribune's* correspondent. "They are seen in conference with delegates at all places, and at all opportunities. They hang on the skirts of preliminary meetings." [19] Together with a rejuvenated Legislative Farmers' Club, the Farmers' Association helped push through an act giving the Railroad and Warehouse Commission the authority to set maximum fares and rates, thereby satisfying the objection of the courts, and forced Beveridge to withdraw his three candidates for the commission and replace them with men acceptable to the association. [20]

◆

But success at the 1873 legislative session hid the limitations of the Farmers' Association lobby and masked powerful divisions within the farmers' movement that would ultimately prove fatal. The rural hierarchy could not long sustain a pressure group catering to the needs of all Illinois farmers. The more radical agrarian spokesmen and the Legislative Farmers' Club opposed the commission bill that became law in 1873. Other legislation backed by the association did not pass at all (the anti-railroad-pass bill demanded by the farmers did not become law in Illinois until 1913). Far more significantly, the state supreme court decision in the *McClean County* case signaled the failure of legislative pressure tactics in a political system dominated, in the view of the grassroots constituency of the Farmers' Association, by the caprice of the courts. The decision induced angry farmers to shrug off the restraining hold of the rural hierarchy and pursue their own brief independent political campaign to reform the courts. [21]

Chief Justice Charles Lawrence's *McClean County* decision was a ringing endorsement of judicial primacy over the legislature. The Railroad Act of 1871 constituted a bid by the General Assembly to use the police power as a tool to establish a politically determined notion of justice—in this case, to restrain Illinois railroads from practicing rate discrimination against local communities. Justice Lawrence recognized the legislature's authority under the common law to prevent unjust discrimination, but he refused to permit the General Assembly, by means of the police power, to determine whether railroad discrimination was just or unjust. Under the 1870 constitution, that authority was reserved to the courts, and the railroad act was therefore unconstitutional. Thus, although Lawrence agreed that railroad regulation was permissible under the common law, legislative initiative in regulation took a back seat to the court's determination of reasonableness. [22]

Unwilling to accept government by the courts, grassroots farmer meetings broke away from their commercial allies. District and supreme court judges in Illinois were elected by popular ballot, and shortly after the *McClean County* decision angry farmers in the Fifth Judicial District banded together to oppose the reelection bid of Chief Justice Lawrence. A March 21, 1873, meeting at Princeton in Bureau County resolved "to secure the selection of a candidate who should reflect the sentiments of the people." [23] Ten days later a farmers' convention nominated Alfred M. Craig for the contested seat and managed to elect him in June, despite great support for Lawrence among lawyers and in the press. Another farmer candidate was nominated for the supreme court in the Second District, and almost a third of the circuit court races included farmer candidates. According to Solon Buck, "in nearly every instance the candidate nominated or favored by the farmers was elected." [24] This action split the Farmers' Association and turned the *Chicago Tribune* against the farmers' movement. The association played no official role in the judicial election, but Secretary S. M. Smith was a key participant in the proceedings, and Vice President M. M. Hooton defended the Princeton endorsement, arguing that the court should "come up to the spirit of the age." [25]

Encouraged by Smith and, with greater reluctance, Flagg, the Farmers' Association embarked on the perilous enterprise of independent-party politics. Spurred by a Livingston County Farmers' Association platform opposing "railroad steals, tariff steals, salary-grab steals, bank steals, and every other form of thieving by which the farming and laboring classes are robbed of the legitimate fruits of their labor," independent farmer candidates ran for county offices in sixty-six Illinois counties in the November 1873 elections and triumphed in fifty-three. [26] In December, the Farmers' Association officially committed itself to the third-party antimonopoly movement. The victories of November were not to be repeated, however. Many farmers who were willing to support local independent candidates refused to undertake a statewide rebellion against the major parties. The membership of the Farmers' Association dropped precipitously. Delegates from seventy-two counties attended the Springfield Convention in April 1873; only twenty-two counties sent delegates to the Association's third annual convention in January 1875. Abandoned by its true constituency, the Farmers' Association was swallowed up in the futility of first the Anti-Monopoly and then the Greenback party and disappeared after 1877.[27]

The Farmers' Association had spent its influence by the time it entered independent politics. A pressure group could bring great force to bear on a legislature, but not on the courts. The rural hierarchy had managed to harness farmer militancy when the din for railroad regulation in Illinois became incessant. After the creation of the Illinois Railroad and Warehouse Commission, the differences between farmers again outweighed their similarities, and the remnants of the farmers' movement wore themselves out on the whirligig of independent politics. But the power of a focused agricultural lobby had been demonstrated and would be remembered in Illinois.

The Alliance Movement and Illinois Populism

Concern over the farmers' place under a government of courts and parties sparked the Alliance movement in much of Illinois during the late 1880s. The diversification of Illinois agriculture freed most Prairie State farmers from the hard times that afflicted the one-crop farm economies of the Plains states and the South. Only the wheat regions of southwestern and extreme southeastern Illinois experienced acute distress. Instead of overbearing economic hardship, governmental inattention to the needs of the farmer motivated Illinois Alliancemen. Angered by the drop in prices in this long-term deflationary period and frustrated by the state property tax (which was thought to hit rural folk much harder than it did city dwellers, who concealed their wealth in intangible property), farmers felt unfairly singled out for financial hardship.

The lack of a single unifying legislative issue, such as railroad regulation, prevented the rural hierarchy from shaping grassroots discontent into productive political pressure. The Alliance movement consisted of a loose confederation of at least five agricultural organizations.[28] Never able to centralize its organization, grassroots radicalism remained far stronger in the Alliance movement than had been the case during the Granger agitation, but even while denouncing the political system as corrupt, the Alliance movement could not devote itself wholeheartedly to independent political action. Further, although many Alliance members elsewhere carried their grievances into the Populist movement, the great majority of Illinois farmers left the fate of the state People's party to a small band of agrarian economic radicals and their allies in the labor movement.[29]

The Alliance movement developed out of successful cooperative ventures in localities across the state. In the southern counties, cooperative marketing experiments by local farmers resulted in the creation of the Farmers' Mutual Benefit Association (FMBA). After five years of sluggish growth, the Illinois branch of the National Farmers' Alliance expanded rapidly in the regions around Champaign County following the 1886 exposure of price gouging by a local grain dealers' association. A successful boycott in 1889 of the binder twine trust included a statewide meeting of farmers in Bloomington that resurrected the spirit of the Granger movement. Although a proposed union of agricultural organizations failed to materialize, a rejuvenated Grange and numerous locals of the Southern Farmers' Alliance from western Illinois swelled the numbers of organized Illinois farmers. By the end of 1890, some 62,000 husbandmen belonged to the organizations making up the Alliance movement.[30]

A theme common to all these organizations was the imperative need to strengthen the farmers' influence in politics. Particular suggestions ranged from the cautious conservatism of the Grange to the sweeping programs emanating from the more depressed strongholds of the FMBA and the radical Southern Alliance, but all called for a full-scale revision of the state tax system, greater popular control over the railroads, and the state provision of uniform public-school textbooks. The farmers' fears of an organized money power resulted in a series of national public-policy demands. The direct election of United States senators, the adoption of the Australian ballot, and the free coinage of silver were intended to return control of American politics and finance to "the plain people."[31]

Hoping to profit from rural discontent, the Union Labor party in 1888 nominated the Illinois agrarian Alson J. Streeter for president and pitched its state campaign to angry farmers. Farmers were reluctant to ally with labor in a third-party bid, however; Streeter received only about 7,500 votes, and the Union Labor gubernatorial candidate badly trailed the Prohibition standard bearer.[32]

Spurning independent political adventures, the Alliance organizations initially followed the path of earlier agricultural success and relied on legislative pressure tactics. As early as 1886 the farmers sent lobbyists to Springfield and flooded the state capital and Washington with petitions, but without central direction or a respectable set of allies, political pressure yielded negligible results.[33] Spurred by harsher demands from southern Illinois, the Alliance movement began to endorse farmer candidates for political office, a policy that still fell short of a third-party bid. Agricultural reform, cautioned the FMBA, would not come about "by forming a new political party . . . but by educating the farmers . . . to use their right of suffrage for men who possess the true qualifications for office."[34] This position was underscored in Springfield on May 2, 1890, at a meeting of representatives from the FMBA, the Farmers' Alliance, and the

Grange (along with the Knights of Labor). Concerned about the possibility of independent political action by disgruntled farmers in the approaching election, Cicero J. Lindly, the staunchly Republican president of the FMBA, overcame the third-party stance of Streeter and pushed through a resolution urging farmers to work as "missionaries" for the agrarian cause within the major parties.

Despite this cautious official stance, a summer drought and the conviction that corruption permeated the existing political system encouraged an independent agrarian campaign in southern Illinois and isolated pockets elsewhere throughout the state. Asserting that "we are not sovereigns but servants, and the office holders are not servants but masters" in a system "teeming with corruption," the Shelby County FMBA declared "that no party can purify itself within itself" and launched an independent local campaign.[35] Independent farmers contested six congressional seats, entered five races for state senator and thirteen for the lower house, and offered local tickets in 24 counties. There was a smattering of local successes, but only three FMBA General Assembly candidates won their races.[36]

Alongside the independent failure, the nonpartisan Alliance strategy appeared to be successful. The Democratic party openly courted farmers' votes, denouncing the unequal distribution of taxes and echoing in its platform the Alliance movement's demands for uniform school textbooks, the direct election of United States senators and members of the state Railroad and Warehouse Commission, and adoption of the Australian ballot. As a sign of good faith, the Democrats in advance of the election named former governor John M. Palmer, who had appealed to rural sentiment in the 1888 campaign, as their candidate for U.S. senator. Gathering support from candidates of both major parties, Alliance supporters elected to the General Assembly seventeen Democrats and eight Republicans pledged to the agrarian program. In their jubilation farm organizations overlooked the school issue, which had led Germans to defect from the Republican fold, and thus took undue credit for the general Democratic victory. Encouraged by the presence of fifty-eight members in the Thirty-seventh General Assembly's Legislative Farmers' Club, they confidently looked forward to the enactment of their legislative demands.[37]

◆

Without a respected and centrally directed lobby to push for one or two specific proposals, the bright promise of the agrarians' expectations quickly faded. The 1901 legislative session tore the Alliance movement apart, revealing its unbridgeable partisan divisions, blundering leadership, and clumsy attempt to play power politics. Believing that the three independent FMBA assemblymen—Hosea H. Moore, James Cockrell, and Herman E. Taubeneck—held the balance of power between the 100 Republicans and 101 Democrats in the General Assembly, the Alliance organizations attempted to force the election of a "practical farmer" to the United States Senate. The ensuing "protracted and sullen contest"[38] tied up the legislature for nearly two months, drained $150,000 from the state treasury, and featured the odd spectacle of three FMBA members refusing to vote for Republican compromise candidate Cicero Lindly, the president of the FMBA, in favor of the independent Alson Streeter, only to have two of the "Big Three"—Moore and Cockrell—then abandon Streeter and give the election to John M. Palmer, the Democratic candidate. These two "independents," who were vilified in the Republican press as the "the Benedict Arnolds of Illinois," in fact were long-time Democrats.[39] Party loyalty proved firmer than agrarian unity. This demonstrated lack of Alliance cohesiveness allowed the General Assembly to ignore the farmers' legislative demands. Of the Alliance program, only the Australian ballot and a reduction of the legal rate of interest became law.[40]

The fragile unity of the Alliance movement crumbled in the wake of this legislative disaster. Within seven months in 1891 the FMBA dropped from a peak strength of over 50,000 to 24,000 members; by early 1893 only 8,000 members remained. The Illinois State Farmers' Alliance suffered a similar collapse, and the Grange gradually withdrew from political activity. The Illinois chapters of the Southern Farmers' Alliance briefly fed off the misfortune of their erstwhile allies, then they too faded into insignificance.[41]

A rump of dedicated agrarian independents took its small following into the Illinois People's party in 1892, which in the next few years attempted to unite the interests of farmers and industrial workers in the name of a producers' antimonopoly movement. The Illinois People's party never enjoyed much electoral success, but in the course of its brief life it endured numerous internal battles as agrarians, socialists, single-taxers, reform unionists, and William C. Pomeroy's corrupt Illinois State Federation of Labor leadership struggled for dominance. After some initial support from farmers in the state's southernmost counties, Illinois Populism became in effect an independent labor party, with its primary strength in the 1894 election centered in Cook County and the bulk of its downstate vote coming from miners and railroad workers. Continuing to resist independent politics, farmers withheld their support from the new party.[42]

◆

The Granger, Alliance, and Populist episodes suggest that late nineteenth-century Illinois farmers were not third-party enthusiasts. Contrary to the implications of the agricultural modernization thesis, the roots of the agricultural pressure groups that took shape in the Progressive Era extended back to the associations constructed by rural notables in the heart of the "agrarian revolt." Nor was the break between traditional and modern agricultural concerns clear-cut. Beginning in the late nineteenth century, state-supported agricultural trade associations such as the State Horticultural Society, the State Dairymen's Association, the Live Stock Breeders' Association, and the Milk Producers' Institute charted the advances of commercial agriculture and worked with state government through the agricultural extension services of the University of Illinois to increase the productivity and efficiency of Illinois farmers. Nonetheless, these manifestations of rural modernization displayed much the same response to the rule of courts and parties as did the farmers in 1873, and, like the associations formed during the agrarian revolt, they failed to break down persistent division within the rural community.

Farmers, Businessmen, and Butter

Even in the heyday of Granger agitation the agrarian movement depended on the support of businesspeople from related industries to push needed measures through reluctant legislatures. With the growth of agricultural trade associations in Illinois, the distinction between those who raise farm products and those who market them blurred considerably in the ranks of the agricultural lobby. The butter lobby in Springfield was one such hybrid pressure group that was no longer agrarian but merely agricultural.

Technological innovations between 1870 and 1890 established the commercial butter industry in northern Illinois. Butter from the creameries of Elgin, which were operated by substantial dairymen, was of a far superior quality to the often impure, occasionally rancid "country butter" from the farm. But oleomargarine, a new, cheaper product made from animal fat, proved to be a stong competitor to butter. Organized dairy interests around the country launched campaigns to regulate the labeling and coloring of oleomargarine, which unscrupulous retailers often sold as butter to unwary customers. The production of oleomargarine in Illinois was a profitable branch of the meat-packing trade carried on by such industry giants as Swift and Armour, whose political clout stalled attempts to regulate the product.[43]

The fight to regulate the color of oleomargarine in Illinois was led by the National Dairy Union, whose leading figure was not a dairyman at all but a commission merchant from the Chicago Produce Board. Early in

1896 the National Dairy Union appointed a committee of twenty to "look after" dairy interests in the General Assembly.[44] With the support of the State Dairymen's Association, National Dairy Union lobbyists worked to pass a law in 1897 preventing oleomargarine manufacturers from coloring their product to resemble butter. Charles Y. Knight, the manager of the Chicago butter trades journal *Chicago Produce,* personally directed the effort in Springfield, speaking in favor of the bill before the legislature and bombarding lawmakers with farmer protests under the guise of his position as secretary of the Illinois Dairy Union. "We will have a stenographer in the House when the bill comes up for discussion," Knight assured House member Lawrence Y. Sherman, "and the speeches and roll call will be printed and sent to the farmers who are interested, of which there have been heard from between 150 and 450 in every legislative district since we began our educational work."[45]

The ensuing struggle over the anticolor bill took the form of Chicago butter dealers donning the homespun of the tillers and denouncing the "Chicago gang" of state senators in a style worthy of the Alliancemen. Knight railed against the obstructionist tools of the packing lords who bottled up the anti-oleomargarine bill in the committee, thus subverting the will of the people and the interests of the "country." *Chicago Produce* claimed that not only northern Illinois dairymen but farmers from across the state had lined up behind the anticolor bill to protest the arrogance of the Chicago politicians.[46] Sherman in turn complained that the Dairy Union was only a sham farmers' organization that concealed "a Chicago monopoly whose purpose [was] to get a grip on [farmers'] pockets."[47]

The anti-oleomargarine bill eventually triumphed when a rural legislator, Senator Orville Berry, introduced a substitute for the bill stuck in committee and pushed it through with the votes of other country members.[48] Support for butter interests surfaced from the farming districts of Illinois, but the primary direction came from sources that symbolized the absorption of farmer groups into a much more varied agricultural products lobby. Appealing to consumer interests, attacking the demons of monopoly and machine politics, and drawing on the sentimental power of the land and those who worked it, the creameries and commission houses nevertheless carried on a professional lobbying effort for a well-organized industry focusing on a single, specific piece of legislation. The Illinois dairymen who supported the campaign also found themselves part of an industrial interest group. With the commercialization of Illinois agriculture, the "producers" had become the united producers, processors, distributors, and retailers.

◆

The scope of their constituency notwithstanding, agricultural trade associations proved no more adept than the Farmers' Association at overcoming the rule of courts and parties. Chicago oleomargarine manufacturers and the urban working class, which liked a cheap alternative to butter, used the courts to block the threat to the new product. At least two judges in Chicago, most notably circuit court judge E. G. Hanecy, declared the anticolor law unconstitutional. The state could not appeal a lower court decision against itself, and so the law was mired in the lower courts. Case after case was thrown out of court until state officials stopped prosecuting merchants and manufacturers who colored oleomargarine. Dairymen moaned that the courts did not provide "a fair interpretation of the law and honest men to interpret it."[49] Ten years passed before the assistant food commissioner successfully prosecuted infractions of the 1897 law before the Illinois bench.[50]

Stymied by the courts, the butter lobby borrowed a page from the Granger movement after the Republican party mentioned Judge Hanecy as a potential candidate for governor in 1900. Waving aside charges of political interference with an independent judiciary from even the agricultural press, the Elgin Dairy Board passed a resolution specifically opposing Hanecy's nomination on the grounds of his anticolor law decision. Visitors to the annual Dairymen's Association convention found pamphlets denouncing Hanecy on their chairs. "This is little less than anarchy," sniffed a state senator.[51] A representative of the National Dairy Union called on the Dairymen's Association to pass a resolution condemning Hanecy's gubernatorial bid. The association approved a resolution that did not mention the judge by name but transparently urged dairy farmers "to scrutinize the record of, and to strenuously oppose the nomination of all candidates for office, who are hostile or unfriendly to the dairy interests of the State."[52] State Republicans nominated another candidate.[53]

♦

The farmer coalitions that temporarily appeared during moments of crisis in the late nineteenth century gradually bowed to specialized trade associations, which achieved more enduring success by protecting the narrow interests of particular branches of agriculture. In the increasing organizational density of the twentieth century, these associations grew more numerous and influential, but in the pursuit of political influence, the differences between Illinois farmers of the late nineteenth century and those living in the "organizational society" were mostly of degree and not of kind. A rural hierarchy allied with various commercial interests tied to agriculture dominated effective "farmer" lobbies from the Illinois State

Farmers' Association of 1873 to the Illinois Agricultural Association of 1916.[54] The efforts of substantial farmers to impose their will over small farmers did not always meet with success in either period. And finally, agricultural organizations in both the age of agrarian revolt and the age of organization exhibited similar frustration with the rule of courts and parties. Organized agriculture would not find a golden age of influence in the Progressive Era, nor, as it turned out, would progressive reformers discover an affinity of interests with progressive farmers.

Public Health and Progressive Agriculture

Nothing was more clearly in the public interest, agreed progressive reformers, than the health of citizens. The minimum standards they constructed for society required sufficient light and air in workplaces and tenements, reduction in the hours of labor for women and children, and the guaranteed purity of meat, milk, and pharmaceuticals. Dairy produce brushed closer against the sensitive progressive notion of the public interest than did any other agricultural product. Butter and especially milk are perishable foods, easily contaminated by filth or disease if carelessly handled. Clean, wholesome milk was essential to the diet of infants and young children, but the unsanitary condition of many town and country dairies and the dangers of unsafe storage and marketing required the utmost vigilance to guarantee that dairy products nourished rather than killed city children. Throughout the nation, public-health officers, social workers, and concerned members of civic organizations fought for the strict regulation of city milk supplies.[55]

American dairy farmers tried to develop a political economy of regulation that balanced the demands of public health with the interests of agricultural producers. State dairy associations were receptive to progressive ideals of high quality and expert supervision embodied in the doctrines of "scientific farming." In some cases, as in Virginia, progressive dairying revived drowsy industries. Organized dairymen elsewhere found political influence by following the creed of efficiency and public health. After Wisconsin dairy interests supported the rise of Robert La Follette, state support for agricultural education, regulation, and research expanded to the point that one historian characterized progressive-era Wisconsin government as an "agricultural service-state."[56]

Central to the political economy of milk regulation was a set of objectives shared by both expert regulators, usually from the professional staff of state dairy and food commissions and the faculty of state agricultural colleges, and the largest, most efficient dairy operators. During the late nineteenth century, food manufacturers discovered that *moderate* regulation of their industries helped ease popular fear of adulteration, and chemists, druggists, and technicians on the state regulatory boards found that the new emphasis on public health enhanced their professional status. Business and science linked fortunes, and so it was with milk regulation. Driven by consumer distrust, urban hostility, and the refusal of many small dairy farmers to adopt sanitary measures, the Illinois Dairymen's Association joined the University of Illinois College of Agriculture in an educational campaign to standardize the quality of dairy products, force out unsanitary and inefficient operators, and ensure the adoption of clean and scientific methods through stronger dairy laws and stricter state inspection.[57]

Progressive agriculture's plan for milk regulation required a precise alignment of science, business, and politics, but when large and small agricultural interests came into contact with urban markets in Illinois, the political economy of milk regulation broke down. Urban reformers absorbed in public-health problems impatiently dismissed the concerns of the dairy industry. "The only safety of the consumer lies in having the city stop the sale of impure milk," declared the Chicago Municipal Voters' League in 1911. The commercial consequences for milk dealers were irrelevant. "The public is not bound to extend considerations to [milk dealers], whether large or small, to the detriment of public health," argued urban progressives.[58] Standards of scientific dairying advocated by the large operators, which small dairy farmers denounced as too extreme, appeared too limited to city health experts. With no common approach to regulation, the quality of milk was determined by the standards of the marketplace—what consumers would drink and what they would pay.

Progressive Farming and a Uniform Product

"This organization is solely educational," declared the president of the Dairymen's Association in 1915.[59] Created in 1874, two years after the establishment of the Elgin Board of Trade, which determined the prices of dairy products for much of the United States, the Illinois State Dairymen's Association reflected the outlook of the large, successful operators of the Fox River valley. With a membership that included not only milk producers but also "manufacturers of milk products, manufacturers and distributors of dairy products, equipment and supplies,"[60] the association took a broad view of the dairy industry. Confronted with the challenge of oleomargarine and the problem of dirty milk, the large operators spread the gospel of progressive agriculture, hoping thereby to make their milk an attractive and uniform product that would allay public suspicions and increase their own revenues.

Persuading the small farmer of the economies and efficiency inherent in scientific dairying was the aim of educational programs. Association meetings led to the creation in 1895 of the Illinois Farmers' Institute. That same year the Dairymen's Association began to receive appropriations from the General Assembly to publish its proceedings and further its work among the dairymen of the state. The association thus joined the Agricultural College of the University of Illinois in the uphill fight to promote "book farming" and establish uniform standards for both the owners of large herds and the farmer who carried the milk of his five cows to the local creamery.[61]

Dairymen's Association officers and professors from the university harped on a constant theme between 1900 and 1920: dairy farming should be treated as a business enterprise, with emphasis on increasing production, efficiency, and quality control. The amount of milk and percentage of butterfat produced by each cow should be carefully measured by the Babcock test, and unprofitable cows should be sent to the butcher. Dairymen should combine into local test associations to monitor the production of their herds. Association president Lewis N. Wiggins declared in 1910 that dairymen "can no more afford to raise grade dairy cows than the modern factory can afford to continue to use, year after year, the old machinery. It is necessary to add from time to time new machines of modern efficiency and perfection. . . . Do not forget the important fact that your cow is a live machine, a most complicated and yet simple one. If she is properly fed the raw material, and you, the operator, use good common horse sense she will turn out for you a good finished product."[62]

University expert W. J. Fraser charged that inattention to business principles allowed a quarter of the state's million dairy cows to return no profit to their owners.[63] Similar carelessness led farmers to confine cattle in shuttered, foul barns, to ignore even the most rudimentary sanitary principles, and to produce milk so revolting that it tainted the entire dairy industry in the public consciousness. "If the purpose were to make the milk unfit even for a calf to drink," marveled another University of Illinois professor in 1901, "human ingenuity could hardly invent a more scientifically complete method than that which is in vogue today on many of our dairy farms."[64]

Not very carefully hidden behind the friendly educational outreach of the Dairymen's Association was a threatening message to slovenly farmers and careless creamery operators. The fortunes of the dairy industry rested on public confidence that butter, cream, and especially milk were pure and safe. In 1892 Chicago authorities revealed that milch cows in cramped, filthy city "dairies" subsisted on illegal "slop"—processed grain obtained from breweries and other industrial enterprises.[65] A decade later the front page of the *Chicago Tribune* screamed "Bad Milk Slaying Babies."[66] It mattered little that the story concerned investigations of tainted milk in New York; Illinois producers were under scrutiny. "There are some people who are not only disgracing the profession but injuring your reputation and taking the money out of your pockets," warned Dean Eugene Davenport of the University of Illinois. These were not association members, but rather "hangers-on that are hitched on to this profession, who ought to be got rid of."[67]

If lax standards, inattention to cleanliness, and even the adulteration of dairy products by Illinois producers and processors withstood the ministrations of college professors and concerned industry leaders, the Dairymen's Association was willing to support state regulation to protect itself and its consumers. President Joseph Newman, one of the largest creamery operators in Illinois, announced in 1904 that "the time is at hand when the dairy laws of the state should be administered by some one clothed with the police power, so that those men who will not produce and deliver milk suitable for human food could be driven out of business."[68]

Self-Policing Regulation

Progressive dairymen and educators believed that tighter regulation of the dairy industry would benefit the public and the farmer. An 1879 Illinois statute forbade the sale of adulterated, diluted, or diseased milk for human consumption but provided no machinery for inspection. A similar 1881 act proposed to ensure the quality of butter and cheese; like its predecessor, it mandated stiff fines for violators. Nonetheless, the overworked state's attorneys in each county charged with enforcing dairy laws could not bring most producers into even marginal compliance.[69]

Inadequate state regulation and an unwillingness on the part of many farmers to voluntarily improve sanitation created a bleak popular image of dairy products, despite farmers' disingenuous praise for "pure country butter" and fresh milk. Dean Davenport reminded the Dairymen's Association what the public saw: "butter made in thousands of places where no decent man would eat his dinner . . . milk loaded with filth visible, constantly suggesting the occasional infection with tuberculosis and typhoid fever; milk that has been watered and milk that has been skimmed; cream that never saw a cow . . . and both preserved by drugs powerful enough to prevent the growth of the organisms it contains until they reach a more favorable habitat in the human body."[70] Dairymen needed to remind consumers that pure dairy products were indeed healthful.

Concern for public health and the well-being of responsible dairymen pushed large operators to the forefront of the pure food crusade in Illinois. Strict controls and rigorous inspection would clean up the dairy industry, but the Dairymen's Association was determined that public-health initiatives not outrun the control of progressive farmers. To that end, it insisted that those "clothed with the police power" over milk production be friendly state officials, often drawn from association ranks, rather than urban public-health authorities.

The pure food movement began in earnest in 1899 with the passage of a law creating the office of State Food Commissioner and arming it with two assistant commissioners and six inspectors. The law specified that one of the assistant commissioners be "an expert in the matter of dairy products."[71]

Early activity of the commissioner's office disappointed the Dairymen's Association. Rather than the "practical dairy man" the association expected, Governor Richard Yates in 1902 appointed a political friend, Chicagoan Rudolph Patterson, as assistant dairy commissioner. One downstate milk dealer joked that the assistant commissioner had learned the dairy trade "in the First Ward."[72] Although recognizing that Patterson attempted to carry out his duties to the best of his ability, association members protested his unfamiliarity with the trade and demanded that he be replaced by a genuine expert as the law required.[73]

Political manipulation aside, the food commission was too weak and unaggressive to adequately enforce higher standards of quality and cleanliness throughout Illinois. Six inspectors could not police nearly six hundred creameries, hundreds of milk depots, and thousands of dairies, especially when they were charged with maintaining sanitary standards in every Illinois establishment that manufactured or sold food. The city of Chicago alone had ten food inspectors in 1902. What was more, the commission failed to prosecute dairies and creameries that violated the law, preferring to file away inspectors' reports with the hope that operators would clean up their premises before the next inspection. "How long, 'oh,' how long will it take such a policy to bring careless or indifferent creamery men to terms?" complained an agricultural newspaper.[74]

Unhappy with the performance of the Food Commission's dairy branch, the state's large operators formally pushed for more effective regulation. In 1905 the Dairymen's Association appointed a three-member committee to meet with State Food Commissioner Alfred Jones and devise amendments strengthening dairy inspection features of the pure food law. The following year a similar committee was empowered to suggest appropriate candidates for assistant food commissioner to Governor Charles S. Deneen. The fruits of increased regulatory activism included the Pure Food Law of 1907, which doubled the state's inspection force, and the appointment of Herman E. Schuknecht in 1906 as the first efficient and dedicated assistant commissioner specializing in dairy matters. More to the point, both Schuknecht and his successor, John B. Newman, were active members of the Illinois State Dairymen's Association. Together they provided scientific dairymen with the friendly, protective regulation the association sought.[75]

◆

Self-policing of the dairy industry through the offices of the Dairymen's Association led to a dangerous regulatory middle ground, however. Unable to control the more freewheeling practices of the state's smaller or uncooperative farmers, and unwilling to adopt the stricter measures advocated by the Chicago Department of Health, the Dairymen's Association presided over a regulatory apparatus that was successful only as an information-gathering body. On the vital health questions of dairy inspection, pure milk, and the regulation of tubercular cattle, the Dairymen's Association found itself caught between numerous small dairymen who resisted all controls imposed by the larger operators and urban reformers committed to protecting the public health. This tangle of interests was further complicated by the association's ambivalent attachment to voluntarism and regulatory coercion.

The Dairymen's Association's decision to push for stricter state dairy inspection owed much to the Chicago Department of Health's initiation, in 1904, of dairy inspections in the countryside surrounding that city. City inspectors visited over 2,800 dairies that year. The growing Chicago milk market turned many ordinary farmers into dairymen on the side.[76] Legions of small farmers, many of them unfamiliar with scientific dairying methods, produced milk under appallingly unsanitary conditions. One expert observed that half the glasses of milk he bought at urban restaurants contained silty deposits of dirt and manure. Faced with the prospect of Chicago inspectors roaming far afield to regulate dairies, the Dairymen's Association intensified its efforts to secure satisfactory statewide inspection—regulation that could be more easily controlled by the larger dairy interests.[77]

State regulation was not, however, a cloak to conceal misdeeds of milk producers. The Dairymen's Association and its representatives in government wholeheartedly joined the pure milk crusade that spread across Illinois in 1906. Assistant Commissioner Schuknecht was a dedicated and vigilant crusader against adulterated milk. After assuming office in April, he inspected the milk supply in thirty-five cities and found the fraudulent sale of skimmed, watered, or adulterated milk in all but three of them.

Unlike his more timid predecessors, Schuknecht did not politely bury his findings but released them to the newspapers of the state.[78] "Publicity is a 'big stick,'" he observed with satisfaction early in 1907, "and it has been wielded lustily."[79]

Schuknecht was not reluctant to swing that stick himself. Declaring that "not more than thirty to thirty-five per cent of the milk sold in the cities of the state was in the condition it should . . . be when offered for sale as human food," the assistant commissioner attacked the complacent boards of health.[80] He described the various types of milk "preservatives" in use, most of them with a formaldehyde base, and denounced the manufacturers of those spurious products as "trafficking in the lives of the babes of the state" when they embalmed city milk supplies.[81] Under Schuknecht the dairy branch of the Food Commission vigorously prosecuted lawbreakers. In 1906 his office filed seventy-six suits for the adulteration of milk products with formaldehyde and fifty-four others for the fraudulent sale of watered or skimmed milk. After his first tour of duty, Schuknecht demanded stronger laws to stamp out threats to public health.[82]

The most dangerous adulteration of milk, that with formaldehyde preservatives, was for the most part the work of city milk dealers. The Chicago commissioner of health, William A. Evans, told the City Club that "in Chicago the law-makers are practically never under pressure from the dairyman, and in consequence it will always be possible to secure a dairy inspection ordinance that will be more effective than will ever be possible through state legislation."[83] Why, then, did the Dairymen's Association move to undercut the better-staffed Chicago Board of Health (by 1911, Chicago had sixty-seven food inspectors to the state's twelve)[84] when the latter began to inspect dairies? Why did it intensify its campaign for state regulation of a problem that threatened cities?[85]

The Dairymen's Association, allied with the agricultural experts of the University of Illinois and the State Food Commission, sought above all else uniformity of standards in a self-reforming industry. Uniform standards of careful sanitation, product quality, and business acumen would provide a safe product to the consumer and a profitable livelihood to the producer. State regulation was the best method for establishing such uniform standards. City regulation introduced variation in regulatory standards and was likely to be carried out by inspectors ignorant of the practical conditions of dairying. The prosperous, "scientific" dairymen of Illinois determined that standards administered on a statewide level provided the best chance for improving dairy products and safeguarding the public welfare.

The theme of regulatory competition between reformers and public-health authorities in Chicago on the one hand and agricultural experts and the organized dairymen downstate on the other dominated progressive-era attempts to ensure the safety and availability of milk. The state emerged more powerful than its metropolis in questions of dairy regulation, but the confidence of the Dairymen's Association that it could secure adequate regulation in Springfield suffered a series of blows at the hands of small dairymen and unrepentant creamerymen, beginning with the enactment of the Illinois Dairy and Food Act of 1907.

Substantial dairymen enjoyed the loyalty of the state agricultural college, but the more numerous small operators were allied with Speaker of the Illinois House Edward Shurtleff. After checking Chicago's regulatory incursions into the countryside, the Dairymen's Association found that it could not prevent less responsible farmers from thwarting key elements of its regulatory scheme. Self-regulation failed because the majority of dairyman refused to be regulated. That failure deepened the antagonism between Chicago pure milk advocates and the dairy industry.

Tying the Gordian Knot

Following passage of the federal Pure Food and Drug Act of 1906, prospects seemed good for securing the stronger pure food act that had eluded Illinois reformers in the General Assembly since 1901. Without a state measure to complement the federal law, Illinois consumers would be flooded with suspect food products banned from interstate commerce by national legislation. Illinois public servants had been content to inject the state's tainted products into the national marketplace, but once it became clear that without corresponding legislation the adulterated food produced by Illinois manufacturers would poison local citizens exclusively, politicians joined reformers in the pure food crusade. Governor Deneen moved with alacrity to enact a satisfactory pure food law in the 1907 legislative session.[86]

The Dairymen's Association and the State Food Commission took advantage of this more favorable climate by drawing up a pure food bill that paid particular attention to the regulation of dairies. Nineteen additional inspectors armed with stricter inspection guidelines formed the core of the bill, which wrested regulatory control from Chicago's roving inspectors and placed it in the hands of state officials in an attempt to assuage public concern over contaminated milk. After the bill was introduced into the House in late January, Assistant Food Commissioner Schuknecht conferred with the Elgin Board of Trade in an effort to tighten several loose features of the bill "in the interests of the general public" and further secure the support of leading dairy concerns.[87] Backed by the authority of the State Food Commission and the foremost advocates of proper sanitary precautions within the industry, the dairy inspection features of the pure food bill appeared certain to pass.[88]

Despite this apparent certainty, however, the Dairymen's Association seriously underestimated the depths of antagonism harbored by modest cow keepers toward the standards of scientific dairying and the large owners who preached them. Small farmers across the United States expressed suspicion and resentment at attempts by "experts" and city-based reformers to "uplift" them. Despite hardships, many rural people were satisfied with their way of life and resisted instructions to alter it. The president of the National Dairy Union bluntly told the 1905 convention that it was impossible to "get the average farmers of the country to attend the state dairy association meetings."[89] Agricultural experts from the state university and Dairymen's Association officers took to the road in a series of one-day meetings and demonstrations to persuade farmers to adopt scientific methods, but the seeds fell on stony soil. In 1919, after years of teaching the financial necessity of testing annual milk production, the association found only nineteen voluntary test associations in the state. Less than 10 percent of the Illinois herd was milked according to association standards.[90]

Frustrated agricultural experts eventually lashed out at the stubbornness of the rural mind. Speaking before the Illinois Farmers' Institute, University of Illinois professor C. C. Hayden announced in exasperation, "it seems that before we can really get on in this matter we must improve the man back of the cow. He must be educated in some way to use his brain. Some dairymen . . . . acquire, no one knows how, a conviction, a belief in regard to the simplest matters and they can no more let go of it than steel of itself can let go of a magnet."[91] Such sentiments did little to win over small farmers to the methods of the professors and their allies in the Dairymen's Association.

Reluctant to adopt the sanitary standards of the Dairymen's Association, small dairymen also rejected regulation for the benefit of public health. The University of Illinois in 1906 offered a special four-week course training dairymen for the special sanitary requirements of producing milk for cities, but many small dairymen either complained that the steps necessary to clean up their barns were too expensive or saw no reason to provide city people with milk better than that which their own families had used for years. Rather than viewing the issue of sanitary milk production in terms of protecting city milk supplies, smaller producers cast the issue in terms of their relations to creamerymen and larger dairymen.[92]

Small farmers who sold milk to creameries or condensing factories claimed that processors fixed prices at absurdly low levels. Compounding the difficulty for the small farmer was the public's refusal to pay higher prices for quality milk. Caught between the "dictum of a mere handler of goods" and "an undiscriminating public,"[93] many small dairy producers adulterated their product. Schuknecht prosecuted seventeen farmers in 1906 for delivering watered milk to creameries or shipping stations. Animosity toward the processor sometimes overshadowed the responsibility to provide a pure product. One farmer caught marketing watered milk explained, "I did not think I was breaking any law, I thought I was breaking the creamery man."[94]

Angry at processors and shippers, defensive of their methods, and distrustful of the consuming public, small dairy farmers believed that the Dairymen's Association intended to drive them out of business with its proposed regulations. Modest farmers bitterly resented the air of superiority so tangible in the association's education campaign. After "listening to some of these great dairymen," one of the small fry wondered whether "the wives of these men . . . would tell the same story. . . . [Whether] the boys of these fathers . . . would tell . . . how they loved to milk 15 to 20 cows, over 700 tons in a years."[95] The teachings of the Dairymen's Association not only called into question the business practices of small milk producers, but threatened their way of life.

◆

The dairy inspection provisions of the 1907 pure food bill became a lightning rod for all the antagonisms of small dairy farmers toward large producers and reformers. Legislative defenders of small dairymen, led by House Speaker Edward Shurtleff, devised a substitute bill that eliminated the strict dairy inspection procedures of the original bill and substantially weakened the Food Commission's powers by erasing definitions of pure milk, cream, and butter. Shurtleff's substitute bill placed the burden of milk inspection at the point of retail sales rather than the place of production. Speaking for many of the state's dairy farmers, the *Prairie Farmer* reported that "the dairy interests of the state had to hustle to keep out of the bill any provisions for purity standards and official inspection of dairies." Although willing to stomach milk inspection, "they didn't want an official inspector around their dairies."[96]

Shurtleff explained that "the original bill was drafted to meet the ideas of the Illinois Dairymen's Association," whose members could maintain standards of cleanliness unattainable by "the man who has three, four, or five cows. . . . Small retail farmers can't keep their places clean as would be required by state inspection under the provisions of the original bill. They are not scientific farmers, and the measure contained a number of requirements which they never could have understood." Unreasonable standards, argued the Speaker, ran the risk of driving small farmers out of the dairy business. The bill "would allow deputy state inspectors to go to the farm of a man who keeps less than half a dozen cows and compel him to make $500 worth of alterations in his barn."[97]

Opponents of the original bill put particular emphasis on Assistant Food Commissioner Schuknecht's close collaboration with the Elgin Board of Trade in amending an early draft of the proposal. Shurtleff claimed that the Food Commission accepted changes in the bill that allowed the large butter and cheese manufacturers of the Elgin district to avoid strict inspection while placing undue pressure on small milk producers to meet unreasonable standards of cleanliness. Schuknecht hotly contested the charge and was backed up by the testimony of pure food expert Edward Gudeman, yet the dairy inspection features of the pure food bill were irretrievably lost. Further amendments cut the number of new inspectors to six. The General Assembly also slashed the Food Commission's request for nearly $200,000 to enforce the act down to a minimal appropriation of $35,520.[98]

Chicago newspapers denounced the maiming of the pure food bill's dairy inspection provisions, but small farmers found an unlikely ally in William A. Evans, the newly appointed commissioner of health for Chicago. Although a firm advocate of strict dairy regulation, Evans acquiesced in striking dairy inspection features from the state law. Aware that any state regulation took precedence over a city ordinance covering the same issue, and that the Dairymen's Association intended the state law to head off Chicago's inspection of country dairies that produced milk for the city market, Evans readily sacrificed downstate milk consumers to protect Chicago's higher inspection standards. He told the Chicago City Club that "so far as the inspection of dairies is concerned, we would be better off in the city of Chicago without the law than we would be with the law." Admitting his stance to be "a somewhat selfish one," he argued that "it did take care of us, and it seemed to me . . . that was my duty."[99]

◆

The Dairymen's Association gambled in 1907 that it had enough influence in Springfield to maneuver around the objections of Chicago health authorities and the bitter opposition of the state's small dairymen and erect a standard of state regulation reflecting its own interest. The gamble failed: the association enjoyed the necessary influence over the regulating agency, the State Food Commission, but not the General Assembly. Although disappointed by its inability to "secure the hearty support of the Legislature in its proposed new bill," the association seemed content with the modest gains achieved by the new pure food law.[100] In 1910 it unsuccessfully petitioned the General Assembly to increase the number of food inspectors to twenty; thereafter, it simply put its faith in the efforts of Assistant Commissioner Newman to enforce a limited law with insufficient manpower.[101]

Effective legislation to guarantee clean and safe milk could not emerge intact from the infighting among the Dairymen's Association, small producers, and Chicago's health authorities, yet each contestant lacked either the power or the inclination to clean up the milk supply on its own. The Dairymen's Association was the most powerful single interest, but its more sweeping regulatory attempts could not pass through the General Assembly. The association's commitment to self-regulation—to voluntary improvements in the industry by way of education—prevented it from protecting strict city standards on the one hand and putting the full weight of its influence behind effective state regulations on the other. The small producers opposed all controls from above, whether by the government or by the industry itself. Chicago authorities pursued high standards, but they were unwilling to compromise for the good of the whole and always rested uneasily under the shadow of state regulation.

Unable to resolve their differences, the dairy industry and Chicago health authorities and reformers became increasingly hostile to each other. Large dairymen advocated voluntary reforms against bovine tuberculosis that appeared onerous to the small farmers and inadequate to frightened city officials. Price controls turned the dairy interests against urban reformers. Turmoil rather than cooperation characterized the remainder of the progressive-era debate over milk.

The White Plague

Neither the Illinois dairy and food law nor the city's own corps of inspectors purified Chicago's milk supply. Professor John Trueman's survey verified that in 1907 milk in Chicago still was often watered and skimmed and, more alarmingly, that these conditions were most prevalent where they could wreak the worst damage—in the city's poorest and most densely populated neighborhoods. In a single month—August 1908—Health Commissioner Evans recorded 719 infant deaths from diarrhea. He attributed about two hundred of those fatalities to contaminated milk. In 1911, the Health Department of Chicago estimated that the filth from one year's supply of milk would "fill four big freight cars."[102] Social workers, doctors, and genteel reformers demanded that the city exercise more stringent control over its sources of milk.[103]

Rendering the mood more inflammatory was an outbreak of tuberculosis—the dreaded "white plague" of progressive-era cities—among the dairy cattle of Illinois. The state veterinarian estimated in 1910 that some 300,000 cattle had contracted the disease.[104] Most medical experts agreed that bovine tuberculosis could be passed on to humans through infected milk. The Dairymen's Association, small dairy farmers, and Chicago authorities responded to the contagion in characteristic fashion. The association launched a campaign for responsible voluntary action on the part of cattle owners to isolate and eradicate the disease, with state controls to seal off the entry of infected cattle from other states. Small farmers and their legislative friends denigrated the efforts of doctors and inspectors and put their faith in the unregulated marketplace. Chicago health officials sponsored extensive new regulations to oversee the production of milk in the surrounding countryside. The ensuing crisis further alienated Chicago health professionals from the state's dairymen, small dairy operators from the Dairymen's Association, and concerned Chicago citizens from state lawmakers.

◆

Whether the tuberculin test should be mandatory was at the center of controversy. The test could determine whether an apparently healthy cow carried the infection. A cow testing positive was slaughtered. Many livestock owners, and by no means only modest ones, distrusted the test. It condemned healthy livestock, they argued, and the test itself could infect a previously clean herd. Giving scientific backing to the instinctive hostility of the farmers were the opinions of Robert Koch, the world's leading medical authority on the disease, who argued that humans could not be infected by bovine tuberculosis and that many animals could recover from the illness if only given time.[105] "There never was a more wasteful and criminal policy affecting the live stock interests," Koch held, "than the killing of an animal just because it reacted to the tuberculin test."[106]

Unpleasant memories of an earlier experiment in compulsory testing underlay dairymen's suspicions of enforced tuberculin testing. An 1899 outbreak of bovine tuberculosis in Illinois had resulted in a gubernatorial proclamation instituting a policy of mandatory testing, with unhappy results. The state veterinarian seized cattle brought into the state without a test certificate. In sixteen months of mandatory testing, 522 animals found to be infected were slaughtered. Farmers received a fraction of appraised value in compensation for the loss of diseased stock.[107] Early in 1901 between 200 and 300 dairymen gathered in Elgin to denounce the compulsory tuberculin test "as a conspiracy of veterinarians to get fees for applying the test to cows" and to remonstrate against it as unreliable, poorly applied, expensive, and unhealthy.[108] In 1903 the Illinois Supreme

Court disallowed state seizure of untested cattle.[109] Mandatory testing for tuberculosis, concluded State Veterinarian James E. Wright in 1909, was not a viable option in the effort to eradicate the white plague among cattle. The lesson of 1899 was that "crusades always meet with disaster."[110]

The Dairymen's Association echoed Wright's opinion that mandatory or indiscriminate testing was not the proper answer to the crisis. To be effective, they said, that policy would entail considerable state expenditure (Wright estimated "at least eleven million dollars")[111] and would require an intolerable expansion of the state police presence along the borders and on the farm. Instead, the association joined the state veterinarian and the agricultural professors at the University of Illinois in a vigorous educational campaign to clarify the seriousness of the threat posed by bovine tuberculosis, to demonstrate the virtually universal reliability of the tuberculin test as an agent to combat the disease, and to press farmers to voluntarily subject their herds to testing.

Dairymen's Association speakers stressed that once in a herd, tuberculosis spread rapidly and that only the tuberculin test, not physical examination, could indisputably determine its presence. The tuberculin demonstration, first conducted at a University of Illinois tuberculosis convention in 1908, became a staple at state fairs, Farmers' Institutes, and the annual meetings of livestock organizations such as the Dairymen's Association and the Illinois Live Stock Breeders. One such test at the Dairymen's Association 1911 convention exemplified the educational effectiveness of live demonstrations. A crowd of curious farmers, far more than usually attended the association's meetings, watched as veterinarians and university professors slaughtered five apparently healthy cows, three of whom had reacted to the tuberculin test, and cut them up to reveal unmistakable tubercular lesions in their lungs and glands. The two cows declared fit by the test were free of lesions.[112]

Wright and the Dairymen's Association insisted that, although strictly voluntary, tuberculin testing should be conducted uniformly and only with state-approved tuberculin. To the Dairymen's Association, uniformity meant state supervision—in this case, by the Illinois State Board of Live Stock Commissioners. Wright declared that cities did not have the means or the trained inspectors to properly conduct the tests. "Competent and . . . reliable men of authority . . . absolutely under state control" should take charge of all testing in Illinois.[113] With proper legislation, state control would also better guarantee adequate compensation to those farmers whose tubercular cattle were slaughtered. "If it is for the public good, then the public should pay for it," reasoned Wright.[114]

The Dairymen's Association gratefully passed resolutions endorsing the work of the state veterinarian and requesting legislation granting state compensation for slaughtered tubercular cattle (initially asking for the full appraised value, but later scaling down the request to a reasonable percentage of value).[115] These suggestions were part of the association's emphasis on voluntary reform backed by protective regulation at the hands of sympathetic state officials. If regulation appeared to be heavy-handed, the association advocated education and voluntary reform; if the state could provide compensation for dairymen's losses, the association welcomed intervention. Ultimately, though, voluntarism and slight controls were inadequate in the face of a free market in tubercular cattle.

Although over thirty states denied entry to dairy cattle that could not show evidence of having passed the tuberculin test, Illinois had no such law. Predictably, the state became a "dumping ground"[116] for animals that could not meet rigid standards elsewhere. Farmers shipped diseased cattle into Illinois; Wisconsin and Minnesota state authorities, as part of their campaign to eradicate the disease at home, sold cattle with positive test reactions on the Prairie State's open market. Even many "healthy" cattle in fact were infected animals fraudulently sold during the thirty-day nonreaction period that followed testing. Equally sharp practices within Illinois hindered attempts to stamp out the disease. One farmer reported selling a diseased cow for slaughter at $15, only to see the same animal sold as a dairy cow the next day for $42.50.[117]

This state of affairs caused dairy experts to call for strong regulations to protect Illinois herds from outside infection. Dairy Association president Lewis Wiggins demanded legislation in 1909 to close off Illinois from the tubercular exiles of other states. Wright also advocated a state law banning the entry of breeding cattle without test certificates.[118] In spite of this advocacy, though, enthusiasm for cutting off the free market did not extend much beyond the leadership of the Dairymen's Association. In 1911 ex-legislator John Stewart told an Illinois House investigating committee that three-fourths of the dairymen in Kane County "do not raise any cows at all. They buy all of their cattle from Iowa, Wisconsin and other states. And to require cattle shipped in with a certificate of having passed the tuberculin test would shut them off."[119] Not until 1911 did the association specifically request the General Assembly to adopt the law Wright had proposed. In the meantime, voluntary testing within Illinois could scarcely be expected to clean up the fraudulent local trade in tubercular cattle.[120]

◆

Despite its limitations, the antituberculosis program of the Illinois Dairymen's Association represented the most public-spirited response to the crisis among cattle owners. Once again, the association's reform efforts were spurred by Chicago's attempt to exert firmer regulatory control over its milk supply.

The threat to city milk posed by tuberculosis heightened a civic uproar that had already seized the attention of Chicago reformers. In the summer of 1908 the City Club, at the urging of Health Commissioner Evans, sponsored the formation of a Milk Commission empowered to establish a uniform standard for certified milk sold in the city—the highest grade (and most expensive) milk available to the public. Supported by a reform community attuned to high quality standards for milk, Evans was unwilling to rely on the dairy interests' voluntary efforts against contagion. Chicago received milk from 12,000 dairies in four states, and neither the dairy industry nor state authorities could police such a collection under existing law. Consequently, in 1908 Evans and his reformer allies pushed through the Chicago city council an ordinance forbidding the entry of milk into the city unless it came from tested cows.[121]

The ordinance, requiring that milk be subject to compulsory city testing rather than state regulation to enter the Chicago market, went into effect at the beginning of 1909. It represented everything opposed by the Dairymen's Association and its state health allies. Even the moderating clause in the ordinance, which allowed pasteurized milk from untested or tubercular cows to enter for five years, upset the secretary of the State Board of Health, James E. Egan, who believed pasteurization to be at best ineffective and possibly harmful. Nevertheless, the Chicago authorities remained adamant. Nearly thirty thousand cows were tested in 1909, and by 1911 the Chicago food inspection force swelled to sixty-seven. That year, thirty-two uncooperative dairies were excluded from the Chicago market.[122] "The dairymen supplying milk to Chicago and to every other city of this country have got to yield to this reform movement," Professor Clarence B. Lane told the City Club.[123]

Twenty-three cities had ordinances similar to Chicago's, but Illinois dairymen protested bitterly against the city's inspectors and the tuberculin test itself. Chief among them was Grace Durand, a notably successful producer of certified milk[124] for the Chicago market until she ran afoul of the Chicago inspectors in 1910. Despite the fact that Durand took dairy courses at the University of Wisconsin, regularly tested her own cows, and produced milk under the highest sanitary precautions, Chicago inspectors found ten reactors among her herd of sixty-five. She claimed that the slaughtered animals exhibited no signs of infection and subsequently appeared before the Dairymen's Association and the Chicago-based Milk Producers' Association to condemn the tuberculin test as worthless, suggest that pasteurization poisoned milk, and question whether tuberculosis in milk could be passed on to humans at all. [125]

◆

Inflamed sentiment among the majority of Illinois dairy farmers doomed the plans of Dairy Association reformers and Chicago authorities alike. The association's bill giving authority to the state veterinarian to test animals on request and providing funds to reimburse the owners of slaughtered cattle died in the General Assembly in 1909, [126] and Speaker Shurtleff, characterizing the Chicago milk ordinance as "without foundation of law, unreasonable, and void," set up a state commission stacked with enemies of the tuberculin test "to determine whether the . . . tests are needful and efficacious." [127] Setting up shop in Chicago to receive evidence "on the milk subject from the producers' standpoint," the committee listened as dairy farmers questioned the necessity of the Chicago ordinance and challenged the competence of Chicago inspectors, one of whom was characterized as a drunk German, "unfit for anything" but, like many of his fellows, intent on finding "something wrong or he would not have a position." [128]

In 1911 the Shurtleff committee made its report. Although it recommended laws requiring test certificates for cattle entering the state and allowed the State Board of Live Stock Commissioners to provide certificates for animals sold to other states, the committee determined that "there is no necessity of adopting the tuberculin test in the State of Illinois." [129] According to the report, physical examinations of cattle were sufficient to detect the disease. In any event, it claimed few children were killed by milk-borne tuberculosis. The committee counted only "sixteen and one-half cases" of bovine tuberculosis passed on to humans through milk in Chicago during 1906. [130] "I am not surprised," Commissioner Evans declared. "The commission was formed solely for the purpose of recommending against the tuberculin test, and it seems to have done its work well." [131]

Complaining that the Chicago milk ordinance "has produced . . . a great element of fear on the part of every dairyman, that his milk supply would be shut off from the market at any particular time when the Board of Health of the city of Chicago sees fit to black-list him," the Shurtleff committee also called for a law "prohibiting any municipality in the State of Illinois from establishing or demanding the tuberculin test of dairy cattle as a means of protecting the milk supply." [132] Shurtleff intended to nullify the Chicago milk inspection ordinance with a state ban on municipal testing. This bill, fumed the *Chicago Tribune*, assumed that "the health of the residents of Illinois cities can be better cared for by the representatives of diseased milch cows than by their own trained sanitary officers."[133]

Despite the anguished protests of the Chicago authorities, on April 6 the House passed the law by the lopsided margin of eighty-nine to twenty. The state senate also approved the measure. Chicago's milk inspection ordinance was struck down; not until 1926 could Chicago again require tuberculin testing for cows supplying milk to the city.[134] "Virtually all interests in Chicago united in favor of milk inspection," writes Steven Diner, "but they lacked the political power to defeat the dairy interests in the state legislature."[135]

On the other hand, the Dairymen's Association also failed to win legislative approval for its program of officially sanctioned voluntary testing. The Shurtleff committee rejected its compensation proposal as too expensive for the state. Until Governor Edward F. Dunne—significantly, a former mayor of Chicago—by proclamation prohibited the entry into Illinois of untested dairy and breeding cattle, the association's effort to close the borders to tubercular cattle made little headway. Not until 1919 did the General Assembly approve limited compensation for the owners of slaughtered tubercular cattle (and then only after the federal government passed a compensation act that required accompanying state legislation). Other agricultural bodies, most notably the Illinois Agricultural Association, played more significant roles than did the Dairymen's Association in this minor triumph. Considering that Frank Lowden, a noted dairy cattle owner, had been in the governor's chair since 1917, the legislative success of the Dairymen's Association was disappointing.[136]

For all the efforts of the Dairymen's Association to provide state assistance for the voluntary eradication of tuberculosis, and Chicago's countervailing attempt to regulate dairy cattle through mandatory use of the tuberculin test, no effective regulation of the white plague among the dairy herds prevailed during the progressive period. "The farmer will simply be left to solve the tuberculosis problem, as he does others," concluded a University of Illinois dairy expert in 1914, "and will have to clean up his herd because it is a good business to do so."[137] Trusting the state's small dairy farmers to adhere to efficient business principles had proven to be an unrewarding enterprise, so Chicago health authorities and the Dairymen's Association hedged their bets by turning to pasteurization. With the aid of civic groups such as the Citizens' Association, Chicago passed a new milk inspection measure in 1912 that required pasteurization for all city milk not certified disease-free by city inspectors. Spurred by an outbreak of hoof and mouth disease, the Dairymen's Association followed suit in 1915 by officially endorsing compulsory pasteurization.[138]

Pasteurization eased the public-health threat from tubercular cows, but the struggle over the regulation of diseased milk permanently alienated Chicago health reformers from the dairymen of Illinois, both large and small. Professional and middle-class defenders of the public health clashed angrily with dairy farmers over attempts to regulate the price of milk. Dairy spokesmen guaranteed that if consumers "should decree that every can of milk should come to the station with a rose on top of the can, and there was an extra 25 cents per can offered for the rose, the rose would be there."[139] But a firm public notion of the just price—"as if it had been written in the Bible," moaned one expert[140]—undercut sanitary efforts.

In 1916 the Milk Producers' Association, an alliance of suppliers to the Chicago market, launched a series of "milk strikes" to boost the price they received from the organized Chicago milk dealers. As the price of milk rose and its availability fluctuated, consumption fell nearly 25 percent in 1917. Alarmed civic officials called on the wartime United States Food Administration to intervene. The resulting Chicago Milk Commission fixed the price of milk at twelve cents per quart for home delivery (a penny less than prevailing prices), but not before the dean of the University of Illinois College of Agriculture quit the commission in protest and dairy members encouraged a boycott of the Chicago market. Dairymen and health reformers had not yet reconciled cheap milk with safe milk.[141]

◆

Varying regulatory efforts failed to create a community of interests among dairymen, health-conscious reformers, and a bargain-seeking public in whose behalf both reformers and scientific dairymen professed to operate. Self-regulation by the dairy industry through the offices of the State Food Commission failed because the larger operators could not control smaller dairy farmers or wield sufficient influence in the General Assembly. City regulation failed because the Dairymen's Association sought milder and more uniform statewide standards and because state power nullified Chicago's stricter guidelines. While city and state health officials decried the production of milk under filthy or diseased conditions, consumers bought the cheapest milk possible, and small dairymen, shrugging off the suggestions of the Dairymen's Association and the undermanned Food Commission, pocketed the change.

Without a shared attitude toward the regulation of milk or a dominant interest to impose its standards, Illinois lurched from crisis to crisis over its milk supply. In times of crisis, the public demanded milk as safe as it was cheap; reformers tried to fix the price of milk; and dairymen poured milk into the streets to raise the price. In this regulatory maelstrom, in which the quality and price of milk were to be expertly blended to the satisfaction of all, even the federal government employing the extraordinary powers of wartime could only patch together an arbitrary stopgap settlement. The one food item that progressives viewed as essential to the public health resisted all attempts to render it uniformly pure, abundant, and inexpensive.

◆

Neither science nor democracy in the countryside produced the heightened awareness of the public interest that progressives believed essential to public policy. Agricultural organization deepened the complex mixture of partisanship, self-interest, and bureaucracy that drove modern American public life. In failing to understand the limited appeal of the public interest as they defined it, urban progressives contributed to the development of a polity based on pluralistic competition rather than the rational cooperation they treasured. As the following chapter shows, industrial reform also escaped the shaping hand of progressive ideals. Progressive attempts to defuse class confrontation by means of factory regulation failed to quell private advantage.

3

Controlling Factory Regulation

The fearful possibility of class warfare in the 1890s deepened progressive commitment to the harmonious ideal of the public interest throughout the nation. In Illinois the impression that society was on the verge of tearing itself apart was particularly acute. After the bitterness and vengeful prosecutions that followed the Haymarket Riot of 1886, renewed violence on the railroads and coalfields in 1894 suggested that employers and wage earners were separating, perhaps permanently, into irreconcilably hostile camps. Sharing with Jane Addams a "constant dread of the spreading ill will," middle-class reformers saw the confrontation as a threat to the stability of the human family. In a poignant example of the progressive tendency to personalize social processes, Addams remembered how the transportation shutdown during the Pullman strike prevented her dying sister's husband and children from reaching the bedside of the sufferer. The shock waves of industrial warfare thus moved beyond the immediate antagonists and upset the web of harmonious relationships on which civilization rested. The casualties of industrial strife, whether they were impoverished families of blacklisted workmen, employers suffused with class hatred, or innocent citizens caught up in the attendant chaos, impressed on Addams "the cruelty and waste of the strike as an implement for securing the most reasonable demands" of the working class.[1]

Mindful of the human cost of unregulated industrial expansion, yet fearing the consequences of direct action by workers, Illinois progressives worked to ameliorate the harsh workplace conditions that triggered destructive conflict between capital and labor. Middle-class reformers such as Florence Kelley, Jane Addams, Graham Taylor, and Ernst Freund and his associates from the Illinois Association for Labor Legislation devoted their expertise and public visibility to the cause of protective state regulation of working conditions. Campaigns for state laws reducing the hours of labor for women and children, requiring protective shielding on machinery, and providing compensation for the families of injured workers furnished immediate relief from the worst features of industrialism, but by transferring conflicts from the shop floor to the General Assembly, progressives embarked on the more important task of transforming class disputes into a public program of social reform. The progressive vision of the public interest demanded compromises that improved society and assuaged class tensions, compromises embodied in the state-sponsored industrial commissions that hammered out many of the successful Illinois protective laws.

For organized labor in Illinois, the emergence of progressive-backed industrial commissions was a pyrrhic victory. As one scholar has astutely noted, progressive innovations in government "sharply reduced the autonomous power of organized labor."[2] Class concerns of labor agitators were lost in the triumph of the progressive concern with the public interest. Even those progressives closest in sympathy to the working class advanced a distinct set of objectives. One example was the Chicago branch of the Women's Trade Union League, headed by Margaret Dreier Robins, which brought together young working-class women and middle-class "allies." The Chicago WTUL labored to organize working women into powerful unions (all the while butting heads with the craft bias of the American Federation of Labor) while simultaneously advocating protective legislation in Springfield. Robins managed to combine both avenues of reform, but she diverged from the goals of class solidarity and power espoused by the trade unionists in the organization. Indeed, Robins remained devoted to a progressive ideal of harmonious democratic rule by selfless citizens. In her later years, she resented what she considered the stunted, narrow focus on class power and personal aggrandizement among WTUL trade unionists.[3]

The shift in emphasis from class advantage to public interest that guided the progressive approach to protective legislation produced ironic consequences for organized labor in Illinois. State industrial commissions brought together representatives of capital, labor, and the public to forge workable solutions to industrial problems. Progressive members of these investigatory commissions expressed sympathy for the plight of workers burdened with long hours and unsafe conditions of labor—but sympathy was not solidarity. Employer associations exploited divisions between progressives and organized labor to seize control of Illinois factory regulation. Guided by the politically sophisticated Illinois Manufacturers' Association, Prairie State employers were better organized than labor and as resourceful as progressives in manipulating public opinion. In a state widely regarded as a stronghold of union power, in which middle-class reform efforts to build coalitions with working-class organizations were particularly active, organized capital ultimately controlled the pace of industrial reform.

The Political Vulnerability of Union Power

The strength and militance of organized labor in progressive-era Illinois was unquestionable. The 243,000 unionized workers in Chicago made the lakefront metropolis, in the judgment of David Montgomery, a fit rival for London as "trade-union capital of the world" in 1903.[4] Downstate coalfields were home to District 12 of the United Mine Workers of America (UMWA) whose 80,000 members in 1903 accounted for over one-quarter of the miners enrolled in the largest single union in the AFL. Bold, independent action accompanied organization. The Chicago Federation of Labor (CFL) coordinated a policy of sympathy strikes that forced the struggle for union shops out of isolated plants and into the public arena of city streets. CFL strategists dared to help organize the polyglot work force in the packing houses. Socialist influences that sparked the most radical initiatives within the UMWA radiated from their District 12 stronghold. Militant coal miners launched a general strike around Springfield in 1917 that stopped police harassment of striking streetcar employees. An aggressive commitment by organized workers to class solidarity and direct confrontation with capital seemed to win concessions at the workplace and recognition of working-class community power from government.[5]

Nevertheless, the foundation on which organized labor reinforced its independent power buckled after 1904. A national campaign by trade associations to impose the open shop shredded working-class solidarity. Taking advantage of an economic downturn, Chicago meat packers first induced a walkout, then imported strikebreakers desperate for work, blacklisted union stalwarts, and routed labor power from the yards until World War I. International Harvester, Pullman, and other Chicago manufacturers purged unions from their works. Throughout the land, organized employers appealed to nonunion workers, slicing through the bonds organizers had painstakingly knotted between skilled workers and their unskilled brethren. Unable to withstand counterattacks on labor's chosen ground of shop floor confrontation, Illinois unions turned to politics and advocacy of protective legislation, but organized labor's ambiguous relationship to the political system had created substantial barriers to independent political influence. Despite their interest in class formation, Illinois unionists could not gain legislative safeguards for workers without substantial support from progressives, who intended to break down class barriers with protective laws.[6]

Political routes to power had not been ignored by organized labor, but they were largely confined to scattered localities. At the insistence of its president, Samuel Gompers, the AFL remained officially committed to the doctrine of "voluntarism," a course of action that opposed affiliation with any political party and proscribed reliance on government for improvements that workers "could accomplish by their own initiative and activities."[7] Nevertheless, judicial support for the open shop offensive in the form of timely antilabor injunctions prompted Gompers in 1906 to loosen restrictions on political participation, and for years before that state and city central labor councils had lobbied in state legislatures and launched independent political movements. In Missouri, California, New York, and Illinois, state labor federations affiliated with the AFL formulated legislative programs and pressured lawmakers to enact them. The unions' legislative agenda sought first to augment labor's economic power by erecting legal safeguards around the right to strike and eliminating unfair competition from convict labor and second to improve safety conditions at the workplace and provide compensation for injured workers. In some cities, such as San Francisco, independent parties guided by city labor councils controlled municipal government. Elsewhere, as in Chicago, city labor federations became influential exponents of a wide range of radically democratic proposals. Too often, however, labor's political power was concentrated in urban centers but weak and divided at the state level, where laws were written.[8]

State labor federations, which suffered from poor funding and inadequate authority, were the weak link in organized labor's chain of political influence. They held no coercive power over member unions and often quarreled with city federations that were more radical or interested in independent political campaigns. The presence in state capitals of highly organized or militant unions engaged in their own lobbying efforts vitiated the claim that state federations were the official political arm of the labor movement. Not surprisingly, state federations chalked up few concrete achievements on their own. Missouri labor lobbyists found greater success when they backed "reform legislation of a more inclusive nature"—in other words, reforms that appealed to the progressive sense of the public interest.[9] It soon became clear that adequate protective legislation for workers could not be enacted without the cooperation of progressive reformers.

Although workers had the most to gain from protective laws, at least immediately, middle-class progressives became the most influential proponents of industrial regulation. Sustained public awareness of specific industrial ills and the measures cultivated to remedy them was a necessary ingredient for the passage of labor laws. Middle-class reformers, who were adept at focusing public attention on the shocking costs of unregulated industry and providing expert testimony in favor of specific legislative solutions, could build such an awareness. For organized workers, the price of factory regulation was the surrender of independent control over the nature and extent of reform.

◆

Illinois unionists shared with their counterparts elsewhere in the nation an inability to move beyond effective local organization and sustain a decisive political presence at the state level. By the end of the Progressive Era the absence of working-class political solidarity was evident even in Chicago. Charles E. Merriam judged city unions to be influential but not decisive factors in Chicago government during the 1920s. "If united in political action," he granted, "they would of course be masters of Chicago."[10] Ironically, organized labor's failure to decisively influence public policy was rooted in its political success at the municipal level in the late nineteenth century. In Chicago, Springfield, and East St. Louis independent labor tickets affiliated with the Knights of Labor prospered between 1885 and 1888, but independent political action did not endure. Instead, "a movement that began by defying the contemporary party system may in the end have left workers even more firmly within its confines."[11] Established party organizations fashioned arrangements with working-class voters that blunted the appeal of independent politics. Chicago workers may have wielded greater political influence within the elder Carter Harrison's Democratic organization than they had in independent parties. Harrison's police force left strikebreakers unprotected and saloon laws unenforced, sealing an informal alliance between labor and the Chicago Democracy.[12]

Despite socialist sympathies in the cities and coalfields, Illinois unions had largely abandoned the alternative of independent political action by the turn of the century. Absorbed in the give and take of municipal politics, organized labor suffered a comparative dearth of influence at the state level. Labor's political clout produced lenient attitudes toward strikers and working-class cultural practices in cities, but not an effective state program of industrial reform. When the open shop assault challenged union power in the cities, organized labor looked to Springfield for protection. Campaigns for legislation regulating working conditions in Illinois were prolonged, extending in many cases over ten years and numerous legislative sessions. To carry on the fight, the state labor lobby needed thorough organization, unity of effort, money, and extreme persistence.

The Illinois State Federation of Labor (ISFL) fell short of those exacting standards. As late as 1905 lawmakers treated its lobby with "supercilious indifference."[13] Divisions within the labor movement further hindered its effectiveness. The radically democratic Chicago Federation of Labor frequently clashed with the cautious state body, and the most influential Illinois unions—the four railroad brotherhoods and the United Mine Workers of America—conducted independent lobbying until 1905. After that the ISFL grew until it considered itself the largest such organization "in the world"; in 1913 it had some 86,000 dues-paying members. Miners and railroad workers remained the primary beneficiaries of industrial regulation, however. Over 35 percent of the labor bills approved by the General Assembly between 1885 and 1919 focused exclusively on railroads or the mining industry.[14]

Troubles within the State Federation of Labor dated from its founding in 1884. Internal disputes between Knights of Labor members and craft unionists threatened to destroy the organization in its infancy. Independent political campaigns absorbed the attention of Illinois unionists in 1888 and 1894, only to result in disillusioning defeat for the Union Labor party and the Populists. Single taxers and socialists battled with "plain and simple" unionists for control of the federation in the 1890s. Even with the sympathetic Altgeld administration in office during the 1890s, the energies of the ISFL were unfocused.[15]

Corruption and infidelity in the ISFL's leadership further stymied legislative efforts. President William C. Pomeroy and his Chicago faction directed the state federation toward moderate unionism and their own profit between 1892 and 1896, when Pomeroy was purged and the Chicago Federation of Labor superseded his city organization as the state's largest central body. Over the next decade the state federation continued to suffer from internal politics and pliable leadership. "The State Federation was bought and sold like a bag of potatoes," recalled one president.[16] Some ISFL officers sought political favors more avidly than they attended to the welfare of the rank and file. At least one president, Barney Cohen (1903–5), was reputedly in the pocket of Martin "Skinny" Madden, the building trades boss who used gangster methods to corrupt the Chicago federation until his ouster in 1906.[17]

Problems raised by inattentive leadership were compounded by the feebleness of the ISFL's Springfield lobby. When funds were available, a legislative committee oversaw the progress of labor bills in the General Assembly, but uncertain finances—in 1903 only a partial legislative committee could be maintained, and even with this economy, ISFL president Adam Menche was forced to leave Springfield in midsession to raise more money—and the multitude of bills entrusted to its care weakened the organization's influence among lawmakers. Its threats to retire unfriendly officeholders proved toothless until 1907, when in keeping with the change in national AFL policy the Illinois State Federation of Labor began to distribute lists of legislative supporters and opponents of labor. Not until 1915 did its annual *Proceedings* regularly include legislative scorecards arranged by district. Further, the federation remained cautious about endorsing new candidates to the General Assembly. One year after the introduction of its *Weekly News Letter* in 1915 there still was no established policy for the favorable mention of major-party candidates endorsed by local labor bodies. Lack of money, disorganization, and hesitancy to offend party loyalties prevented the federation from utilizing its membership to apply political pressure.[18]

Weaker than the sum of its parts, organized labor in Illinois cooperated with the regulatory commissions favored by progressives. Organized employers participated in the commissions as well, but in contrast to labor, Illinois capital had been forged into a solidly united and politically sophisticated legislative force. That force can best be understood by turning to the history of the Illinois Manufacturers' Association.

The Political Mobilization of Business

The promise of cooperative action by a reform community that included women settlement house residents and socialites, male and female trade unionists, respected professionals, and sympathetic state officials launched the career of perhaps the most powerful state business organization of the Progressive Era. Thrown together in 1893 to combat provisions of the landmark child labor law approved by the Altgeld administration, the Illinois Manufacturers' Association (IMA) managed to destroy or muzzle most attempts to regulate factory conditions in Illinois. By 1913 the IMA was a large, powerful, integrated enterprise with two headquarters, ample finances, and a great deal of influence over political issues affecting its narrowly defined interests. Many of the firms in the association were relatively large units tied to national or international markets. They had experienced at first hand the impact of the transportation revolution and the emergence of big business. Changing circumstances in a competitive marketplace taught them the value of centralized administration and the rapid manipulation of resources. These business perceptions determined the political course of the organization. The IMA built united sentiment among manufacturers and used it to wrest regulatory control of industrial working conditions from reformers and labor.[19]

Mansel Blackford has found that California businesspeople between

1890 and 1920 at first turned to political action only after their problems eluded private solutions. As the state developed economically, however, business interests joined wholeheartedly in the contest of organized interest groups to extract their pound of flesh from government. A similar pattern of business organization in the face of economic change and growing demands for government regulation appeared across the nation. The desire to stabilize industries, counter regulatory initiatives, and erect a united front against the demands of their workers encouraged businesspeople to form active trade associations. As many as five hundred such organizations existed in 1905. As business associations grew in the Progressive Era, they broadened their activities, absorbed local groups and established ties with national organizations, and produced vigorous leaders who set priorities and directed policy.[20]

The Illinois Manufacturers' Association conformed to this pattern, yet it also built an independent national reputation. IMA leaders cooperated with the open shop campaign of the National Association of Manufacturers (NAM), the leading business advocate of the early twentieth century, but the midwestern group pioneered in the development of antilabor legislative lobbying. Its membership between 1910 and 1920 remained about one-third the size of the NAM. Such numerical strength, combined with commercial rivalries between midwestern producers and some of the NAM's eastern firms, led Illinois businesspeople to rely on the IMA as their principal weapon against the regulatory initiatives of progressives and organized labor.[21]

◆

Prior to the election of Governor John Peter Altgeld in 1892, Illinois manufacturers faced little in the way of legislation benefiting working people at the expense of their employers. Safety laws for the mining industry—the most active area of state regulation—troubled few manufacturers, and the Railroad and Warehouse Commission provided businesspeople with the low, uniform shipping rates they desired. Nevertheless, Altgeld came into office with a determined sympathy for beleaguered workers and a dedicated corps of lieutenants led by Bureau of Labor Statistics director George Schilling, a former Anti-Monopolist, and Chief Factory Inspector Florence Kelley of Hull House.[22]

Ongoing concern in Chicago about the conditions under which women and children labored in the garment trades took legislative shape in 1893 with the enactment of the Factory and Workshop Inspection Law, commonly known as the sweatshop act. Supported by city unionists and the Hull House community, Florence Kelley compiled a detailed report of the frenzied atmosphere in small shops that scrambled to assemble clothing for larger manufacturers. Her efforts ushered in the pattern of independent investigation, public outcry, and regulatory response that characterized the reform of working conditions during the Progressive Era. Assisted by activist lawyers and buoyed by a rush of public enthusiasm, Kelley drafted a bill intended to curb the exploitation of children and women workers. The resulting law, the sweatshop act, spurred both the push for industrial regulation in Illinois and the political mobilization of Prairie State businesspeople. Few protested the child labor provisions of the bill, but the act also prohibited any factory from employing females for more than eight hours a day or forty-eight hours a week and created a department of factory inspection to guarantee compliance with the law. Altgeld appointed Kelley to head the new department.[23]

Factory owners, claiming that the Illinois law gave the advantage to out-of-state competitors, drew together to resist the most stringent features of the law. Chicago employers of women formed the Manufacturers' Protective Association with intent to overturn the eight-hour provision of the law. By 1894 two hundred manufacturers had joined, and the group was incorporated as the Illinois Manufacturers' Association. The IMA hired first-rate legal counsel, raised funds, and set out to challenge the constitutionality of the sweatshop act.[24]

The ensuing legal struggle called forth the resources that made business organization a potent influence over progressive-era public policy. IMA officials wanted to delay enforcement of the disputed law until their test case made its way through the Illinois Supreme Court, but Kelley rigorously brought suit against violators of the sweatshop act. Association money paid for the defense of member firms. All thirteen IMA firms convicted under the law had their appeals financed by the organization; nine of those cases reached the state's highest court. Organized business had reservoirs of time and money to pour into its cause, resources that organized labor was unable to match, and it produced results. In March 1895 the Illinois Supreme Court in *Ritchie v. People* declared unconstitutional the eight-hour provision of the sweatshop act.[25]

Success in the eight-hour fight suggested the advantages of permanent organization, but without an immediate threat to unite them, Illinois businesspeople drifted from political activism. Association members wanted to expand markets, ease costs, and prevent unwanted regulation of their enterprises. Without a firm directing hand to channel those concerns into specific public policy stances, the intersections of legislative politics and business interests were too infrequent to generate the degree of compelling group identification necessary to sustain effective organization. By 1898 the IMA had dwindled to a stagnant collection of forty-three firms. Then it found a dynamic leader whose political expertise propelled the resources and interests of a moribund business lobby into legislative power.

John M. Glenn, who at the age of thirty-eight became secretary of the IMA, knew how to sway opinions and pull strings in public life. He had worked as a journalist, mostly for Republican newspapers, and had served briefly as secretary of the Chicago Civil Service Commission. Glenn knew how to direct public opinion toward political ends, was familiar with the inner workings of government, and had ties to the press and politicians. He was also a prodigious organizer and tireless lobbyist. Glenn inundated manufacturers, lawmakers, and the press with association bulletins, adding the journal *Manufacturers' News* as an IMA mouthpiece in 1912. In his frequent appearances before General Assembly committees Glenn established a reputation for persistent and unflagging energy in pursuit of the association's goals.[26]

Growing pressure from progressives and organized labor for expanded state regulation of business was the most effective spur to IMA growth. Many anxious businesspeople, awakened into political consciousness by some pending regulatory intrusion, were attracted to the IMA by Glenn's aggressive insistence that "power is in acting together."[27] The push for stronger factory safety laws in 1907 coincided with the creation of an IMA membership committee that divided Illinois into districts and systematically prosyletized manufacturers. Between 1909 and the American entry into World War I, IMA membership fluctuated from 1,100 to 1,500 firms; the roll swelled to over 2,300 companies in 1922. But the concentration of Chicago interests that gave the IMA its financial power limited its appeal outside the Windy City. At no time during the Progressive Era did more than 10 percent of Illinois manufacturers belong to the IMA, nor did the powerful Peoria distilleries or many East St. Louis concerns come within the fold.[28]

Despite its somewhat narrow appeal, the IMA built itself into a preeminent legislative force because of its influential members, its willingness to expand its activities, and its ability to influence politicians without threatening their control of government. Important corporate members helped the IMA gain a respectful hearing in Springfield. Historians generally have considered the employers' associations that flourished between 1890 and 1910 as the representatives of small and medium-sized businesses, but some of the largest corporations in the nation, along with many firms of great local importance, were early and active members of the IMA. Meat-packing giants Armour and Swift joined leading producers of agricultural implements such as the McCormick Harvesting Company, John Deere, Moline Plow, and the Rock Island Plow Company in the association's ranks. Another large member was the Illinois Steel Company, whose South Chicago works, one of the biggest manufacturing establishments in the nation, employed over six thousand workers. Other members included American Steel & Wire, Latrobe Steel, Western Electric, Link-Belt (a leading exponent of the scientific management techniques of Frederick Taylor), Elgin Watch, Conrad Seipp (the nation's ninth-largest brewer), and dry goods leaders John V. Farwell, Montgomery Ward, and Mandel Brothers, along with prominent Chicago clothing and shoe manufacturers, printers and publishers. Dominant regional industries such as Rockford furniture makers were also active in the association. Numerous small manufacturers also belonged to the IMA, but the vocal participation of Illinois big business lent special weight to its political activities.[29]

Influence also came from Illinois politicians who trusted their business interests to the IMA; these ranged from Republican national committeeman Graeme Stewart to Cook County Democratic boss Roger Sullivan. Influential Republican, erstwhile Chicago city council "gray wolf," and later prominent congressman Martin B. Madden was IMA president in 1901. His Western Stone Company, "the largest and most completely organized concern for the quarrying, handling and marketing of building stone in the world," employed 2,700 workers in 1895.[30] Sullivan operated the Ogden Gas Company, the product of a spectacular city council franchise scheme, until he and his partners unloaded it for six million dollars in 1906. Five years later, by then affiliated with the Cosmopolitan Electric Company, Sullivan served on the IMA legislative committee. Respectable as well as suspect politicians served in the IMA over the years, including Chicago alderman Frederic W. Upham, William Meese (trusted aide of Governor Frank Lowden), Treasury Secretary Franklin Mac-Veagh, and Edward Hurley, vice-chairman of the Federal Trade Commission. Such connections ensured that the IMA was never politically naive.[31]

The second key to IMA effectiveness lay in its increasing involvement in public affairs. As the association's activities expanded, the web of interconnections in industrial society linked the interests of manufacturers with those of a much broader business class. The IMA's legal challenge to the sweatshop act, for instance, soon took on institutional permanence as a legal bureau that issued formal written opinions on recently passed laws. Overspilling the special concerns of manufacturers, the legal bureau functioned as a clearing house for information pertaining to government regulation of business. Just as the seeming coherence of expanded government authority was the product of a patchwork of discrete influences, the dynamic public role of business in progressive-era Illinois took shape as specific regulatory initiatives and labor activism called forth sharp reactions that widened the scope of the IMA.[32]

The IMA helped business exert direct pressure on lawmakers and strik-

ing workers. In 1898 Glenn discovered irregularities in the passage of a
fire escape law that IMA attorneys were challenging in the courts. The
association set aside its test case and demanded that the General Assembly repeal the offending act, underlining its seriousness by arranging for a
large crowd of disgruntled businesspeople to meet with key legislators at
Chicago's Grand Pacific Hotel. The law was repealed at the next session;
thereafter, the IMA carefully groomed the techniques of mass mobilization of businesspeople, cascades of telegrams, and forceful public meetings
that had proved decisive in this instance.[33] In addition, IMA ties to other
business associations sustained direct action against labor. In Chicago,
IMA money and personnel helped the local Employers' Association battle
workers in the streets. Teamsters, guards, and detectives provided by the
IMA broke a 1903 strike against the Kellogg Switchboard Company. Two
years later, during the epic Teamsters strike, the IMA raised $22,000 to
bolster the Employers' Association and shared the services of its legal
counsel, Levy Mayer. Afterward, IMA member Montgomery Ward, a
principal figure in the strike, occupied a central position in the Employers'
Association.[34]

Perhaps the most important reason for the continued influence of the
business lobby was the IMA's refusal to compete with politicians for control of government. A central tenet of progressive belief was that politicians should be ousted from the management of public affairs and be
replaced by incorruptible, efficient public servants. Progressive public-
policy initiatives invariably contained at least rhetorical challenges to the
close ties between party organizations and government administration.
Despite the widespread progressive-era enthusiasm for applying "business
methods" to government (that is, rigid economy, centralized direction,
and, above all, efficiency), the organized representatives of business interests in the Prairie State mostly kept quiet about such matters. To be
sure, the lure of efficiency drew some businesspeople and professionals,
many of them moderate progressives, into campaigns for "businesslike"
government. Exasperating expense and inefficiency in municipal administration in particular led some businesspeople to advocate the adoption
of commission government in several downstate cities and then to dominate the triumphant city commissions. For most Illinois businesspeople,
however, organized efficiency meant membership in activist business associations, not direct intrusion into public office. Popular sentiment influenced public policy, and public policy had expanded into questions formerly considered private. Businesspeople needed to mold that sentiment
in their favor if they were to counteract the policy initiatives of organized
labor and its progressive allies. To meet that pragmatic rationale, the
IMA claimed it was "the big unit. It takes care of the big questions. It is
cumulative action."[35]

Protecting their competitive market position was the overwhelming concern of IMA members. If government regulation strengthened their position, they supported it; if government activity proved a threat, they opposed it. Self-interest dictated IMA opposition to most factory regulation, and it prompted Association endorsement of the Illinois Railroad and Warehouse Commission's maximum rate rulings and a more powerful Interstate Commerce Commission.[36] The IMA cut directly to the public questions that affected it, blandly declaring its interests synonymous with the public good. Uninterested in social justifications for government activity, its one consistency was to keep to the path of personal advantage no matter what terrain it crossed.

An unwavering focus on a limited set of concerns without any broader political ambitions allowed the IMA to influence politics without threatening politicians' hold on government. Leaders of the association's legislative committee harangued businesspeople for paying too little attention to politics, but suggestions for greater involvement fell short of a call to shoulder aside the politicians and seize control of the state. The IMA did not share the urge to "clean up" government that motivated business and professional reform clubs such as the Civic Federation. Manufacturers were advised to know their representatives, to aid their election campaigns, and thereby gain access for legislative favors. "If you expect to influence [the General Assembly] by your presence here," an IMA speaker reminded a group of manufacturers in Springfield, "it must be because you are at least on friendly terms with the members from your home district."[37] After striking up a "personal acquaintance," concerned businesspeople could "take up discussion of pending bills with their members in a free and detailed way."[38]

Instead of grappling with lawmakers, the IMA used its resources to ensure a smoother working relationship with legislators. This strategy conceded the realm of politics to the politicians; it insisted only that the interests of the manufacturers be protected.[39] The place of businesspeople in the political structure of the Progressive Era allowed them to outdo their trade union rivals in political influence. Unions simply lacked the organizational resources for political mobilization that the IMA could muster. Because organized labor sought to build legislative protection for working people, and businesspeople aimed to obstruct or limit those gains, the business lobby had the additional advantage of a defensive legislative posture. Middle-class progressives had more access than did workers to the centers of political power, but their suspicion of politicians prevented easy influence. Progressives appealed to the public interest and relied on the force of public opinion to accelerate their drive for reform. IMA leaders, however, proved fluent in the progressive language of public responsibility.

Whenever possible, IMA officials linked their self-interest to broader images of public concern. Business opposition to the renewal of the Bell System's Chicago telephone franchise in 1907, for instance, portrayed itself as a consumer revolt against unprincipled corporate power. Such an approach boldly drew on the popular wave of anger against municipal utility corporations that, antithetically, was molding in American cities a constituency favorable to progressive reforms.[40] Chicago Telephone's refusal to implement unlimited business service, its intention instead to introduce more costly measured service, and its failure to connect with independent lines over long distance upset manufacturers. However, because many Chicagoans relied on Chicago Telephone, the IMA declared itself the champion of the consumers in a struggle against a haughty and indifferent monopoly. Warming to its unaccustomed role, the association adopted the methods of progressive reformers to whip up popular feeling against the company. It investigated telephone rates in European and American cities and distributed charts detailing Chicago Telephone's inadequate service and unjustifiable charges. With the voice of a civic reformer, Glenn pronounced Chicago Telephone "one of those public utility transgressors upon whom nothing but the strong arm of the law and the fear of real competition has had any effect."[41]

The IMA foray into the telephone business produced mixed results at best. Chicago Telephone won its franchise renewal in late 1907, but the city obtained some rights to rate regulation along with the shadowy possibility of future municipal ownership. IMA activism on behalf of consumers proved both fleeting and unconvincing. The public interest was in truth only a tributary emptying into the association's mainstream of private concerns. Nonetheless, the telephone controversy demonstrated the willingness of business advocates to use the progressive tools of investigation and publicity for their own ends. Lessons absorbed in this and other public campaigns were successfully applied by Illinois businesspeople to the vital issue of state factory regulation.[42]

Managing Reform by Commission

The state-sponsored investigatory commission symbolized progressive attempts to remedy the injustices of industrial life through compromise. In theory, these commissions were to utilize the expertise of particular interests to uphold the public weal. Eagerly advocated by middle-class reformers, the commissions also afforded labor organizations a greater degree of influence and public support than normally attended their legislative efforts. Alive to the necessity of shaping public opinion, the IMA was inevitably drawn to the commissions as well. If legislative changes were to come—and the appearance of commissions was a sign of a public demand for change—then the active participation of organized business representatives could encourage modest reforms that satisfied public demand and undercut labor's more extensive aims. The IMA's ability to bend this instrument of reform to its own purposes profoundly damaged progressive hopes that social harmony could be achieved through public cooperation.

Spectacular reminders of the dangers inherent in industrial labor, such as the 1911 Triangle Fire in New York, incited popular demands for reform in the Progressive Era.[43] A comparable Illinois tragedy transformed the quietly simmering private conflict over industrial accident compensation into a public uproar requiring immediate legislative attention. On November 13, 1909, fire swept through a mine in the gloomy town of Cherry, killing 274 miners. A shaken Graham Taylor, inspecting the site as a member of the Illinois Mining Investigation Commission, published a series of articles detailing the horrible deaths of the immigrant miners, who were sealed inside the burning shaft, and the anguish of their destitute families. Inadequate financial compensation for their loss compounded the agony of the survivors. "In the absence of any workingmen's compensation law or compulsory insurance," Taylor grimly reported, "at least $100,000 more in charity is needed to compensate for the lack of justice to those who hazarded everything and lost all in the dangerous occupation of mining."[44]

Progressives seized the opportunity to redress that shortcoming when Governor Charles Deneen called a special session of the General Assembly in December. Illinois Association for Labor Legislation president Ernst Freund persuaded Deneen to ask the legislature for a commission empowered to investigate industrial accidents and recommend proper compensatory legislation. Freund then drafted a bill creating the Illinois Employers' Liability Commission, composed of six employers and an equal number of labor representatives appointed by the governor, which the legislature passed and furnished with a $10,000 appropriation.[45]

Organized labor and capital quickly filled the open positions. Deneen allowed the Illinois State Federation of Labor and the Chicago Federation of Labor to select the labor commissioners. Prominent IMA members constituted half the employers' delegation, and association director Charles Piez assumed the chair (replacing the deceased original nominee). The remaining employer representatives included two railroad presidents and the secretary of the Illinois Coal Operators' Association. Recognizing the extent of public support for workers' compensation, Piez and his colleagues accepted the idea. The commission mailed questionnaires to IMA members and labor organizations and reaped a mound of data

clearly establishing the need for a standardized compensation system paying higher damages to accident victims. In 1908 Cook County alone reported 600 deaths from industrial accidents. The commission investigated
149 nonrailroad fatalities for which detailed records existed and discovered that in 70 cases "not a penny was recovered, either in court or out
of court."[46] But drafting a model bill produced tension and disagreement.
Through 1910 business and labor commissioners clashed over the size of
benefits and the principle of employers' liability[47]

Both sides knew that changes were necessary. The lack of an adequate
compensation law often shattered the families of fallen breadwinners.
Nearly 400 of the approximately 1,000 industrial fatality cases examined
by the commission had disappeared from the record, leading the commission to conclude that "hundreds of families became broken up and migra-
tory."[48] One persistent commission investigator found the widow of an
accident victim working as a prostitute to support her four daughters.[49]

Reliance on the courts and common law dissatisfied both employers
and injured workers. Courts awarded damages in only 24 of the 641 fatality cases traced by the commission, but fear of extensive litigation and
unpredictable damages occasionally awarded by sympathetic juries moved
employers to settle many cases out of court. Insurance men and lawyers
consumed the lion's share of damages: lawyers demanded between 50 and
60 percent of the claims sought by the families of the Cherry victims.[50]
Mindful of this, the commission thrashed out an approach intended to
force compensation questions out of the courts. Those employers who
refused to accept the compensation schedules established by the proposed
legislation would lose their right to the legal defenses of the fellow servant
doctrine, assumption of risk, and contributory negligence in any common-law injury suit initiated by an employee who had accepted the provisions of the act. On the other hand, an employee who agreed to the
act's compensation plan forfeited any right to common-law action against
participating employers.

Beyond this basic outline the commissioners could not agree. Piez and
the other employers considered the suggested rates of compensation to be
too high and objected to a provision that retained an employer's civil
liability if state safety regulations had been consciously ignored. Meanwhile, labor's fragile unity fractured. The labor commissioners believed
the suggested compensation inadequate, but miners and ISFL representatives supported a workers' compensation bill as a more workable answer
to industrial injuries than an employers' liability law. On the other hand,
commissioners from the Chicago Federation of Labor and the Railway
Brotherhoods, John Flora and M. J. Boyle, respectively, refused to accept
workers' compensation unless it was preceded by the enactment of a liability law stripping away employers' common-law defenses altogether.

Shortly before the 1911 legislative session, a "voluntary commission" that replaced Flora and Boyle with two members picked by ISFL president Edwin Wright, and otherwise identical to the Employers' Liability Commission, completed the draft of the proposed workers' compensation law and submitted it to the General Assembly.[51]

Seeking to patch the growing rift with the Chicago federation, the ISFL submitted an old draft of an employers' liability law to the General Assembly, but the CFL refused to "be bound by any action of the commission appointed by President Wright of the Illinois State Federation of Labor" and dispatched lobbyists to "prevent as far as possible the enactment of a workmen's compensation law or employers' liability law that has not been endorsed by the Chicago Federation of Labor."[52] An uncertain General Assembly passed both the workers' compensation bill and an employers' liability measure. With labor's forces scattered, however, the IMA dropped its cooperative stance and attempted to rout them. IMA leaders recognized that workers' compensation enjoyed popular support and that the bill regularized compensation proceedings, but they fastened onto its distasteful features and organized an efficient campaign to force Governor Deneen to veto both bills.[53]

Deneen agreed to hold hearings on the bills in the state senate chambers on May 26, 1911. Glenn immediately gathered an impressive business delegation. "Governor Deneen will not veto the measure unless the industries of Illinois demand it," he reasoned. "Two or three hundred telegrams and a delegation of fifty or a hundred men cannot produce the result."[54] With an eye on labor's troubles, Glenn arranged a preliminary conference to iron out any difficulties before the official hearing. As a result of Glenn's prodding, nine railroad cars loaded with Chicago manufacturers rode to Springfield, where three hundred businessmen jammed the senate chamber on the 26th.[55]

IMA unity at Springfield contrasted sharply with labor's disintegration. ISFL loyalists charged that a lobbyist claiming CFL credentials personally aided Glenn against the compensation bill and that CFL and railroad union lobbyists joined the IMA secretary in defeating the state body's liability bill. Chicago Federationists hotly replied that ISFL president Wright sat with Glenn at the Springfield hearing and subsequently brought out "the steam roller" to crush his opposition at the 1911 ISFL convention. Unable to resolve the dispute, the Chicago federation broke with the state labor body. In Springfield, the Joint Labor Conference established in 1905 between the ISFL, the CFL, the United Mine Workers of America, and the railroad brotherhoods fell apart, hamstringing attempts to carry on a unified legislative program. The various lobbies issued separate reports until 1915.[56]

Glenn's intensified opposition helped worsen labor divisions and encouraged Deneen to veto the liability bill, but it could not persuade the governor to veto the compensation act. IMA predictions of life under the compensation law were colored by depictions of industrial anarchy. "A stick of dynamite during a strike might give you fifteen or twenty permanently injured people who would be weights to your business as long as they had the breath of life," read one dark warning. And if manufacturers refused to accept the plan, "the jury can take the plant away from you or the bread and butter from your children if it sees fit."[57] Despite these dire prophecies, the obvious need for legislation, public support for compensation, and business participation in the commission that drafted the model bill overwhelmed the IMA's eleventh-hour opposition. Deneen signed the bill, but he allowed for court tests until the following May, when the compensation law took effect.[58]

Once the bill was passed into law, the IMA ceased to communicate feverish visions and devised the best method to conform to the new situation. Piez suggested the formation of the Illinois Manufacturers' Casualty Company to insure members under the terms of the law. Because the compensation law determined awards "with sufficient definiteness to avoid acrimonious litigation" and provided for the simple payment of claims, in-house coverage was more attractive than the high rates demanded by commercial insurance.[59] The resources of mobilized businessmen in Illinois seemed to meet every contingency.

◆

Organized, powerful, and realistic, the IMA inserted itself between the business community and an active public policy. Progressives believed that reform by government commissions provided the best chance to resolve industrial conflicts on the broad terms of the public good without damaging the vital interests of capital or labor. Capital made better use of these commissions than did labor. As the workers' compensation episode unfolded, the IMA displayed a deft touch: compromising when necessary without losing its unity of purpose, softening the proposed regulation to acceptable levels, and still severely injuring the Illinois labor movement. Even on the unfamiliar progressive terrain where the public interest was the ultimate priority, the IMA strode confidently toward its private goals.

The Political Campaign against Labor

The running battle between the Illinois Manufacturers' Association and organized labor formed the core of IMA activities and only occasionally crossed the public interest. The IMA's career as a strikebreaker and stalwart in the national open shop movement displayed a single-minded ferocity that it carried into its legislative lobby. Through the first two decades of the twentieth century the IMA and organized labor shadowed each other's movements in a competitive *pas de deux.*

After 1905 the legislative fortunes of organized labor began to brighten. That year the four major labor lobbies at Springfield—the United Mine Workers of America, the Railway Trainmen, the Chicago Federation of Labor, and the Illinois State Federation of Labor— coordinated their efforts through daily meetings of an eighteen-member conference. This Joint Labor Conference proved so vital to the protection and advancement of labor legislation that it was known as the "third house" of the legislature.[60] The ISFL's influence was boosted by the infusion of 300 United Mine Workers of America locals into the organization in 1908, doubling the federation's receipts for 1909, and by ISFL president Edwin Wright's friendship with Governor Deneen. The spate of health, safety, and hours legislation introduced in the Forty-fifth General Assembly marked a commitment to regulation of working conditions unknown in Illinois since Altgeld. Following Deneen's two terms, Edward Dunne encouraged even greater industrial reforms.[61]

IMA officials exaggerated the strength of the labor lobby to encourage an increased legislative presence capable of countering the schemes of a wily and persistent foe. IMA president LaVerne Noyes told Montgomery Ward in 1909 that "the forces which we are battling maintain a lobby at Springfield during the entire session which makes it doubly important that manufacturers manifest their interest by occasionally visiting the capital and showing their interest in the measures we are advocating and their opposition to the bills we are opposing."[62]

The IMA stepped up its Springfield activity in 1907, publishing the first of its special legislative bulletins. The bulletins followed bills through the General Assembly, appraised members as to their likely impact, and provided the names of key legislators along with messages intended to sway their votes. This added pressure so strengthened legislative intransigence to labor initiatives in 1907 that a member of the CFL's legislative committee vowed never to return to Springfield as a lobbyist, holding that "the Federation might better throw its money away than spend it in further lobbying."[63] "On almost every occasion," complained ISFL president Edwin Wright, "we have been told to agree with our opponents (our employers) and present 'agreed legislation.'"[64] By 1913 the IMA issued weekly legislative reports, and in 1915 it instituted a daily news service from the capital called the "pink sheet."[65]

The struggle against labor initiatives and industrial regulation drew the

Illinois Manufacturers' Association deep into legislative politics. In 1912 the IMA's legislative organization committee created subcommittees arranged by state senatorial districts. Ranging from two to fifteen members apiece, they were to serve as liaisons between local businesspeople and their state representatives. The subcommittees established personal relations with lawmakers and arranged for candidates to meet with businesspeople and employers' organizations. They also coordinated local business response to legislation and selected employers' delegations to testify before the General Assembly. By 1915 all fifty-one senatorial districts were organized, and the IMA had established headquarters in Springfield at the Leland Hotel, the capital's central political gathering place.[66]

The institutionalization of business advocacy in Illinois reflected national trends during the Progressive Era. As state legislatures came under growing pressure from both progressives and unions to regulate factory conditions, employers feared the economic consequences of uneven regulatory development. This was especially true where industrial pockets conformed to geographic rather than political boundaries. Political mobilization by businesspeople in one state nearly compelled similar vigilance elsewhere. On the other hand, widespread demands for industrial regulation somewhat lessened the political challenge for business interests. If employers exerted enough influence to limit protective regulation to the general outlines of existing laws in other states, they lost no competitive ground. If they could tailor it a bit more to fit their wishes, they won a victory. Thus, even though Illinois joined other industrial states in extending greater governmental controls over conditions in the workplace, the IMA's ability to shape that regulation made it a formidable power. Still, the IMA objected to the "mania" for "wild cat legislation" in Springfield and measured its success by the number of bills it blocked. In 1915 its legislative committee happily reported that of 1,541 bills introduced in the General Assembly that session, only 271 were passed into law.[67]

♦

Union lobbying and progressive appeals to public opinion managed to chisel past the granite opposition of organized business on several occasions. Progressives, labor advocates, and the IMA were particularly active in the Forty-sixth General Assembly in 1909. In that session twelve labor bills became law, fifty-one failed to pass, and two were vetoed by Governor Deneen.[68] Most of the bills that passed were minor, but extreme pressure forced the IMA to compromise on a factory safety measure and retreat on hours regulation for women workers.

Illinois had long possessed one of the feeblest sets of factory health and safety regulations in the nation. Industrial accidents were so routine, observed a union official to the Chicago City Club, "that no wood worker working in a factory in the city is recognized as a mechanic if he has all his fingers."[69] Illinois lacked statutes ensuring adequate factory ventilation or requiring protective guards over moving machinery, leading Chief Factory Inspector Edgar Davies to confess, "I hang my head in shame."[70] Eager to improve this dismal record, Governor Deneen commissioned Davies in 1905 to study factory laws in Europe and America with the intent of drawing up a model safety bill for Illinois. The familiar progressive coalition of civilian experts and government officials set to work on the project, completing its task in 1907. IMA officials decried the model bill, however, complaining that it gave "czarlike" power to the state factory inspector and created a situation in which "the whim of the Factory Inspector may become the law, and the business men of the State become criminals, because of their inability to anticipate his next whim."[71] Despite the bill's popularity, the IMA killed it in the senate.[72]

Sheer refusal to cover exposed machinery nevertheless was not a realistic stance for the business lobby to adopt in the steady light of publicity. Determined to make the best of the situation, IMA officials pressed the governor for the creation of an industrial commission to recommend proper health and safety standards. Late in the 1907 session the General Assembly approved the formation of a nine-member commission representing the interests of employers, employees, and the public. Deneen appointed three IMA members as the employers' representatives, who joined such luminaries as Graham Taylor and David Ross of the State Bureau of Labor Statistics. Factory Inspector Davies, Charles R. Henderson of the University of Chicago, and John R. Commons of the University of Wisconsin aided the commission's work, while reform groups such as the Women's Trade Union League freely made suggestions.[73]

Public expectations for the commission's success persuaded each of its three factions to offer concessions in the interest of producing an acceptable measure. The IMA endorsed the bill that emerged from the investigation, and in 1909 Illinois moved in one bound from the very rear to the forefront among states in factory safety regulation. With a nod to the public and a wink to businesspeople, the IMA later boasted that its work concerning factory safety "has been both Constructive and Protective."[74]

IMA defenses against the women's ten-hour bill proved neither constructive nor sufficiently protective. Every eight-hour bill that appeared in the General Assembly during the Progressive Era was beaten down with the help of the IMA, but the 1909 measure championed by the Women's Trade Union League cleverly asked for a ten-hour day based on the precedent of the recent *Muller v. Oregon* decision of the United States

Supreme Court. The bill was passed by the General Assembly, but it was struck down by the Cook County Circuit Court after a challenge from the IMA in the name of the same firm—W. C. Ritchie and Company—that had been involved in the 1893 suit against the sweatshop act. Any similarities with the events of the 1890s ended at that point. Backed by public opinion and legal expert Ernst Freund, Louis Brandeis and Josephine Goldmark of the National Consumers' League appealed the decision before the Illinois Supreme Court with a 600-page replica of the famous brief assembled in the *Muller* case. On April 21, 1910, the state court upheld the women's ten-hour law completely and in all its particulars. Not even politically mobilized business interests could expect faithful support of public-policy positions from the courts.[75]

◆

Aggressive lobbying created bad blood between the IMA and industrial reformers. The manufacturers' association regarded unions as havens for dangerous agitators and radical "walking delegates" who did not have the real interests of working people at heart. IMA spokespeople termed organized labor "a conspiracy as criminal as the Molly Maguires or Ku Klux Klan" and, during World War I, as akin to "kaiserism."[76] Lurid articles in *Manufacturers' News* stressed the violence of "labor thugs"; as for the union leadership, Glenn charged that they were "mentioned in connection with the anarchistic movements which the police of the large cities are trying to suppress."[77]

Nor did Glenn spare progressives who assisted the cause of industrial labor. The secretary considered them either the allies or the dupes of the "labor dictators." He scornfully linked "the labor unions and sociologists" and decried the "misguided public sentiments created by certain social settlement people in Chicago and union labor agitators."[78] Association official Dorr E. Felt went even further, hinting dramatically of the "marked similarity between the teachings of Trotzky [sic] and those of the average social worker."[79]

Illinois social reform advocates displayed a comparable hostility toward the IMA. After IMA pressure helped block the 1907 factory safety bill, Raymond Robins blamed the group for "two more years of the harvest of industrial cripples in this state."[80] Graham Taylor in 1910 denounced Glenn as unfair, unethical, and a disgrace to the state of Illinois.[81] Frustrated reformers regarded the IMA as a brake on progress, a powerful and obstructive organization clinging to corporation privileges that were relics of a bygone age. Above all, progressives resented the IMA's uncanny ability to influence politicians.

◆

Although the politics of factory regulation in progressive-era Illinois led to some improvement in the material conditions of Prairie State workers, it produced no rationale for public policy beyond stark self-preservation. Whatever hopes organized labor may have harbored for a distinctive working-class democracy were lost in the necessary alliance with progressives that underlay the public campaigns for protective legislation. Progressive intentions to heal social fractures with the balm of public interest were blocked by the political mobilization of business. No competing vision of public life superseded the public interest. Despite the IMA's legislative success, the web of relationships between businesspeople and lawmakers envisioned by some of its leaders never materialized. Manufacturers in Illinois were acutely conscious of their rights, but they responded to threats only as they arose. As judged by their actions, mobilized businesspeople believed that the IMA's task was to influence politics without attempting to hold office or dictate overall party policy. As long as the unions were kept at bay, the politicians could have the rest.[82]

In the same vein, the leadership of the IMA failed to develop any consistent viewpoint as to the proper role of government in a highly developed economy. The IMA's only measure was that of self-interest. It developed finely honed legislative tactics to pursue that interest, and understood the power of public opinion, but it had virtually no ideas about government per se. Consequently, it shrilly rejected the centralization of authority in the office of the state factory inspector and a revamped Board of Tax Commissioners while ardently defending regulation of public carriers and pressing for greater municipal control over the Chicago telephone monopoly.

◆

One of the broad themes of progressive reform was a desire to unify society. Middle-class reformers attempted to break down class antagonisms, eliminate ethnic rivalries, and ease the distrust between country and city. In their place, progressives would construct a compassionate, yet efficient state that served the public interest. In this ideal scheme, unruly partisans of particularistic interests became public-spirited citizens and order was imposed on a chaotic world. Organizations like the IMA, which entered the public arena to further private goals, dashed cold water on that hope.

Singleness of purpose in the pursuit of private interest by the Illinois Manufacturers' Association subverted the progressive attempt to reconstruct the relations of capital and labor along lines intended to promote the greater harmony of society. That clash symbolized the weakness of the public interest as a determinant of public policy. Similar organizations involved in other intensive conflicts frustrated most attempts to rationalize the government of Illinois and retool its creaking machinery to meet the more complex needs of the twentieth century—indeed, manufacturers and unions were far from the only organized interests in the state descending on Springfield with narrowly conceived sets of demands and a strong unwillingness to compromise. As Illinois society grew denser after 1890, and the political parties began to shed their role as havens of cultural identity and unified outlook, hundreds of groups organized around trades, localities, or beliefs and pursued their conflicting goals with fervor. Illinois politics had long witnessed interest-group lobbying and selfish legislative demands, but the scale and ferocity of the competition among interests grew crazily after 1900, overwhelming institutional attempts to manage it and meet the changing needs of the state. The state tax system remained a disgrace; Chicago failed to gain a new charter; and Illinois fumbled its attempt to write a modern constitution. Like many organizations of the time, the Illinois Manufacturers' Association was committed, powerful, and short-sighted. That unhappy combination helped ensure that Illinois government remained shackled to outmoded forms. Unable to define the public interest, Americans celebrated interest-group pluralism, in which the values of the marketplace determined public policy.

PART TWO

Reforming the City: Efficiency and Democracy in Chicago Public Life

There is little doubt that Chicago
will be cleaned up.

—Lincoln Steffens, 1903

4

Defining Home Rule: Mainstream Reform, Alternative Culture, and the Chicago City Charter Movement

"The Twentieth Century opens with two distinguishing features—the dominant city and militant democracy." So wrote Frederic C. Howe, protégé to Cleveland mayor Tom Johnson. Howe was confident that the challenges of urban life would usher in a new spirit of democratic citizenship in American cities. The "strait-jacket" of state control heretofore had prevented urban self-rule. Lack of independence, he claimed, allowed selfish or private goals to dominate urban government and institutions. Possibilities inherent in civic patriotism and shared purpose went unrealized as long as city dwellers lacked the power to shape their institutions, but Howe felt that liberation from archaic state restrictions would bring on an urban renaissance. He predicted that "home rule would create a city republic" distinguished by an outpouring of civic dynamism and talent reminiscent of Athens, Rome, and Florence at the height of their glory. [1]

Such were the buoyant hopes of progressive city builders. Graham Taylor, among other Chicago reformers, shared Howe's conviction that the city must come to represent unselfish ideals of common identification rather than the self-destructive temperament of individualistic advantage. [2] If American civilization were to advance in the twentieth century, then its most compelling modern manifestation, the city, would have to be reformed. Urban America was the acid test of these progressive ideals.

Central to the civic resurgence envisioned by Howe was urban home rule. The ability of progressive-era cities to act creatively in the face of overcrowding, industrial expansion, and deteriorating public services was hampered by state-imposed limitations on urban power. Urban reformers tried to break free from state restrictions by means of new city charters, municipal ownership of public-service franchises, and more extensive popular control of government. Rather than unleashing cooperative democratic movements that transformed civic life, however, the quest for urban home rule reinforced deep social, class, and intellectual divisions that flourished in progressive-era cities. Democratic reformers such as Johnson and Howe, city central labor councils, and socialist and working-class organizations understood home rule to mean urban independence from outside interference and popular control within the city. Upper- and middle-class businesspeople, professionals, and educators defined home rule as a consolidation of civic functions that transferred power from state legislatures and urban immigrant and working-class populations to more "responsible" city residents such as themselves. In the rough and tumble of urban politics, each of these "home-rule interests" splintered into more specialized blocs that prevented any single group from dominating home-rule reforms and often produced unforeseen consequences. The consolidation of independent towns into greater New York in 1897, for instance, launched by the city's commercial, real estate, banking, and reform elites, ultimately worked to the advantage of Republican state boss Thomas Platt.[3]

The progressive-era movement for a new Chicago charter shows how home-rule notions worked as a stumbling block to urban reform instead of as a key to urban unity. Chicago was a striking anomaly in the 1890s—an industrial giant growing frightfully larger each year but governed under an 1872 state law that limited the city's tax base, stunted its bonded indebtedness, and divided it into autonomous financial principalities directly responsible to the General Assembly, the governor, or any number of judges and commissioners. Public opinion in the city agreed that the situation was intolerable and demanded remedy, but consensus stopped there. Chicago was not one but many cities—neighborhoods, classes, and communities with distinct sets of values, customs, and priorities that were often hidden from one another or locked in conflict. Each stressed a different understanding of home rule. Their confrontations over the proposed city charter divided reformers, angered protectors of morality and defenders of ethnic customs, and pitted the city against the rest of Illinois.

The proposed charter was first advocated by the prosperous business and professional residents of Chicago. Unsettled by financial and administrative restrictions on the city, private citizens' clubs devised a charter that would consolidate these public functions of city government. This "nonpartisan" effort fell short of the goals sought by other Chicagoans, however. Democratic reformers led by the Chicago Federation of Labor demanded that such measures of popular government as municipal ownership of utilities and the referendum not be sacrificed to achieve administrative efficiency. Immigrant residents of Chicago, upset at downstate attempts to regulate public drinking in the city, complained that a home-rule charter that did nothing to protect the established customs of city residents was a sham. Downstate interests intervened in the charter dispute. Rural representatives in the General Assembly tied the fate of the charter to restrictions on Cook County's political power. The Anti-Saloon League of Illinois pressured Chicago charter supporters to help enforce state laws closing saloons on Sunday and yoked a local option law to the charter in the legislature. Assailed on all sides, the charter was defeated and Chicago remained administratively divided against itself, a division that accurately mirrored the social, cultural, and political condition of the metropolis.

How could progressives have been so mistaken about the shared public spirit of the city? How could they have misunderstood so completely the desires of the majority of Chicago citizens? In the case of Chicago charter reform, the progressive idea of the public interest provides the answer. For the mainstream middle-class reformers who wrote and supported the Chicago charter from 1905 until 1907, practicality and idealism led them to demand the consolidation of city administration as the necessary first step to civic improvement. Frustrating daily experience in a city that smelled bad, that could not coordinate public services, that wallowed in political corruption, and that had to rely on the goodwill of the state to improve matters persuaded these reformers that, above all, Chicago must have financial and administrative independence. However, the charter they constructed to gain that independence had to be approved by the General Assembly. Because sources of tension between Chicago and downstate Illinois, such as the explosive question of saloon regulation, could threaten the basic goals of the charter, mainstream reformers compromised on these "lesser" issues. That was practical enough. These mainstream reformers based their actions on the assumption that Chicago voters shared a conception of the public interest that placed financial and administrative reforms above local control of saloons as a civic priority.

In fact, however, Chicago immigrants and their children, especially those of central European origin, placed a greater emphasis on local control of public drinking. Fellowship in family saloons, fraternal associations, and private clubs formed part of a deeply rooted "alternative culture" in Chicago that did not seek to overturn dominant "American" standards but did insist on preserving an independent outlook and identity.[4] For many Germans, Bohemians, and Poles in Chicago, state interference with Chicago's tolerant public drinking regulations represented a disruptive challenge to their cultural autonomy. The United Societies for Local Self-Government organized to repel that threat. Alternative Chicago interests did not deny the need for financial and administrative consolidation, but they refused to allow it at the expense of their own civic priorities; consequently, they worked to defeat the Chicago charter. The public interest promoted by mainstream reformers did not represent the beliefs of the largest segment of Chicago's population.

Democracy revealed not the unity of progressive-era cities but their division. The flawed attempt to reform Chicago government pointed not back to the civic culture of city-republics but rather ahead to the racial antipathy, bureaucratic jumble, and political misrule of urban America in the twentieth century.

The Case for Administrative Reform

To the young, efficiency-minded professionals who worked in Chicago, nothing made as little sense as the patchwork, financially restricted, and confusing administrative organization of city government. Existing state controls over Chicago could not cope with rapid urban growth, while fearful and partisan downstate lawmakers appeared unwilling to offer any remedy. "Renowned for business system, enterprise, and success throughout the world, Chicago must match its business triumphs with a fitting municipal advance," declared Alderman and University of Chicago professor Charles E. Merriam.[5] Citizens had not only to tame the political machine but also to attain home rule for the city.

Following the Great Fire, private organizations labored to temper Chicago's rapid expansion as a population center and commercial headquarters with orderly city government and efficient public services. Prominent businesspeople, galvanized into action in 1874 by the threat from fire insurance companies to remove all coverage of Chicago property, founded the reformist Citizens' Association and dragooned a reluctant city council into reorganizing the city's patronage-laden fire department into an effective unit. Similarly, the foul condition of the Chicago River drew the Citizens' Association into a decade of activity that resulted in the creation of a large-scale planned sewage system.

In both campaigns, the Citizens' Association found city government alternately unwilling and administratively unable to act forcefully for the provision of basic urban services. The association hired experts to devise solutions to problems fostered by ineffective public works and then crafted partnerships between reformers and government to implement privately subsidized plans. Experience from the late nineteenth century thus produced a group of prominent, public-spirited citizens wedded to the use of independent experts, conscious of the weakness of corrupt and restricted municipal government, and eager to restructure administrative authority so that Chicago could adequately govern itself.[6]

The Civic Federation of Chicago carried this reformist tradition into the twentieth century. Like the Citizens' Association, the Civic Federation was founded in an atmosphere of crisis. After the Haymarket riot of 1886 clarified the reality of class hatred, and as the depression of 1893 settled over the city, English journalist William Stead added a further shock with *If Christ Came to Chicago*, a muckraking account of urban iniquity. Stead arranged for a public meeting on November 13, 1893, to address concerns his book had raised among the civic-minded. Out of that gathering a coalition of businesspeople, professionals, labor leaders, and social workers created the Civic Federation. Soon the organization was busy distributing relief to the city's growing army of the unemployed. Businesspeople and professionals quickly came to dominate the federation, however, turning it to the middle-class purposes of cleaning up city hall and promoting efficiency in the conduct of public business.[7]

Late nineteenth-century annexations of middle-class suburbs to Chicago and the vigorous campaign of the Civic Federation's political offshoot, the Municipal Voters' League (MVL), changed the composition of the Chicago Common Council. In 1889, the towns of Hyde Park, Lake, Lake View, Cicero, and Jefferson elected to join Chicago, bringing with them middle-class voters inclined to support administrative reforms. George Cole, the diligent head of the MVL, maintained contact with voters by means of ward-level organization and cooperative Chicago newspapers, which published the MVL's evaluations of council candidates. Cole astutely combined reform appeals in outlying wards with practical local politics in immigrant districts. Newly annexed wards provided the MVL with the great majority of its early victories, but by 1900 MVL-approved aldermen made up two-thirds of the city council. Added to the civil service law of 1895, this change so improved municipal conditions that in 1903 Lincoln Steffens expressed "little doubt that Chicago will be cleaned up."[8] For a brief time, the Chicago city council received national acclaim as a model for municipal government.

◆

Reform of the city council improved Chicago government, but without consolidation of municipal authority the city could not provide adequate services or efficiently allocate resources. Indeed, without the consolidation of suburbs into Chicago, the MVL's effort to elect better aldermen would have been severely handicapped. State law divided authority in metropolitan Chicago and restricted the financial power of the city. A wider campaign to remove structural impediments was necessary before the city could achieve anything resembling administrative rationality.

The 1870 Illinois Constitution was the primary source of restrictions. Operating to curb legislative abuses, the constitution limited the power of the General Assembly to pass special laws incorporating municipalities or altering their charters. Lawmakers met constitutional requirements by enacting a general incorporation statute, the Cities and Villages Act. In 1875 Chicago relinquished its outdated special charter and came under the jurisdiction of the act. In consequence, during the period of its most spectacular growth Chicago shared the basic administrative features of much smaller cities. The General Assembly could not alter Chicago's financial structure or lengthen the term of its mayor to four years without first amending the constitution to allow special legislation for the metropolis. In the meantime, groused Alderman Milton Foreman, "such laws as were enacted were grotesque compromises, efforts at averages, somewhat as might have resulted from an attempt to make a suit of clothes that would fit both a giant and a child."[9]

Thirty years of growth in metropolitan Chicago under the general incorporation law created a patchwork of competing government jurisdictions with a public financial base ludicrously underutilizing the wealth available in the city. By the turn of the century, eight separate taxing and governing bodies competed in Chicago: Cook County, city hall, the Chicago Board of Education, the Chicago Public Library Board, three separate park boards, and the Chicago Sanitary District. Each of these answered to a separate authority. The mayor appointed members of the school board and the library board, but on appointment they became free agents. The governor appointed members of the West and Lincoln park boards, whereas Cook County circuit court judges named the South park board. Voters chose the Cook County and sanitary district boards. This nightmare of overlapping jurisdictions produced five separate police forces, four electric lighting plants, two waterworks, and four bodies charged with maintaining the streets. Citizens paid a confusing array of taxes and voted to fill one hundred offices every four years.[10]

The spur that this fragmented authority gave to political factionalism can well be imagined, but its impact on city finances was devastating. The tax structure under the welter of competing governments in Chicago is a landmark in the history of chaotic administration. Before 1898, the state, Cook County, the city, and various boards levied taxes without regard to what the others were doing. Some competing districts assessed the taxable property of their rivals; for example, Cook County assessed property for taxation in Chicago. Worse yet, the county relied on the notoriously inaccurate reports of township assessors, who somehow remained in office after their communities had been annexed by the city.[11]

Fraudulent property assessment and tax evasion plagued governments across the United States in the late nineteenth century, but the problem was particularly severe in Illinois. Illinois was the fourth-largest industrial state in 1880, yet its per capita personal property assessment lagged behind all other industrial states. In 1900, Illinois property assessment reflected only 14.1 percent of market value. By contrast, assessment in Massachusetts totaled 77.5 percent of market value, in New York over 64 percent, and in Ohio more than 47 percent. The gap between Illinois and other industrialized states widened in ensuing years. Uniform property assessment, locally elected township assessors, an inefficient Illinois State Board of Equalization filled with political placeholders, and massive corporate tax evasion created a serious revenue problem in the Prairie State.[12]

Chicago's assessment and taxation difficulties were far worse than those elsewhere in Illinois. The second largest population, manufacturing, and banking center in the nation could not provide adequate municipal services to its citizens. Administrative partition and inaccurate property assessment hamstrung Chicago. The system was so confusing and riddled with corruption that in 1898 the General Assembly eliminated township assessors and fixed assessment for tax purposes at 20 percent of actual value. Because state law limited district tax rates to about 5 percent of assessed valuation, metropolitan Chicago at the turn of the century was reduced to a tax base of 1 percent of the actual property wealth in Cook County. City taxes were restricted to 2 percent of *assessed* valuation. Experts estimated that continuing fraudulent assessment lopped off nearly one-third of what remained.[13]

Despite the shrunken tax base of Chicago, the city's fragmented administration produced a multitude of levies that angered city residents. State attempts to impose order failed. The Juul law of 1901 proposed to limit the combined tax rate of Chicago's separate governments to an aggregate of 5 percent of assessed valuation. Unhampered by a common authority, the competing taxing bodies of metropolitan Chicago refused to adjust their rates. Instead, each one imposed extraordinarily high taxes so as to ensure its share of the pie. The county clerk was left with the thankless task of scaling down actual levies to fit the aggregate set by the state.[14]

In the meantime, the various local governments could not accurately forecast their available funds for operating each year. Each therefore applied to the General Assembly for an increase in its taxing power. In 1906, for example, the levy of the South park board was made under the terms of ten separate laws. Surveying the damage inflicted by the flood of special acts and amendments, an expert declared "the Juul Act so modified as to make it practically inoperative and void."[15]

For advocates of a united and efficiently governed Chicago, this was the worst of all possible cases. The vast wealth of the city remained un-

tapped for public purposes; taxing power was divided among eight bickering and separately administered districts, so revenues could not be centrally allocated according to specific annual needs; the various taxing
bodies were relying on the General Assembly for special tax legislation,
even further subverting the authority of city government; and the citizenry was convinced that it was oppressively overtaxed.

Nor was this the end of Chicago's financial miseries. Taxation by 1906
produced but one-third of public income in the metropolis. Constitutional limitations on the city's bonded indebtedness further sapped its
financial strength. Constitutional and legislative stipulations combined
to reduce Chicago's borrowing power to 1 percent of its actual property
values. According to Charles Merriam, these restrictions left Chicago
with a municipal debt "proportionately far below that of any other great
city in the world."[16] Even including the obligations of independent
boards within Chicago and the city's share of the Cook County and sanitary district debt, Chicago's bonded indebtedness in 1906 was some
$60,000,000. New York's debt at the same time was approximately
$400,000,000.[17]

♦

Unable to tax or borrow adequately, Chicago manipulated the system
of divided authority to absorb some of the costs of urban government and
sought alternative sources of money. Each independent government in
metropolitan Chicago was responsible for its own maintenance, which
eased the burden for city hall but increased the chances that Chicagoans
would periodically suffer from breakdowns in public services as financial
crises engulfed local administrations. When the need for additional municipal services arose, Chicago had to embark on a complicated series of
maneuvers between concerned citizen groups, city government, and the
General Assembly to secure improvements.

The services so tortuously acquired could be as basic as adequate sewage facilities. The long road to the creation of the Chicago Sanitary District illustrates the machinery of divided government in Chicago at its
most ponderous. When the Citizens' Association commenced agitation
for an improved city sewage system in 1879, it found city government a
roadblock to reform. Limited mayoral power left the issue in the hands of
the city council. Not until 1886 did the council authorize the creation of
an expert commission to study the Chicago sewer system. By that time,
an independent Citizens' Association investigation determined that a regional system of sewage disposal was required. City government lacked
adequate authority to pursue a regional system, and its bonded debt limit
prevented Chicago from absorbing the cost. A coalition of private civic

associations therefore turned to the state, resulting in the creation in 1889 of an independently administered sanitary district with its own bureaucracy and taxing power. Although 92 percent of the Chicago Sanitary District lay within city limits, the city council had no authority over its administration. Under Chicago's restricted powers, the cost of improving the city's drainage system was the loss of control over its own sewers. Elite reformers who fought to improve the drainage system were rewarded with a new bureaucracy and payroll on which Chicago's political factions could feed.[18]

Middle-class reformers learned that public life could function under the system of divided authority and financial limitation, but the cost in time, enhancement of political patronage, and social discord was too great to bear. Saloon licenses contributed much of the city revenue unobtainable through property taxes—especially after 1906, when the cost of a license rose to $1,000—but such sources of income were insecure and troublesome. Divisive attitudes toward saloon regulation wedged themselves into the debate concerning Chicago government, and fueling city government on high saloon licenses invited political manipulation and fraud. Chicago's divided system of government also produced administrations of widely varying means, composition, and ability. The South park board was patronized by civic-minded businesspeople and professionals open to suggestions from planning advocates. It participated enthusiastically in the parks movement launched by settlement workers in the late 1890s. By contrast, West park district residents paid higher taxes than their southern neighbors, but "the West Board remained a Republican stronghold, more interested in padded payrolls and patronage than progressive reform."[19] Dependable city government could come only with financial independence from the state and administrative consolidation of city functions. Chicago must have home rule.

Home Rule through Charter Revision

Weary of the squandering of inadequate revenues, the lack of centralized administration of public business, and Chicago's dependence on state government, mainstream reformers demanded government efficiency through home rule. By the late 1880s, municipal reformers across the country were turning from the mugwumpish reliance on "good men" and putting new emphasis on rebuilding the structure of city government. Revised city charters helped free late nineteenth-century cities from administrative control and political interference at the hands of hostile state legislatures. Boston, Philadelphia, Los Angeles, Baltimore, and New York obtained new charters between 1885 and 1898. Some prosperous reformers, such as Tom Johnson of Cleveland, intended home-rule charters to sweep away obstacles to direct popular control of urban government. Most mainstream charter reformers, however, laid greater stress on building rational, efficient city government by creating a strong executive and separating politics from administration.[20]

Elite Chicago reformers emphasized the administrative aspects of home rule. In 1884 the Citizens' Association advocated charter reform; fifteen years later the Greater Chicago Committee proposed to extend the city limits to the borders of Cook County. Conditions in Illinois made charter reform difficult to achieve, however. An amendment to the state constitution legalizing charter revision was necessary first, and then the charter had to be passed by the General Assembly. Neither the enabling amendment nor the charter would become law until approved by voters.[21]

Downstate bitterness toward Chicago complicated matters further. Although, one urban historian has found that "deference to local opinion was . . . basic to the legislative process in late nineteenth-century America,"[22] Illinois state lawmakers did not defer so readily to Chicago opinion. The downstate majority in the General Assembly feared Chicago as a menacing center of corporate arrogance, political corruption, and moral degradation that threatened to swallow the entire state. As early as 1890 the legislature dragged its feet when reapportioning state senatorial districts to reflect the population growth of the metropolis. After 1901, when Cook County controlled over one-third of the seats in each house, the General Assembly simply refused further reapportionments and openly worked to restrict Cook County's representation permanently. Even partisan bonds weakened from the hostility between the state and its largest city. "Dam them kind of [Chicago] Republicans," cursed a GOP official from central Illinois, "thay are not like the boys in old McDonough."[23]

All sectors of Chicago society complained of state interference in the affairs of the city. Faintly praising the "homely virtues of the country," the *Chicago Tribune* blasted the "impudent and preposterous" attempt of downstate legislators to restrict the "great activities and marvelous usefulness" of Chicago.[24] Chicago Democrats resented the Republican-dominated legislature's control of patronage in metropolitan Chicago. Catholics and Germans angrily recalled the nativist Edwards education law passed by the General Assembly in 1889. Saloonkeepers and their patrons hated the statewide Sunday closing law and feared that the state would compel city authorities to enforce the statute. Advocates of popular government distrusted rural Illinois legislators, considering them a barrier to democracy.

State impediments to independent action on the part of Chicago and the animosity they aroused hampered charter reform in two ways. Obviously, legal restrictions and legislative hostility made it more difficult to obtain a new charter. The second barrier was more ironic and probably more dangerous. Because all Chicagoans seemed to oppose certain features of state guardianship over the city, mainstream reformers assumed most Chicago residents shared a commitment to home rule. However, the administrative home rule mainstream reformers attempted to enshrine in the charter did not reflect the home-rule aspirations of those seeking cultural autonomy or popular control within the city. As a slogan, home rule had sweeping appeal in Chicago; as a blueprint for city government devised by mainstream business and professional interests, it laid bare basic conflicts over the future of the city.

The young businesspeople and professionals who seized the initiative in the charter campaign were not especially arrogant or narrow-minded individuals. Charles Merriam and Ernst Freund, who provided the theoretical and legal underpinnings for charter revision, were learned, sensitive laborers for the public good.[25] Paradoxically, it was this devotion to the public interest that restricted the outlook of most mainstream reformers. For progressive upholders of the public interest, as Martin Schiesl observes, "public policy was not the result of thorough discussion by various interest groups."[26] Because they thought that truly efficient "nonpartisan" administration should not be subject to the compromises of everyday political methods, Chicago charter advocates listened to representatives of diverse opinions during deliberations on the new charter, yet they consistently voted down minority viewpoints. They expected dissenters to swallow individual disappointments and, for the sake of civic improvement, support the fruits of united effort.

Mainstream reformers perhaps anticipated widespread public acceptance of their proposals because they already had tailored the national municipal efficiency doctrine to fit the special circumstances of Chicago government. Unlike reformers who pared away the influence of political parties by means of commission government or at-large council elections, Chicago's middle class remained content with the mayor-council form of government. The modest advances of late nineteenth-century reform, confidence in the rising public spirit of the city, and the powerful hold of party identification even on reformers left mainstream efficiency backers reluctant to tamper with the internal machinery of Chicago government.

Commission government was out of the question in Chicago. A large city with a highly diverse population needs a charismatic mayor as a symbol of civic unity and authority. Besides, Mayor Carter Harrison appeared amenable to measures designed to streamline the internal administration of the city bureaucracy. For example, in 1900 the Chicago Merchants' Club complained of poor accounting procedures within city departments. Harrison hired a distinguished outside expert who centralized city accounting within two years.[27]

The prospects of the Chicago Common Council also appeared promising. By 1900 the days of aldermen passing transparently corrupt franchise laws against the interests of the public seemed to be over. The MVL's reform campaign had transformed the council into a respectable city legislature. A satisfactory settlement of the city's dispute with local streetcar companies appeared inevitable. In an era marked by increasing surrender of power by municipal legislatures to the central authority of mayors, the Chicago city council maintained a notable vitality. Although later events would dislodge their confidence, most mainstream reformers at the turn of the century were satisfied with the work of the council. A majority in the Charter Convention supported the retention of ward-based council representation in the city. The at-large system of representation that appealed to progressives elsewhere seemed unnecessary in Chicago. Besides, the city's thicket of political factions and ethnic neighborhoods doomed any attempt to root out ward politics.[28]

Mainstream reformers did not conceive of charter revision as a power struggle between elements within the city. Constitutional limitations on city government and state hostility toward Chicago monopolized their concern. Satisfied with the basic components of city government, they labored to remove the system of independent outside authority that clogged administrative efficiency. In so doing, they refused to reorganize the internal power structure of the city in ways that would allow greater popular control over government. To the surprise of mainstream reformers, their efforts to create home rule prompted a struggle over rule at home.

The Charter Conventions

From the outset of the lengthy process of charter revision, Chicago business and professional organizations outmaneuvered elected officials and other rivals to set the agenda for efficient change. At the same time, these mainstream reformers emphasized the need for a united front against downstate hostility if consolidation of local government functions were to be achieved. The firm conviction that their stance embodied the public interest allowed charter proponents to exaggerate the representativeness of two city charter conventions and then brush aside objections from the few popular government supporters who did attend the proceedings.

Mayor Carter Harrison was the first to be nudged aside. Troubled by

mounting revenue problems in 1901, Harrison asked the city council to
devise constitutional amendments to centralize local taxation under city
authority. Because the proposed alterations affected four articles of the
state constitution, and state law prohibited the General Assembly from
amending more than one article per session, this plan required a constitutional convention. The Civic Federation refused to allow a gathering
of downstate lawyers to reconstruct the city, however. Instead, it called
on Chicago citizens to write an amendment allowing revision of the city
charter and then to construct a new home-rule charter. The legislature
could pass the entire package in four years. Harrison liked the scheme
and, in 1902, tried to ease back into control by calling on elected officials
to assume leadership in the charter movement. Nonetheless, the federation pressed on with its private campaign.[29]

At the invitation of the Civic Federation, representatives from twenty-
four public and private organizations met in October as the New Charter
Convention. Although sponsors claimed that "no prominent organization, municipal, industrial, or political," would be excluded and promised
a "full exchange of views," it was apparent that mainstream reformers
from business and professional organizations were in complete control of
the proceedings.[30] Harrison and a handful of aldermen and county officials
were outnumbered by delegates from the Civic Federation, Citizens' Association, MVL, City Club, Bar Association, Merchants' Club, and so
on. Two delegates from the Chicago Federation of Labor represented the
working class. Immigrants had no direct representation. Keynote speaker
Bernard Sunny, president of the Civic Federation, sounded the dominant
theme from the outset: "The federation has come to the conclusion that
our only hope for constitutional modification depends entirely and absolutely on the unity of the people and press of Chicago as to a specific
plan," he urged. "Anything short of this is of no value whatever."[31] Supporters of a constitutional convention were routed in short order, and a
committee report echoed Civic Federation suggestions for an enabling
amendment and a charter convention. The proposed amendment placed
independent boards and county jurisdictions inside the city limits under
Chicago's authority. The city assumed the debts and liabilities of the absorbed authorities and increased its bonded indebtedness to 5 percent of
full property value. These administrative and fiscal measures satisfied the
home-rule aspirations of most convention participants.[32]

Mainstream reformers closed ranks against democratic dissenters. Judge
Edward F. Dunne, supported by CFL delegate James Linehan, attempted
to add provisions to the enabling amendment for municipal ownership of
utilities, the initiative on petition by 10 percent of city voters, and the
referendum. The committee spokesman complained that Dunne's pro-

posal "would give too small a percentage of the voters a chance to be always stirring up trouble."[33] Dunne's amendments were buried, and, in January 1903, the enabling amendment was sent to Springfield for approval by the General Assembly.

The enforced "unity" of the New Charter Convention covered up but did not resolve tension between mainstream reformers, Chicago politicians, and adherents of popular democracy. Now the General Assembly refused to play its part. Downstate lawmakers tried to link the enabling amendment to measures restricting Cook County's representation and revising tax laws to the advantage of rural Illinois. Chicago representatives managed to thwart those designs and pass the enabling amendment, but not without changes. The legislature specified that the independent authority and governing bureaucracy of Cook County and the Chicago Sanitary District would remain intact under a new charter. Administrative consolidation would not be complete.

Mainstream reformers took the legislature's alterations in stride. Arguing that the basic features of consolidation and revenue enhancement remained intact, the Civic Federation urged voters to approve the amendment at the November 1904 election. The city council also endorsed the amendment, but the CFL broke the facade of unity and opposed adoption. Labor resistance was not in response to the General Assembly's actions; instead, the CFL belatedly complained that the exclusion of popular democratic measures from the amendment favored the interests of business at the expense of the people. The CFL made its objections public just before the election, and they had little effect on the popular vote. Chicago voters approved the amendment in landslide proportions, and it won the necessary statewide victory.[34]

The first phase of Chicago charter reform, ending in 1904 with the adoption of the enabling amendment, established the basic characteristics that marked the remainder of the charter campaign. Mainstream reformers identified the primary goal of home rule as the attainment of centralized, efficient, and fiscally secure city administration. Business and professional charter proponents assumed that anyone concerned with the future of Chicago shared that central goal. The General Assembly could be expected to tamper with the details of charter revision, but as long as the central features of administrative consolidation remained in place such interference could be tolerated. Yet once the city received the power to revise its charter, the right of mainstream reformers to speak for Chicago was challenged by groups that demanded an equal voice in fashioning public authority in their city. The drive for home rule sparked an internal power struggle.

◆

Mainstream reformers managed to write a city charter that reflected their desires, but this time they had to weather sterner opposition. As soon as voters ratified the enabling amendment, the executive committee of the 1902 convention authorized seven men (including Sunny, Harrison, and three executive committeemen) to begin work on a charter. The CFL immediately submitted a proposal for electing delegates to a convention. Neither bid to organize a convention made any headway, and after the General Assembly unsuccessfully tried to take control, the Chicago city council seized the initiative. Luckily for mainstream reformers, most of whom were Republicans, the GOP had the advantage in the council. After some wrangling, Republican aldermen pushed through their plan in June 1905.

The council plan was both partisan and conciliatory. It skillfully catered to the interests of the various bodies then governing metropolitan Chicago. The convention would consist of seventy-four appointed delegates, including fifteen aldermen selected by the council, fifteen Chicago state representatives picked by the chief officers of the General Assembly, fifteen delegates appointed by the mayor and fifteen by the governor, and two appointees each from the governing boards of the county and the sanitary district, the school board, the library board, and the three park boards. Republicans controlled all but two of the appointing bodies; each set of delegates reflected the political allegiance of its sponsor. All but five of the delegates were businessmen or professionals. Many of them were active in civic reform clubs. Mainstream reform had not lost its grip on the charter movement.[35]

Thanks to Edward Dunne, the convention did incorporate a broader range of opinion than had the 1902 proceedings. Running on a platform of municipal ownership of streetcar lines and expanded popular control of government, Dunne was elected mayor in April 1905. His appointments to the convention included CFL officials, supporters of the Chicago Teachers' Federation, middle-class champions of popular democracy such as Raymond Robins and Louis Post (editor of the single tax journal *The Public* and Dunne-appointee to the school board), and representatives of Chicago's immigrant communities. These delegates kept up a constant demand that the new charter award voters greater power over municipal affairs.[36]

During the time the Chicago charter convention was in session, the city was bitterly divided over Dunne's attempt to "democratize" public affairs. Violent strikes by packing-house workers, streetcar employees, and teamsters had convulsed Chicago over the previous five years, but within the city council chambers, where the convention met, a distinguished body of mainstream reformers shut out the evidence of turmoil and stressed a shared public commitment to rational, centralized city administration. In Walter Fisher, George Cole, Milton Foreman, Walter Clyde Jones, Charles Merriam, Raymond Robins, and Graham Taylor, the convention enjoyed the counsel of some of the nation's foremost reform spokesmen. For some of them, most notably Merriam and Taylor, administrative efficiency was but a first step in building a unified society. All except Robins, however, defined consolidation of city functions as the key public demand to be incorporated into the charter. Even before the convention opened, portions of the proposed charter were hurried through the General Assembly to speed the process of centralization. A new professional municipal court system in Chicago replaced the ragtag and often venal proceedings of the city's fifty "justice shops." Another law lengthened to four years the terms of Chicago's mayor, city clerk, and treasurer; it also took the city attorney off the ballot and made the office appointive. The charter promised to consolidate power in Chicago, not to broaden it. [37]

◆

Between November 30, 1906, and March 1, 1907, mainstream reformers constructed a city charter that matched their vision of the public interest. According to convention chairman Milton Foreman, charter framers worked "not for their own purposes, not for their own use, not for their own benefit, but for the benefit of all the city for all the time." [38] Charter sponsors stressed the broad representative character of the convention. To them, the presence of a few ward heelers, radical democrats, and labor officials in the debates signified widespread public endorsement of the charter idea and an implicit acceptance of the document that would emerge from the convention deliberations. The changes that mainstream reformers sought to enact seemed so obviously necessary, so "nonpartisan" in application, that only selfish factionalists would oppose them. Bolstered by faith in the public interest, the majority of convention delegates evaluated opposition proposals and citizens' petitions according to how those measures would affect the prospects of municipal consolidation.

Charter provisions addressed concerns that were common among mainstream critics of urban government. More than anything else, the new charter would give Chicago centralized government authority, streamlined city administration, and strengthened public finances. The park, library, and school boards came under the control of city hall. Delegates reduced the school board from twenty-one to fifteen members and placed a powerful superintendent and business manager at its head. Civil service procedures were extended to the municipal court system. City department heads received the authority to dismiss inefficient employees. Aldermen obtained increased pay and a longer, four-year term in office. The new charter also reorganized the council. Gone was the dual representation thirty-five ward system, replaced by an arrangement of seventy wards, each electing a single alderman. Overlapping authority would not be permitted, even among municipal legislators.

The charter also encouraged moderate electoral reform and gave grudging assent to a slight extension of popular democracy. Delegates approved a direct primary law, removed the party circle from Chicago ballots, and added a corrupt practices act. The 1904 Mueller bill grant of municipal authority to take over the city's street railway system was broadened to include all public utilities. Nevertheless, democratic measures were accepted only to the extent that they did not impair government stability and efficiency. Delegates ignored the initiative and the recall and limited the referendum to franchise awards. The fact that Chicago voters endorsed the initiative and referendum in advisory votes in 1902 and 1904 had no more effect on the convention than a similar vote supporting an elected school board.

Charter positions on issues of popular control occupied the middle ground between the aims of "the classes and the masses," a reflection of the progressive belief that the public interest would be best served by practical measures that would draw antagonistic groups toward the center. Such was the case with the referendum. Chicago Federation of Labor officials demanded that referenda be held on petition by 5 percent of city voters. Conservative delegates suggested that the extreme step of a public referendum should not occur unless one-fourth of Chicago voters specifically requested it. Mainstream reformers helped engineer compromises that eventually reduced the requirement to 10 percent, but compromises in the face of clearly expressed public sentiment and uncertainties in the law eroded the common ground that mainstream reformers offered to radical democrats. The compromise referendum did not open up Chicago government to popular control. The direct primary proposal in the charter was based on a legally precarious state law, soon to be struck down by the courts. And, much to the disappointment of the militant Chicago Teachers' Federation, municipal women's suffrage was not included in the charter.[39]

The barrier between mainstream reformers and popular government sponsors was most apparent in the debate over Chicago schools. Mayor Dunne had made popular control of public schools a principal objective of his administration, but he encountered violent opposition from the city's educational establishment and administrative efficiency supporters. The controversy spilled into the charter convention as delegates tried to reconstruct the board of education. With the backing of several Dunne appointees on the school board, the CFL petitioned the convention to reduce the authority of the superintendent, provide for a popularly elected board, and compensate board members so that working-class representatives could afford to serve the city. The convention majority, led by mainstream reformers, retained the appointive board and active superintendent, squelched the salary bid, and reduced the size of the board. During a sometimes angry debate, radical democrats and mainstream reformers talked past one another. Clergyman Rufus A. White, a member of the school board and the Civic Federation, argued that public service without compensation was an honor for responsible citizens. Introduction of salaried positions would "deteriorate" the board. CFL representative Linehan charged that White's ideal of public service installed millionaires on the school board while it "disfranchised" the working people whose children were educated in Chicago public schools.[40]

The education debate revealed the place of democracy in mainstream reformers' conception of the public interest. "There is a curious idea that seems to be voiced quite generally in the Convention," complained school board member Raymond Robins, "that seems to put the business efficiency of the school board as its supreme function." Not so, argued Graham Taylor, Robins's mentor at Chicago Commons and chair of the convention school committee. Taylor held that the chief goal of educational administration was to protect the public interest. Expert administrators, each an "agent of the people," would guard against financial waste, shoddy facilities, and political factionalism in the public school system. Democracy was fully realized by pursuing the public interest, not by partisan majority rule. Although the CFL platform was "very well intentioned" and "right in theory," Taylor found it impractical and misdirected. While supporting "as absolute a democracy as can be made efficient," Taylor cautioned "that nothing can be worse for democracy than inefficiency."[41] The stern virtues of common purpose outweighed numerical advantage as a determinant of responsible democracy. Sacrifice advanced the public interest, loyalty to anything but the needs of the "whole people" tore it apart.

The convention rejected or modified most proposals for increased popular control, not because the majority of its members were hostile to democracy, but because they were strongly committed to administrative reform. Taylor and Merriam, who at other times called for extensions of participatory politics, simply considered majority rule within Chicago a lesser immediate need than rationalizing municipal government and achieving financial independence commensurate with the city's commercial standing. Under the existing system, Chicago interests languished in the General Assembly. State lawmakers refused to spend time untangling

Chicago affairs.[42] Without administrative reform, other initiatives would be meaningless. Moreover, radical democratic measures could stir down-state passions against the metropolis and disturb safe passage for the charter. Mainstream reformers would not encumber administrative home rule with controversial baggage.

Charles Merriam told the City Club in 1907 that Chicago's "greatest troubles in city government have been (1) the lack of adequate power, and (2) the lack of unity and responsibility in government."[43] The new charter remedied those administrative deficiencies. As Merriam and his colleagues shored up the unity of public functions, however, they failed to appreciate the disunity that characterized attitudes toward public life in Chicago. Compromises and appeals to the public interest did not build support for the charter among those who identified the public interest with expanded democracy; even worse, mainstream reformers underestimated the home-rule expectations of Chicago immigrants and their children. Issues of liquor regulation and Sunday observance that charter enthusiasts treated as secondary concerns were at the core of an alternative culture that steadfastly refused to surrender to state control. When charter supporters proved inattentive to those concerns, the authentic public voice of Chicago made itself heard.

Alternative Culture and Home Rule

The home-rule demands of alternative Chicago were articulated by the United Societies for Local Self-Government, a coalition of immigrant social clubs, fraternal orders, and benevolent societies. The development of this group paralleled the rise of private associational activity that had dominated mainstream reform in Chicago for a generation and prompted the charter movement, but the tradition of alternative culture in Chicago was hostile to mainstream reform—"puritan" or "Yankee" ideals that scorned the values of the foreign born and sought to mold immigrants into citizens with homogeneous "American" ways of thinking and acting. The ethnocultural struggle between advocates of personal liberty and those of moral regulation became an important component of late nineteenth-century party politics.[44] In Chicago, the battle between mainstream reformers and immigrant Americans swirled with particularly ferocity around the control of alcohol and the custom of the Continental Sunday.

The experience of nineteenth-century Chicago proved saloon regulation to be an extremely sensitive public issue. In 1841 the General Assembly enacted a statewide Sunday closing law, which Chicago authorities generally ignored. Two mayors attempted to enforce the law, with disastrous consequences. Nativist mayor Levi Boone ordered saloons closed on the sabbath in 1855. The resulting street uprising by the city's German population became known as the "Lager Beer Riot." Soon Boone and enforcement of the Sunday closing law were only memories. Not until after the Great Fire did another mayor seek to reapply the state law. That executive was the kid-glove reformer Joseph Medill of the *Chicago Tribune*. Germans did not riot after Medill's 1872 edict; rather, they allied with the Irish in a temporary "People's Party" that helped drive the newspaper publisher out of office. Two years later a city statute authorized saloons to remain open on Sunday if the front shades were drawn and patrons entered from the rear.[45]

Politicians thereafter trod warily around the Sunday closing question, but in immigrant Chicago (particularly among Germans) the memory of attempts by nativists and mainstream reformers to abolish the Continental Sunday remained sharp. After 1890, wary Germans, Bohemians, and Poles linked mainstream reform efforts to a repressive urge to curtail their innocent social customs. A German newspaper in 1894 painted an ideal picture of the Continental Sunday: "After six days of work and toiling, the Germans want to enjoy life freely on Sunday. As they see the Sabbath, some people will go to the Church in the morning. Many more people will go in the afternoon to theaters and afterwards to cafes and restaurants. Some other people will stay at home or flock to saloons to meet old friends and make new acquaintances. Sunday nights should be reserved for family affairs." This agreeable scene was "in bitter opposition to the Puritan standpoint, as voiced by the Anglo-American Press, which wants to give to the American people a dead Sunday, with the silence of a graveyard and bare of any joys of life."[46]

Conflict over the Sunday law grew between Germans and temperance activists in the 1890s. Controversy over the Edwards English language education law of 1889 left Chicago Germans organized in defense of their cultural traditions.[47] When middle-class native-born Americans banded into organizations such as the Sunday Closing Association, Germans answered with associations such as the Alliance for Personal Rights. In 1892 plans to close the Columbian Exposition on Sunday prompted an organizational drive in alternative Chicago that presaged the charter campaign. "Whenever the Anglo-Americans granted us something, they were not prompted by love, but by fear," newspaperman Anton C. Hesing reminded two dozen German social clubs. "We must demonstrate to our opponents that they will feel our strength at the ballot box if they deny us our rights." Hesing recommended "a mass-meeting in a large hall, and afterward a torch-light procession with music to make our demands

known." Mass meetings, public protests, and the threat of political action
were tactics of organized pressure groups that were becoming increasingly
common in the final decade of the nineteenth century. Hesing suggested
that Germans also "unite with the Bohemians and Poles to enlarge our
forces."[48] The seeds of an immigrant mass movement were planted in the
1890s; the hothouse atmosphere of saloon regulation in Chicago caused
them to flower during the charter debate in 1906.

♦

The bulk of charter enthusiasts in 1907, remembering the divisiveness
of past conflicts between the alternative culture and moral Americanizers,
desperately worked to keep the question of saloon regulation out of the
charter deliberations. Most business and professional reformers placed administrative concerns far above ethnocultural matters in importance. In
the face of these efforts, temperance and personal liberty forces adopted
organizational techniques to press the liquor issue on the convention as a
matter of public policy. Thus, old disputes over alcohol flared up in the
early twentieth century, stirring up renewed cultural conflict and hostility
between Chicago and rural Illinois and entangling the charter in the bri-
ars of saloon regulation. In the process, the balance of power in the city
began to tip away from mainstream reformers and toward alternative Chicago. Within a generation the children of immigrants would control Chicago politically.

Weaknesses in Chicago government compelled private bodies to prosecute public business at the turn of the century. One reform path led to
charter revision; another collided with the saloon and alternative Chicago. The suppression of vice seemed to be among the most urgent of
public necessities, and the saloon became a particular target for mainstream moral regulators. To reformers intent on eradicating crime, political corruption, and disease from the city, the saloon elicited no ambivalence. It was a bastion of drunkenness and destroyer of families, a
headquarters for pothouse politicians, and a haven for prostitutes, pick-
pockets, and other species of degraded criminality engaged in a general
war on social convention and civilized behavior. Elements of this picture
were substantially accurate in Chicago. The first-ward levee district, with
its saloons, cathouses, and large "floating" vote purchased with a drink
and guided to the polls by henchmen of aldermen Michael "Hinky Dink"
Kenna and "Bathhouse John" Coughlin, stood as a mocking confirmation
of Chicago's reputation as a wide-open city. In 1905 there were over eight
thousand licensed saloons in Chicago and thousands more unlicensed
"blind pigs." By that time, associations such as the Anti-Saloon League
of Illinois and the Chicago Law and Order League were pressuring city

hall to curtail drunkenness, vice, and corruption through the regulation and gradual elimination of the saloon.[49]

But the saloon also fit another, entirely different description. This view emphasized the saloon's role as a welcome and vital component of the immigrant and working-class neighborhood, seeing it as a semipublic place that served as an extension of the crowded working-class home and as a refuge from the toil of the workplace and the bustle of the street. As a slogan of the day put it, the saloon was the "poor man's club." The number of saloon patrons on an average day in Chicago during the 1890s totaled half the city's population. Parents at factory gates would send children with a pail to a saloon, from which the youngsters returned with a nickel's worth of beer. The majority of saloons in Chicago offered the famous free lunch, a welcome alternative for many poor families. But the saloon provided far more than drink, food, and fellowship. With a safe and a ready supply of cash, the saloon functioned as a bank in working-class neighborhoods. It furnished halls for meetings of ethnic and neighborhood associations and served as an employment agency. The saloon was also one of the few establishments in the city with public restrooms. Finally, it offered working-class people a chance to set up a small business on fairly easy terms.[50]

In short, there were different kinds of drinking places: bars downtown away from neighborhoods, saloons where vice flourished, and quiet ethnic taverns in residential areas. To complicate matters still further, many immigrant clubs and fraternal associations that were not properly saloons at all held liquor licenses and served alcohol. Threats to these clubs by moral reform groups drew alternative Chicago into the charter debate.

◆

Temperance reformers intensified their pressure on city government in 1905 with assaults on Mayor Dunne, who supported the Continental Sunday. Appeals to the courts and county prosecutor to force Dunne to comply with the Sunday closing law or face indictment brought no action. Then, in December, a distraught teenage girl killed herself in front of the America Dance Hall in Chicago. Thousands of such establishments had appeared in American cities since 1900. The dancing craze scandalized parents: not only did youth shed its inhibitions on the dance floor, but most of the clubs served alcoholic drinks, and some were rumored to be recruiting dens for prostitution rings. Newspaper reports confirmed the worst fears. "Young boys and girls learn the way to crime in the drunken orgies of public balls," warned one.[51] Special licenses allowed the dance clubs to sell liquor until three o'clock in the morning, two hours after state law closed saloons.[52]

Legal officials who had earlier rebuffed temperance reformers now sprang into action against special bar permits. Cook County state's attorney John J. Healy broadcast his willingness to prosecute Dunne unless the mayor closed all liquor establishments at one o'clock. Shortly after Dunne was summoned before the grand jury, the city council ceased issuing special bar licenses to clubs. Chicago edged closer to compliance with state regulations.[53]

Respectable ethnic clubs that held special permits fumed that the suspension of licenses placed their organizations "on the same level with the orgies of the condemned and criminal vice dens."[54] A popular movement of Chicago's alternative culture rapidly formed in defense of its institutions and customs. Unwilling to rely on quiet court challenges or disparate individual protests to reverse the council's action, representatives of German, Bohemian, and Polish organizations made a public display of the united strength of the immigrant community. While officers of ethnic clubs monitored the city council license committee, the movement's activists perfected careful plans for a mass meeting, including speeches in English to draw in "liberal thinking citizens of all nationalities."[55]

On March 25, 1906, some 35,000 members of ethnic singing societies, gymnastic clubs, and fraternal associations, carrying banners and accompanied by ten bands, marched from all sides of the city to a mass meeting at the Armory Hall. There they called on the city to reissue the special licenses and on the General Assembly to give municipalities "the absolute right to regulate the customs and pleasures of their inhabitants in their own way."[56] Chicago immigrants had endorsed municipal home rule, but on their own terms and with their own agenda. Within a month, over 60,000 members of ethnic clubs banded into the United Societies for Local Self-Government. By June, the city council passed an ordinance reviving special bar permits. Committed to the "repeal of . . . obsolete laws" that threatened the autonomy of Chicago's alternative culture, the United Societies next demanded that the home-rule movement sanction personal liberty.[57]

◆

The United Societies for Local Self-Government had been carefully organized as a representative, firm, and respectable public advocate of personal liberty. Despite the dominance of Germans, Bohemians, and Poles in the confederation, highly visible positions were held by Croatians, Hungarians, Swedes, Danes, Swiss, Italians, and Belgians. On the other hand, sharp tensions kept Chicago's Irish and central European communities at arm's length. The Irish were reluctant to share their powerful position in the Democratic party with other nationalities and lacked a cultural attachment to beer halls and the Continental Sunday. Nevertheless, two prominent Irishmen served as president and attorney of the United Societies; as public spokesmen for the confederation, Charles Gilbert, a well-known lawyer, and former congressman Edward Noonan provided names more euphonious to native-born ears than those of John Cervenka, Fritz Glogauer, or Anton Cermak. Political control was centralized in Cermak's hands. Named permanent secretary of the organization in 1907, the Bohemian Democratic assemblyman used his position on the House Charter Committee to strengthen the United Societies. Cermak would later use the organization as his springboard to power as Chicago's first mayor from among the "new immigrants."[58]

Such immigrant unity reflected the intensity of the threat to the autonomous alternative culture of Chicago. The city's Poles traditionally were divided among themselves and loath to cooperate with other nationalities. Politically, they had been concerned primarily with electing fellow Poles such as Stanley Kunz and John Smulski to office, ignoring party differences between these men. Nonetheless, when Kunz supported the 1906 increase in the cost of Chicago saloon licenses, his countrymen voted him off the city council. Republican city attorney Smulski joined the United Societies, and other Poles actively participated in its affairs. Over time, Poles even accepted the Bohemian Cermak as their political representative, which they had refused to do with Bohemian Jew Adolph Sabath.[59]

Temperance reformers denied the legitimacy of the alternative culture, claiming that Illinois liquor interests financed the United Societies. The Anti-Saloon League dismissed the confederation as a front organization for the brewers' associations and liquor manufacturers. "You must not confound the United Societies with the brewers," Noonan told the City Club.[60] Yet thirteen brewers, liquor dealers, and saloonkeepers were United Societies officials; and the Bohemian Saloonkeepers' Association was a member organization. State liquor associations lavished praise on the confederation. Before the first public rally of the immigrant protest, a retail liquor trade journal promised the assistance of "nearly every saloon-keeper in Chicago."[61]

In fact, Illinois liquor interests did spend money to influence legislation. Peoria distillers allegedly were major contributors to the infamous "jackpot" maintained at Springfield to oil the General Assembly. In 1904 the Brewers' Association offered a gubernatorial candidate $25,000; the next year the Liquor Dealers' State Protective Organization solicited lobbying funds. It seems likely that liquor interests contributed to the United Societies. According to his biographer, Cermak received money from brewers and, to a lesser extent, distillers, but few knew of the practice, and no one has traced the flow of cash.[62]

Whatever financial support may have been provided, there is little substance to the charge that the United Societies fronted for brewers and distillers. A fairer conclusion would be that the liquor industry hitched its fortunes to the popular movement for an autonomous immigrant culture. Moral commitment and voting strength (155,000 qualified voters by 1909) made the confederation the chief public defender of the pro-liquor position. Although United Societies representatives condemned "the abuses and temptations of 'saloon life,'" they emphasized the legitimacy of the liquor trade.[63] To that degree, Chicago's alternative culture and the organized liquor interests shared common goals, but liquor barons did not control the United Societies.

Temperance reformers nevertheless maintained that Chicago's immigrant community should play no role in the public life of the city. The United Societies' vision of home rule and personal liberty struck them not as a reasonable safeguard for cultural diversity but rather as a direct threat to dominant American values. A Methodist Episcopal minister detected "the spirit of lawless unrest and anarchy" behind the rhetoric of personal liberty and anticipated "a foreign invasion" of alien folkways.[64] The Chicago Law and Order League expressed concern that a referendum proposal under discussion in the charter convention would provide immigrants a powerful voice in the formulation of public policy. On questions of governance, the league held, "it is better to have the more conservative and more American sentiment of the country to help us rather than to leave the whole matter to the population of Chicago."[65]

◆

Thrusts between the United Societies and its temperance critics cut to the heart of the home-rule dilemma. Retracing the steps of the Citizens' Association and Civic Federation, the United Societies demanded Chicago's liberation from the confining and inappropriate purview of rural Illinois, but the immigrant movement asked questions that the administrative reform clubs had not anticipated. If Chicago should have the power to govern itself freely, to adjust its finances to suit its needs, should not its citizens also have the power to protect their social customs? Should not citizens possess the democratic tools to rule their city? As the alternative culture of Chicago pressed the charter convention to meet its demands, the Chicago Federation of Labor and a small circle of democratic reformers rallied around the United Societies. Saloon regulation became a test of the democratic possibilities of home rule.

In December 1906 the United Societies called on the charter convention to fortify the charter with strong provisions giving the city council explicit authority to regulate Sunday closing and the sale of liquor by private clubs. Although a handful of United Societies members and allies (most notably George Thompson of the CFL) were delegates to the convention, the confederation submitted demands through its committee on charter legislation. Emphasizing that its proposals reflected "the sentiment of four-fifths of the voters of our city," the committee promised that an unfavorable response would force "the very unpleasant duty of appealing to our membership to vote against any and all laws" deriving from the charter.[66]

Saloon regulation was just the sort of contentious issue that government rationalizers had sought to keep out of the charter. Achieving financial independence and administrative orderliness for Chicago was in their eyes the most important goal of the charter. Other issues were secondary, and if these jeopardized the attainment of the charter movement's principal concerns, they should be avoided. The General Assembly had to approve the charter before it went before the voters, and the more specific provisions the charter contained, particularly on such emotional topics as saloon regulation, the greater the chance that the legislature would strike it down. Provisions for the direct primary, referendum, and moderate municipal ownership already put the charter at risk. Common sense dictated that caution rather than boldness should mark the convention's decision on the United Societies' proposal. It passed a home-rule clause that guaranteed Chicago greater financial and administrative powers yet asserted municipal primacy only in matters "not in conflict with any general law of the state."[67] That clearly left open the question of Sunday closing enforcement.

The United Societies refused to back down. Complaining that the convention's stand "not only denies home rule on our proposition, but abrogates some of the great local powers now possessed by the city," the federation renewed its demand for specific charter protection for the Continental Sunday and private liquor permits.[68] Publicity brought more ethnic clubs into the organization, and a liberal Sunday coalition took shape. The Chicago Federation of Labor officially endorsed the United Societies' position. The Chicago Law and Order League stepped up its insistence that the charter bow to state law. The convention had to confront the saloon question.[69]

Chairman Milton Foreman confessed that saloon regulation was "the most complicated and embarrassing obstacle which the Charter Convention encountered."[70] Some delegates allowed that Chicago should have the power to set its own liquor policy. "If there is any question which properly comes within the question of local self-government," admitted

Lessing Rosenthal, "this is certainly one."[71] Others, such as Republican businessman (and future member of the Progressive party) Alexander Revell, argued that a home-rule stance necessitated adoption of the United Societies' demands. "Is it reasonable to propose," Revell asked, "that remote portions of the state, with a scattered agricultural population shall enact laws and compel city populations to observe them?" If the convention did not challenge state control over Chicago saloons, the city would witness "the spectacle of an unenforcible law—a failure of law."[72] Many convention delegates not connected in any way with the United Societies were driven by their home-rule convictions and desire for order to a sympathetic consideration of immigrant demands.

The convention still refused to place the entire charter in jeopardy for the sake of local saloon regulation. Veteran legislator David Shanahan argued against putting the saloon proposals in the body of the charter. That would "bring on a great fight" and ensure "that every person who is opposed to an open Sunday will oppose the entire charter."[73] Instead, Shanahan recommended attaching the two liquor proposals as separate questions accompanying the charter. This would allow the General Assembly to submit the questions to voters apart from the charter itself. The convention unanimously adopted the compromise, and so the matter stood when the convention adjourned in March 1907 and sent its handiwork to Springfield for the consent of the General Assembly.

◆

The compromise reflected the curious position of Chicago's alternative culture in the home-rule movement. Confident that Chicago voters would endorse its liquor referenda, the United Societies agreed to the compromise. Immigrant Chicago was at best a stepchild of the charter campaign, however, and the United Societies had to look to its own resources to protect the liquor proposals from hostile attacks in the legislature. Noonan and Nicholas Michels, already in Springfield to lobby against the latest Anti-Saloon League local option bill, turned their attention to the House Charter Committee.[74] With only lukewarm backing from charter proponents, they found few friends in the legislature.

State lawmakers struck down the Chicago liquor control bills without hesitation. Lawrence Y. Sherman eschewed the customary silence maintained by the Senate president and urged rural representatives from both houses to quash the charter's open Sunday proposal. "There is not a man in this legislature, native born or of alien birth, who can tamper with the conscientious scruples of the people of this state on the subject of Sunday observance," he railed. No one could vote for open saloons on Sunday "without violating the inheritance which he had from his mother."[75]

Tempers flared between Chicago and downstate members of the House Charter Committee. "I am greatly troubled by the thought of what would happen to a German citizen of Chicago if he didn't get his drink regularly," jibed Charles Allen. "I don't know how a German or a Bohemian would look if he had to get over a Sunday without a drink or had to go to a wedding where none was served." The committee killed the Sunday regulation bill and threatened to throw the special bar permit measure "into the waste basket" unless Chicago representatives agreed to support the bogged down local option bill.[76] The special permit bill was discarded before the charter came to a final vote.

The General Assembly buried many charter provisions. Hints of trouble had surfaced when several legislative delegates to the charter convention refused to adopt the charter as written. The House Charter Committee, which had strong ties to the Republican faction of newly elected Chicago mayor Fred Busse, trimmed the charter to fit his political needs. It left the charter's consolidation and revenue articles largely untouched but gutted the electoral reform and anticorruption features. The General Assembly refused to extend civil service to the new municipal court system, rejected the direct primary in favor of ward conventions, eliminated a corrupt practices act, and returned the party circle to the ballot. Worst of all, it reorganized Chicago into fifty wards outrageously gerrymandered in favor of the Republican party, with the provision that no reapportionment occur until after the 1920 census. Under the new arrangement, the previous balance between the parties in Chicago shifted to a Republican advantage of thirty-two to eighteen.[77]

Even in this altered form, the charter nearly failed to pass through the hostile legislature. Cook County senators narrowly defeated Sherman's bid to permanently restrict the county's representation in the General Assembly. Prospects were so bleak that Chicago representatives had to trade support for the statewide local option bill to squeeze the amended charter through, in early May 1907, with a bare constitutional majority. Lobbyists helplessly stood by as the local option bill was "bound to the chariot wheels of [the] charter, and under the whip and spur, dragged to its final passage."[78]

◆

The General Assembly had destroyed the tenuous common ground joining Chicago's alternative culture and popular democrats with the city's mainstream efficiency advocates. Supporters of popular control mourned the loss of home rule, but consolidationists judged the essentials of the charter intact and pushed for its adoption in September. Charles Merriam argued that democratic controls could be salvaged under the amended charter. "In granting broad powers of local government," he maintained, the charter "lays a foundation for efficient democratic government."[79] Lost reforms could be restored by a more powerful city. If the present charter were rejected, a hostile General Assembly could prevent any constructive change. Other charter enthusiasts were less solicitous of disenchanted democrats and immigrants. Administrative home rule— increased revenue, greater borrowing power, centralization of city departments—had been achieved. What more could the city require? As convention chairman Foreman naively put it, "every feature of the charter that Chicago really wants . . . is in the charter just as it was on the day it left the Charter Convention."[80]

As the summer wore on, cracks in the brittle home-rule coalition widened into chasms. The Civic Federation, the Citizens' Association, and the Republican party campaigned for adoption of the charter, but elements of mainstream Chicago withheld approval. George Cole of the Municipal Voters' League cooled his enthusiasm as the September election approached. The South park board, marked for extinction by the charter, publicly worked for its defeat, as did the Woman's Suffrage Association. Some reformers, noting the advantages the GOP would gain from the charter, denounced it as a fraudulent cover for corrupt politics. Harold Ickes said the city faced "a boss rule charter sought to be imposed upon Chicago by an unsavory alliance" of political factions.[81] "Let the plunderers of the people keep their poisoned bread" advised Raymond Robins.[82]

Groups outside the mainstream power structure of the city organized to reject the charter. A loose alliance consisting of Democrats, the Chicago Federation of Labor, the Chicago Teachers' Federation, and the United Societies for Local Self-Government conducted the anticharter campaign. A CFL report linking business and professional support for the charter to the suppression of working-class democracy captured the tone of the alliance. "This class who have most loudly demanded reform," it claimed, "have the most to fear from the inauguration of any real reform. They constitute the class who fear the rule by the whole people. They are the class who in this Charter seek to curb the power of the electorate."[83]

Members of Chicago's alternative culture used the crisis to protest their place in the political system and to assert their independent power. The United Societies employed the democratic language of the anticharter alliance but understood it in a wholly different sense. Immigrant representatives at first played down the defeat of the liquor bills, emphasizing instead their disapproval of the restrictive and undemocratic features of the charter. For the United Societies, however, the issue at hand was not electoral reform, working-class democracy, or "rule by the whole people";

instead, it was the vital necessity of Chicago's alternative culture to establish itself as an independent political force able to protect its distinctive
customs from the oversight of the "whole people."[84]

For this reason, the United Societies refused to surrender its independent campaign against the charter. Overtures from the Democratic party
and William Randolph Hearst's Independence League to centralize anticharter operations were rebuffed. United Societies strategists were especially careful to remain apart from party organizations. Central Europeans
resented Irish domination of the Chicago Democratic organization and
were unwilling to further the impression that they rested in the pockets
of Democrats. Political parties had insulted immigrant voters over the
years. "The Republicans treat us always as voters who can be herded like
cattle," charged a Polish Catholic newspaper in 1896; a Bohemian journal complained in 1909 that an Irish Democrat proposed to "buy the
Czechs for a keg of beer."[85] Alternative Chicago would not be drawn into
a party fight over the charter. By mobilizing in defense of their self-
defined interests, immigrant voters alerted politicians and reformers that
Chicago's foreign community would carve out its own agenda.

Led by the United Societies, immigrant Chicago developed a political
organization that reflected neither callous manipulation by machine politicians nor a searching critique of American democracy. Anticharter
pamphlets, printed by the United Societies in a variety of languages and
containing detailed instructions on how to mark the ballot, filtered
through immigrant neighborhoods in the summer of 1907. The immigrant confederation took pains to demonstrate that the foreign-born voter
was as good a citizen as the Yankee, but the 90,000 eligible voters attached to the confederation were not motivated, as one scholar has suggested, by a conviction that "fundamental American democracy require[s]
direct citizen participation in decision-making."[86] Democratic forms were
used to reinforce cultural autonomy. Fear of cultural disruption from stringent state enforcement of saloon regulations, as well as reluctance to pay
higher taxes to "reform" Chicago, made up the core of immigrant hostility to the charter. United Societies official Nicholas Michels bluntly
stated as much to the City Club. Home rule was a defensive measure for
Chicago's alternative culture, not a path to additional reforms. Before and
after the charter campaign, immigrant voters showed little interest in
electoral reforms and a frank hostility to middle-class reformers.[87]

Conflicting bids for home rule and personal liberty led to unorthodox
political configurations in the final days of the charter campaign. The
United Societies had deserted Mayor Dunne, leader of the popular government forces, over the issue of special bar permits and supported the
successful candidacy of Republican spoilsman Fred Busse in 1907. Busse,

described by Harold Ickes as a "near hoodlum," promised to support the confederation's charter position,[88] but after the General Assembly gerrymandered Chicago wards in favor of the Republicans, Busse climbed on the charter bandwagon. In September he threatened to close saloons on Sunday if the United Societies did not drop its public opposition to the charter. Three days before the charter referendum, Busse's election board attempted to exclude working-class charter opponents from the vote by designating the referendum a special election, for which workers did not receive time off from their jobs, instead of a general election. The standard alignments of progressive-era politics fell into disarray in 1907 Chicago. Middle-class charter enthusiasts such as Merriam and Ernst Freund assured alternative Chicago that state saloon regulations would remain a "dead letter." Meanwhile, the city's dominant machine politician turned his back on immigrant and working-class constituencies and threatened to replace customary urban practices concerning saloons with state laws. Good government proponents in the Civic Federation and Citizens' Association found their hopes for the passage of a reform charter dependent on the political trickery of a most disreputable bedfellow.[89]

Busse's gamble backfired. In a demonstration of solidarity and power, 35,000 members of Chicago's alternative culture gathered in Grant Park on September 15 to denounce the charter and its adherents. Fritz Glogauer, editor of the *Abendpost*, presented the bill of indictment against mainstream Chicago. "The reactionary element," he told the crowd, "are trying to suppress us with the charter. We were not consulted in its planning. They insolently rejected our two amendments and now we are also using our rights to reject the bill." According to Glogauer, reformers and newspaper editors assumed that immigrants, "solely from caprice, stand in the way of 'progress,'" but reformers should take warning, for immigrants "are thoroughly tired of being regarded as hangers-on. In their own opinion they are not an inferior, unchained mob, but full-fledged citizens, who have as much a share in the progress of the city as the natives have had, and hence insist that they receive the consideration due them. The immigrant voters, who with their immediate descendants by far make up the majority, will not accept a city charter which was drafted by the 'upper classes' to promote their own interests only."[90]

Two days later voters firmly rejected the charter 121,935 to 59,786. Democrats, unionists, and businesspeople opposed to higher taxes also cast negative votes, but alternative Chicago clearly communicated its position, saying that it would "no longer tolerate the audacious tutelage of the presumptuous hypocritical throng" and that "the sooner the ruling party recognizes this and acts accordingly, the better it will be for it."[91] Charter reform not only had failed to unify administrative authority in

Chicago, it intensified existing social, cultural, and political divisions among city residents. Consensus on public-policy issues would henceforth be even more difficult to achieve.

◆

Charter proponents, bewildered by the defeat of a measure that they judged essential for the improvement of Chicago, attempted to analyze what went wrong. Most argued that the spirit of compromise completely broke down after the General Assembly mutilated the charter, but it was also clear that procharter arguments failed to engage the interest of many voters. Only about half the registered voters in the city even cast a ballot on the referendum. Most damaging of all to progressive faith in the public interest was the realization that the people of Chicago were simply not interested in the reform package presented to them by the convention.[92]

The charter movement never recovered. Some discouraged efficiency seekers, unwilling to trust the legislature or the electorate, abandoned the charter idea and instead pressed for a constitutional convention to remedy the deficiencies of Illinois government. Once a skeptic about useful results from a constitutional convention, Charles Merriam in 1916 sponsored a Chicago city council resolution requesting one. The Civic Federation turned its attention to the twin goals of opposing the initiative and referendum and reforming the state system of property assessment and taxation. Renewed attempts to pass a charter failed in 1909 and 1914, and the issue disappeared from the progressive-era political agenda.[93]

Conflict over Chicago saloons continued unabated after the demise of the charter. State's Attorney Healy, assisted by Chicago Law and Order League zealots, hauled saloonkeepers into court for breaking the state Sunday closing law. Chicago juries turned them loose. The Illinois Anti-Saloon League attempted to force local option onto the Chicago ballot. Chicago's alternative culture blocked the effort. All the while, Anton Cermak tightened his control over the United Societies for Local Self-Government and steered it into broader political action. In 1908 he created an adjunct voters' organization called the Liberty League, which endorsed candidates in municipal, county, and state elections. That year Cermak's friend John E. W. Wayman defeated the incumbent Healy in the race for state's attorney. Cermak and the United Societies held off Sunday closing until 1915, when Mayor William Hale Thompson went back on his word and ordered city saloons closed on the sabbath. Then came prohibition. More importantly, however, after years of growing influence in the Democratic party, Chicago's alternative culture entered the mainstream of political power. In 1931 Anton Cermak defeated Thompson for mayor, and the children of immigrants finally received "the consideration due them" as "full-fledged citizens."[94]

◆

The interplay between the Chicago charter movement and the city's alternative culture illustrates the troubles that beset progressive public policy. Despite vigorous efforts by a talented body of reformers, it became increasingly difficult to isolate social and political problems, construct suitable legislative remedies, and win approval for them in a democratic setting. Society had become too complex, too dense, for any single class or group to dominate the formulation of public policy. Neither government nor private groups could achieve preeminence. Private interests bartered with state government over local powers, but political parties continued to guard the legislative gate and demand tribute. Nineteenth-century political issues such as temperance and personal liberty had a continuing appeal, but now, with the maturation of the organizational impulse, their advocates were less restrained by the collar of party loyalty. Finally, the cumbersome structure of Illinois government discouraged efforts at broad reforms of power and authority. These required painstaking attention to the demands of a myriad of organized groups to build effective coalitions. How much easier it was to be satisfied with smaller victories, to press a narrower interest, to become a thorn in someone else's side, to demand appeasement and be rewarded.

The Chicago charter movement failed not simply because of new difficulties in the process of influencing government but also because its vision was flawed and its proposals were inadequate to meet the needs of all Chicago citizens. Alternative Chicago had no clearer grasp of the public interest. No doubt many charter opponents failed to appreciate how the consolidation of administrative authority could improve the services demanded of a great city by its people, but immigrant voters did no more than assert the power vouchsafed them by democratic institutions. The majority of charter backers had not considered this possibility, and thus the liquor question that civic reformers treated as a side issue became a principal determinant of the charter's fate. In the process, the business and professional interests of Chicago lost their monopoly as critics of parties and government in Illinois.

Streamlining urban government proved a more formidable task than the progressive notion of the public interest suggested. Democracy did not speak with a united voice against inefficiency and injustice, nor would it prove easy to democratize city services in Chicago. As the following chapter shows, another tangle of interests bogged down attempts to reform Chicago schools and its mass transportation system. Reforming a city that was not a community held many perils.

5

The Public versus the People: Controlling Schools and Streetcars in Chicago

Progressives shared a belief that city life was in disorder at the turn of the century. Private interest and the force of ethnic, neighborhood, or economic loyalties had diluted the bonds of citizenship, weakening the sense of civic purpose that alone could provide the foundation for a rational, comprehensive solution of urban problems. Sprawling, decentralized, and chaotic, large cities shrugged off the limited authority of legitimate government and settled under the control of the "inner organization"—an informal government system administered by political machines and oiled by graft. Chicago progressive Charles Merriam called this intolerable substitute government the "Big Fix,"[1] under which city schools and streetcar lines, fixtures in the lives of city residents, had become links between private avarice, parochial selfishness, and corrupt political organizations. Urban progressives sought to remove the public school and transportation systems from their corrupting entanglement with municipal politics and operate them under expert supervision for the benefit of the public interest.

These progressives were not to be unopposed in this project, however. In seeking to overturn the "Big Fix" and return the schools and streets to the community under the stewardship of the public interest, urban reformers collided with an alliance of groups excluded from Chicago's mainstream power structure. Attempts by professional school administrators to centralize authority in the Chicago public school system aroused bitter opposition from the Chicago Teachers' Federation (CTF). All female, largely Irish Catholic, and employed in elementary schools, CTF members constituted the least powerful group within the education hierarchy, but they were also the most direct link between the city school system and neighborhoods that were heavily immigrant, working class, and Catholic. The CTF demanded democracy in the schools, including job control for teachers and popular control of education policy. The Chicago

Federation of Labor, the city's powerful central labor council, endorsed the CTF position. This teacher-labor alliance declared the school issue part of a broader struggle between democracy and elite domination that included the initiative, referendum, and public ownership of utilities. In 1905 the coalition tied its fortunes to the mayoral campaign of Democrat Edward F. Dunne, who sought to bring schools and streets under popular control by means of a more open board of education and immediate municipal ownership of streetcar lines (IMO). Dunne's election placed public schools and municipal transit squarely in the center of city politics.

Controversy over Dunne and the teacher-labor alliance tore apart Chicago's reform communities. Neither democracy nor expertise emerged triumphant. Centralization of Chicago public education was not fully achieved until 1917, but then, with the regime of William Hale Thompson, city schools came more deeply under the control of the Big Fix than ever before. Dunne's bid for municipal ownership of streetcar lines was blocked, but no decisive settlement was reached during the Progressive Era. Without a shared municipal sense of the public interest, the competing reform aspirations of efficiency and democracy could not draw schools and streetcars "out of politics."

The Problem of City Schools

There was abundant national evidence of corruption and disorganization in urban public schools. Lincoln Steffens reported that textbook publishers tempted teachers and principals with money and women. Mayor Hazen Pingree of Detroit had four school board members arrested in 1894 after they demanded payoffs from a school furniture salesman. In Philadelphia, ward politicians placed janitors as their agents in the public schools; an incredulous journalist saw one of them issue peremptory instructions to a school principal in 1904.[2]

Chaotic administration further hampered the effectiveness of urban public school systems. The typical city school system of the 1890s included a large board of education (either elected by ward or appointed by city officials) and numerous ward-based subsidiary boards that actually controlled the finances, curricula, and personnel of local schools. Local boards could stymie the superintendent or the central school board. In addition, power struggles between city councils and school boards further eroded central direction. Buffalo suffered under a system in which "the mayor appointed janitors, the superintendent teachers; the city council bought sites for new schools, while the department of public works erected them."[3]

In the absence of centralized direction, city schools became adjuncts of local political machines. Philadelphia's teachers and principals were assessed for campaign expenses as if they were officeholders. Almost everywhere, teachers needed "pull" with their ward board for placement in a neighborhood school. Petty tyrannies and job pressures turned many city schools into dreary places to work or learn. Joseph Rice documented the worst characteristics of urban schools in a series of magazine articles in 1892: mechanical repetition of memorized passages by straight-backed children, listless instruction by worried teachers, and an overall atmosphere of dread lest performance by either pupil or instructor fail to please roving local authorities.[4]

The situation in the Chicago public schools matched the bleak nationwide picture. Political patronage choked efficiency. School janitors won promotion through political service rather than efficient job performance. Weary principals petitioned the school board in 1902 to base janitorial promotions on monthly progress reports from principals, so that school officials would have "at least an indirect supervision" over these independent employees.[5] Nor were Chicago's public school teachers highly regarded. Joseph Rice judged Chicago teachers less qualified and competent than their counterparts in Philadelphia and New York. Although Rice noted the kindliness of many elementary school teachers, he pronounced some of their teaching "by far the most absurd I have ever witnessed."[6]

◆

To a new generation of professional educators and their civic-minded supporters, a public school system splintered by competing authorities and staffed by inadequately trained teachers was as great a threat to the public welfare as unregulated street railways. Neither the school nor urban transportation system could improve until it was taken "out of politics" and placed under the guardianship of disinterested experts. The school reform movement coalesced around a group of university presidents, education professors, and sympathetic businesspeople. Led by Columbia University president Nicholas Murray Butler, these "administrative progressives" dominated the National Educational Association during the 1890s and by the end of the decade presided over major school reform campaigns in the nation's largest cities. The administrative progressives attempted to shore up urban school systems by centralizing authority in a powerful school superintendent, removing school boards from political (and popular) control, and professionalizing the teaching force by toughening qualification standards and developing a promotional system based on merit.[7]

◆

The school centralization campaigns enjoyed notable success. Between 1893 and 1913 the size of school boards in twenty-eight American cities over 100,000 dropped from an average of 21.5 members to 10.2. Men from the business and professional classes filled the majority of positions in the new smaller school boards. The campaigns also had their detractors, however. School centralization aroused intense opposition from working-class, ethnic, and Catholic neighborhoods, whose inhabitants saw in centralization a loss of popular control over the schools, and from teachers, especially women, who feared a loss of job security and control. The ward-based public school system tended to soften the Protestant character of public education in Catholic neighborhoods, partly because local school committees in Chicago often placed teachers in schools located in their home neighborhoods. For many city residents, popular control of the schools meant local control. To the administrative progressives, it meant inefficient parochialism.[8]

Teachers stood the most to lose from school centralization. Higher professional standards denigrated their training, ignored their experience, and darkened their chances for promotion. Administrative progressives expected a high standard of performance. "Progressivism cast the teacher in an almost impossible role," observes Lawrence Cremin. "*He* was to be an artist of consummate skill, properly knowledgeable in his field, meticulously trained in the science of pedagogy, and thoroughly imbued with a burning zeal for social improvement."[9] Public school teachers, however, particularly in the lower grades, were almost exclusively women who assumed their positions after a stint at the local normal school or a short apprenticeship (as was the case in Chicago). These women felt the sting of the administrative progressives' reforms. They fought back with an alternative vision of the public schools.

Resisting the Professionalization of Education in Chicago

President William Rainey Harper of the University of Chicago initiated the fight to centralize authority in the Chicago public schools. From his position at the dynamic new university, Harper widened his power base by chairing the Chicago Civic Federation's education committee. Supported by the university's school reformers and the city's principal good government association, Harper won appointment to the Chicago Board of Education in 1896. That same year, Harper's friend E. Benjamin Andrews, the former president of Brown University, became Chicago's superintendent of schools. Administrative progressives then looked to expand their influence.[10]

In December 1897 the professional educators got their chance to reform Chicago's school administration. Mayor Harrison named Harper to an eleven-member Chicago Education Commission created to study the nation's schools and suggest a reorganization plan for Chicago. Harper had great influence over the appointments and rapidly assumed chairmanship of the committee. Chicago lacked the ward committees that hamstrung school centralization in other cities, and the school board was appointed by the mayor, so the primary tasks of centralization were to streamline the size and functions of the school board and increase the authority of the superintendent. With that in mind, the Harper commission spent the next year investigating school centralization, leaning heavily on the expertise of the Butlerite professional education establishment.[11]

The commission's lengthy report became the basis for a new school bill introduced in the General Assembly in 1899. It was a characteristically progressive solution to educational disorder. The Harper bill reduced the Chicago Board of Education from twenty-one to eleven members, gave to the superintendent a six-year tenure and full executive power, and created a business manager with the power to direct the financial affairs of the city school system. Teachers came under the direct authority of the superintendent, who was given the power to hire and fire them. Women teachers especially were threatened by Harper's suggestions. The commission noted a scarcity of men teachers and recommended a separate, higher pay scale to induce men into the schools (all fifty-four "advisers" to the commission were men).[12] Hiring and promotional changes favored university graduates over those who, like most women in the system, attended the Chicago Normal School, and merit-based pay and promotions relied more heavily on scholarly attainments.[13]

Unlike other cities, Chicago's administrative progressives did not overwhelm the opposition to school centralization. The Harper bill did not pass in 1899, and its subsequent incarnations from 1901 until 1917 died in the General Assembly. By March 1900 a discouraged Andrews had resigned as superintendent, and Harper was dispatched from the school board. Counterattacking Chicago politicians and the CFL harassed administrative progressives, but the principal opposition to centralization came from the Chicago Teachers' Federation, whose supporters had absorbed John Dewey's message that the health of society depended on an intellectually vigorous, democratic school system. Although Dewey was at the University of Chicago from 1894 until 1904, he played no active role in the struggle over public schools, yet the philosopher's abstract and idealized commitment to educational democracy took concrete form in the hands of his "wisest" student, Ella Flagg Young, an assistant superintendent of schools who in 1909 would become Chicago school superintendent. Young warned that hierarchical systems of educational administration such as Harper envisioned would crush the democratic possibilities of education by destroying teacher autonomy. According to Young, "teachers, instead of being the great moving force, educating and developing the powers of the human mind in such a way that they shall contribute to the power and efficiency of this democracy, tend to become mere workers at the treadmill" under the weight of administrative progressivism. CTF leaders developed these themes into an articulate class indictment of expertise in the schools.[14]

♦

A growing threat to the already tenuous status of women elementary school teachers prompted the formation of the CTF in March 1897. Women teachers in the 1890s were isolated from the educational establishment. Herded into elementary schools, denied promotion to administrative positions, and lacking a voice in the National Educational Association, they nursed a deep resentment of their menial official status. Teachers attending the Chicago Normal School between 1896 and 1899 benefited from the teaching of Francis Parker, a pioneer of progressive child-centered education, but the demand for higher professional standards along with a twenty-year freeze on teacher salaries threatened to transform teaching from a working-class livelihood to a temporary middle-class occupation. Between 1880 and 1900 the number of women teachers from blue collar families dropped from nearly half to 35.6 percent of the Chicago teaching force, while the number of daughters of middle-class parents rose from fifteen percent to over a quarter of Chicago public school teachers.[15]

Standing between women elementary school teachers and further hardship was a teachers' pension law shepherded through the General Assembly in 1895 by Governor John Peter Altgeld. Arvilla C. De Luce, a teacher at the Calhoun school in Chicago, had launched a grassroots pension movement among Chicago teachers in 1892. Another Chicago teacher, Catherine Goggin, whose cousin was a superior court judge and former school board member, used her influence to persuade Altgeld that teachers needed protective legislation. Altgeld, reasoning that teachers deserved the security afforded civil servants, added a tenure clause to the pension bill, freeing Chicago teachers from the painful system of annual contracts. Backed by the school board, principals such as Young, and Goggin's personal appeal before the legislature, the bill was approved. Tenure helped make the pension law of 1895 a badge of respectability and professionalism to the embattled teachers.[16]

But the pension law disrupted the school hierarchy. During the grassroots pension campaign of 1892 Chicago school principals occasionally refused to circulate pension petitions among their teachers, and after the pension system became law they complained that it unfairly favored women teachers. Principals and male teachers, because of their higher salaries, contributed more to the pension fund and had to serve five years longer than women to qualify for benefits, but the benefits were uniform—$600 annually for life—for all pensioners. School principals called the 1 percent salary deduction that funded the pension an unjust tax and in 1897 supported a substitute pension bill that, among other things, eliminated the tenure clause.[17]

The Chicago Teachers' Federation grew out of meetings organized by women teachers to counter the threat to their pension plan and push for a salary increase. Elementary school teachers occupied the bottom rung of the Chicago school system's pay ladder (the CTF complained that the laborers and barn foreman employed by the school board earned more than experienced teachers), averaging $600 annually, with a top salary of $800 for those with over seven years' experience. A handful of activists, contending that "without the proper material conditions about the teacher little *real* improvement could be accomplished in the schools,"[18] organized the CTF to represent the interests of elementary school teachers. Membership was confined to "those actually engaged in the work of *teaching*," excluding even sympathetic principals and supervisory teachers.[19] High school teachers remained aloof from the organization, defeating an attempt in 1899 to combine Chicago's eight teacher associations into a common federation. "There are but few things in common between high school and grade teachers," announced one high school teacher. "Many teachers are politicians first and then teachers."[20] Militantly alone, the CTF persuaded the General Assembly to defeat the substitute pension bill and, on the strength of a petition signed by 3,568 teachers, won from the school board pay increases for experienced teachers running to a new maximum salary of $1,000 for those with ten years of service.[21]

The CTF quickly came into bitter conflict with the administrative progressives on the Chicago school board. Harper opposed a $50 salary increase for teachers, explaining to an inquiring committee of teachers that they already earned "as much as his wife's maid."[22] With the appearance of the Harper commission report in January 1899, the CTF went on the offensive against Harper and Andrews, known derisively among the teachers as "Bulletin Ben."[23] Blasting the report as a scheme for undemocratic, dictatorial rule, the CTF developed tactics against the adoption of the Harper bill that soon became the trademark of the organization: mass meetings to arouse public anger, intensive lobbying of public officials by the federation's representatives, and close ties with organized labor.

Elements of the Chicago reform community opposed to centralization

of the public schools on the terms of the administrative progressives in-
structed the CTF in opposition politics. Frances Temple, the dominant
force in the Chicago Women's Club, persuaded Margaret Haley, the
emerging leader of the teachers' federation, that the CTF must oppose
the establishment of a school system in which the superintendent "was
assumed to be an educator . . . and six thousand teachers in the system
merely takers of orders."[24] Ella Flagg Young electrified the teachers with
a scornful denunciation of the Harper bill. Mayor Harrison gave a committee of teachers the use of the city council chambers to confer with
General Assembly members. A sympathetic male high school teacher
steered Haley toward the Chicago Federation of Labor as a useful ally in
the legislative fight, and former governor Altgeld and Clarence Darrow
arranged the meeting that sealed the partnership.[25]

Supported by the capitol's labor lobbyists and armed with a petition
against the education bill signed by 3,300 CTF members, Goggin and
Haley led a six-woman CTF delegation to Springfield. Labor veterans put
the teachers in touch with important legislators, but in her remarks before
the House Education Committee Haley demonstrated that the CTF
would not depend on quiet diplomacy. She boldly stated that only Jesus
Christ could fulfill the Harper bill's requirements for a superintendent
who was "omnipotent," "omnipresent," and "capable of perfect justice,"
adding that Harper himself fell considerably short of that standard.[26] The
Harper bill died in committee, and the CTF served notice that henceforth it would lead the opposition to the administrative progressives.[27]

The consolidation of power by Margaret Haley and Catherine Goggin
in the CTF was the source of the organization's assertiveness. The daughter of an Irish Catholic radical who once pulled his children out of a
meeting after an orator "spoke sneeringly of Susan B. Anthony," Haley
directed the CTF with passion and utter fearlessness. Imbued in her youth
with the egalitarian ideals of the greenback movement, Haley was introduced to the ideas of Henry George during a year of study at the Illinois
Normal School in Bloomington. She enjoyed an unusually rich exposure
to progressive educational principles during her studies under Francis
Parker and William James at the Cook County Normal School (later the
Chicago Normal School) and the Buffalo School for Pedagogy. Entering
the Cook County school system in 1882, Haley taught in the sixth grade
for sixteen years between 1884 and 1900 at a school close by the Union
stockyards on Chicago's South Side. The pension fight brought her into
the teachers' federation, and she quickly demonstrated uncommon skill
and persistence as a lobbyist. As the paid business agent of the CTF,
Haley attended every session of the General Assembly from 1898 to 1935.
After the CTF affiliated with the Chicago Federation of Labor, Haley also

served on the CFL's five-member legislative committee, leading a field of ten male aspirants in the 1906 CFL election. Stubborn, tactless, and extremely talented, Haley put her personal stamp on the CTF. [28]

Catherine Goggin shared the leadership of the CTF with Haley. Goggin, who had taught in the Chicago schools since 1872 without normal school training, was a leader in the pension fight. Her cool, earnest demeanor balanced the flamboyance of the impetuous Haley. The two women worked as a team, planning strategy at the federation's Unity Building headquarters and then continuing their work at the lodgings they shared. Together they dominated the CTF until Goggin was killed by a truck while hurrying from a federation meeting in 1916. [29]

Shortly after defeating the Harper bill, Haley and Goggin solidified their control of the teachers' federation. The Harper report had opened a rift between Haley and Goggin's radical faction and a group, including CTF president Elizabeth Burdick, who questioned the wisdom of opposing Harper's reforms. Three CTF officers in fact lobbied for the passage of the Harper bill. Determined to purge these elements and broaden the federation's agenda, Haley put Goggin forward as a candidate for the CTF presidency in 1899. Opposed to the radical ticket was a "peace party" slate advocating a less controversial role for the CTF. The contest was "bitter and uncharitable in many instances." [30] Opponents within the CTF preyed on Goggin's Catholicism. A spurious announcement, claiming "we Catholics are in the majority and if we stand together shall surely win," circulated through the teaching force just before the election. [31] Convinced that Goggin had been counted out in her 1898 presidential bid, Haley insisted that the election be conducted by secret ballot under the watchful eyes of clerks, tellers, and judges selected by the opposing factions. Amid great excitement, and with policemen standing by, Goggin defeated the peace party candidate, Lucy Laing, 1,701 to 543. Haley later reminisced, "we had tasted blood and we liked the taste." [32]

Guided by Haley and Goggin, the Chicago Teachers' Federation openly challenged the basic assumptions of the administrative progressives. The CTF considered the popular control of public education a greater good than centralized professional control. CTF officials also argued that education proceeds more smoothly when teachers exercise independent authority in the classroom. Proposals such as the Harper committee's for upgraded professional standards for teachers and a promotional system directed by the superintendent would demean teachers' abilities and sabotage their efforts to teach effectively.

Job control in the classroom was not a rhetorical issue in the Chicago schools. In November 1902 Jane McKeon, a teacher at the Andrew Jackson school, was suspended for one month without pay and transferred to another school after resisting her principal's order to reinstate a boy she had removed from class for using "intolerant language."[33] McKeon, an active CTF member, charged that Superintendent Edwin Cooley pressured the Jackson school principal into filing the insubordination charge "to oust [her] from the schools."[34] The local community stood behind its accused teacher; school children demanding McKeon's return boycotted classes with the consent of their parents. Alderman John Powers brought the matter before the city council, and a sharp dispute over the merits of centralized versus local school control briefly flared on the school board. Shaken by the militance of the teachers and the dismaying outbreak of "strikes" among school children, the *Chicago Tribune* reminded teachers that in Chicago "employment means work, not argumentation. The school system is not a debating society."[35]

Nonetheless, the CTF effectively used the school system to publicize its opposition to administrative centralization. Each school served as a neighborhood headquarters for the CTF, from which teachers distributed circulars, organized local meetings, and got out the vote on election day. The CTF press committee fed information to the newspapers; federation officials developed a particularly close relationship with correspondents from the Hearst papers. In 1901 Haley launched the *Chicago Teachers' Federation Bulletin* as a mouthpiece of the movement. The *Bulletin* spread the CTF doctrine of job security and popular control of education among disaffected women teachers and demanded action from public officials. The Chicago school system had become less a debating society than a battleground.[36]

◆

The CTF's role in the defeat of the Harper bill also revealed a growing schism among Chicago's educational reformers. A collection of Deweyite educators supported the teachers in their resistance to Harper's centralization scheme. Ella Flagg Young introduced a series of advisory teachers' councils into the school system, thereby providing teachers with a voice in educational policy formulation. Others, however, professional educators and good government reformers alike, condemned the CTF as a reactionary obstacle to the necessary reorganization of an antiquated, unwieldy school system. *The Dial*, a genteel literary publication, stressed the importance of professionalizing the school system and complained that the CTF "used the weapons of the politician rather than those of the educator," particularly by enlisting the aid of organized labor.[37] Instead of confronting the problems exposed by the Harper commission, "such words as 'autocracy,' 'tyranny,' and 'despotism' have been freely used, and the magic word 'democracy' has once more been worked into the service of the reactionary party."[38]

Chicago's elite reformers, represented by the Civic Federation and Commercial Club, became estranged from the Chicago Teachers' Federation. A Civic Federation Commission of One Hundred reasserted its commitment to the ideals of the Harper commission in 1900, but two bills intended to centralize Chicago schools, one prepared by the Civic Federation and the other the work of new school superintendent Edwin Cooley and Clayton Mark of the Commercial Club, fell before CTF lobbying in 1903. Haley's disingenuous claim that both proposals meant to place Chicago schools under state control, despite the Civic Federation's well-known advocacy of home rule, further antagonized administrative reformers. Hostility deepened at the Chicago Charter Convention. After the Cooley–Civic Federation plan for school administration appeared in the proposed charter, the CTF joined vigorously in the coalition that defeated its adoption in 1907.[39]

Superintendent Cooley tried to outflank the CTF's political influence by reorganizing the administrative hierarchy within the school system. Like Andrews, Cooley believed with a technician's certainty and a reformer's zeal that cost-cutting efficiency in the allocation of resources and authority in the person of a professionally trained superintendent would build a superior and socially responsible school system. Unlike Andrews, however, Cooley possessed the administrative polish necessary to build support on the school board and among reforming clubmen. Through administrative adjustments Cooley took over many of the diffuse powers of the school board. To combat political "pull" in teacher appointments, the superintendent persuaded the board to transfer its appointive power to him. Cooley next restructured fourteen committees into four bodies overseeing school management, buildings and grounds, finance, and compulsory education. Lost in the shuffle were the district committees, whose ties to neighborhoods and local politicians had seriously limited the superintendent's authority. Cooley reduced the number of semi-independent district superintendents from fourteen to six and made them roving assistants subject to his direction. Allies in the press took Cooley's resourceful methods of building his authority as "pretty good proof that he will use his power wisely."[40]

Once the Chicago Board of Education gave him a vote of confidence in November 1901 in the form of a $10,000 salary and a five-year contract, Cooley moved to assert control over the refractory teachers. He cut salaries and introduced a promotional merit system based on written examinations and confidential evaluations by superiors. The CTF complained that the merit system ignored seniority, and because teachers scoring below a mark of seventy could not appeal their score or even see their examinations, it blasted the plan as a subjective "secret marking" system intended to terrorize and pacify the teaching force. Cooley answered by heaping on coals, abolishing the advisory teachers' councils in 1903. These were hardly welcome moves to adherents of democratic schooling. John Dewey feared that, "in their zeal to place the centre of gravity inside the school system, in their zeal to decrease the prerogatives of a non-expert school board, and to lessen the opportunities for corruption and private pull which go with that," school administrators had "tried to remedy one of the evils of democracy by adopting the principle of autocracy."[41]

From School Reform to Social Reform

The school question in Chicago cut to the heart of the progressive dilemma: how to balance the efficiency of expert control with the freedom of democracy. Business-oriented reform clubs pressed for rational control of public education through centralized administration. Reformers affiliated with settlement houses or women's causes, even the elite Chicago Women's Club, backed the teachers' fight for higher pay, job security, and local control of the schools. Opportunistic politicians such as Mayor Harrison, who carefully measured reform currents before swimming with them, waited for the stronger constituency to emerge. Even before Cooley finished restructuring the school board, however, the CTF altered the terms of the debate. Haley charged that administrative progressives were not disinterested educational experts but rather corrupt participants with the major Chicago utilities in a scheme to defraud the schools of tax revenue and crush democratic resistance to corporate domination. Thoroughly radicalized, the CTF affiliated with the Chicago Federation of Labor and endorsed a wide range of proposals—including women's suffrage, municipal ownership of utilities, and a popularly elected school board—designed to increase popular control of public affairs.

Teacher militancy was fueled by the collapse of the 1898 salary increase for experienced teachers. Teachers received the initial seventy-five-dollar increment in 1898, but the school board suspended further planned increases the following year and in January 1900 revoked the 1898 salary schedule altogether. The board explained that insufficient revenue and a transfer of existing funds between departments left no money for teacher salaries, but the city taxes that sustained public schools had risen. Intrigued by newspaper allegations of massive corporate tax evasion, Margaret Haley visited the Cook County clerk's office during her 1899 Christmas vacation and hounded the assistant clerk into allowing her to examine the state auditor's reports on the assessment of corporate property by the Illinois State Board of Equalization. Haley discovered that, when assessing property for taxation, the board consistently failed to add the value of capital stock and franchises to the physical valuation of Cook County utility corporations. In 1899 the franchise value of Chicago's street railway, gas, light, and power companies went completely untaxed. This meant that millions of dollars' worth of taxable property escaped assessment, and revenue that could have funded the teachers' salary increases went uncollected.[42]

With the permission and encouragement of school board president Graham H. Harris, who saw no reason to further antagonize city teachers, the CTF authorized Haley and Goggin to pursue their investigation of Cook County corporate taxes as paid representatives of the federation. Neither woman ever worked in a classroom again. They spent the next two years wading through auditors' reports, haranguing the mayor and the tax bodies of Cook County, tracking down elusive members of the state board of equalization, and conferring with judges and attorneys. In November 1900 the federation sued the equalization board to compel proper assessment of the intangible property held by five Chicago public utility corporations (organized into twenty-nine companies) that, according to the CTF, owed over $2,350,000 annually in unpaid taxes.[43]

Chicago's mainstream reformers encouraged the teachers' tax suit. Jane Addams and liberal clergyman and Civic Federation member Rufus A. White expressed support in a rally at Chicago's Central Music Hall, while Haley flayed the "tax dodgers." Legal advice from Altgeld and Clarence Darrow carried the CTF through state and federal courts, until the Chicago utilities were ordered to pay $597,033 in back taxes in July 1902. The press, public, and even Nicholas Murray Butler offered congratulations.[44]

◆

It was not a total victory, however. The tax fight also revealed the power of capital over the governing system of courts and parties. Under pressure from the utilities, the board of equalization made a hasty assessment of the corporations' capital stock and franchises shortly after the CTF initiated its suits. The compliant board declared a modest value of $12.5 million, over $220 million below the CTF estimate. State courts invalidated the forced appraisal, but a federal injunction secured by the utilities set aside the higher assessment ordered by the state. The final judgment rendered by the federal court reduced the utilities' tax bill by more than two-thirds. Meanwhile, the 1901 General Assembly eliminated compulsory deductions from the teachers' pension law, badly weakening the system. Haley protested to Assemblyman David Shanahan and absorbed a lesson in Illinois civics. Women teachers usually received protection, explained the crusty Republican leader, but when teachers "attack these great, powerful corporations, you must expect that they will hit back." From that moment, Haley vowed to overturn the corrupt alliance between business and government.[45]

The CTF soon included administrative progressives and the school board in the cabal. Flushed with success, the teachers expected the taxes their efforts had secured for Chicago to be used to revive the 1898 salary schedule. In this they were frustrated. Police and firemen had pay cuts restored by the city council, but the board of education refused similar treatment for stunned teachers, instead using money from the CTF suit to improve classrooms, fortify the building fund, and pay the coal bill. Another CTF lawsuit, this time against the school board, was necessary before the teachers recovered their share of the tax proceeds. Circuit court judge Edward Dunne ruled in August 1904 that, as diligent creditors, the teachers had a prior claim on the back taxes awarded to the school board. The CTF gained an ally in Dunne. More decisively, Haley now concluded that corporate tax dodgers, enemies of the pension, and the backers of the revived Harper bill from the Civic Federation and the board of education were all of one corrupt, dictatorial piece.[46]

◆

With the purifying logic of a conversion experience, the tax battle transformed Haley's opposition to school centralization into a systematic social critique and ringing call to arms. In a statement to CTF members, Haley attacked "the power of intrenched, organized human greed," bolstered by "the machinery of law," against which "alone the school is powerless." Nevertheless, she maintained, the CTF, women's clubs, and organized labor—representing the democratic power of the school, home, and factory—could through political action reestablish the rule of law, "adjust the social relation and restore equilibrium."[47] Powered by Haley's democratic theories and attracted by the 200,000 votes of the Chicago Federation of Labor, the CTF voted to affiliate with the CFL on November 8, 1902. Jane Addams cautiously encouraged the move, but Haley bluntly demanded that CTF conservatives step aside and cease "stopping the wheels of progress." CTF president Ella Rowe condemned the vote as "a political trick, accomplished by a thoroughly oiled political machine," and resigned from the federation in protest.[48] At most only 485 federation members attended the meeting, and many opponents of union affiliation had departed before Haley rushed the issue to a vote. Nevertheless, the new course was clear, and before the month ended the CTF elected thirty delegates to the Chicago Federation of Labor.[49]

Following Haley, women teachers plunged into reform politics. CTF votes were crucial in breaking the hold of building trades boss Martin "Skinny" Madden over the CFL in January 1903. The triumphant reform faction, led by John Fitzpatrick and Edward Nockels, worked closely with Haley and the teachers' federation. Haley was one of the most conspicuous and effective lobbyists before the Forty-third General Assembly in 1903, representing the CTF, the CFL, and the Illinois Federation of Women's Clubs. Aside from defeating the school bills prepared by Cooley and the Civic Federation, Haley helped push through child labor and compulsory education laws that forced children out of factories and into schools. The legislature rejected the CTF plan to open the Chicago Board of Education to popular election, but Haley pressed on for other popular controls. In Chicago she developed close ties with the Municipal Ownership League (MOL) and boldly used school children to circulate petitions requesting a citywide advisory vote on the desirability of primary elections and municipal ownership of railway, gas, and electric companies. Following the successful city election of April 1902, school children again fanned out with petitions, this time to request a constitutional amendment providing for a state initiative and referendum law. Illinois voters endorsed the idea in November, but the 1903 General Assembly refused to enact the amendment.[50]

Practical as well as ideological considerations prompted the outburst of teacher activism. For example, municipal ownership of utilities, aside from the question of popular control, would prevent tax evasion and protect future salary increases for teachers. Further, because Illinois women voted in school elections, the CTF could outmaneuver administrative progressives on an elected school board. The CTF's agenda was wider than that, however; Haley's justification for CTF political activity went beyond issues of salary and job control to the role of public education in a democracy. Speaking before the 1904 meeting of the National Educational Association, she argued that dominant educational theories glorified knowledge too exclusively and overzealously pursued rational organization, forgetting that "the public school is the organized means provided by the deliberate effort of the whole people to free intelligence at its source—and through freed intelligence to secure freedom of action."[51] The public schools were the incubators of democracy.

According to such a view, it is the duty of teachers' organizations "to preserve and develop" democratic ideals, not only in school administration but in the schools' relations with the public. Teachers' organizations therefore should not ignore public questions but rather seize on them to provide a model of democratic citizenship. Confident that "there is no possible conflict between the interest of the child and the interest of the teachers," Haley dismissed charges that teacher activism would turn selfishly inward and damage children's education. As for the CTF's affiliation with organized labor, she argued that "there is no possible conflict between the good of society and the good of its members, of which the industrial workers are the vast majority."[52] Both the public school and organized labor sought to preserve the democratic ideal against the rising industrial ideal that hallowed commercialism. Both the good of the child and the mission of the public school demanded that teachers ally with labor and enter public affairs.

The press and the educational hierarchy nevertheless roundly condemned the teachers' federation for affiliating with the CFL, and the praise elicited by the tax fight turned to bitter denunciation. The *Chicago Tribune* treated a series of classroom uprisings in late 1902 as student strikes, creating the impression that unionized teachers soon would paralyze the schools with disruptive labor disputes. The school board's committee on school management declared in June 1905 that public school teachers had "absolutely no moral right to assume partisan attitudes and deliberately take the side of one portion of the public against the other," and it expressed "unqualified disapproval" of the CFL affiliation.[53] Butler in 1907 encouraged regulations that "would remove from the school service any teacher who affiliated himself or herself with a labor organization."[54] Although Jane Addams worked with the CTF for the child labor bill of 1903, other former allies abandoned the teachers. The Civic Federation's Rufus White considered the CTF's decision "unwise, anomalous, and undemocratic." The mainstream progressive support briefly enjoyed by the CTF flickered out.[55]

◆

By 1905 the CTF occupied an exposed and highly vulnerable position on the left wing of Chicago's reform spectrum, but the enthusiasm for popular control generated by the campaign for the municipal ownership of city streetcar lines temporarily overshadowed the danger. By linking its fortunes with the municipal ownership mayoral bid of Edward Dunne, the teacher-labor alliance achieved its greatest political triumph against administrative progressives. Dunne and his supporters alienated many mainstream reformers, however, and lacked a massive popular following to counterbalance that loss. Unable to push through either municipal ownership of street railways or popular control of public schools, the Dunne administration of 1905–7 succeeded only in entangling both issues in controversies that suffocated the programs of administrative progressives and radical democrats alike.

Streetcar Politics

The discovery that business corrupts politics created the mass constituency that supported progressive reforms in the United States. Nowhere was the corrupt partnership between corporate arrogance and venal politics so visible as in the street railway systems of late nineteenth-century American cities. The dealings of political rings with streetcar companies filled the pages of muckraking journals; Lincoln Steffens reported such illicit connections in St. Louis, Pittsburgh, and Philadelphia.[56] In Detroit, Cleveland, Milwaukee, and scores of smaller cities, popular outrage at poor service and extensive bribery by streetcar franchises ushered in a new era of civic reform. The Windy City was not to be outdone, however; in the brazenness of its political manipulation, the cynicism of its corporate directors, and its casual disregard of efficiency and public convenience, the Chicago streetcar system had no equal.

Inefficiency and corruption characterized Chicago public transit from its beginnings. The first corporations received rights to city streets for twenty-five years in 1858. Five years later, three separate companies operated horse-drawn streetcar lines in different sections of Chicago and refused to issue transfers for passengers forced to switch lines. By 1885, when Charles Tyson Yerkes arrived from Philadelphia and completely overhauled the northern and western streetcar lines, the struggle between consumers, the city council, state government, and the companies formed a well-established pattern. Chicago aldermen were willing to provide favors to the streetcar companies for a price but resisted long-term franchises. The General Assembly proved to be more pliant, and streetcar magnates regularly attempted to bypass the city council through long-term franchises granted by the state. In 1865 the General Assembly enacted a ninety-nine-year extension of Chicago streetcar franchises over the veto of Governor Richard Oglesby, but the constitution of 1870 and subsequent legislation gave the city control over franchise extension and limited any renewal to twenty years.[57]

Yerkes mixed managerial brilliance with cynical opportunism. Through a complicated series of mergers, he acquired control of the northern and western Chicago streetcar lines, as well as franchises in adjoining towns later annexed by the city. Yerkes also controlled three of the five new elevated rail lines in Chicago. He replaced horse-drawn cars with ones powered by cable, but he also packed hapless commuters into inadequate space, extracted double fares by dividing routes between companies, and neglected to maintain the lines he built. The entire operation bobbed on a sea of watered stock. By means of holding companies, dummy construction outfits, and the practice of ignoring the depreciation of physical assets Yerkes capitalized his enterprises at nearly twice their actual worth. Excess capital financed extensive bribery of Chicago aldermen and secured friendly ordinances. Yerkes' methods of influencing politicians were so storied that Carter Harrison took pains never to be in a room alone with the traction magnate.[58]

The poor service and political corruption so visibly attached to the streetcar system operated by Yerkes provoked a popular reform outcry in Chicago. Seeking a longer franchise extension than the voracious gray wolves on the city council could provide, Yerkes turned to the General Assembly in 1895. It passed two measures granting the Chicago city council authority to extend streetcar franchises for ninety-nine years and severely hampering the ability of future competitors to challenge the Yerkes monopoly. Shaking off a Yerkes bribe, Altgeld vetoed the "monopoly" bills with a stinging message. Two years later, the Yerkes forces managed to pass the Allen bill, which empowered city councils to grant fifty-year franchise extensions, and secured the approval of Governor John Tanner. When the franchise ordinances were introduced in the Chicago city council, however, they faced the vocal opposition of an aroused community. Mayor Harrison, elected in 1897 with a pledge to defend the public interest in franchise matters, vowed to veto any extension. Street demonstrations denounced the proposed extensions, and when the matter came to a vote in December 1898, angry citizens carrying nooses monitored the proceedings from the gallery. The franchise extensions failed to pass, and at the next legislative session the Allen act was repealed. The Municipal Voters' League, strengthened by popular outrage over franchise bribery, began to reform the Common Council. Yerkes reorganized his deteriorating lines into the Union Traction Company, unloaded it at an inflated price to Philadelphia buyers, and left Chicago in 1901.[59]

◆

The municipal ownership movement grew from the rubble of Yerkes' legacy. Badly in need of repair, swollen with watered stock, and with franchises set to expire in 1903, the former Yerkes holdings proved too much for the new owners to handle and passed into a receivership administered by federal circuit court judge Peter Grosscup. Grosscup personified the union between the courts and corporations in Illinois. His injunction had temporarily blocked the CTF tax suit, and now he worked to revive the streetcar lines. Grosscup resurrected the ninety-nine-year franchise act of 1865 and made arrangements with the House of Morgan to consolidate the city rail system. Concomitantly, sentiment for municipal ownership had been growing in Chicago following Altgeld's unsuccessful race for mayor in 1899. Nonbinding public-policy votes in 1902 and 1904 supported city-run utilities. Mainstream politicians and reformers took note. In 1903 a coalition including Harrison and the city council, elite reform clubs, the Referendum League of the MOL, and the CFL sponsored the passage of the Mueller law. This act gave Chicago the power to purchase or construct streetcar lines on voter approval and set up a financial apparatus by which municipalization could be funded. Last ditch attempts in the Illinois House to paralyze the Mueller bill prompted a near riot in the chamber featuring an assault on Speaker John H. Miller.[60]

Despite the Mueller law, Harrison felt outflanked by Grosscup's judgment on the ninety-nine year leases. Shrugging off popular votes for immediate municipal ownership and against franchise extensions for streetcar companies, Harrison made an arrangement with Chicago City Railway, the South Side's major line, by which the company's franchise was extended for twenty years and in return it abandoned claims to the ninety-nine-year lease. Harrison's compromise provided for eventual purchase of the lines by the city, but his disregard of public opinion triggered renewed agitation for immediate municipal ownership.[61]

Radical democrats, upset at Grosscup's arrogance and Harrison's caution, forced municipal ownership into the political mainstream. The aging radical Henry Demarest Lloyd, backed by the settlement house contingent, the CTF, and the CFL, helped put the Mueller law on the public-policy advisory ballot of 1904. In 1904, after Harrison ignored the five-to-one majority for implementation of the Mueller law, two circuit court judges, Dunne and Murray F. Tuley, assumed leadership of the immediate municipal ownership forces. Tuley published an open letter in January 1905 urging Dunne, an adherent of the Altgeld wing of the Illinois Democratic organization, to become the movement's candidate for mayor in 1905. Sensing his untenable position, Harrison stepped aside, and Dunne became the regular Democratic candidate. In November Dunne became mayor of Chicago, defeating Republican John M. Harlan, a moderate advocate of gradual municipal ownership, by 25,000 votes.[62]

The CTF enthusiastically attached itself to Dunne's campaign. Margaret Haley believed that a gang of "tax-dodging" corporations and public officials was smothering the popular will in Chicago, which had been expressed clearly by advisory public-policy votes since 1902, and that only new political leadership could break its grip. Further, Harrison had surrendered to Grosscup and the public utility corporations during the teachers' tax suit and again in the streetcar fight. In July 1903 the CFL petitioned Harrison to appoint five labor representatives to the Chicago school board. He instead named five businessmen to the posts. As public support for IMO grew, Harrison could not see "how municipal ownership is to be accomplished."[63] He and the CTF became implacable enemies. Haley came to despise him as "a cowardly, subservient tool to big business" who had betrayed the children and taxpayers of Chicago.[64]

Dunne, on the other hand, shared the CTF's democratic aspirations. He supported the teachers' tax suit and endorsed the teacher-labor alliance's use of advisory public-policy elections as a form of moral referendum. Where Harrison scoffed at the feasibility of immediate municipal ownership of utilities, Dunne anchored his campaign on its necessity and practicality. Most importantly, Dunne signaled that he would approve the teachers' bid to democratize the school board if the influence of "low ward politics" were excluded.[65]

Dunne, Democracy, and Disaster

Dunne's election appeared to be the crowning achievement of a popular reform movement dedicated to immediate municipal ownership and resurgent democracy, but in fact, the new mayor's administration rested on unstable ground. Widespread dissatisfaction with Harrison's proposed streetcar settlement apparently drew more votes to Dunne than did the plan for IMO. In the 1904 city election, 152,434 Chicago voters favored the implementation of the Mueller law, but the number endorsing IMO fell to 120,744. More than one-quarter of those voting ignored the IMO measure altogether. The 1902 public-policy question on municipal ownership and the 1904 IMO question drew approximately the same number of voters, but the majority favoring municipal ownership dropped in two years from 115,000 to 70,000.[66]

Dunne's insistence on IMO cost him the support of Chicago's moderate reform element. The *Chicago Examiner* and the *American,* two Bryanite newspapers in the Hearst chain, backed Dunne in the 1905 mayoral campaign; the remainder of the Chicago press lined up solidly against him. Most newspapers endorsed the *Chicago Tribune's* judgment that "the immediate acquisition of the street railway systems by the city would be an unqualified misfortune."[67] Prominent members of the Civic Federation and Municipal Voters' League predictably supported Harlan, but settlement house progressives Graham Taylor and Raymond Robins also rejected Dunne in favor of the Republican candidate. Dunne was able to win election without the aid of the newspapers or moderate reformers. Governing effectively without their support, however, was another matter.[68]

◆

Edward Dunne did not find himself at the head of a united consumers' movement such as the one that pioneered progressive reform in Wisconsin. Instead, Dunne's power rested on the loyalty of two irreconcilable groups: radical social reformers—the CTF, the CFL, their allies among settlement house workers, and old Altgeld partisans—and the Democratic ward organizations that had thrown over Harrison. Because Harrison loyalists controlled much of the Democratic party organization, Dunne was forced to rely on the support of powerful ward leaders such as John Powers, Michael Kenna, and William Dever, who expected to profit from the new mayor's election. In policy matters, however, Dunne sought advice and assistance from the social reformers, few of whom were well-placed in party circles. Once in office, Dunne was reluctant to make wholesale patronage appointments, preferring only a few changes in crucial policy-making positions. Denied their patronage reward, ward leaders, many of whom were aldermen without a personal commitment to IMO, refused to support the mayor in the city council. Stripped of the advantage gained by an alliance with ward organizations, Dunne also suffered when Chicago's moderate reform forces—the Civic Federation, administrative progressives, and the *Tribune*—denounced the "machine" base of his government. [69]

Alienated from Chicago's moderate reform organizations and unwilling to indulge the appetites of ward bosses, Dunne's administration leaned heavily on the support of its radical backers. Municipal ownership enthusiasts, single-taxers, and CFL and CTF representatives proved less adept at the art of political compromise than the common run of municipal politicians. Politically isolated, inexperienced, and uncompromising, the Dunne administration absorbed a series of concussive blows that sidetracked IMO and created havoc and bitterness on the school board.

◆

Symptomatic of the difficulties that plagued the Dunne administration was the violent Chicago teamsters strike that erupted in April 1905, just days before the new mayor took office. For three long months, the CFL and the Employers' Association formed to break the strike battled in the streets. Over 560 union members were arrested during the strike, as were 187 strikebreakers hired by the Employers' Association, while the mayor fruitlessly attempted to restore order. Dunne appointed a Commission of Inquiry, chaired by Graham Taylor, to get at the facts behind the strike, but to little avail. The commission relied on the voluntary cooperation of witnesses, and without the authority to compel testimony, it was unable to question reluctant employers and unwilling to conduct each session in public as the CFL demanded. The commission soon collapsed. Attempts

to arbitrate the strike through the city council also failed. Escalating violence forced Dunne to expand the police force and threaten state intervention. Caught between his labor allies—the CFL remained among the
staunchest supporters of IMO—and an angry public, the bewildered
mayor could only watch as the Employers' Association crushed the
strike.[70]

Dunne's performance during the crisis drew criticism from both camps.
The *Union Labor Advocate* noted with disappointment that "had the
mayor been wise and strong the strike must have ended in ten days. But
he proved weak and vascilating [*sic*], truckling for a while to both sides."[71]
From the other side Dunne was linked to the misdeeds of the strikers,
most notably strike leader Cornelius Shea, who during the height of the
conflict frolicked with his lieutenants at a bordello called the Old Kentucky Home. Because of Dunne's attachment to the CFL, which refused
to denounce Shea, and his reluctance to challenge the "wide open town"
preferred by ward leaders, the mayor could be tarred with that unsavory
brush. Worse yet, the entire debacle diverted attention from IMO. Years
later, Dunne attributed the strike to "a conspiracy between the foes of
municipal ownership and Con Shea."[72]

Dunne's IMO program also stalled before the uncooperative city council. Once in office, he realized that his plan to condemn the streetcar
lines and initiate a new municipal system under the Mueller law faced
lengthy delays and legal uncertainties. The mayor therefore shifted his
allegiance to a new plan that authorized five public-spirited citizens to
issue bonds and begin construction on a streetcar system, with proceeds
going into a sinking fund to finance eventual city purchase. By working
through a "private" company, the city would avoid the legal pitfall of
Chicago's debt limitation and its unresolved relation to the Mueller law's
financial apparatus. Dunne was thwarted in this also. The city council set
aside the mayor's plan and opened new franchise negotiations with the
streetcar companies. Dunne later recalled that after each council meeting, the newspaper headlines read "Mayor Snubbed Again."[73]

A series of misadventures further imperiled Dunne's position with the
recalcitrant aldermen. In February 1906 James Dalrymple, a Scottish expert commissioned by Dunne to evaluate the Chicago streetcar system,
came to the embarrassing conclusion that the city's most efficient course
lay in extending the current franchises of the streetcar companies.
Dunne's attempts to conceal the report caused public ridicule of IMO.
Dalrymple's report came on the heels of another embarrassment, the resignation of special traction counsel Clarence Darrow. Late in 1905 Darrow announced that the mayor could not work with the city council until
several obstructionist aldermen were removed from office in the 1906

election, but Dunne would not wait, and when he resubmitted his proposal for an outright city takeover of streetcar lines Darrow resigned in frustration. IMO and Dunne's reputation were on the ropes.[74]

Events in early 1906 created a spirit of compromise in the administration and the streetcar companies that broke the logjam. A suit initiated in the Harrison regime struck down the companies' claim to the ninety-nine-year lease law, eliminating their strongest bargaining chip, and in an abrupt reversal of form, the city council passed Dunne's most radical municipalization proposal and submitted it for voter approval. The Big Fix was behind the turnaround. Fearful that the streetcar corporations had written off IMO, aldermanic gray wolves changed course to jolt the companies out of their complacency and loosen their pockets. But referenda in April brought a dangerously low majority of 3,300 backing the issuance of Mueller certificates to fund a city takeover of the lines and an outright failure to reach the 60 percent approval margin necessary to operate the lines under the Mueller law. With public support for IMO rapidly declining and the constitutionality of the Mueller certificates under review, the situation was ripe for compromise.[75]

The eventual settlement of the streetcar question reflected not the radical IMO outlook of Dunne and Darrow but rather the moderate approach of Republican reform. Walter L. Fisher, late of the Municipal Voters' League, replaced Darrow as traction counsel and orchestrated a compromise that received the mayor's support. In extended negotiations, Fisher, a commission of experts, the transportation committee of the city council, and the streetcar companies hammered out a set of ordinances that essentially surrendered IMO in return for improved streetcar service. The companies agreed to issue universal transfers, to electrify their systems, and to expand their lines according to the will of the city. They also pledged five million dollars for the future construction of a city-owned subway. Experts employed by the city would oversee the maintenance and financial operations of the companies. Beyond a 5 percent profit on investment, revenue would be split, with 55 percent going to the city and 45 percent remaining with the companies. Twenty-year franchises, revocable on six months' notice, were issued to the companies. It was a typically progressive settlement, balancing public and private claims, reducing conflict through expert supervision, and furnishing increased efficiency.[76]

Dunne at first approved the so-called settlement ordinances, but his radical allies considered them a betrayal of municipal ownership. The *Union Labor Advocate* charged that the streetcar companies, "camped upon the streets of our city like an invading army of Cossacks," used a calculated decrease in service to create a mood conducive to a quick set-

tlement. [77] Hidden in the ordinances by deceitful lawyers and venal aldermen, the labor journal claimed, were "jokers" undercutting the professed
devotion to public interest and eventual municipal ownership. Confronted with the anger of his most loyal constituents, Dunne reversed his
field and opposed the adoption of the settlement ordinances unless
amendments intended to eliminate any "tricks" lurking within them were
accepted. The city council ignored the amendments and passed the ordinances on February 4, 1907, whereupon Dunne vetoed them. But Dunne
was powerless. The council resoundingly overrode the veto, fifty-seven to
twelve, and in April voters approved the ordinances by a 33,000 vote
majority. Chicagoans were willing to accept an imperfect settlement in
return for more reliable streetcar service. IMO died quietly in the winter
of 1907. [78]

The plan for municipal stewardship did not solve the mass transportation problem in Chicago. Another utility baron, Samuel Insull, gained
control of the elevated lines in 1911, and by 1914 Insull was the dominant figure in Chicago's streetcar network. Insull improved the by now
legendary poor service on the rail lines, but he also attempted to break
away from municipal oversight. With the help of state Democratic boss
Roger Sullivan, Insull influenced the General Assembly to create a State
Public Utility Commission. Insull preferred that his electric and transportation network be subject to the more predictable regulation of a state
body. The commission, intended to remove utilities from the intrigue of
municipal politics, went into operation on January 1, 1914, but the city
council retained control over franchises, so the old pattern of cooperation
and blackmail between Chicago politicians and utilities persisted. [79]

The End of Democratic Schools

The incompatibility of radical and moderate reform visions that doomed
IMO created bitterness over Dunne's school policy as well. A vocal proponent of educational democracy, the mayor supported the Chicago
Teachers' Federation against administrative progressives on the school
board. Each year the mayor was allowed to appoint seven new members
to the twenty-one-seat Chicago Board of Education. Aided by Margaret
Haley and the CTF, Dunne used this power to offset the influence of
businesspeople and professional educators on the board with advocates of
popular democracy and representatives of labor, immigrants, and neighborhoods. His first picks included two settlement house reformers, the
founder of Francis W. Parker's progressive School of Education at the
University of Chicago, the former president of the Referendum League, a

member of the CFL's committee on schools, and representatives of the city's Polish and Jewish communities. Three of the new school board members were women: Jane Addams, whom Haley nominated and then persuaded to accept the position; educational philanthropist Anita Mc-Cormick Blaine; and settlement house physician Cornelia De Bey, renowned for mediating the Chicago stockyard strike of 1904. In 1906 Dunne added Louis Post, the radical editor of the *Public*; well-connected settlement house reformer Raymond Robins; CFL officer John J. Sonsteby; Methodist Episcopal minister Wiley Wright Mills (like Post a devotee of the single tax); and municipal ownership backer Philip Angsten.[80]

The Dunne board, as it soon became known, reversed the trend toward centralized authority under Superintendent Cooley and initiated a series of actions beneficial to the CTF. The new school board dropped its predecessors' resistance to the teachers' salary suit, proposed to restore teachers' councils, commissioned a highly critical study of Cooley's merit system, and adopted Post's plan for a more "democratic" system of teacher ratings and promotions (including salary increases for 2,600 teachers). It supported legislation to restore compulsory contributions to the teachers' pension fund, add interest on school taxes to the fund, and protect teachers from dismissal unless written charges were filed with the city's board of education. These measures were enacted into law by the General Assembly in 1907.[81]

The aggressive stance of the CTF created fissures between moderates and radicals on the school board. Rufus White, reappointed by Dunne in 1906, had broken with the CTF over union affiliation in 1903 and distrusted its influence over school affairs. Several of Dunne's appointees resisted Post's promotion scheme as impractical, complaining that it would bankrupt the school system. Jane Addams came to view Haley as an ideologue with a self-destructive tendency to refuse compromise. Addams and several others made known their disappointment when the CTF failed to distribute the spoils of the tax fight to all Chicago public school teachers and instead confined the money to federation members. Haley, who derisively referred to Addams as "Gentle Jane," in turn expressed regret that Chicago's First Citizen valued compromise more highly than justice and hinted that perhaps Addams feared offending the wealthy sponsors of Hull House.[82]

Weakened internally, the Dunne board nevertheless followed the lead of the CTF and CFL and challenged the *Chicago Tribune*, the most powerful newspaper in the Midwest and an influential proponent of moderate reform in Chicago. The controversy centered on a ninety-nine-year lease the *Tribune* had held since 1885 on land owned by the Chicago schools. In 1895 school board president Alfred S. Trude, who was also a *Tribune* attorney, struck out the original lease's revaluation clause and fixed the rent on one of Chicago's prime downtown locations at $30,000 annually. In 1905 the rent rose to $31,500 for the duration of the lease. The CTF and CFL argued that the true rental value of the property was $95,000 and that the paper's cozy lease was yet another corporate attempt to withhold money from the public schools. The Dunne board filed suit against the newspaper in May 1907, hoping to invalidate and then renegotiate the lease. After three years of acrimonious litigation, the Illinois Supreme Court ruled in favor of the *Tribune*. [83]

Bold action and the neglect of political fences left the Dunne board without many friends. No Democrats had been named to the board in 1905, and its radical members had alienated the press and reformers, such as Addams, who desired compromise. Thus, few defended the Dunne board against the missiles launched by administrative progressives and the newspapers. The *Tribune* and Victor Lawson's *Daily News* and *Record-Herald* led the stoning in the press. A *Tribune* editorial in October 1906, characterizing the Dunne appointees as "freaks, cranks, monomaniacs, and boodlers," drew a libel suit from Robins and Post. [84] Nicholas Murray Butler complained that the Dunne board was "a collection of rare specimens" for whom "no experiment was too rash or foolish" and called for "a big, strong, vigorous personality" to redirect the school board and discipline unruly teachers. [85]

The fate of the board was settled in April 1907, when Dunne lost his reelection bid to veteran Republican politico Fred Busse by 13,000 votes. School board appointments were for three years, but Busse wasted little time in purging CTF sympathizers. He prepared letters of resignation and sent them to twelve board members on May 17, 1907. An unseemly tangle of disputatious school board meetings, lockouts, and rump assemblies of the ousted board members followed, until the Illinois Supreme Court reinstated five of the Dunne appointees six months later. In the interim, however, Busse's board protected Cooley, killed the Post plan, and soft-pedaled the *Tribune* suit. The democratic hopes of Dunne and the teacher-labor alliance abruptly crashed to earth. [86]

Three strands of educational reform had become knotted together in Chicago. Administrative progressives strove to centralize school operations and policy under professional leadership. They believed that tight standards and a uniform curriculum would eliminate the public school failings Joseph Rice had catalogued in 1892. The teacher-labor alliance worked to "democratize" public schools. The alliance held that neighborhood groups, parents, and teachers in direct contact with the children should control the schools, not a university-trained elite that applied "business principles" to education. A third group of "nonpartisan" reformers such as Jane Addams, containing elements sympathetic to both efficiency and democracy, desired above all to bring the schools "out of politics." Political patronage and interference had corroded the effectiveness of schools, argued this group, but business interests also had sought to manipulate the schools for their own ends. In 1907 none of these viewpoints had won out. By 1919 they were all defeated by the Big Fix.

For several years after 1907 the teacher-labor alliance harassed the education policies of administrative progressives. The Commercial Club of Chicago sent former school superintendent Cooley to Europe in 1910 to study Continental systems of vocational education. Cooley returned with praise for the efficient German dual education system, and with the backing of the Commercial Club, Chicago Association of Commerce, Illinois Manufacturers' Association, and Chicago Civic Federation a vocational education bill reflecting his findings appeared in the 1913 General Assembly. The proposal created separate vocational and general school tracks after the sixth grade. Supporters of the bill pointed to the dual system instituted in Wisconsin in 1911 and argued that a separate vocational track would increase industrial efficiency and dampen radicalism. The CTF resisted the bill, however, branding it a plan for educational segregation intended to cultivate a permanent and docile labor caste. With help from Dunne, now governor, Ella Flagg Young, now school superintendent, and City Club education committee chair George H. Mead, the teacher-labor alliance blocked the Cooley bill.[87]

Setbacks also stalled the teacher-labor alliance. In 1913 the school board moved against the CTF. Jacob Loeb, Mayor William Hale Thompson's new school board president, saw no room in the schools for "lady labor sluggers" such as Haley. On September 1, 1915, the board passed the Loeb Rule, which prohibited teacher affiliation with labor unions. Nine months later Loeb and his supporters suddenly fired sixty-eight teachers. Thirty-eight of the blackballed women were CTF members who had received job evaluations of "superior" to "outstanding." Included in the mass firing were all CTF officers still actively teaching, three officers of the newly organized American Federation of Teachers, seven delegates to the CFL, three delegates to the Illinois Federation of Labor, and four members of the Chicago Teachers' Pension Board. In April 1917, in a judgment Young termed the "Dred Scott decision of education," the Illinois Supreme Court upheld the validity of the Loeb Rule.[88] Soon thereafter the CTF severed its ties with the CFL. Teachers were soothed with a state grant of tenure, but the same law gave Chicago educators a smaller eleven-member school board.[89]

Neither the defeat of the teacher-labor alliance nor the trimming of the school board took the Chicago schools out of politics. Mayor Thompson fought with the city council and the courts over the control of the school board, and when the twenty-one-member board returned by court order in 1919 Thompson locked out its choice for superintendent. And cash began to flow. "New schools went up like mushrooms on the prairies," Haley recalled, "not because they were needed, but because their building was part of the political system, benefitting builders, contractors, and other friends of the machine."[90] The corruption and patronage that riddled the Chicago schools under Thompson prompted a grand jury investigation in 1922. The result of progressive-era attempts to reform Chicago schools was neither popular control, professional control, nor impartial public service. It was the Big Fix.[91]

◆

The politics of schools and streetcars in Chicago did not forge a united movement of citizens and consumers against political spoilsmen and their corporate allies. Instead, it exacerbated differences in reform ranks and revealed the vast gap between the progressive vision of the public interest and the ideal of popular control cherished by Margaret Haley and Edward Dunne. Progressives such as Graham Taylor and Jane Addams saw themselves as guardians of a responsible middle ground between corporate interests and working-class demands. This progressive tendency to favor compromise, to mediate differences for the sake of social peace, thinly concealed a paralyzing ambivalence over the comparative merits of democracy and efficiency. Up to a point, the assaults on corporate irresponsibility embodied in the program of the CTF and IMO converged with progressive notions of the public interest; thereafter, they veered sharply apart. Where Dunne and the teacher-labor alliance saw the need for stronger measures to root out business control over public affairs, progressives saw unwarranted political encroachments on the conduct of public education and visionary meddling with a viable streetcar compromise. Progressives and radical democrats alike feared the unsavory union of business and politics, but they offered incompatible solutions to the threat. For the teacher-labor alliance, democracy meant trusting the working-class majority of Chicago to run the city. For most Chicago progressives, democracy ultimately meant unselfish public service and not majority rule. Unable to drum up a shared commitment to dedicated citizenship and frustrated by the audacity of the Big Fix, progressives moved to extinguish the links between partisanship and government. If the people would not support the public interest, then a nonpartisan government would have to enforce it.

PART THREE

Political Machinery: The Irony of Progressive Reform

I wisht I was a German an' believed
in machinery.

—Mr. Dooley, 1900

6

Nonpartisan Reform and the New Politics, 1893–1912

Partisanship seemed to frustrate the public-policy objectives of progressives at every turn. It took many forms: localism in the countryside and an insistent devotion to ethnic autonomy in the city; the search for class power or commercial advantage; even uncompromising calls for popular rule. None of those positions approached the ideal of disinterested, mature citizenship that progressives believed was central to the public interest. Still, progressive political activists were unwilling to renounce the possibility of social harmony enshrined in the idea of the public interest. Nor were they able to entertain the notion that their public-interest stances represented a distinctive cultural, class-specific, and attitudinal point of view no less "partisan" than those adopted by their antagonists. They continued to believe that true democracy was efficient and that enlightened efficiency was democratic. The central barrier to the creation of a government attuned to those values, progressives argued, was not a lack of popular support; it was the power self-interested political organizations exercised over public life. Devising measures to transform the state of courts and parties into a state directed by the public interest became the overriding concern of Illinois political progressives by 1912.

The progressive drive to build a just and efficient state could not succeed without a fundamental reconstruction of party government. Party considerations determined appointments in state administration and shaped public policy. Progressives viewed corruption, incompetence, and a low regard for public institutions as the natural consequences of a system that linked government to partisan advantage. Redemption depended on the creation of a "politics without politicians" through ballot reform, professional administration, and rigid civil service codes.[1] Nonpartisan reform would break the destructive grip of politicians on Illinois government.

But nonpartisan reforms did not extinguish partisanship in Illinois. Instead, governors John Peter Altgeld, Richard Yates, and Charles S. Deneen developed a new style of executive leadership that absorbed reform energies and constructed powerful personal political organizations. In the hands of resourceful governors nonpartisan reform became partisan reform. Public-policy stances borrowed from reformers provided governors with distinctive "issue identities" that attracted support. At the same time, "nonpartisan" election laws, administrative reorganization, and legislative programs were used by governors to weaken party rivals and consolidate their own power within the party. Too late did progressives realize that their reforms had not rooted out party government but rather had nourished the growth of more powerful personal machines. Partisanship and reform were firmly bound together by the close of the Progressive Era.

The Crisis of Party Government

The seeds of partisan reform first took root, as did so many features of progressive-era Illinois, in the late nineteenth century. Illinois Republicans awoke to an unfamiliar and disturbing political world in the 1890s. For over a generation, the party of Lincoln had dominated state government, confident in its role as the political voice of optimism and progress. The Republican party "has in it the elements of growth," boasted Illinois's Robert G. Ingersoll in 1880. "It is full of hope. It anticipates. The Democratic party remembers." [2] It would soon find reason to appeal to past glories, however. As the nineteenth century wound to its end amid GOP factional squabbles, organizational difficulties, and the insistent demands of farmers, workers, and immigrant groups, embattled Republicans looked to the past for security, justifying the party's right to rule by the deeds of the Civil War generation and its pantheon of visionary heroes. A Belleville Republican suspected of factional disloyalty to Governor Joseph Fifer in 1892 relied on his performance as "the *only Cavalry* Division Commander under the Gallant P. N. Sheridan who escaped censure in the field" to restore his party credentials. During the senatorial deadlock of 1891, another distraught Republican tried to come to grips with the forces that allowed "this foolish craze called the farmers movement to come in and destroy the party which saved this country from dissolution" and "builded up one of the greatest nations the world has ever known in a little more than one decade of time." [3]

One by one, the tangible links with the party's glorious past faded as the Civil War generation aged and died. John A. Logan passed on in 1886, and through the following decade the bell tolled for William

Tecumseh Sherman, Benjamin Butler, Hannibal Hamlin, and even Confederate vice president Alexander Stephens. Their passing symbolized the end of a political era in Illinois. Mocking critics in 1892 laughed as the Republicans "put the old bald heads in front" and charged "bravely upon an army whose bones are now mouldering in the cemeteries upon a thousand hills."[4] "Private Joe" Fifer, the Republican governor of Illinois, did not exude the optimism and confidence of the Republican creed in 1892. Before a surprised crowd of farmers in Joliet, Fifer rambled through a series of doleful pronouncements, voicing his sentiment that "our country was filled up. There was no west to go to. . . . The farmers were always poor and always would be poor. . . . Just so certainly as I stand here this Government will fall. All tends to wealth, wealth to luxury, luxury to weakness, and weakness to lapse."[5]

Fifer's bleak outlook reflected the moribund state of the political system that governed Illinois in the 1890s. Republican party government in the late nineteenth century depended on consistent voter support, the promise of office, and the ability of the party to organize a responsive General Assembly. Loyalty, patronage, and adherence to the dictates of the party caucus were the cardinal political virtues. (All Republican candidates for city offices in Bloomington paid an assessment to the party campaign fund. The city central committee threatened to drop shirkers from the ticket, and campaign workers who failed to support the complete party slate were fired or went unpaid.) Fidelity brought the promise of office. "The boys are preparing 'to cut a water-melon,'" confided a political insider immediately following the election of the Republican state ticket in 1896.[6] State institutions—prisons, insane asylums, schools for the blind and the deaf—were jammed with political appointees, who continued their party work while in office. By the time civil service was extended to state institutions, over 2,234 employees came under its provisions. Where no position existed, it could be created. Charles Deneen's lieutenant, Roy O. West, requested a General Assembly job "worth about $4 per day" for a deserving ward supporter in 1899. "He had a job of that kind last session," assured West. "I think he wound a self-winding clock or watched the sunsets on the dome of the Capitol or performed some other function, incident to law making."[7]

The vigor of the Republican electoral and patronage network could not offset serious challenges to the nineteenth-century notion of party government. Legislative custom and popular opinion in the late nineteenth century demanded short legislative sessions, and observers grew suspicious when the General Assemblies of the 1890s ignored the sentiment for adjournment at "corn-planting time" in early April and instead remained in session from early January to mid-June.[8] "There is grave fear that the Illinois legislature will stay in session for some time after they repeal the laws of the last session," complained the Democratic *Peoria Herald* in 1899. "If this be the case the next legislature will be called on to do that much more business."[9] Such criticism was not mere partisan sniping. When the Democrat-controlled General Assembly in 1893 tarried too long in Springfield, a Democratic editor could find "absolutely no excuse for its long and practically useless career."[10]

Republicans stood the most to lose from the lengthy sessions of the General Assembly because they revealed the party's inability to expeditiously organize state government and conduct its business. Republican factionalism and Democratic competition produced a series of legislative deadlocks over the election of senators, the naming of Speakers in the House, and party organization within the General Assembly that hampered the work of the legislature and prolonged its life beyond the limits of public patience. During the two-month senatorial impasse in 1891, newspapers denounced "the Illinois monotony" and its paralyzing effect on government. Similar deadlocks and internal fights wracked Illinois Republican conventions in 1892. The party of progress appeared to be unable to govern.[11]

As the GOP's internal discipline wilted in the 1890s, it lost its hold on some voters. German Lutheran Republicans, angered by the Edwards compulsory education law of 1889, which threatened German language education, adamantly refused to support Fifer's reelection in 1892 and helped boost Democrat John Peter Altgeld to the governorship. More troubling to the party professionals, who expected the Germans eventually to resume their Republican loyalties, was the appearance of independent, issue-oriented voters. Voters immune to the appeals of party were anathema to the late nineteenth-century American political system. "It is my doctrine that we should all believe in some political creed, for which we are willing to do battle and make sacrifices," intoned Republican governor John Tanner in 1898, "and I should far rather a man be a Democrat, bad as I think that is politically, than be a mere political non-entity—too good in his own eyes for political association with his fellow-citizens."[12] In 1897 a Chicago bicycle club asked Assemblyman Lawrence Y. Sherman to support a bill reducing the baggage charge for bicycles on trains, then threatened to vote him out of office if he did not comply. The astonished Sherman declared that "the wheel has risen superior to the principle which divides political parties. The implied threat . . . is that the Associated Wheelmen of that club will bolt their ticket when it contains the name of one who has voted against the bill in question. . . . I can not believe that any person of any political convictions will test his party fealty by his wheel."[13] Nevertheless, Chicago Republicans considered the bicycle law vital to the success of the party in the city elections and asked Sherman to work for it.[14]

◆

The new attitudes that so bewildered party stalwarts Tanner and Sherman in the 1890s were expressions of a fundamental political transformation from a distributive polity, in which the political parties functioned as the principal conduit for goods and favors between government and the electorate, to a regulatory polity, in which government shouldered greater responsibilities and brokered the claims of particular interests. This shift marked "the end of the party period" because the initiative in the handling of goods and services passed into the hands of government executives, their agencies, and expert advisory commissions. Formerly the agents of governance, parties now assumed a role secondary to the dominant personalities and ideologies in office.[15] This shift corresponded with the antiparty, or more properly antimachine, sentiment that so strongly emerged in the Progressive Era. Demands for the Australian ballot, primary elections, initiative and referendum, and civil service were targeted at professional politicians, and such features of regulatory government as the government commission, the budget, and the legislative agenda were intended to replace party interests with the public interest.

The challenge for state party organizations during this period of voter realignment, progressive-backed electoral reforms, and the growing role of government was to adjust party goals to a new issue-oriented politics. Political organization everywhere grew more centralized and professional as primary elections vitiated the old system of caucuses and slate making and as ticket splitting and a dip in voter loyalty cut into the ranks of party regulars. The search for voters led to herculean feats of organization among party professionals. In 1908 the Nebraska Republican central committee gathered detailed information on about 70,000 voters, nearly one-third of the state total. More intensive work was not enough, however. A new kind of party politics became necessary. "We must organize the State as it was never organized before," insisted an Illinois Republican official in 1892. "The old political cranks must step aside for new men. Our speakers *must* be in touch with the common people."[16] The new political men of the 1890s adopted merchandising techniques to draw uncommitted voters to particular candidates. Political advertisements appeared in Illinois newspapers soon after the introduction of primary elections.[17]

Nonetheless, the most striking feature of the new politics was not the refinement of organization and electioneering methods among professional party workers. It was the emergence of a new set of executive officeholders who identified themselves with particular issues, built personal organizations within their parties, and seized the initiative from the old party professionals. Thomas Collier Platt, the state boss of the New York Republican party, struggled to adjust to the new political conditions, making concessions to interest groups within the party and wooing independent-minded urban voters, but he was replaced as party leader by Governor Charles Evans Hughes, who galvanized public attention by identifying a corrupt link between business and politics and built popular support by proposing a concrete program of reforms to correct the situation.[18] In an age of primary elections, attacks on boss domination of parties, and intense reform agitation, political leadership passed from party organizers to officeholders. Politics in the form of government service became a profession in the Progressive Era. State legislators in this period served more terms in office than had their late nineteenth-century predecessors, and many made a career in politics.[19]

Yet a politics of issues dominated by officeholders did not sap the importance of party affiliation, at least not in Illinois. Reform and antireform factions, as well as aspirants to executive leadership, fought their gravest battles within their respective parties. Illinois voters remained overwhelmingly loyal to the Republican party, so much so that internal Republican feuds accounted for the only Democratic state administrations of the period (in 1892 and 1912). The persistence of party loyalties in Illinois meant that reform and partisanship were minted together, as indivisible as the two faces of a coin. New election laws coexisted with lingering remnants of distributive politics. "The voters here are used to getting something for their votes," a correspondent from rural Shelby County informed a candidate during the 1912 Republican primary campaign.[20] Candidates were expected to pardon felons, contribute to church building funds, provide loans to start businesses, distribute money to unemployed miners, and furnish voters with beer and cigars. Politicians did not always fulfill these requests, but the assurance that for "the price of about three or four kegs of beer I think every thing would be alright for you here" diminished the threat that the direct primary would radically transform the political system.[21] Party concerns dominated the actions of reform governor Charles S. Deneen from 1907 until 1912 as greatly as they did those of antireform stalwart governor Len Small after 1920. Politics indeed changed in Illinois after 1892, but partisanship controlled the shape of progressive reform.

Altgeld and the New Politics

The Illinois Republican party revived from its crisis of the 1890s with a new emphasis on personal leadership and executive initiative in government, but the model for the new politics in Illinois was Governor John Peter Altgeld, the Democratic beneficiary of the defection from the Republican party by dissatisfied Germans in 1892. Earlier historians portrayed Altgeld as an historical anachronism, a reformist John the Baptist preparing the way for a compassionate, activist liberalism but condemned by his times to wander unappreciated through the wilderness. Iconoclastic ethnocultural historians, intent on destroying the "myth" of Altgeld, treated him as a typical midwestern governor, highly partisan and willing to provide troops to put down "dangerous" labor unrest.[22] Altgeld's most enduring political impact in Illinois, however, was as a pioneer of the new politics of personality and executive leadership, combining reform and partisanship.

Altgeld took pains to identify himself, rather than the national election or Democratic party policies, as the central element of the 1892 gubernatorial campaign. His strategy was unorthodox. Shortly after his nomination, Altgeld embarked on an exhaustive tour of Illinois that featured no campaign speeches but allowed him to size up the temper of the state, to meet voters, and to impress on them through direct contact the force of his personality. In Rockford the local Republican newspaper painted Altgeld as a corrupt millionaire intent on using his well-stocked "barrel" to buy his way into office, but when the candidate appeared there in mid-May, he ignored political talk, scotched plans for a formal reception, and instead shook hands with people on the street and chatted amiably in the newspaper's office. By the next morning he was gone, leaving the *Register-Gazette* admiring a man "thoroughly onto his job."[23] Five months later Altgeld was back in Rockford, in the midst of his second state canvass, this time presenting in great detail his political creed and the issues his administration intended to address. Altgeld's new style of campaigning puzzled a Jo Daviess County Republican, who reported that the Democratic candidate's speech "only touched *State* issues, or rather issues made *by him* and that bear no relation to either platform. It was the most *selfish* and *greedy* speech ever delivered here."[24]

Altgeld's style of ideological, executive-led politics made him, rather than the Democratic party, the central force of his administration. The governor attracted a personal cult of admirers, who for years remained slightly outside the regular Democratic organization. Similarly, his detractors maligned the man more than the party he represented. Many joined

Joseph Medill of the *Chicago Tribune* in his abhorrence for "the jesuitical little socialistic demagogue."[25] Altgeld's highly individualistic actions in opposing President Grover Cleveland's intervention into the Pullman strike and pardoning the remaining Haymarket anarchists ruined his administration's effectiveness by driving away the mainstream support necessary to enact his legislative program. Nevertheless, although his critics sought to dismiss his political style as an anomaly, Altgeld outlined the future course of political organization and governance in Illinois.

Altgeld's brand of personal politics walked a tightrope between his reform ideology and the partisan imperative. When the new governor presided over a legislative reapportionment that was little more than a Democratic gerrymander and then cleaned house in the state's charitable institutions, critics then and now judged that Altgeld had surrendered to the party bosses.[26] However, a closer examination of Altgeld's dealings with state institutions—the major form of public responsibility in the late nineteenth century—reveals his effort to create a new style of executive leadership that would yield both partisan and reform benefits. Altgeld's attempt to build a personal organization that was committed to his own ideological agenda but remained within the party became the model for gubernatorial leadership in progressive-era Illinois. His policy toward the state's charitable institutions illustrates the crucial distinction between "nonpartisan" reform, as advocated by progressive civic groups, professional organizations, and settlement workers, and reform carried out under the exigencies of partisan politics. Because Altgeld developed a mechanism that pursued reform without destroying party organization—close executive supervision of state services and centralization of decision making within government—progressive-era Republican leaders such as Governor Charles Deneen managed to build powerful organizations of loyal government insiders even as they publicly worked to streamline administration. To officeholders there was no such thing as nonpartisan reform. The same road of executive authority was traveled by John Peter Altgeld and Len Small.

◆

State prisons, hospitals for the insane, homes for the physically handicapped and aged veterans, and county almshouses overseen by the Board of State Commissioners of Public Charities were the objects of a battle in Illinois between nonpartisan administrative professionals and party patronage networks for control of the state's expanding commitment to the welfare of its least fortunate citizens. Since its creation in 1869 the public charities board had primary responsibility for investigating and improving the facilities that provided care for state dependents. An advisory body to the governor, dependent on the cooperation of the General Assembly, the board's influence relied on the talent and dedication of its secretary, Frederick H. Wines, an internationally acclaimed authority on crime, pauperism, and prisons who served from the board's inception until 1893. He incessantly prodded the General Assembly for improved state facilities and, with the assistance of Dr. Richard Dewey, designed the innovative detached ward plan for the Eastern Hospital for the Insane at Kankakee. This hospital was a pioneer among mental institutions. For example, while on staff at Kankakee from 1893 until 1895, Dr. Adolf Meyer introduced the practice of clinical rigor and careful attention to the individual case histories of patients that would help usher in modern American psychiatry. Under Wines's determined leadership, and despite inadequate appropriations, the board worked to improve record keeping in state institutions, authored laws to perfect regulatory oversight, struggled heroically against poor conditions in jails, almhouses, and asylums, and tried to prevent their political spoilation by Republican office seekers.[27]

Party politics was a double-edged sword for Wines and his colleagues. On the one hand, Republican victories accounted, in part, for the secretary's longevity in office and thereby gave strength to his efforts to professionalize the state institutions. On the other hand, party considerations habitually frustrated the board's attempt to introduce efficient, economical administration of the institutions. The Southern Hospital for the Insane at Anna was located far from needed water sources, and it took great expense to remedy that oversight. The bill authorizing construction of the Kankakee hospital made special provision for the commissioners of the Joliet state penitentiary to bid for the construction contract, which the appointees won for themselves in 1878. The state senator who steered the bill creating the Pontiac State Reformatory through the General Assembly was appointed superintendent of the new institution after its completion in 1891, at an annual salary of $3,500.[28]

Financial mismanagement wasted state funds, and untrained personnel and political appointees led to ill treatment of those most dependent on the skilled care of others. The state prisons and reformatories were favored havens of political appointees, resembling campaign headquarters in some election years. "In the government of the prison," the public charities commissioners vainly argued, "politics in the ordinary acceptation of the term has no more place than it would have in a church or in an astronomical observatory."[29]

Political maneuvering and an abundance of inadequately qualified staffers provoked serious consequences in the treatment of the insane. Angry social workers reported that the Cook County Board of Commissioners distributed appointments by drawing job lists out of a hat. Subse-

quent appointments to the Cook County Insane Asylum included ignorant supervisors, inexperienced doctors, and vicious attendants, "the
refuse of appointments," one of whom kicked a patient to death.[30]

A series of scandals during Governor Fifer's administration tarnished
the reputation of the state's charitable institutions. Illinois law stipulated
that the most violent and unmanageable patients should be handled by
the state hospitals, but in 1889 the superintendent and trustees of the
Northern Hospital for the Insane at Elgin, nearing the hospital's quota for
patients from Du Page County and weary of dealing with two particularly
troublesome female patients, transferred the women to the Du Page
County almshouse. The supervisor of the almshouse, "a good farmer, and
probably a good man, but wholly inexperienced in the management of
the insane," could not handle the unruly inmates, who tore off their
clothes and fouled their cells. Completely at sea, the supervisor confined
each patient in a cell "little more than seven feet square," lined the walls
with zinc for easier cleaning, and bound the women's hands with twine.
The county commissioners and almshouse supervisor completely lacked
facilities and training to deal with the violently insane, whereas state
hospital officials were negligent and cost conscious to the point of derelic-
tion of duty (one of the patients was returned to county care because she
was a German national).[31] Shortly thereafter, newspaper reports alleging
brutal mistreatment of the insane at the Central Hospital for the Insane
in Jacksonville drew the admission from the state commissioners that "in
all large hospitals for the insane attendants are at times employed who are
incompetent, and who lose their temper under provocation,"[32] but the
board assured its critics that offenders were promptly dismissed.

Wines and his colleagues used these sensational reports to enlist public
support for their efforts to introduce more professional operating procedures in state institutions and to expand their patient capacity. Stories of
brutality (such as the elderly suicidal pauper shackled to a tree in Iroquois
County) or callousness (such as the judgment of a Menard County almshouse visitor that the presence of a two-hundred-pound inmate "shows
that she, at least, has not been starved") were part of the board's perpetual
struggle with politicians to upgrade state facilities and free them from
political interference.[33] The belief among professional social workers that
state boards of public charities should rigidly exclude political considerations in the oversight of state institutions and strictly adhere to an ideal
of nonpartisan public service was sounded by a national committee of
charity experts, chaired by Wines:

> The duty of a State Board, with reference to the collection and expenditure
> of public funds, is to see that money is not taken from the tax-payer upon

false pretences, nor in amounts larger than is really necessary to accomplish the purpose in view in making a specific appropriation; that it is properly accounted for, and not stolen, either directly or indirectly; and that it is not wasted by the employment of useless supernumeraries, or the payment of extravagant salaries, or by extravagance and display in the buildings pertaining to a public institution. A thoroughly conscientious and upright Board of State Commissioners cannot do otherwise than frown upon nepotism and political favoritism in the appointment of institution officials and employees. It regards incompetency as the worst form of waste, a wrong to the beneficiaries of institutions as well as to the public treasury, and an absolute bar to the execution of the popular will in their creation and maintenance. But there is some degree of incompetence wherever there is inexperience. Hence it is opposed to political rotation in office in institutions, where the competency and integrity of the officials in charge are not questioned.[34]

The professionals' desire for completely nonpartisan administration of an institutional network that was part of the machinery of state could not be shared by politicians, reformers though they might be. Even when elected officials spoke the same language as the professionals, their goals were different. John Peter Altgeld was deeply committed to the alleviation of human suffering, penal reform, and the proper administration of state institutions, but Altgeld was a partisan reformer. The currency of stories of incompetence and maladministration in the state charitable institutions gave Altgeld an effective political weapon against the Republicans in 1892. He used it for both partisan and reform purposes.

Altgeld stressed that the lamentable state of affairs in the charitable institutions reflected Governor Fifer's poor executive abilities. The indictment was twofold. First, charged Altgeld, Fifer had turned state institutions into political machines. A case in point was the state penitentiary in Joliet. To swing the balky Will County Republican organization behind his reelection effort, Governor Fifer replaced the nonpolitical Joliet warden with an appointee "who knew nothing of prison management and was simply master of the caucus."[35] Prison employees ignored their duties and devoted their energies to the governor's campaign. This political intrigue, Altgeld charged, was accompanied by inefficient administration of state institutions. The Democratic candidate complained of hidden payrolls, neglected patients, the improper use of convict labor, and deteriorating facilities.[36]

Fifer indignantly denied Altgeld's accusations, but he was peculiarly vulnerable to charges of inattention and overt political manipulation of state institutions. Early in his term, Fifer had distributed state appointments between his own supporters and friends of the United States senator Shelby Cullom. Aside from the routine duties of office, Fifer at this time took no extraordinary steps to oversee the performance of the state charitable institutions. Then in 1891, he broke with Cullom's chief Illinois lieutenant, John Tanner, who worked to deny Fifer the gubernatorial nomination in 1892. Confronted with this sudden and bitter challenge, Fifer turned to supporters in the state institutions to salvage his political fortunes. As Altgeld had charged, Fifer placed Henry D. Dement as warden at the Joliet penitentiary to secure Will County from the Tanner forces. Warden E. J. Murphy of the Illinois Southern Penitentiary also focused on the political struggle against Tanner. Among other prominent Fifer Republicans serving in the state welfare system were public charities commissioner Dr. A. T. Barnes, chairman of the McLean County Republican central committee, and southern Illinois prison commissioner J. B. Messick, a member of the state GOP executive committee.[37]

Fifer's desperate, belated attempt to assemble a personal machine in the state institutions stumbled badly. Tanner Republicans held positions of power in many of them. Samuel R. Jones, a commissioner of the Joliet penitentiary (the institution singled out by Altgeld as the bastion of Fifer's machine) was a member of the "Springfield Ring" opposed to Fifer and a close ally of Tanner. Another of the three Joliet commissioners was later appointed chief trustee of the Northern Hospital for the Insane by Tanner.[38] Because he had initially shared state patronage posts with Cullom and Tanner, Governor Fifer was compelled in 1892 to intervene directly and for the most transparent political reasons in the state institutions. He managed to secure the Republican nomination, but at the cost of drawing greater attention to their unsatisfactory condition.

Fifer's supervision of state charitable institutions had been lax, and now, under the glare of Altgeld's scrutiny, he could not shore up their administration. The governor was hamstrung by inefficiency and local disputes. At the state reformatory in Pontiac, Superintendent B. F. Sheets and the institution's overseers quarreled over whether new buildings under construction should face the town or the railroad. The resulting barrage of conflicting work orders, charges of insubordination, and calls for resignations and support drove both the contractor and the governor to distraction. Such comic episodes were grist for Altgeld's mill. Fifer was equally vulnerable to charges of ruthless political manipulation and wasteful administrative inefficiency.[39]

◆

Following his victory over Fifer in the 1892 election, Altgeld quickly moved to establish his authority over Illinois's charitable institutions. In January 1893, letters to the trustees and superintendents of state prisons and hospitals requested their immediate resignation so as to make room for appointees "in thorough harmony with the executive and dominant legislative party."[40] Several defiant officials refused to step down. Luther L. Hiatt of the Northern Hospital for the Insane claimed that "the institution is now free from political machinery, the question of POLITICS never entering into the employment of Superintendent, Assistants, or other help. . . . I am opposed to making a political machine of The Northern Hospital for the Insane, and can not in conscience aid in so doing."[41] These protesters were removed from office. The public charities board also was swept clean, and Wines lost his position as secretary. Anguished psychiatrists and social workers would charge later that Altgeld introduced the spoils system into the state institutions and that his Republican successors Tanner and Richard Yates followed his lead.[42]

Altgeld was acting as a partisan reformer more than as a spoilsman. This distinction was perhaps immaterial to penologists and physicians who desired complete freedom from political interference, but it was critical in the development of executive leadership in Illinois. Altgeld intended to pursue his own program of reform for the state institutions and so moved to assert greater control over the system than had Fifer. His attitude toward administration of the prisons and hospitals was different from that of Wines and the institutional professionals. The governor believed that longevity in office bred stagnation and corruption, so that rotation in office—"the new broom," as he termed it—was not harmfully disruptive but rather salutary. New ideas, a more original and vigorous attempt to solve problems, and public accountability would come with new leadership. Altgeld rejected the notion that only trained experts could properly oversee the humane treatment of criminals and the insane. He held instead that politicians and private citizens, if honest and dedicated to the faithful performance of the offices entrusted to them, could provide exemplary public service.[43]

The complex nature of partisan reform and executive leadership emerged in the two most celebrated cases of politically motivated dismissals under Altgeld, those of Dr. Richard Dewey and his successor as medical superintendent at the Kankakee hospital, Dr. Shoval V. Clevenger. Dewey was a distinguished psychiatrist, but there were reports of partisan Republican activity, financial irregularities, and mistreatment of patients during his tenure. Clevenger had made his reputation by exposing corruption in the Cook County asylum, but when he encountered interference from members of the General Assembly and the trustees at Kankakee (among them an unsympathetic brewer) he suffered a nervous breakdown. Obsessively concerned with misdeeds both real and imagined, Clevenger became ineffective and was removed from office.[44]

Altgeld actively sought to promote the interests of the Democratic party, but not at the expense of his leadership or his reform program. Most of his new appointees were Democrats (one trustee placed by Altgeld was soon rewarded with a postmastership by President Cleveland), but he offered positions as well to Republicans whom he admired. One such was R. W. McClaughry, Chicago superintendent of police and the former warden at the Joliet penitentiary, appointed by Altgeld to head the Pontiac reformatory. Influential Livingston County Democrats, unable to obtain sinecures for relatives in the institution, claimed that McClaughry favored Republicans for reformatory jobs. Despite their unrelenting opposition, Altgeld stood by his appointee. The governor alienated other Democrats by appointing women to important posts and by ignoring requests to offer state employment to relatives of prominent party officials.[45]

An outspoken proponent of penal reform, Altgeld exercised close personal supervision over the state welfare system. The keenness of his interest in prisons is reflected by the fact that he altered the uniforms worn by the inmates. Intent on eliminating wasteful expenditures in the state hospitals, Altgeld replaced the unregulated activities of purchasing and business agents with a system of competitive bidding for supplies. He ordered that future reports from the state institutions contain detailed records of all employees, the nature of their duties, and the salaries they received. Overcrowding in the state hospitals for the insane was another problem that confronted Altgeld. The state's institutions contained five thousand patients, another two thousand received inadequate care in county almshouses, and the number of afflicted citizens was growing. The General Assembly provided for the expansion of two state hospitals to meet the swelling need, but Altgeld vetoed the bill, arguing that increased capacity would only lead to greater inefficiency and poor treatment. Instead, Altgeld led a successful effort to construct two entirely new hospitals and even suggested the appropriate architectural style (Tudor Gothic) for the buildings.[46]

Altgeld made the public charities board his regulatory agent for the reform of state institutions. The board, whose most vigorous member was settlement house reformer Julia C. Lathrop, made a detailed investigation of the condition of the state hospitals, and on its recommendation Altgeld introduced the appointment of interns selected by competitive examination to the medical staffs of the hospitals, added women doctors and assistants, and attempted to upgrade the staff's interest in pathology and professional developments. Knowing that the board's initiatives could be smothered by unsympathetic trustees and superintendents, Altgeld on two occasions called his appointees to Springfield and lectured them on their public responsibilites. "If you do not intend to make yourselves thoroughly masters of all the details of your institutions," he reminded the officials, "and to look after everything, even the minutest matter, with scrupulous care, then you are making a mistake in holding on to your office."[47] He checked on conditions by making personal visits to the kitchens and living areas of the institutions. Some officials resisted Altgeld's efforts, and abuses continued to occur, but there was no doubt about the governor's direction of policy.[48]

Altgeld's style of executive leadership extended beyond Illinois's prisons and charitable institutions. With great personal commitment, he sponsored the development of the University of Illinois into a respectable academic institution. He created the Illinois Department of Factory Inspection to investigate conditions of industrial labor and appointed another Hull House resident, Florence Kelley, as its chief. Altgeld named labor spokesman George Schilling to head the Illinois Bureau of Labor Statistics, then authorized him to investigate the inequities of Illinois tax law. The resulting report, wrote an enthusiastic former opponent of Altgeld, should "be placed in the hands of every farm laborer, every coal miner and workingman in this state; and I wish it had a trumpet voice that would call into the ears of every editor of a so-called Democratic paper in this state, in the whole country, until they would give it and its subject the notice they deserve."[49]

Altgeld was less successful in rallying the legislature behind his proposals. He twice chided the General Assembly for ignoring his request to reorganize or eliminate ill-working courts and government commissions, and he could never gather a cooperative majority of legislators. On the other hand, Altgeld also frustrated his lawmaking foes. He made use of the veto far more readily than had his predecessors, striking down legislation twenty-three times, and in so doing set a precedent for the vigorous executive oversight of the General Assembly that characterized the administrations of progressive-era governors.[50]

◆

Altgeld's political career disastrously unraveled in 1896. He was a Democrat in a fiercely Republican state and stood little chance to win reelection even without pardoning the Haymarket anarchists and defying President Cleveland during the Pullman strike. The pardon, and the extraordinary outburst of abuse that followed it, doomed any hope of a second term. Altgeld focused on Bryan's national campaign in 1896, turning his back on the successful strategy of 1892. He was defeated handily by Republican John Tanner, who then in unprecedented fashion refused the outgoing governor the courtesy of a farewell address on inauguration day. Illinois Republicans seemed intent on eradicating the memory of John Peter Altgeld and his administration.

Nonetheless, the new politics of executive leadership, personal organization, and partisan reform introduced by Altgeld endured. The next three governors of Illinois, all Republicans, attempted to assume party leadership through the executive power. The next two governors following Altgeld, John Tanner (1897–1901) and Richard Yates (1901–5), confirmed that assertive governors could devote the expanding power of the executive to purely partisan concerns. Charles S. Deneen (1905–13), like Altgeld, combined a reform consciousness and a commitment to personal partisan advantage in a blend that attracted but ultimately disappointed "nonpartisan" reformers. Progressives believed that an executive-dominated government was more "businesslike" and efficient, less vulnerable to partisan debasement, but the governors of progressive-era Illinois fashioned nonpartisan electoral and administrative reforms, such as civil service systems and primary elections, to the needs of their personal political organizations.

Executive Power, Factions, and Partisan Reform

The governor was the key figure in party organization and governmental authority in progressive-era Illinois. Political factionalism, particularly within the Republican party, and the clamor for electoral and administrative reforms fed the growing willingness of Illinois governors to expand the authority of their office. Within the GOP, a bitter struggle between rival patronage networks—the "federal crowd" of postmasters, internal revenue inspectors, and other federal officials appointed through the influence of Illinois's elected representatives in Washington, and the "state crowd" of institutional trustees and appointees—reflected the contest between the senior United States senator from Illinois and the governor for control of the state party. The turbulence of this conflict fragmented the Illinois Republican party into several competing factions divided by organizational jealousies and ambitions and by ideology.[51] With a shattered party consensus, the office of governor became the most secure base of party power.

The new politics of executive authority, expressed through a legislative program and a firm direction of policy toward the state institutions, allowed the governor to build a stronghold of personal supporters in the General Assembly and the state service that could withstand the assaults of factional party rivals. Besides the construction of a personal organization within the party, the new politics of executive leadership built a following outside the professional structure of the party by identifying the governor with a particular set of reform proposals.

Charles S. Deneen, the state's first two-term governor in a generation, was the most successful practitioner of partisan reform along these lines. Despite his lack of personal warmth (various contemporaries characterized him as the "iceberg" and the "cold storage Governor"),[52] Deneen managed through his support of civil service reform and primary elections to create a formidable political machine. Although genteel reform clubs and organizations of social workers applauded Deneen's introduction of "nonpartisan" methods into state service and the selection of elected officials, Deneen's factional rivals complained that his control of the state institutions and manipulation of the direct primary confounded their efforts to unseat him.

◆

Factional politics and mismanagement of state institutions paved the way for Deneen's success. Disgruntled medical professionals complained that governors Tanner and Yates "out-Heroded Herod" in their subordination of the state hospitals and institutions to party concerns.[53] Tanner filled the chief trustee position at the Kankakee hospital with Len Small, a Kankakee Republican who became the mainstay of the "regular" factions allied to Tanner, Yates, and Chicago congressman William Lorimer, and briefly dropped Altgeld's practice of listing employees and salaries paid at the state institutions.[54]

Yates, the son and namesake of Illinois's Civil War governor, proved more adept than Tanner at applying Altgeld's methods of executive leadership in the struggle for factional supremacy within the GOP. Embroiled with Lorimer in a fight against Charles Dawes of the federal faction, Yates took personal control of patronage decisions following his election in 1900. He dismissed all members of state boards and commissions and then rearranged them to his liking. Again following in Altgeld's footsteps, Yates gathered the trustees of the state institutions to clarify his administrative policies. But Yates's pursuit of partisan control was more painstaking than Altgeld's direction of partisan reform. Yates immersed himself in the political minutiae of each state institution, in some cases causing "the Superintendent to look up the political pedigrees of every small employee and to report to Springfield upon it, with the result that many changes [were] made in consequence directly by the Governor."[55] Yates also appointed and dismissed deputy factory inspectors without the knowledge of the chief inspector.[56]

Critics deplored the governor's interference in the state institutions. Two members of the charities board, Julia Lathrop and Dr. Emil G. Hirsch, resigned their positions after Yates pressured the board to name J. Mack Tanner, son of the late governor, as secretary. It soon became clear that the state institutions had become weapons in the political arsenal of Yates and his allies. "Send any competent committee to Chester, the Reform School, the Kankakee Asylum, the West Chicago Park Commissioners or the Lincoln Park Commissioners," wrote a Republican enemy of the Yates-Lorimer faction, "and there can easily and quickly be found the most abundant evidence to sustain any suspicion you may have respecting Lorimer's relations to the 'business' of the State."[57]

Allegations that Len Small, at the time a state senator, had turned the Kankakee hospital into a political machine and that significant patient abuse occurred during his trusteeship were discounted by a board of public charities investigation. Newspapers and social work journals denounced the board's bland conclusions as a "nerveless" whitewash.[58] Other reports, more resistant to the soothing words of official spokesmen, accumulated through the remainder of Yates's term: that the governor levied a 5 percent assessment on all institutional employees; that Yates attempted to remove two officials from the Soldiers' Orphans Home "because they were unable to control delegations in his favor at the McLean County Republican Convention"; and that he fired employees of the southern Illinois prison at Chester for similar political transgressions.[59]

The excesses of the Yates administration led to an outcry for civil service reform in state institutions. Prodded by the Illinois Civil Service Association, elite reform clubs, and an anti-administration Republican faction led by Lawrence Y. Sherman, Yates in October 1902 appointed a commission to investigate the application of the merit system to these facilities. Despite this move, the governor's enthusiasm for civil service legislation quickly came under question. Three of the commission's five members held office in state prisons, hospitals, and on the public charities board, and both Yates and his commission spokesman, Warden E. J. Murphy of the Joliet prison, claimed that a practical system of civil service was already operating in the state institutions. A statute was nevertheless drawn up in 1903, but when Sherman unexpectedly gave it his support, the lower house attached an amendment invalidating the bill unless it received the endorsement of the majority of voters casting ballots at the next general election. Incensed by this partisan maneuver, the two reform members of the commission, Edgar A. Bancroft of the Civil Service Association of Chicago and John H. Hamline of the Union League Club, dropped their support of the bill. No acceptable alternative was found, and the state's institutions went unreformed.[60]

♦

Intense factionalism deadlocked the Republican convention in 1904 and denied Yates renomination. After nearly one month and seventy-nine ballots, Charles Deneen emerged as the Republican gubernatorial standard bearer. Deneen's background was well suited for a champion of civil service and other progressive causes. His grandfather was a Methodist minister, his father was a college professor, and Deneen himself made his reputation as a state's attorney in Chicago, operating under the principle that "the criminal with influence and friends will be prosecuted with greater vigor than the one who is penniless and friendliness."[61] But Deneen's keenest instincts and fullest devotion focused on partisan politics. A staunch Republican (his father was also a member of the Grand Army of the Republic), Deneen at various times in his career formed alliances with such antireform Republicans as West Side Chicago boss Lorimer, downstate spoilsman Small, and self-promoting Chicago mayor William Hale Thompson. During the 1904 campaign he declared, "I am not a civil service reformer or civil service agitator. Not at all. I believe that positions ought to be held out as inducements for political work."[62]

Deneen believed in reforms that would yield political advantage. His two outstanding traits as governor were an exceptional talent for political organization and extreme caution. Deneen consulted freely with reformers and took care to listen to the suggestions of powerful newspaper publishers (most notably the Chicago newspapermen denounced by Lorimer as the "trust press"), but he would act only if public interest were sufficiently aroused or if his actions solidified his authority as governor and party leader. Such was the case with primary election laws and civil service reform in state institutions.[63]

There was considerable pressure for the enactment of an effective primary election law in Illinois in 1905. Good government reformers had long advocated primaries as a weapon to break the stranglehold of political bosses over party nominations and restore the political initiative to the people. The depredations of the Yates administration and the wearying Republican deadlock of 1904, plus the spur of direct primary laws passed by eight states since 1901, intensified the demand for a remedy in Illinois. A statewide advisory public-policy vote in 1904 recorded a seven-to-one majority in favor of direct election. Deneen promised to deliver a compulsory primary law during the 1904 campaign, but he preferred a moderate solution that retained convention nominations to the more radical idea of a direct primary selection of candidates.[64]

Political circumstances transformed Deneen into an advocate of the direct primary. Four primary laws were enacted during his administration between 1905 and 1910. The first three were invalidated by the Illinois Supreme Court on technical grounds. Deneen's cautious bills of 1905 and 1906 drew opposition from conservatives reluctant to scale down party machinery and from a small minority of progressive Republicans intent on more far-reaching changes, only to be struck down by the court after surviving the legislative contest. The invalidation of the 1905 law was particularly damaging, occurring as it did at the height of the primary campaign in April 1906. His leadership challenged, Deneen promptly called a special session of the General Assembly, which then passed the 1906 bill. Passage of a strong primary election law that would stand up in the courts had become a test of the governor's effectiveness. [65]

Deneen was boxed in. He had vowed to produce a primary law, but the compromises necessary to gain the support of regular Republicans (namely, the retention of convention nominations in Cook County) made the laws unconstitutional. After the Illinois Supreme Court struck down the second primary law in October 1907, the governor went for broke and pushed for a direct primary law. The House Republican leadership, including Speaker Edward Shurtleff, rebelled, shrugged off Deneen's special message, and went through a series of recesses without taking action on the direct primary bill drafted by John G. Oglesby. Deneen answered with a dose of the new politics. He toured fifty-three counties to arouse support for the Oglesby bill, turned away from the senior members of the House to ally with a group of young Republican legislators (the "Band of Hope"), and accepted thirty Democratic votes to get the bill through the lower house. A complicated battle in the senate ensued, but a version preserving direct nomination based on plurality (with an advisory vote for United States senator) emerged triumphant. "That is the Best Bill that was ever enacted in the State of Illinois," enthused one citizen. "It practically does away with the Rings and fixes it so Decent men can get into office. . . . I will do what I can to help the present Governor to hold his office." [66] Another constitutional objection, this one in June 1909, facilitated a redrafting of the law in 1910, but direct primaries remained in operation and became the linchpin in Deneen's political organization. [67] "Under this primary law," complained a rival, "it is practically impossible to defeat the Governor in office for nomination if he uses his office to renominate himself." [68]

Deneen won the praise of charity reformers and civil service advocates by renouncing the practice of assessing officeholders in state institutions, sponsoring a 1905 law that brought most state hospital employees under civil service rules, and displaying a renewed commitment to the improvement of services in the state hospitals. Deneen returned Lathrop and Hirsch to the public charities board and pledged not to interfere in its operations. On the governor's suggestion, a conference of state hospital superintendents and medical experts met in October 1906 to consider improvements in state care. Deneen was an active and enthusiastic participant in the discussions. Delighted with this official cooperation,

Charities and The Commons devoted most of one issue to a laudatory review of the "inspiring opportunity" presented by Deneen and "his progressive State Board of Charities" and beseeched the General Assembly to adopt their program.[69]

Deneen's assertion of leadership was natural for a man who scoffed at the notion "that all a governor has to do is sit in his chair and obey the Constitution."[70] The fight for civil service and institutional reform was part of his struggle to establish authority over the General Assembly. Deneen could get only a compromise civil service bill through the 1905 General Assembly, and legislators then tried to smother it by providing no enforcement appropriation. He survived this test of wills by transferring the necessary amount from his contingency fund.

Deneen did not intend to fill the state institutions with his political followers. To clear his flank, he apparently agreed to retain most of Yates's appointees. Then, to get action out of the General Assembly, he refrained from making new appointments for several months in 1905, suggesting that support for his legislative proposals would expedite the appointive process. Finally, by publicly identifying himself with popular reform programs such as those concerning civil service, institutional improvements, and primary election laws, Deneen proposed to build enough public support to overwhelm his legislative and factional enemies.[71]

The civil service reforms enacted did little to hamper the power of the governor. Deneen appointed the three members of the civil service administration who monitored examinations and appointments. The top positions in the hospitals—trustees, superintendents, chief clerk, and stenographer—did not come under the provisions of the law, and current employees acquired civil service protection without taking the examinations. Just before the law went into effect in November 1905, Deneen made a flurry of appointments to the state institutions.[72]

Deneen made it clear that civil service was a tool to help him govern more effectively, not a device to bind his hands. A doctor at the 1906 conference complained that Altgeld had interfered too readily in hospital affairs and expressed concern that Deneen's decision to reinstate two officials dismissed by their superiors indicated the continuation of that disruptive tradition. Deneen angrily reminded the assembled experts that "the Governor is responsible for these institutions" and that, as in the case of Altgeld, many of the reforms they applauded were the direct result of executive intervention.[73]

Primary legislation and civil service reform were part of Deneen's overall political strategy, and beginning in 1906 he relied on the goodwill he had built up among reformers to sustain him as he moved to solidify control of the Republican party and work for reelection. After the deadlocked

1904 convention, Deneen bought peace with both the Yates group and the anti-Yates legislative faction headed by Lawrence Sherman by allowing many of Yates's appointees to linger in office and naming Sherman his lieutenant governor. Thereafter, Deneen let Sherman wither on the vine, and in 1906 he moved against Yates. Yates believed that Deneen would support him for United States senator in 1906, but the governor was not forthcoming with aid. It was a declaration of factional warfare. Complicating matters was the growing alienation from Deneen of Speaker Shurtleff and the old-guard Republicans in the General Assembly. Deneen's attempt to dominate legislative policy led to a complete break with Shurtleff in 1907. Both Yates and Shurtleff would run for governor against Deneen in 1908.

Once again, state charitable institutions became a campaign issue. Reports of injuries to several patients in state care prompted a full-scale House investigation in 1908. Sparks flew between the governor and his detractors as the investigation proceeded. Shurtleff privately expressed the wish that the investigation would unveil Deneen as "one of the most notorious hum-bugs, hypocrites and four-flushers of the twentieth century."[74] The House committee presented a report bulging with charges of incompetence, payola, and political favoritism and proposed a reorganization of administration under a central board of control just before Deneen's primary renomination campaign got under way in the summer of 1908.[75]

Deneen was one step ahead. In October 1907 he commissioned a joint committee of private citizens and Board of State Commissioners of Public Charities members to investigate public charity administration in other states and recommend improvements for Illinois. The committee report appeared in May 1908, at the height of the controversy over the House investigation. Its model bill was a masterful compromise that deflated the House's suggestions. Rather than advocating a salaried board of control to replace the public charities board, the model bill devised a dual system for Illinois. A centralized five-member Board of Administration would assume the powers of local boards of trustees and the current public charities board. A second five-member board, the Charities Commission, would exercise the independent investigatory role of the current charities board. No more than three members of the Charities Commission could belong to the same political party. The plan blended centralized supervision with local watchdogs. Charity experts dismissed the House report as a crude effort to sabotage Deneen and instead effusively praised the recommendations of the governor's expert committee. After some amendment, the model bill was enacted into law in 1909. In the meantime, the House report fizzled.[76]

Considerable opposition to Deneen's renomination remained. Southern Illinois Republicans distrusted the governor's legislative program, particularly an expensive deep waterway project, and derided the special sessions of the General Assembly he called. Lingering reports of corruption alienated others. A former Yates supporter, allowing that the ex-governor "was more crooked than a ram's horn," concluded "that Governor Deneen has been following in the same corrupt lines."[77] Factional enemies abounded. Shurtleff, playing on downstate resentment of the metropolis, characterized Deneen as a Chicago loyalist and vowed to restrict Cook County's representation in the General Assembly. Yates, Small, and Lorimer banded together against the governor. Small ran Yates's campaign, and Lorimer used his influence with Chicago Democrats to amass a large crossover vote for Yates in the August primary.[78]

The direct primary law saved Deneen. Under the old system, he would have faced the prospect of a deadlocked convention, but the direct primary, wailed one opponent, eliminated the sound judgment "found in a state convention of sensible leaders. The matter is now with the 'dear people,' easily led by demagogues."[79] Forced into the governor's game, Shurtleff and Lorimer crony Willard McEwen deferred to the candidacy of Yates, and the anti-Deneen combination posed as the true friends of the primary. With the aid of Chicago mayor Fred Busse and John Smulski, Deneen fashioned a friendly Cook County slate, but Lorimer histrionically shrank from such "a violation of the primary idea," and Yates blasted the Deneen organization as "Primary Law Nullifiers."[80] The Lorimer-Yates campaign of melodrama and manipulation weakened Deneen, but the governor barely eked out a majority and was renominated. Without the direct primary, judged Charles Merriam, "the nomination of Governor Deneen would have been almost impossible."[81] The irreconcilable Lorimer-Yates combination refused to back Deneen in the November general election, dropping his majority nearly 56,000 votes behind that of William Howard Taft. Nevertheless, Deneen became only the second Illinois governor to succeed himself.[82]

◆

"Civil service and the Board of Control have completely disorganized the Republican party," mourned a fourteen-year veteran of the Western Illinois Hospital for the Insane in 1912,[83] but Deneen had used electoral reforms and the power of his office to assemble a formidable personal organization within the party. Since 1905 Deneen and a conclave of Chicago politicians known as "The Big Five"—Fred Busse, Postmaster Daniel Campbell, James Pease, James Weber, and John Hanberg—

prepared primary slates for Cook County and dominated the Cook County and, increasingly, the state Republican conventions. Neither Yates, Lorimer, Small, nor Shurtleff attended the 1908 state convention. In 1910 Deneen had the platform printed before the convention opened. State Republican committeemembers, elected by the people under the primary law, placed a Deneen majority on the state central committee.[84]

Despite intense factional opposition in the General Assembly and plunging popularity, Deneen's organization secured his nomination for an unprecedented third term in 1912. Civil service laws did not prevent the Deneen machine from making use of the state charitable institutions in the primary campaign. In Rock Island County a former trustee of the Lincoln Asylum for Feeble-Minded Children and a former clerk of the Western Illinois Hospital organized the Deneen forces. A chaplain at the hospital attempted to line up church voters for the governor. The Deneen organization in Danville tried to quiet criticism by dangling before citizens the possibility of a new state hospital in the city.[85]

Other government boards and commissions also came under the control of Deneen's personal organization. Secretary James E. Egan of the Illinois State Board of Health "has used the office for political purposes until he has completely lost the confidence of the medical profession," complained the editor of the *Illinois Medical Journal*, and "he now claims to have ensconced himself under the Civil Service Act."[86] An extensive web of alliances furnished Deneen's government machine with enough editorial support and cash to overwhelm his primary rivals. Two of the three newspapers in Rockford were partly owned by loyal Deneen appointees. When rhetoric faltered, the governor's organization was able to sway opinions with more stable currency. The close primary race of 1908 was broken open in Rockford after the Deneen forces hired workers away from Yates at the climax of the campaign. In 1912 the financial health of the administration machine was still robust. "The Deneen element are . . . spending money like drunken sailors," glumly reported a Small worker.[87] Judicious, executive-led reform had actually bolstered partisanship in Illinois.

The Politics of Antipartyism, 1909–1912

In 1908 most Illinois reformers supported Deneen. Four years later the governor had to rely on his machine to win renomination. Seven candidates challenged him in the primary, among them Lorimerite Len Small and Walter Clyde Jones of the newly formed Illinois Progressive Republican League. By the 1912 general election Progressive Republicans had bolted to form their own Progressive party and fielded a state ticket against Deneen. Other Republicans refused to support their party's nominee, and Deneen suffered a humiliating loss to Democrat Edward F. Dunne. The Illinois Republican party was in a state of collapse.

The rejection of partisan reform by the good government forces in Illinois ensured Deneen's downfall. The governor had built his administration on a curious blend of openness to "nonpartisan" reforms and an efficient personal machine within the Republican party. Between 1909 and 1912, however, Deneen's commitment to reform and his ability to control the General Assembly came into question. This failure of leadership came just as a shocking political scandal—revelations of bribery in the selection of a United States senator and allegations of a permanent corruption fund in the General Assembly—plunged popular confidence in representative government to its nadir in Illinois. To the unforgiving eyes of good government Republicans Deneen now looked like a machine politician, and his program of partisan reform took on the appearance of an insidious fraud.

The efficacy of Deneen's executive leadership and his electoral reforms were immediately challenged in the 1909 General Assembly. Determined to unseat Shurtleff as Speaker, Deneen organized a Republican caucus to unite behind an administration candidate, but Shurtleff's Republican supporters combined with nearly the entire Democratic membership of the House to reelect Shurtleff, who had publicly recorded his opposition to the governor's legislative proposals. Deneen's inability to organize the legislature threw the deficiencies of his primary law into stark relief. Before the General Assembly convened, the Chicago City Club had expressed dismay at a number of election frauds in the 1908 primary, and in January, in the first stage of a crisis that would shake the foundations of the Republican party in Illinois, uncertainty over the advisory primary clouded the General Assembly's task of electing a United States senator.[88]

Albert J. Hopkins, the junior senator from Illinois, received a forty-one percent plurality in the advisory primary and argued that legislators should be bound by the state returns. Factionalism negated any such easy solution. Hopkins was a conservative backed by a faction directed by Chicago mayor Fred Busse and Chicago postmaster Dan Campbell, two members of the Big Five. Members of Deneen's Band of Hope, many of whom had begun to outdistance the governor in reform sentiment, distrusted Hopkins, and many refused to vote for him. A third faction of Shurtleff and Yates followers headed by William Lorimer believed Hopkins had betrayed Yates in the 1908 primary and was determined to prevent his election. The General Assembly, meeting in convention, rapidly became deadlocked. Factionalism, the bane of Republican party government, had returned.[89]

The senatorial deadlock droned on to the end of May. During the frustrating proceedings, Deneen held a number of conferences with his erstwhile foe Lorimer, who tried to persuade the governor to take the Senate seat. Deneen was amenable, but his reform allies in the press recoiled at the possibility of state control falling into the hands of Lorimer, and the deal fell through. Then in May the Blond Boss from Chicago's West Side began to make his own move. The son of a Scottish Presbyterian minister, Lorimer had risen from humble jobs in Chicago packing houses and streetcars to six terms in Congress and immense political influence in Illinois by turning the twists of fate and Republican factionalism to his advantage. Conversion to Catholicism and loyal service to the packers, manufacturers, and lumber producers of his district solidified Lorimer's standing with immigrants and businesspeople. Never one to let opportunity slip by, Lorimer saw the chance to fill the contested seat himself. He successfully lined up enough Democratic votes to overwhelm Hopkins and the other Republican candidates and was elected United States senator on May 26. Deneen and Senator Lorimer talked of burying the hatchet, but Deneen's reform followers in the press and legislature would have none of it. The two Republicans soon resumed their mutual antagonism,[90] but Deneen's contacts with the notorious symbol of boss rule cast suspicion on the genuineness of his reform sentiments.

Then, in the spring of 1910, the bombshell burst. Four General Assembly members claimed that they had received money in return for their votes to elect Lorimer. For the next two years revelations of bribery and political manipulation in Illinois surfaced as both the General Assembly and the United States Senate investigated the Lorimer scandal. Deneen testified before the Senate that a corruption fund called the "jackpot" was assembled by the railroads, Chicago utilities, meat packers, and liquor interests to influence legislators on close ballots.[91] "Lorimerism" became the supreme political issue in Illinois. The Senate expelled Lorimer in July 1912. Long before the politicians took action, elite good government reformers, speaking in a tone of injured innocence, vowed to redeem the shame that engulfed Illinois.

At the urging of Chicagoan Harold Ickes, nearly a hundred progressives gathered in Peoria on June 27, 1910, to discuss solutions to "the breakdown of representative government in Illinois."[92] Members of Deneen's legislative faction attended the conference and listened to familiar appeals for independent voting and civil service from the likes of George E. Cole of the Chicago Municipal Voters' League, Edgar Bancroft, Merritt Starr, Judge Lewis Rinaker, and Robert Catherwood of the Chicago Civil Service Association. On the next day, however, friends of the governor heard disturbing words. "Legislators no longer feel the responsibility to their constituents that is desirable and necessary," the conferees resolved, "but rather give their allegiance to political 'leaders,' treating with indifference and disrespect the sustained efforts of public-spirited citizens to secure needed legislation."[93] The reformers looked not to Deneen but rather to the people for aid. The Peoria Conference demanded the passage of an initiative and referendum law, a corrupt practices act, and a comprehensive civil service law. A Committee of Seven was appointed to organize the effort to submit these issues to a public-policy advisory vote in November.[94]

The Peoria Conference marked the birth of the Progressive Republican movement in Illinois. Spurred by the leadership of Raymond Robins and Charles Merriam, citizen conferences on the Peoria model popped up across Illinois during the next few months. Each of the three demands of the Peoria Conference acquired the requisite 110,000 signatures to appear on the advisory ballot in 1910, and all three received substantial majorities at the polls.[95]

Deneen struggled to keep up with the new insurgent spirit. He put an initiative and referendum plank in the 1910 Republican platform and managed to pass a broad civil service bill through the 1911 General Assembly. In 1910 and again in 1912, Deneen stumped across the state denouncing "bipartisan jackpotism." But it was to no avail. The governor was caught in a no-man's land between reform and reaction. Deneen could not prevent the renomination of Shurtleff and his other legislative enemies at the 1910 primaries. Illinois "now has no political leader of prominence," declared Charles L. Capen, chairman of the Peoria Conference. "Who are the Republican leaders, who state public sentiment, who guide public opinion?"[96] Progressive political sentiment had bypassed Deneen.

Deneen failed to retain the loyalty of many reformers because, at the height of antiparty agitation in Illinois, he refused to take any steps that would threaten his party organization. The Peoria Conference reformers joined in the national fight to reduce the power of Speaker of the House Joseph Cannon, who had spoken against the direct primary in 1908 and was an implacable enemy of electoral reforms. Deneen shrank from any criticism of Cannon, preferring to uphold the standard of true Republicanism against the bipartisan alliance of the Lorimer-Shurtleff faction. Busse, Pease, and Campbell, the governor's occasional allies in the Big Five, were among the "reactionaries, bosses and tools of special interests" the Peoria reformers had vowed to eradicate from the Republican party.[97] As Progressive Republican sentiment in Illinois began to back the presidential aspirations of Theodore Roosevelt, Deneen cautiously remained uncommitted. Then, after the Republican national convention, he allied with the incumbent William Howard Taft.

The good government forces began openly to distrust Deneen's legislative initiatives. Disappointed civil service reformers acknowledged the
governor's aid in passing a civil service law in 1911 but then complained
that he appointed a political ally to administer civil service hiring on the
Chicago West park board. "Mr. Mugler will be called upon to eliminate
politics and political influence from the parks whenever Mr. Mugler, the
Fifteenth ward boss, Mr. Mugler, the county central committeeman, or
Mr. Mugler, Governor Deneen's patronage secretary, attempt to evade the
law," declared the exasperated Catherwood.[98] After a proposed constitutional amendment establishing the initiative and referendum failed to
pass in the General Assembly of 1911, some former allies doubted Deneen's commitment to the idea.

More damaging was Deneen's reluctance to support the independent
Republican campaign of Charles Merriam for mayor of Chicago in 1911.
Alderman Merriam's city council commission uncovered a great deal of
inefficiency and corruption during the Busse administration, and Peoria
Conference reformers rushed enthusiastically to his standard. Merriam
defied the regular Republican organization, establishing Progressive Republican clubs and calling for Democratic reform votes. Deneen saluted
Merriam for his primary victory in March, but he quietly withheld his aid
in the general election as the Big Five, led by Busse, sabotaged Merriam
and gave the victory to Carter Harrison. Merriam's enraged campaign
manager Harold Ickes announced "that Merriam had not been defeated
by Harrison, but by a Republican Governor, Deneen; a Republican Senator, Lorimer; and a Republican Mayor, Busse."[99] Deneen responded
poorly, accusing the Merriam campaign of buying votes. Three months
after the mayoral campaign, in July 1911, the Peoria Conference reformers formed the Illinois Progressive Republican League and backed Walter
Clyde Jones for governor.[100]

Deneen struggled to retain the progressive label. Thoroughly alienated
from the powerful Cook County Progressive Republican League, the governor nevertheless had enough support among downstate reform legislators to prevent the formation of a united Republican movement against
him. Republican legislators attending a July conference with the Chicago
group reaffirmed their loyalty to Deneen and expressed reservations concerning the initiative and referendum, effectively destroying the possibility of any agreement. In Chicago, elite good government Republicans
representing the city's universities, newspapers, businesses, and reform
clubs such as the Civic Federation organized the Committee of One Hundred to pursue reforms that would not harm the Republican party or experiment with the initiative and referendum. Deneen partisans controlled
the committee.[101]

Deneen's claims to progressive leadership received a further boost with the entry of a Lorimer candidate into the primary race. The embattled senator formed the Lincoln Protective League in July 1911 to carry on his fight against proposed electoral reforms and named Len Small as his gubernatorial candidate. Small had been appointed United States subtreasurer in Chicago on Lorimer's recommendation in 1910. He was well known as Lorimer's chief downstate lieutenant. Small and the "Lorimer-Lincoln League" provided Deneen with a target for his campaign against "jackpotism" during the primary. Anti-Lorimerism and the inability of Deneen's opposition to settle on a single candidate resulted in the governor's triumph over a field of seven contenders in the April 1912 Republican primary, despite the fact that he only received 35 percent of the vote. Small finished second with 20 percent. Progressive candidate Jones came in seventh. [102]

Organization and a crowded primary enabled Deneen to win renomination, but he could not control the Republican party. His conservative opponents sat out the election, more willing to endure Democratic victory than to aid the governor. The Progressive Republicans followed Theodore Roosevelt into the new Progressive party. Although not strongly committed to Taft, Deneen refused to bolt. Some Roosevelt enthusiasts resisted efforts to field a state Progressive ticket, but the dominant Cook County group won out and in August nominated Frank Funk to head the Illinois Progressive slate for the November election. [103]

In the final stages of the campaign, Deneen appealed to Roosevelt supporters not to let their devotion to the charismatic Rough Rider imperil Republican rule in Illinois. "Irrespective of your preference as to presidential candidates," Deneen's circulars warned voters, adherence to the Republican state ticket was the only legitimate alternative to Democratic misrule. "A vote for Funk is a vote for Dunne" became the desperate motto of the partisan reformer. [104]

And so it turned out to be. Dunne swept to victory with 38 percent of the vote, as Deneen (27 percent) and Funk (26 percent) split the usual Republican majority. Roosevelt crushed the hapless Taft by over 150,000 votes, but Woodrow Wilson finished almost 20,000 votes ahead of Roosevelt. [105] The 1912 election marked the low point of Illinois Republicanism.

◆

The Progressive party in Illinois was founded on the belief that party government had broken down. Veterans of the Peoria Conference, stung into action by the painful revelations of the Lorimer scandal, demanded electoral reforms that would introduce the ideal of "politics without pol-

iticians." Deneen's brand of partisan reform they thought a sham, a cynical concession to the worst political instincts of the age. The leaders of
the Republican party were throttling Illinois, wrote Progressive attorney
general candidate Fletcher Dobyns to Deneen:

> You have been Governor for eight years, and have proved yourself unwill-
> ing or unable either to take the control of the party from these men, or to
> control their actions in the interests of the people, and I believe it would
> be vain to hope that you would do in a third term what you have failed to
> do in the two terms which you have already served. . . . A progressive is a
> man who will fight for the overthrow of rule by bosses and special interests,
> and the restoration of government to the people and who will employ as
> his weapons certain measures which experience has proved to be effective
> and indispensable to that end. He will stand for the initiative, referendum,
> recall, direct primaries, short ballot, civil service reform, direct election of
> United States senators, direct election of delegates to national conven-
> tions, women's suffrage, and the other measures that are embodied in the
> national progressive platform and in the progressive platforms of the vari-
> ous states. . . . What have you done and what will you do to drive the
> bosses out of your own party and to establish the rule of the people by
> means of these progressive measures? In the past you have gone before the
> people and in the counsels of your party have advocated actively but one
> of these measures—a primary law. . . . You took this step as a means of
> holding power in your own hands rather than of restoring it to the people.
> Since that time you have sat for days in caucuses with notorious bosses of
> this County and State fixing up slates to be forced upon the voters in vio-
> lation of the spirit of the primary law. . . . Whenever you have signed a
> civil service bill you have done all in your power to diminish its usefulness
> by your numerous appointments made in support of your machine. . . .
> The impartial historian will say that you were weak, evasive and self-seek-
> ing; that you worked with political bosses and were one of the bulwarks of
> the spoils system in your State, and therefore responsible for conditions
> that have disgraced it.[106]

Progressive good government reformers denounced Deneen as a mere
partisan leader, but the Progressive party fared no better as a model of
"nonpartisan" reform. The Illinois Progressives were almost exclusively a
band of exiled Republicans. Despite Democratic gubernatorial candidate
Edward Dunne's enthusiastic espousal of the reforms contained in the
Peoria Conference platform, support for his candidacy was never seriously
entertained by the Progressives. The 1913 General Assembly contained
twenty-five Progressive representatives and two senators, holding the balance of power between the Democratic and Republican contingents, but
the Progressives could not take advantage of the possibilities thus offered.
"We are undisciplined," observed state Progressive party leader Medill

McCormick, "and like most reform parties liable to disintegration, because of untrained individualism and faction spirit."[107] Two Progressives voted against an initiative and referendum resolution, depriving it by one vote of the two-thirds majority necessary to send it on to the public as a constitutional amendment. In Chicago Ickes and Merriam resisted McCormick's attempt to control the party, while a downstate faction arose against Chicago domination. Within two years most Progressives had drifted back into the Republican party.[108]

The new politics of executive leadership made reform gains possible in progressive-era Illinois. "In his new role the governor becomes the virtual boss and shapes the course of legislation for the general benefit, instead of for private and special interests," wrote an admiring political scientist.[109] Many political reformers were less sanguine. They disliked the partisan aspect of reforms initiated by governors who were also attempting to become party leaders. In 1912 they rebelled against it, but the enactment of a strictly nonpartisan program of political reform proved impossible. For good or ill, both partisan and reform initiatives lay with the governor and his party followers. After 1912 progressives put their faith in administrative reforms that were meant to cauterize government services from the corrupting influence of partisan designs, but streamlined bureaucracy was no less susceptible to direction from a self-interested executive; indeed, it was more so. The public interest did not replace partisan reform. After 1920, however, the improved machinery of state came under the control of dedicated partisans who scoffed at reform.

7

The Failure of Administrative Reform, 1912–1922

The reformers who attended the Peoria Conference in June 1910 were not radicals. Indeed, Walter Fisher of the Chicago City Club took pains to describe them as "progressive conservatives."[1] Numbered among them were some of Chicago's most respected citizens: university professors, members of the city's elite good government clubs, and advocates of civic virtue and "decent" government. Nonetheless, their pronouncements in the wake of the Lorimer scandal were alarming. "Here in Illinois representative government has ceased to exist," maintained Walter Rogers, chairman of the Committee of Seven. "Not only did the last Legislature not represent the people, but it was an actual menace to the welfare of the state."[2]

The Peoria reformers traced the crisis in Illinois government to a growing reliance on government services without corresponding controls on the "shrewd and resourceful men" who directed politics. As population increased and natural resources dwindled, municipalities, counties, and the state were forced to spend money to provide roads and sewers, to house criminals and the infirm, and to regulate commerce and award public utility franchises. "The political boss," lamented Fletcher Dobyns, "saw that if he could build up a machine, if he could get the power to nominate men for office, he could control their action after they were elected, and that, so doing, he could control the letting of contracts, the granting of franchises and the passing of legislation."[3]

The structure of Illinois government abetted the power of political organization. The state's unique system of cumulative voting protected local party organizations and discouraged innovation in the General Assembly. Cumulative voting was introduced in the 1870 Illinois Constitution as a means to counter the extreme concentration of Republicans in the northern counties and Democrats in the south, thus providing representation to the minority party members in both sections. Each voter cast three ballots, in any combination desired, to fill the three seats in the lower house of the General Assembly accorded to each district. Members of the minority party, such as Democrats in Winnebago County, could amass their three votes behind a single candidate and so elect one of their own to the General Assembly. Unfortunately, this effort to provide minority representation resulted in a noncompetitive political system that helped entrench local machines. Throughout Illinois the rival parties divided each district's three seats. The majority party would put up two candidates in the election and the minority party would offer a single candidate. All three were then elected. Party organizations were certain of at least one seat—and its privileges—each term and had no incentive to disrupt this comfortable, predictable state of affairs. Limited voter choice at home and political stagnation at Springfield resulted. "Our minority representation plan has made representative government impossible," fumed George Cole of the Municipal Voters' League.[4]

The program of the Peoria reformers sought to dry up the reservoirs of jobs, franchises, and money that sustained government by organized political factions. Some of their means were those of traditional elite reform—civil service and stringent regulations on the use of money in political campaigns through corrupt practices legislation. So greatly did these "progressive conservatives" distrust officeholders, however, that they moved beyond the rhetoric of "government by the people" to forcefully demand the introduction of such instruments of popular government as the direct primary and the initiative and referendum. Some even moved beyond criticism of Republican party government to form the opposition Progressive party. Nevertheless, neither democratic electoral reforms nor a "nonpartisan" political movement could prevail against the nimble strength of political organization in Illinois.

Internal bureaucratic reform offered greater possibilities. Scholars have emphasized the divergent strains of democracy and efficiency in the reform programs of the Progressive Era. Proposals for greater popular control of government—direct primaries, direct election of senators, and the initiative and referendum—were joined by innovations that reduced the political role of the average citizen—at-large elections, the short ballot, and regulatory commissions. Often, the impulses toward democracy and efficiency came into conflict, but for the dominant group of progressive political activists in Illinois, especially the Chicago reformers in the City Club, the two impulses were linked by their common challenge to the control of government by political organizations. Extreme circumstances generated by the Lorimer scandal, described at the Peoria Conference as a crisis of representative institutions, propelled moderate reformers to place exaggerated reliance on popular democratic measures in the hope these reforms would pry loose the grip of political organizations on government. After the General Assembly rebuffed their demands, however, the web of reform associations centered in Chicago shifted their emphasis to the restructuring of Illinois government by means of administrative centralization and constitutional revision.

Renewed calls for governmental consolidation and bureaucratic tightening quickly overshadowed the democratic proposals of the Peoria Conference. Deneen's personal organization had smoothly integrated electoral reforms into his machine; on the local level, organization politicians like Fred Busse appeared more adept at controlling voters than were reformers like Charles Merriam. The Progressive party floundered in the 1912 election, then lost its cohesion during crucial votes in the General Assembly. Good government reformers simply could not compete with organization politicians in the "democratic" arena of elections and legislatures. Still, administrative reform could knock the props out from underneath the politicians by restricting and carefully monitoring the flow of money in government, and it could centralize power in the hands of a few responsible public officials so that government could function effectively. "You cannot make a ramshackle government responsive," insisted Richard S. Childs, secretary of the National Short Ballot Organization. "You must give your governments single brains before they or any other organism will work."[5] The culmination of progressive political activity in Illinois was a drive not for democracy but rather for efficiency and economy in government.

The hopes that political progressives infused into the movement for efficiency and economy were immense. Government efficiency would not only isolate political organizations from their source of power but also slash through the regional, class, and cultural tensions that had long paralyzed government in Illinois. In their search for social harmony, reformers too often downplayed powerful and sometimes irresolvable conflicts between citizens over economic, political, and cultural issues, casting the disputes instead in terms of an administrative imbalance or deficiency in government that allowed small groups of powerful individuals to defy the public good. Rural legislators in Springfield, unwilling to face the facts of population and commerce, used the General Assembly and the state constitution to block home rule for Chicago. Decentralized schools, abundant independent government boards and commissions, and competing government hierarchies gave selfish politicians the opportunity to hold tyrannical sway over their local pockets of influence. The absence of clear regulatory authority even allowed defiant dairymen to shrug off expert advice and continue selling unhealthy milk.

Administrative reformers noted the irreducible interest conflicts that swirled around these issues, but they failed to recognize their tenacity. The recurring progressive invocation of the "public interest" in the face of sharp divisions within communities indicates that the reformers' believed harmony to be the natural accompaniment of responsible conduct in public affairs. Conflicts or abuses could be traced to imperfections in the administration of government and justice, errors that could be remedied by expert hands. "This illusion—that administration would dispel social conflict—was the greatest single flaw in the progressive conception of government," judged one penetrating analysis.[6] In Illinois, administrative reform produced genuine innovations in government organization but could not overcome the crippling assumption of its supporters that the consolidation of authority was sufficient to harness political organizations and dampen social conflict.

◆

The career of the Chicago Bureau of Public Efficiency, founded just three weeks before the Peoria Conference, represented the developing consciousness of administrative reform. In the summer of 1909 Charles Merriam headed a city council commission investigation of Chicago municipal expenditures that uncovered a pattern of carelessness and favoritism in the conduct of city business on the part of Mayor Fred Busse. Altered records, inside agreements, and shabby administration permitted the mayor's political friends to reap excessive profits from city contracts. One duplicitous contractor dug through soft clay to install a sewer line but charged the city an additional $45,000 for the removal of a phantom bed of shale. He was devising a plan to sell the clay back to the city in the form of bricks when the Merriam commission unearthed the scheme. Several of Busse's political associates, municipal appointees, and even the mayor's personal secretary became mired in a string of such scandals. Resignations and sixteen criminal indictments followed over the next two years.[7]

None of Busse's henchmen landed in jail, but the evidence obtained by the Merriam commission spurred a committee of the Chicago City Club, including Merriam, Walter Fisher, and philanthropist Julius Rosenwald, to organize the Chicago Bureau of Public Efficiency on June 8, 1910. The new body, patterned after the New York Bureau of Municipal Research, undertook to examine and publicize the flow of money through Chicago's bureaucratic maze of local governments. Payrolls, accounting procedures, and the handling of contracts within the various governing bodies of the metropolis were the particular targets of their gaze and subsequent public reports. The purpose of this scrutiny was to pressure public officials to practice efficiency and economy in their civic duties.[8]

Within a short time the bureau had moved beyond simple oversight of municipal spending to advocate broad administrative changes intended to thwart the structural chaos of urban government and the political organizations that prospered off its disarray. Constitutional strictures that subjected Chicagoans to 19 separate taxing bodies and 236 elective officials institutionalized inefficiency and confusion. In 1913 the bureau advocated the unification of local governments and the short ballot. Four years later, as William Hale Thompson exercised his extravagant reign as mayor of Chicago, the bureau added the introduction of the city manager plan to its list of remedies. A taut administrative structure and centralized policy direction would enable democracy to act responsibly; therefore, removing the elective office of mayor and eliminating popular participation in the selection of other public officials, argued the bureau, enhanced democracy rather than diminished it. "The power of the people is dissipated and weakened when delegated power is divided among different independent elective authorities instead of being centralized in one responsible body," reasoned the bureau in defense of the city manager plan.[9] There were, however, constitutional obstacles to such centralization. A thorough restructuring of Chicago government could not proceed without extensive revision of the state constitution to give Chicago administrative independence, and so the Chicago Bureau of Public Efficiency became a vocal proponent of a new constitutional convention.[10]

The increasing thoroughness and centralizing tendencies of the public efficiency bureau's administrative reform program mirrored the statewide effort that dominated Illinois politics in the second decade of the new century. The first stage emphasized efficiency and economy in the existing administrative structure of state government. Beginning with the administration of Governor Edward Dunne in 1913, particular attention was devoted to the flow of money and legislation through the government labyrinth. The Legislative Reference Bureau charted the course of bills through the General Assembly; it also kept tabs on appropriations requests from the array of independent boards and commissions reporting to the governor in the process taking the first rudimentary steps toward the development of the executive budget.

The second stage of statewide administrative reform comprised administrative consolidation and centralization of authority in the executive. The control of money, in the form of taxes and appropriations, and direct gubernatorial supervision of state administration were the prime objectives. At the request of Governor Dunne, an efficiency and economy committee investigated the organization of state government and recommended a thoroughgoing revision of state administration into several departments directly responsible to the governor. After his election in 1916, Governor Frank O. Lowden adjusted the committee's recommendations to further centralize authority in the executive and put the new system into practice in the form of his Illinois Civil Administrative Code. Lowden also revamped the state's tax system by eliminating the elective Illinois Board of Equalization and replacing it with a tax commission appointed by him. Lowden's reorganization of Illinois government, which firmly established executive control over the budget and state services, was greeted with great acclaim and imitated by other states.

The final stage of administrative reform in Illinois entailed the revision of the state's 1870 constitution. The construction of an efficient state government, one capable of responding effectively to the needs of an industrial society, required clearing away the statutory underbrush that made the state constitution (which ran to a remarkable length of fifty pages) such a constrictive document. Not only did the constitution bar Chicago from meaningful home rule, but it blocked the absolute administrative centralization of Lowden's Civil Administrative Code and his tax commission. Because the amending procedures of the constitution were so laborious—only one article of the constitution could be amended at each legislative session, and before adoption each amendment had to attract approval from a two-thirds majority in each house of the General Assembly and then receive endorsement from a majority of voters participating in the next general election, at which point further amendments to the article in question were prohibited for four years—Lowden favored a constitutional convention as the only feasible mechanism to speedily remove the many roadblocks to administrative efficiency.

Signs of the broad appeal elicited by administrative reform influenced progressive political activists to put undue faith in the harmonizing powers of centralization. Government efficiency and economy was a "bedrock" reform that attracted diverse political personalities, few more diverse than governors Edward Dunne and Frank Lowden, the political sponsors of the government consolidation movement. Dunne was a Democrat, an Irish Catholic supporter of the radical wing of the Illinois Democracy, who as mayor of Chicago attempted to achieve immediate municipal ownership of the city's streetcar lines and as governor expressed his devotion to the initiative and referendum and supported a wide range of social welfare measures. Lowden, on the other hand, was a Republican, a successful businessman and gentleman farmer, the son-in-law of George Pullman and former director of the Pullman Company, who dismissed direct primaries and the initiative and referendum as dangerous "new fads" and made plain his intention to run the affairs of Illinois as he would a large industrial enterprise.[11] Both men nevertheless identified the need to overhaul the administrative organization of Illinois government as a vital component of their otherwise divergent agendas.

The need for fundamental changes in the structure of Illinois government, and especially constitutional revision, was plainly evident to all reformers, but it was especially compelling for those from Chicago. Strong identification with the plight of Chicago's hamstrung government undoubtedly influenced Dunne and Lowden in their commitment to administrative reform. Chicago's constitutional and administrative straitjacket prevented solutions to problems that democratic politics could not resolve. Inadequacies in the state tax system were irksome throughout Illinois, but special constraints in the constitution made the system particularly damaging in Chicago. Bitter memories of the failed charter of 1907 convinced many in Chicago that home rule for the city would never come from the General Assembly. Any clear-eyed observer in the metropolis recognized that a new constitution was imperative before complete administrative efficiency could become a reality in Illinois government.

Uniform agreement on the necessity of administrative reform and progressive faith in smoothly operating government machinery shrouded two deficiencies that fatally weakened the effort to outflank political organizations and unify society through administrative reorganization. First, the centralization of government administration fed into a movement that was in itself profoundly political—the new politics of executive leadership. Unable to combat the influence of political organizations in elections or in the General Assembly, the "nonpartisan" reformers were thrown into an alliance with the public official who stood the most to gain from administrative centralization, the governor of Illinois. Partisan reform—the combination of a reform agenda with the development of a powerful personal political organization—had characterized the most enlightened state administrations in the recent Illinois past; as recently as the Deneen administration, the Peoria Conference reformers expressed distaste with this formula. Administrative reorganization would afford a reform-minded governor a better chance of functioning effectively, but the office of governor (and its partisan benefits) would remain no less political.

The inability of administrative centralization to blot out partisan reform was dwarfed by the fact that not all governors could be expected to be reformers in the first place. Increasing the authority of the office did not guarantee that honorable men would occupy it. The trend in Illinois politics for powerful political organizations to gather around the governor increased the chances that an extreme partisan could wield dangerous power under the new system. As Lowden's biographer recognized, "an administrative structure which centralized so much power in the chief executive could become a mighty engine of spoils politics."[12] With the election of Len Small in 1920, those fears were realized. By itself, administrative reform could not remove the blight of politics that so distracted progressives.

The second deficiency was even more debilitating. Administrative reform could not sidestep democracy or diminish conflict. Instead, and particularly so in the creation of a new state constitution, the many conflicts between Chicago and the downstate (e.g., disputes over the rights of labor and the demands of radical democrats, uncompromising stands on the liquor question, and other divisive issues) overwhelmed the administrative reforms meant to quiet them. The proposed state constitution of 1922 was the ironic cap of Illinois administrative reform. It represented the culmination of years of effort by political progressives and marked the inadequacy of their vision. Despite the governmental reorganization that preceded the constitutional convention of 1920–22, as well as the superficial unity of the war years, nothing had diminished the rancor that Illinois citizens harbored over fundamental social conflicts; those conflicts exploded anew during the convention debates and destroyed the charter that was supposed to serve as the foundation for modern government in Illinois.

Administrative Reform Takes Shape

Assertive Illinois governors had been informally centralizing state administration to their advantage since the days of Altgeld, but a comprehensive effort to fundamentally reorganize state government did not commence until the administration of Edward Dunne in 1913. Dunne did not share the sentiment growing among many progressives that democracy benefited more from centralized administrative power than from widened popular participation in government. Dunne believed in the wisdom and efficiency of direct democracy. Early in his term, he made clear that the enactment of the initiative and referendum was the "chief ambition of his administration" and accused its opponents of "raising a false and pharisaical cry for tax reform and a revision of the state constitution" to bury his democratic proposal.[13] Dunne opposed a constitutional convention, contending that the inadequacies of the state charter would best be resolved by loosening its restrictive amendment clause, which, in concert with the initiative and referendum, would open the constitution to effective popular control.[14]

Organized labor supported Dunne's call for greater democratization, and in turn the governor was the warmest friend of labor to occupy the executive office during the Progressive Era—endorsing wages, hours, and health and safety measures throughout his tenure. Dunne's commitment to the popular control of government, active concern for the well-being of the working class, and opposition to sumptuary laws characterized the outlook of "urban liberalism," the distinctive reform style developed by ethnic politicians who moved from big city Democratic organizations into important state offices during the second decade of the twentieth century.[15]

Despite his differences with "progressive conservatives," Dunne also recognized the necessity of administrative reforms that further centralized power in the hands of the governor. He declared the state board of equalization "a departmental fiasco," and sought to replace it with a five member tax commission appointed by the governor. At Dunne's prodding, the General Assembly created the State Public Utilities Commission, consisting of five commissioners appointed by the governor, to regulate utility rates and service throughout the state. Neither initiative contradicted Dunne's "urban liberal" values. The elective equalization board, Dunne explained, failed to assess corporate property adequately, thereby unduly lightening the tax burden of industry "at the expense of the people." His compact tax commission "would be more efficient in action, more responsive to the public demand for equitable taxation, and more easily and directly held responsible for any errors and mistakes which might be made."[16] Dunne's proposal for the utilities commission included an important provision extending regulatory "home rule" to Chicago over local utilities, clearing the ground for eventual independent municipal ownership. In both cases, administrative consolidation aimed at tightening public control over corporate wealth.

Handicapped by the lack of a Democratic majority in the General Assembly, Dunne's program of democracy and efficiency met little success in the 1913 legislative session. The initiative and referendum were struck down, the tax commission bill died in the senate, and the Chicago home-rule feature of the State Public Utilities Commission law was eliminated. Roger Sullivan and Carter Harrison, heads of the most powerful Democratic factions in Chicago, urged Dunne to veto the amended public utilities bill, but he refused to sacrifice the partial gains it achieved and signed the measure into law. Chicago interests suffered a further blow as the General Assembly, in defiance of the governor and the specific demands of the constitution, refused to reapportion state senatorial districts to reflect population changes detected in the 1910 federal census. Despite its tremendous growth, Chicago would get no more seats in the General Assembly. It was a disappointing legislative session. Political fights over the organization of the legislature and the election of two United States senators produced delays that stretched the Forty-eighth General Assembly out to an unprecedented six months, yet only 240 of the 1,600 bills

introduced in the mammoth session reached Dunne's desk. "If the legislature would adjourn for five years the state would be better off," concluded one unhappy participant.[17]

The disorganization of Illinois government frustrated any coherent legislative program. Lack of coordination in the General Assembly and the
state administration led to hastily devised and conflicting laws, needless
duplication in administrative services, and overall financial waste and
confusion. Legislators were swamped by the sheer volume of bills they
encountered in Springfield. "Imagine for a moment being confronted
with one thousand pieces of prospective legislation, with respect to each
one of which you are supposed to arrive at some just conclusion, as this
conglomerate mass is hurled at you from day to day," sighed state senator
Frank Schmitt in 1907.[18] Parliamentary tactics inflated the disorder, as
lawmakers hid or delayed bills until the final frantic days of the session,
then rushed them through a frenzy of roll calls before adjournment. Much
of the resulting legislation was poorly drawn or flatly contradictory. Two
laws passed in 1911, for instance, contained conflicting guidelines for the
appointment of state mine inspectors.[19]

The haphazard proliferation of state administrative agencies further
stymied coherent policy direction. A product of many impulses—the progressive thrust for regulatory commissions, professional organizations' demands for expert oversight, partisan reform's tendency to create patronage
positions, and the General Assembly's penchant for ad hoc solutions—
administrative growth flowered during the Progressive Era without any
systematic plan to coordinate the functions of the various boards. By 1913
over 100 independent boards, commissions, and agencies, ranging from
the Department of Factory Inspection to the Stallion Registration Board,
clogged state administration; thirty-four of them appeared between 1909
and 1913. Most existed in an administrative no-man's land between the
inattentive General Assembly that funded them and the overburdened
governor who appointed their members but could not supervise their
disparate activities. Overlapping authority and financial waste were the
natural results. Each board submitted a separate request to the General
Assembly for money, and without any central oversight of spending,
appropriations soared from just under $20 million in 1909 to nearly
$38 million in 1913. Deficiency appropriations increased threefold be-
tween 1911 and 1913 as the General Assembly struggled to keep up with
expenditures.[20]

Disorganization and inefficiency impeded the new politics of executive
leadership. Governor Dunne's ambitious "urban liberal" proposals were
expensive and difficult to enact without a Democratic majority in the
General Assembly. Illinois's decentralized, improvident state administra-

tive system and the General Assembly's helter-skelter approach to legislation worsened matters by vitiating Dunne's ability to influence lawmakers and direct policy. To control spending and reinvigorate executive
authority, Dunne accompanied his "urban liberal" reforms with efficiency
measures favored by "progressive conservatives." He consolidated the "inefficient, wasteful, and extravagant" fish commission and the office of
game commissioner into a single body in 1913, thereby shaving $50,000
off the 1911 appropriations for the two agencies.[21] "The more needless
offices that the Governor abolishes, the more respect we will have for the
chief executive of the state," a country newspaper responded, "provided
that the Governor does not create a number of 'commissions' to take the
place of the offices he has abolished."[22] Dunne also successfully sponsored
the creation of the Legislative Reference Bureau in Springfield.

The Legislative Reference Bureau symbolized the intersection of administrative reform with executive primacy in Illinois. The first such legislative reference bureau was developed in Wisconsin at the turn of the
century by Charles McCarthy, a clerk in that state's Free Library Commission. McCarthy and his assistants compiled information on various
legislative topics and provided lawmakers with impartial expert guidance
in the technical matter of drafting bills, with the aim of producing laws
that could stand the test of the courts. "We have seen the courts equipped
with the highest talent which we could furnish, sitting in judgement upon
laws made by farmers and business men, by men who were honest, but
who were not expert in making those laws," McCarthy told the Chicago
City Club. "We must put the expert behind our representative."[23] Illinois
reformers agreed. Walter Clyde Jones reported that General Assembly
members routinely ignored existing statutes when drafting bills and often
submitted bills so poorly written as to render them worthless. "Since I
have been a member of the legislature I have marveled that any law that
has ever entered a statute book could be sustained by the courts, considering the methods by which those laws are prepared," he testified.[24]

Beginning in 1907, Jones and others tried to create an Illinois legislative reference bureau along the lines of the Wisconsin model, but without
success. Veteran legislators distrusted the reform, believing that it would
increase the influence of younger General Assembly members in the Band
of Hope at their expense. There were also administrative problems. Mc-
Carthy and his legislative experts were supported by Wisconsin's efficient
state library. The Illinois state library was divided into three parts, with
separate legal and historical collections, and there was no Illinois library
commission to sort out the consolidation of materials necessary to build
an effective legislative reference service. The Legislative Voters' League
filled the gap with a voluntary reference bureau that provided information

and encouragement to reformers in the 1907 General Assembly, but the league went bankrupt in the effort. [25]

When Dunne finally established the Illinois Legislative Reference Bureau in 1913, it was fundamentally different in form and function from the Wisconsin body of impartial clerks and librarians. The Illinois bureau was formed to provide increased executive supervision over legislative spending. Officeholders dominated the bureau. Its five members included the governor (as chairman) and the chairs of the Appropriation and Judiciary committees in both houses of the General Assembly. Like its Wisconsin predecessor, the Illinois bureau (directed in these endeavors by its permanent secretary, University of Illinois professor John A. Fairlie) gathered statistics and information on legislative questions, catalogued bills, and helped properly draft legislation. Its most important duty, however, was to prepare an estimated state budget for the General Assembly based on the appropriations requests made by state agencies. Dunne had not yet created an executive budget, but he had begun the process of binding both state administration and legislative action to a uniform program developed by the governor. [26]

The cornerstone of Dunne's effort to concentrate power in the executive was the investigation of state administration conducted by the Efficiency and Economy Committee. Similar committees formed in Massachusetts and New Jersey in 1912 were given the task of reorganizing the administrative structure of those states. Five states, including Illinois, joined the movement in 1913. Dunne had recommended the formation of such a committee in his inaugural address, and the General Assembly promptly created the eight-member joint legislative Efficiency and Economy Committee, authorized it to devise improved accounting procedures for the state and to suggest a reorganization plan for state offices, and supplied it with $40,000 to carry out its task. The committee, whose most active members were Democrat Walter I. Manny and Republican Logan Hay, met on August 1, 1913, and decided to devote its attention to administrative reorganization. A team of academic experts led by Legislative Reference Bureau secretary John Fairlie thoroughly investigated the existing administrative structure and suggested ways to improve it. After a series of meetings and public hearings attended by officials of the various state boards and commissions, the committee published its report in 1915. [27]

The report minced no words in presenting a comprehensive indictment of administrative incompetence in Illinois. "A condition of disorganization and confusion exists in the executive departments of the State government which necessarily produces inefficiency and waste in the State services," it concluded. [28] Offices, often with closely related duties, were not gathered in a central location but rather were scattered throughout Springfield and Chicago. Supplies were purchased piecemeal by each authority, although they could be had more cheaply through bulk orders after competitive bidding. Salaries varied widely; a seat on the State Board of Pardons paid $3,500 annually, whereas the commissioners of labor each received only $150 per year. State inspectors in different departments were paid different amounts for similar work. Other officials received no compensation. Regulation of agriculture, industry, working conditions, financial institutions, and the public health was carried out by numerous boards working independently of one another. Officers from various departments could conceivably visit the same establishment and issue contradictory orders to the proprietors. Reports were filed irregularly and to different authorities. As a result of all this, the General Assembly was poorly informed, money was misspent, and the governor, saddled by public opinion with the responsibility for state government, was ill served.

To remedy this situation, the committee recommended providing the governor with the means to exercise his responsibility by consolidating state administration into ten concentrated departments over which the chief executive could maintain effective supervision. The ten proposed departments—finance, charities and corrections, education, public works and buildings, agriculture, public health, labor and mining, trade and commerce, law, and military affairs—differed in organization. Most were headed by a single official appointed by the governor, but the departments of public works, charities, education, and most importantly, finance were to be administered by commissions. The committee favored such organization "only for functions where consultation and consideration of several persons is advisable" or when the revamped administration could not bypass elected officials, such as the superintendent of public instruction, whose positions were created by the Illinois Constitution.[29]

Governor Deneen's successful 1909 reorganization of the state charitable institutions under a central board of administration undoubtedly boosted the committee's faith in the efficiency of executive commissions. In the case of the finance department, the committee divided responsibility between a state comptroller, tax commissioner, and revenue commissioner. The three-member Finance Commission would assume the duties of the inefficient twenty-six-member State Board of Equalization, the State Tax Levy Board, and the Court of Claims, all three of which the committee would abolish. Each of the commissioners would then perform a centralized function: the comptroller would prepare the state budget, the tax commissioner would assess property for taxation, and the revenue commissioner would oversee the collection of other moneys. Two elected officials, the auditor of public accounts and the state treasurer, would sit as ex-officio members of the commission.

This arrangement symbolized the tenor of the entire report. Adjustments were recommended that did not require a substantial revision of statute law or amendments to the constitution. Constitutional officers were worked into the system, often to the detriment of absolute efficiency, and lent a thin strand of popular control to the streamlined administration. Above all, however, the ability of the governor to set policy and control its operation was sharply increased.

Dunne commended the report to the General Assembly in 1915. Unwilling to gamble on the passage of an omnibus measure, the governor, at the request of the Efficiency and Economy Committee, submitted the proposed reforms in a series of separate bills, but the Forty-ninth General Assembly was a disaster for Dunne. Only two minor suggestions of the committee were enacted into law. "At that time my term as governor was half over, the Legislature was Republican, the patronage at the disposal of the governor had been distributed," Dunne later remembered.[30] Republicans preferred to wait for a change in administrations before fundamentally reorganizing state government. When that change came, a governor with a belief in the curative powers of administration stronger than Dunne's presided over administrative reform.

Lowden and Centralization

Few Illinois citizens could work up a genuine dislike of Edward Dunne, but he was a Democrat, and state spending escalated during his term. "A yellow dog would win on the Republican ticket next Fall," proclaimed one contestant for the 1916 GOP gubernatorial nomination.[31] The Republican choice for governor did defeat Dunne in 1916, but Frank O. Lowden was not as common as a yellow dog. As a millionaire lawyer and industrialist successful in the direction of several large corporations, a breeder of prize cattle at his country estate, "Sinnissippi," and a former congressman who longed to bring the efficiency of the large corporation to state government, Lowden carried a pedigree and vision that distinguished him from other Illinois Republican leaders. "I believe in the short ballot in business just as I believe in the short ballot in politics," Lowden affirmed. "I believe in placing power and responsibility with executives and holding them to a strict accountability."[32]

Lowden's primary campaign stressed his ability to unite the divergent factions in the Republican party. Lowden had been William Lorimer's choice for governor in 1904, and downstate suspicion concerning his attachment to Chicago "boss rule" was renewed in 1915 when Chicago mayor William Hale Thompson began working for Lowden's election. Some of Lowden's downstate friends openly expressed fears of "a recrudescence of the Lorimer machine," with Thompson and his political mastermind, Fred Lundin, acting as Lowden's sinister puppeteers.[33] Lowden's campaign took pains to distance itself from Thompson without sacrificing the benefits of the volatile mayor's extraordinary political organization. Lowden's campaign manager, William H. Stead of Ottawa, shut out Lundin from the downstate effort and worked behind the scenes to reduce his influence in Chicago. Stead assured supporters that talk of revived Lorimerism was "idiotic" and that Lowden was "not the candidate of the City hall or of any other faction of the Republican party" but would accept the support of Thompson or any other Republican to end factionalism within the party.[34] Meanwhile, Thompson and Lowden avoided appearing together at downstate functions, and Lowden emphasized his avocation as a farmer and his attachment to his estate in Ogle County.[35]

As Lowden eased the doubts of downstate Republicans, he also drew in administrative reformers and Progressive party members. Stead gathered a mailing list of 200,000 Republicans and former Progressives outside Cook County and took care to include a Progressive in the initial Lowden effort in each precinct downstate. During the spring primary campaign, Lowden pitched his administrative consolidation proposals to a reform audience. "Our present system of haphazard appropriations has proved subversive of the very principle of democracy, fostering 'boss rule' and 'invisible government,'" he wrote in an open letter to Medill McCormick. "I believe the budget system to be one of the most potent instruments of democracy."[36] In addition to the executive budget, Lowden called for a constitutional convention and surprised many by endorsing universal women's suffrage. At the same time, the candidate deflated several troublesome "Chicago issues" by defending state regulation of all Chicago area public utilities that crossed municipal lines and pledging to sign a county option bill to regulate saloons.[37]

Lowden's strategy worked. By the end of the primary campaign he had gained the support of many current and former Progressives. In August he defeated Morton D. Hull, a former Progressive favored by Deneen and the Anti-Saloon League, by 110,000 votes to gain the Republican nomination. Dunne stood little chance in the November general election. Lowden defeated him by a 150,000 vote majority.[38]

◆

Governor Lowden briskly set about the business of administrative reform in January 1917. He believed that government could attain effi-

ciency only if public officials, and especially the governor, were granted
expanded power. "Democracy has been afraid of itself, and of its own
chosen officials," he later recalled, "and has hedged them about with so
many restrictions that genuine efficiency has been well-nigh impossible."
In Lowden's view, the creation of responsible state government required
centralization of authority in the executive and the elimination of statutory restrictions that hampered the executive's freedom of action. A
streamlined state administrative structure with clear lines of authority and
a new constitution to replace the statute-choked charter of 1870 formed
the core of Lowden's effort to afford the governor "power commensurate
with his responsibility."[39]

Using Dunne's Efficiency and Economy Committee report as a foundation, Lowden suggested a reorganization scheme that formalized in law
the new politics of executive leadership. The new plan, called the Civil
Administrative Code, retained the committee's recommendation to consolidate state boards and agencies (by 1917 there were over 125 of them)
into central departments, but it pared the number of departments to nine:
finance, agriculture, labor, mines and minerals, public works and buildings, public welfare, public health, trade and commerce, and registration
and education. Beyond that Lowden broke new ground. He rejected the
committee's proposal to place commissions in charge of some departments, arguing "that it is individuals who do things and not bodies of
men. We have acquired the habit, of late years, of creating a commission
every time something goes wrong."[40] Lowden insisted as a first principle
of administration that all power in each department be concentrated in
one person who would report directly to the governor. Advisory boards
and regulatory commissions were to be absorbed into this executive
structure.

The major goal of the Civil Administrative Code was to separate the
legislative, judicial, and administrative functions of state government so
that the chief executive could operate freely and efficiently. For a generation, Illinois lawmakers had created administrative offices on boards and
commissions and provided detailed sets of responsibilities and procedures
for those offices. "The result has been that administration as well as legislation has been written into our statute law," complained Charles E.
Woodward, Lowden's principal adviser on the code. "The extreme of
popular control was secured; energy and efficiency of administration were
sacrificed."[41] The code was intended to sweep away legislative meddling
in administration and replace it with a flexible and responsive structure
fortified by clear lines of authority. Certain general duties were assigned
to each department, but the details of implementation were left open for
the directors to arrange as they saw fit. This corporate model of responsi-

bility freed administrators from statutory control by the General Assembly yet tied them more firmly to the policy directives of the governor. Except where prohibited by the state constitution, each official under the code served a four-year term commensurate with that of the governor.[42]

The strengthened hand of the governor was evident everywhere in the code, but nowhere more so than in the finance department. Through it Lowden controlled the flow of government money more precisely than any previous chief executive. The finance department controlled the spending of the other eight departments and coordinated their relations. "It is the eye of the Governor in the expenditure of all appropriations made," Lowden stressed.[43] The department's director was furthermore authorized to prepare a state budget for the governor to submit to the General Assembly. This executive budget gave the chief executive the upper hand in formulating a legislative program. Lowden celebrated the Illinois Department of Finance, and in particular the executive budget, as "a new conception in our state government—and in that of government in any American state."[44]

Lowden aggressively pushed the Civil Administrative Code through the General Assembly. Learning from Dunne's troubles, Lowden presented the entire code in a single bill and refused to make any patronage appointments until the legislators passed it. Opposition to the code fell into two camps. First, the various professional, agricultural, and labor organizations that had gained a hearing at Springfield through the numerous state boards and commissions feared a loss of influence in the proposed consolidation. Lowden met privately with representatives of such groups and assured them that their voices would not be shut off from the reorganized departments. Second, objections also came from "politicians who think that the abolition of any political office is an interference with their vested rights," the governor confided. "I am attempting to meet this latter kind of opposition through public sentiment—the only effective way to overcome it."[45] Lowden nevertheless agreed to place elective offices in the state administration outside the purview of the code, confining its supervision to appointed officials.[46]

Whether Lowden's minor compromise, his withheld appointments, or a general sympathy to the new plan influenced lawmakers the most is unclear, but the Civil Administrative Code sped through the General Assembly in three months and was approved nearly unanimously by both houses in March. By July the new system was functioning. In March the General Assembly also arranged for the question of a constitutional convention to be put to the people by way of a plebiscite set for November 1918. In 1919 Lowden further centralized his control over state finances with the creation of the long-awaited Illinois Tax Commission.

The Civil Administrative Code made Lowden an instant celebrity. Theodore Roosevelt and other luminaries inquired about the Illinois reforms. Soon Lowden was touring state legislatures as the spokesman for government efficiency. In Massachusetts he was fulsomely introduced to the General Court as "the pioneer and originator" of the executive budget.[47] By 1923 seven states had copied the Illinois Civil Administrative Code and a half-dozen others had made partial advances along the same lines. Lowden became a strong contender for the 1920 Republican presidential nomination.[48]

Illusions of Harmony

America's entry into the First World War in April 1917 heightened the appeal and exaggerated the benefits of administrative reform. In its first biennium of operation, the Civil Administrative Code yielded a budgetary surplus, but the redirection of state spending toward the war effort accounted for most of the savings in the nine executive departments. Several construction projects authorized under the code were abandoned for the duration of the conflict. Meanwhile, high wartime prices and the mobilization effort shot total state expenditures over the $46 million mark set by Dunne. The real advantage of the code was more emotional than financial. It provided an example of centralized, united effort that helped ease the transition into a wartime economy. Under the code, "the spirit of cooperation is everywhere manifest," reported the director of the Illinois Department of Education and Registration, as the directors developed an "interested, enthusiastic, and completely harmonious fellowship" in their joint pursuit of public efficiency.[49]

Efficient state government and public cooperation became a patriotic necessity as the United States geared up for the conflict overseas. Lowden's reorganization of Illinois government coincided with the apparent unity of sentiment behind the war effort to create the illusion that administrative reform had fostered social harmony. As reformers Merriam, Ickes, and Robins volunteered for military service and dashed off to Europe, Illinois prepared for war with additional administrative centralization. In May 1917, shortly after the Civil Administrative Code became law, Lowden and the General Assembly created the State Council of Defense to coordinate war production, conserve needed resources, stimulate popular morale, and generally organize the war effort in Illinois. Its fifteen members included public utilities magnate Samuel Insull, who served as chairman, industrialists J. Ogden Armour and Charles Wacker, Republican officeholders John G. Oglesby and David E. Shanahan, Chicago Democratic boss Roger Sullivan, Illinois Manufacturers' Association counsel Levy Mayer and officer Fred W. Upham, and Illinois State Federation of Labor president John H. Walker and secretary Victor A. Olander, along with representatives of the press, women's organizations, and other prominent interests.

The war seemed to erase deep conflicts between the disparate members of the council. Before the 1916 election, Walker, a former Socialist, expressed the opinion there was no "abler, shrewder, or more mercenary enemy of the labor movement" than Frank O. Lowden.[50] With the declaration of war, however, Walker denounced "the Kaiser and his autocracy" and accepted Lowden's appointment to the State Council of Defense with alacrity, backed by a favorable vote of 790 to 6 from ISFL members. Once on the council, Walker found Lowden "an exceedingly agreeable surprise" who protected the rights of labor in a number of wartime crises.[51]

With the cooperation of nearly 400,000 workers organized down to the school district level, the defense council brought the war home to every community in the state, even to the point of regulating Christmas gift giving. Planning, bank loans, and specially trained laborers from cities and towns coaxed a bumper wheat and rye crop from Illinois farms. The council's war drives brought in so much money that it turned a profit. The council promoted an "organized state of mind" by means of publicity committees, touring Four Minute Men, and a massive propaganda effort by the cooperative Illinois press—some country newspapers between 1917 and 1918 contained only dispatches from the front, support for state wartime organization, and appeals for prohibition. The council's massive centralized campaign limited fuel and food use and helped prevent paralyzing labor disputes. Many unions agreed to work in open shops during the conflict. Insull proudly remarked that the council brought "uninterrupted social and industrial peace" to Illinois in the time of its greatest need.[52]

The passage of the Civil Administrative Code and the performance of Illinois's wartime government cemented the triumph of administrative reform over social and "democratic" proposals. The hope of political progressives that economy, efficiency, and expertise could not only secure good government but promote social harmony as well received a tremendous boost from Lowden's administration. For the majority of Illinois reformers absorbed in the war effort, and impressed by the unity of effort achieved by centralized direction, the "progressive conservatism" of Lowden and Walter Fisher seemed more effective than the legacy of social activism derived from Altgeld and Jane Addams. Administrative reform could bring both efficiency and democracy.

As if to cap off the war with a further endorsement of administrative reform, Illinois voters in November 1918 approved by 74,000 votes the calling of a convention to draft a new state constitution. The General Assembly scheduled the election of constitutional delegates for November 1919. After 1919, however, there were no more triumphs for administrative reform in Illinois.

Coming Apart

Administrative reform eventually failed because it was burdened with too many hopes. Expanded executive authority, streamlined administration, and a sensible budget allowed the state government to function more effectively, but these reforms could not extinguish social discord or eliminate the influence of political organizations in Illinois. Violent outbreaks of hatred during the war and in its immediate aftermath testified to the deep divisions that remained unchecked between citizens of the Prairie State. A mob of inflamed patriots in the Madison County town of Collinsville lynched a hapless German workingman in April 1918 and then were acquitted of the crime. Other German residents of Illinois were roughed up and forced to perform humiliating demonstrations of loyalty. Lowden denounced such vigilantism, but these incidents hinted at the divisive social currents coursing beneath the surface harmony of a people at war.[53]

Outbreaks of vicious racial violence made the social disaffection even more plain. Illinois had long been an inhospitable land for its black residents. Progressive reformers largely ignored their struggle for work and housing, the respectable middle class dismissed them as frequenters of gambling dives, and the working class reviled them as strikebreakers. With the outbreak of war, however, employment beckoned in the booming war industries, and blacks began to leave their homes in the southern states and pour into Illinois cities. Chicago's black population leaped from 44,000 in 1910 to nearly 110,000 a decade later. In East St. Louis, white unionists complained that employers were importing black southern migrants to destroy labor organizations in that city, a claim endorsed by State Council of Defense member John Walker after outbreaks of racial violence in May 1917. On July 2 a savage riot broke out, and forty-eight people, the vast majority of them black, lost their lives. Local police and the Illinois National Guard failed to quell the violence. Many stood by as white mobs fired on blacks and burned their homes; several even joined in the gunfire. Two years later, racial tension in Chicago over jobs, housing, and city politics exploded into violence. Thirty-eight people died in that riot; over five hundred were injured. Again the official response was tardy and inadequate.[54]

The riots exposed more than bitter racial antagonism. The angry struggle between capital and labor would soon throw off the uneasy wartime truce. Chicago endured more strikes in 1919 than any American city except New York. As early as fall of 1918, the Chicago Federation of Labor pushed for the formation of an independent labor party. In March of the following year, the membership of the Illinois State Federation of Labor overwhelmingly endorsed the idea. The crushing steel strike of 1919 and renewed stirrings of the open shop campaign helped persuade Walker to drop his cooperative stance toward Lowden. In 1919 he joined the Farmer-Labor party and in 1920 ran for governor of Illinois on its ticket. Samuel Insull's hope that industrial "teamwork" would extend beyond the war emergency proved futile. [55]

For Governor Lowden, the problems of loyalty, race, and industrial strife all converged in the person of Mayor Thompson of Chicago. Thompson was a difficult politician to classify. Born into the wealth and prominence of an old-stock family with roots in Boston and Chicago, he spent his youth as a Nebraska cowboy and Chicago football star. He entered politics as a loyal protégé of Lorimer and, like his mentor, profited from Republican factionalism. Alternately shrewd and clownish, Thompson juxtaposed support for older immigrant groups such as Irish, Germans, and Swedes with anti-Catholicism and insensitivity toward newer immigrants (epitomized in his "Tony, Tony, where's your pushcart" jibe directed at Bohemian leader Anton Cermak in 1930) and combined public works projects that glorified Chicago with an acceptance of organized crime that tore down its reputation. He served three terms as mayor, from 1915 until 1923 and from 1927 until 1931. During his first term, "Big Bill" constructed a powerful organization based on his settlement of a 1915 streetcar strike and his ability to maintain the popular nickel fare, his courteous attention to black Chicagoans (which won him the loyalty of the city's fastest growing voting bloc), and a fast-flowing river of graft. Lowden cultivated Thompson's support in the 1916 campaign but denied him patronage rewards after the victory. The subsequent feud deepened into actual conflict when Thompson adopted an antiwar stance in 1917. After a pacifist group called the "People's Council" had been chased out of several midwestern towns, Thompson offered them the hospitality of Chicago for an antiwar meeting. Although wholly without authority to do so, Lowden ordered Chicago's chief of police to dissolve the meeting and then ordered in the National Guard when Thompson blocked him. The pacifists had finished their business before the troops arrived, but the break between Lowden and Thompson was now permanent. [56]

Relations between the two officials deteriorated rapidly over the next two years. In 1918 Lowden rejected Thompson's request for a special legislative session to authorize increased revenue for Chicago. Later in the

same year Thompson ran for United States senator, but the governor
threw his support to Medill McCormick and Thompson was defeated in
the Republican primary. Nevertheless, "Hizzoner" seemed unassailable in
Chicago, brushing aside Republican opposition from Charles Merriam
and Judge Harry Olson and winning reelection as mayor against Democrat
Robert Sweitzer in a close contest in 1919. Then, in July, the mayor was
shocked as the contending parties in a city streetcar strike spurned his
mediation efforts and turned instead to the State Public Utilities Commission. Against Thompson's protests, Lowden allowed the commission
to mediate the strike and rubbed salt into the wound by attending the
proceedings. The utility commission's settlement of the dispute included
an arrangement by which wage increases would be partially covered by
higher fares on the streetcar lines. In one stroke, state regulation threatened Thompson's position as the controlling force in Chicago affairs and
abolished the symbol of his popularity, the nickel fare.[57]

The State Public Utilities Commission became the issue over which
Lowden and Thompson acted out their antipathy. Thompson pronounced
Lowden and the commission toadies of the traction plutocrats and vowed
to restore "home rule" over Chicago utilities. Lowden's representatives
asserted that the cunning Thompson played on the "prejudice against
public utilities" to assail the governor. The old fear of public utility out-
rages "has been seized upon by the head of the 'Chicago Tammany' and
his satellites as a political asset," an administration statement warned,
and was then spread "by demagogical appeals and misrepresentation."[58]
The Chicago race riot erupted at the height of the streetcar controversy,
and the unwillingness of the mayor and the governor to work together
allowed the violence to escalate needlessly. Illinois government was not
functioning peacefully or responsibly in 1919.

Gathering the Spoils

Unabated social conflict and resurgent machine politics framed the de-
nouement of Illinois progressivism. The hopes that "progressive conservatives" had placed on administrative reform were dashed as Lowden's
reorganized government became the foundation for the most highly developed spoils machine in state history, and the proposed modern state
constitution floundered to an inglorious demise.

Thompson's battle with Lowden carried over into the 1920 election.
The mayor strenuously opposed the governor's bid for the Republican
presidential nomination and organized a state ticket against Lowden's designated successor, John G. Oglesby, and the entire administration slate.

Len Small was Thompson's choice for governor. Despite his ties with Lorimer, Small had retained his knack for holding office, serving as state treasurer for two years as part of Lowden's unity ticket. Good government Republicans were horrified by the Thompson-Small combination, but Lowden's poor judgment helped it secure victory. The governor's presidential ambitions crashed to earth after Louis Emmerson, Lowden's secretary of state, could not explain why he had handed $5,000 to a pair of Missouri delegates to the Republican National Convention. Lowden foolishly rewarded the blundering Emmerson by endorsing him for reelection on the state ticket. Thompson and Small had their ammunition, and they expended it with gusto. "Each candidate on the Lowden-Oglesby Utilities ticket represents a link in the chain of corporate greed that grinds the people," cried Small's campaign circulars. Small promised to dismantle the State Public Utilities Commission, to ensure that the Pullman Company paid its just tax burden, and to provide for public ownership of Chicago's streetcar system with a restored nickel fare.[59]

The colorless Oglesby could not compete with Thompson's organization. Small's 76,000 vote majority in Cook County gave him a narrow 8,000 vote victory over Oglesby for the Republican nomination. "The best administration in Illinois history" had been overcome by "the worst," brooded the *Peoria Transcript*.[60] "I was mad before and after seeing the sad spectacle of Mr. Len Small, in person, I am now in a frenzy of rage," wrote one Oglesby supporter after the primary. "I will not be a party to the crime of electing Len Small."[61] Lowden and Oglesby overcame their misgivings, however, and endorsed the party choice. Small rode the Harding landslide to a half-million vote majority over Democrat J. Hamilton Lewis, although he polled nearly 375,000 fewer votes than the GOP standard bearer.[62]

For the next eight years, Small presided over an administration that, according to a contemporary observer, "for waste, mismanagement, inefficiency, intrigue, manipulation, and downright disregard of the public interest [had] few parallels in the history of the United States."[63] In Small's hands, the clear channels of executive authority developed by Lowden became arteries for a vast patronage network. Small cast aside civil service restrictions, removing unwanted personnel on the transparent grounds of "incompetency."[64] The governor placed his son at the head of a newly created department of purchases and construction, through which all government supplies were procured. He named his son-in-law administrative auditor of the State Department of Finance. In addition to providing employment for his family, the government of Illinois doubled as Small's personal political organization. He amassed over a half-million dollars for campaign expenses in 1924 from assessments of state employees and used government resources to distribute his campaign material.[65]

Disclosures of corruption dogged the Small regime. Word spread in 1921 that during his term as state treasurer Small had diverted state funds into a secret account from which he made high-interest loans. The state received the minimum rate of interest from the money under Small's care, and Small pocketed the excess—estimated at over $1 million. In a trial that aroused public suspicion, the governor was acquitted of embezzlement charges, but he eventually agreed to return $650,000 to the state treasury. Lieutenant Governor Fred Sterling was indicted for similar misdeeds, and in 1928, the United States Senate denied admittance to Small ally Frank L. Smith after the corrupt use of money in his primary victory of 1926.[66]

Small nonetheless retained his popularity, winning reelection in 1924 despite the charges of graft. He was a master of interest-group politics. Before the 1920 election he played up to the Anti-Saloon League; then, for the 1924 campaign, Small attracted labor support by adopting an anti-injunction stance and won the endorsement of the newly powerful Ku Klux Klan by providing meeting space for the Invisible Empire on the state fairgrounds. Above all, however, the key to Governor Small's appeal was an ambitious road-building program that cleverly revived the distributive politics of the late nineteenth century. Good roads had been an issue in Illinois politics since the 1890s, yet for many years the issue had only limited appeal. Bicyclists, fledgling motorists, and certain prosperous farmers demanded that the state's atrocious mud roads be surfaced with hard pavement, whereas the majority of rural dwellers decried the expense of any improvements. By the 1920s, however, the fuller extension of the market and the popularity of the automobile helped the special interest nature of road reforms dissolve in a broader community of interest. Dunne's administration had created a state highway commission in 1913, and Lowden's had passed a $60 million bond issue for highway construction in 1918, but little actual work took place before Small's inauguration. Small knew what to do when a political opportunity fell into his lap, and he immediately launched a torrid road-building program that expanded the paved surface of Illinois from 700 miles to 7,000 miles, more than any other state.[67]

Road construction became the primary link between Small's political organization and the citizens of Illinois. "A few miles of completed road on the proposed Route would increase the faith of our people in our administration and would make things much easier for us," a Crawford County Republican informed Small in a typical exchange concerning the merits of highway construction.[68] Small countered adverse publicity with public works. People read about graft in the newspaper, but they could see a new road. (For those needing further evidence, Small had the state printers publish thirty pages of "before and after" photographs documenting his improvements of state highways, bridges, and road markers.) Automobile license fees funded the bond issue, so there were no direct taxes to complain about. During Small's reelection campaign in 1924, Illinois built a record 1,230 miles of road, and the governor promised more through an additional $100 million bond issue. Government by political organization had reached its culmination in Illinois by using centralized administrative reform as a stepladder to power.[69]

◆

Small's ability to appease individual interest groups while staking out a general policy that attracted mass support stands in direct contrast to the failure of the Illinois Constitution of 1922 to satisfy anyone. The efforts by Lowden and the major progressive political reform organizations in Chicago to construct a new state charter were part of a progressive-era surge in constitutional revision in the northern states most affected by immigration, industrial expansion, and urban growth. Between 1912 and 1922, Ohio, Massachusetts, New York, and Illinois held constitutional conventions. Voters rejected the New York and Illinois constitutions, and the Supreme Judicial Court of Massachusetts invalidated that state's document. Reformers applauded the Ohio charter, but its success was tempered by voter indifference and charges of special interest domination. The overall failure of constitutional revision during the second decade of the twentieth century represented what Morton Keller has called "the Strange Death of American Progressivism: the inability of the polity, as it was then constituted, to respond effectively to the demands of a new society."[70] Alterations in the structure of government could not harmonize the interests of a diverse society. The hopes of Illinois "progressive conservatives" that a reorganized state administration and a new constitution could do so reflected the extent of the progressive malaise.

Governor Lowden and the reform clubs of Chicago engineered the movement for the new state constitution. Before the 1918 public referendum on the convention, George Cole of the Citizens' Association of Chicago, which had worked since 1912 for a convention, called a meeting in Lowden's office to organize the public campaign for a new constitution. Justice Orrin Carter of the Illinois Supreme Court was put in charge of the publicity effort that resulted in public approval of the convention call. The Chicago City Club, the Chicago Civic Federation, and the Chicago Bureau of Public Efficiency joined in the convention preparations along with business and professional organizations. Downstate support for the convention concentrated in agricultural and banking organizations desiring alterations in the state tax system, but the proposed adjustments to the constitution were heavily weighted toward the concerns of Chicago interests and supporters of Lowden's administrative reforms: repeal of the cumulative voting system, introduction of the short ballot, strengthening of the state supreme court, overhaul of tax practices, and Chicago unification and home rule.[71]

There was nothing "nonpartisan" about the selection of delegates or organization of the convention. Nonpartisan reformers in the City Club favored the nomination of delegates by petition, but the Citizens' Association and the Constitutional Convention Campaign Committee helped persuade the attorney general that the proper constitutional procedure called for nomination by way of primary elections. Selection of the 102 delegates (2 from each state senatorial district) therefore became a partisan issue. The September 1919 primary and November general election produced a lopsided Republican convention majority of eighty-five to seventeen. Lowden put the partisan imbalance to use, organizing the Republican delegates in a caucus before the convention opened in January. The Republican majority elected Lowden aide Charles Woodward as convention president, and Woodward excluded Democrats and Thompson supporters from important committee posts.[72]

Neither the Chicago reform clubs (nine City Club members were delegates) nor the governor could dominate the convention. The most powerful force at work in Springfield between January 1920 and September 1922, when the discouraged convention dragged to a close, was the unresolved tension in Illinois society. Conflicts between Chicago and the downstate fractured the convention into irreconcilable factions. Chicago demanded greater power than the downstate elements were willing to concede, including an expansion of the state supreme court from seven to nine justices, with both additions coming from the Chicago district. Downstate delegates urged that Chicago's legislative representation in Springfield be permanently limited. On June 23, by a vote of forty-eight to twenty-three, the convention adopted the majority report that limited Chicago's General Assembly contingent to a third of the upper house and seventy-six seats in the lower, one less than a majority. The Citizens' Association warned, "should that proposal be finally adopted as a part of the proposed new constitution it will undoubtedly meet with defeat when submitted to the voters of Cook County and will be likely to carry to defeat the remainder of the proposed new constitution."[73] In December, the limitation was formalized, and the convention ground to a halt. Several Cook County chairmen resigned from their committee posts. The

City Club announced that "the convention's long drawn out course has ended in recognized failure."[74] On the brink of dissolution, the convention adjourned until September 1921.

Calls for democratic reforms further divided the convention. A public-policy advisory vote in 1919 recorded a majority favoring the inclusion of an initiative and referendum in the new constitution. Former governor Dunne, reformers such as Charles Merriam, and organized labor rallied public support behind the proposal, but Lowden distrusted the reform, and downstate interests feared that it would enable the population of Chicago to dictate policy. The convention killed the initiative and referendum and inserted into the proposed document a bizarre section specifically intended to obliterate any chance of their reappearance: "the republican form of government of this State shall never be abandoned, modified or impaired."[75]

The convention bogged down in a ludicrous display of futility. Delegate absenteeism became common, and each time the General Assembly convened, the convention had to surrender the House chamber it occupied. With no alternate meeting place, the delegates had to disperse and await the conclusion of the legislative session. By 1922, the dreary proceedings revived enough to push through some compromises that gave the constitution a faint hope of approval at the hands of the voters. The biggest compromise restricted the Cook County limitation on representation to the lower house of the General Assembly. Still, few were happy with the document. Labor, already embittered by the rejection of the initiative and referendum, feared the expanded power of the judiciary to issue injunctions and disrupt unions. The Anti-Saloon League wanted greater restrictions on Chicago's political power. Business interests disliked the new income tax; others thought it unduly favored the wealthy (the maximum rate was frozen at three times the minimum rate). Those willing to endorse the new constitution as better than nothing implored the convention to submit controversial items separately to voters. Such a formula aided the passage of the Ohio constitution in 1912, and Lowden, now out of office, had endorsed a similar procedure for Illinois. Nevertheless, the convention decided to submit its work to the voters in a uniform package. Fragile compromises and the convention's reluctance to leave open the possibility of a public vote on the initiative and referendum underlay that final extraordinary action.[76]

Although the City Club swallowed its losses and, in a straw poll, voted 549 to 214 to approve the new constitution, the document stood virtually no chance of adoption. Governor Small was outspoken in his criticism of the constitution, Harold Ickes and Dunne organized the People's Protective League to oppose its adoption, and the majority of the state's organized interest groups urged its disapproval. The special election in December 1922 came as an anticlimax: the new constitution was rejected by a vote of 921,398 to 185,298. Cook County shouted it down by a twenty-to-one margin. With it, the Progressive Era in Illinois staggered to a close. [77]

Marketplace Pluralism

Progressive hopes for the construction of a public policy fueled by the public interest, in which the community of democratic citizenship envisioned by Dewey sanctified the efficient conduct of public business, went unrealized in Illinois and in the nation as a whole. Too often, in their confidence and sense of mission, progressives failed to appreciate the strength of partisanship in American life, the degree to which practical ties of self-interest, trade, locality, and ethnicity overwhelmed attachments to such abstract constructions as Citizenship and the Public. More systematically, progressives were unable to overcome, or even to recognize, the extent of their own partisanship—the ways in which their priorities of public concern reflected sometimes narrow outlooks shaped by race, culture, social position, and family experience and the manner in which their relationship to the party system limited their range of reform options. Still, the reform energy of Illinois progressives was breathtaking. The progressives chose to confront rather than to cover up the fundamental problems of their society. Candid discussions of contemporary issues from a diversity of viewpoints were standard fare in the public forums of progressive-era Illinois. Confident in people's ability to transform society, reformers were open to political experimentation. Finally, despite their setbacks, the efforts of Illinois progressives helped make the lives of working men, women, and children healthier and more secure; stirred middle-class concern for the welfare of immigrants and the poor, heretofore left to their own devices in the squalid anonymity of back-street tenements; and forced people to critically examine their society and seek ways to improve it. Their inability to forge public solutions to the problems of their age achieves greater significance because of their intensity and commitment.

The progressive political faith in administrative reform nevertheless was misplaced. The shape of party government was transformed by the new politics, but it was not replaced. Administrative centralization not only failed to separate politics from government, it unintentionally became the foundation for Small's highly developed state machine. Chicago political organizations also achieved tighter control over government through centralized personal machines. Municipal and Democratic party control were merged by Anton Cermak, Edward J. Kelly, and Pat Nash, and were brought to a culmination of centralized direction by Richard J. Daley.[78]

The twentieth-century American polity was based on marketplace pluralism, not the public interest advocated by progressives. By the time of the New Deal, organized interest groups competed with one another for the attention of governments broken down into bureaucratic fragments. Amid the calls for legislation, accommodation, or protection, not all segments of American society exercised equal influence or received sympathetic attention. The polity rewarded winners and punished losers. As a result, the sense of a shared American public life idealized by progressives suffered. Instead of monuments to a common spirit of citizenship, twentieth-century American cities became symbols of the enduring gulfs in a society patterned by the marketplace, examples of the sagging commitment to public education, and the central arenas in which recurring episodes of racial strife continue to be played out. Prosperity, security, beauty, and international influence were also achieved by modern American society, but marketplace pluralism produced a public life that was often inefficient, unduly influenced by powerful social groups, and remote or uninteresting to many citizens. Illinois limped on without a new constitution until 1970. Meanwhile, the Illinois Manufacturers' Association continued to maintain an influential lobby in Springfield. In 1984 the IMA, still devoted to "killing other people's weird ideas," was named by General Assembly members as the third most powerful state lobby. "We have become a General Assembly of special interests," declared a state senator.[79]

Progressives were ill suited for such a future. "Focusing always on what was morally right, and finding that invariably in a state of mind that looked beyond self and class, the progressives felt defeated by any 'reform' that accepted special claims and honored them," Otis Graham wrote in describing aged progressives' hostility to the New Deal. "Aimed at unifying the American people, progressivism would produce few men who, even after the social education acquired during lengthy careers in public affairs, could accept frank class legislation."[80]

Partisanship overwhelmed the progressive notion of the public interest in Illinois. The ties between politics and government remained fast. Ethnic, class, and regional antagonisms did not dissolve into a harmonious union of citizens. A highly subjective blend of personal motivation, class outlook, and rational turn of mind shaped the progressive definition of the public interest in the first place, but very little in the experience of Illinois from 1870 to 1922 indicates that it was a widely shared ideal. That is not cause for harsh criticism of the progressives, however, and still less for celebrating self-interested pluralism. Freedom to dissent from an imposed declaration of the public interest is an American strength; the inability to define or act on the public interest is not.

8

Conclusion: Progressivism and American Politics

Americans in the Progressive Era attempted to fashion practical, humane responses to the challenging conditions of modernity. Their successes and their failures have since become our own. A generation ago, Ray Ginger celebrated a burst of creative energy in Illinois at the turn of the century that broke through the crass American ethic of getting and spending to reach a new plane of compassion, insight, and reformist intentions. He generalized the spirit of the endeavor with the label "Altgeld's America" and summed up its creed with the motto that ideals "must set the standard toward which we try to shape reality."[1] Altgeld is an appropriate symbol for the checkered legacy of progressive politics as a whole. His public career was marked by painful and never fully successful attempts to reconcile his personal and political ambition with his passion for justice and crowned by the loss of power and influence as the price for his one great act of conscience, the pardon of the remaining Haymarket anarchists. Altgeld's progressive contemporaries and subsequent upholders of the political reform tradition had reason to applaud the ideal of public service that he brought to state government, as well as the material accomplishments of his administration in the form of protective and social welfare legislation, but in terms of institutional politics, Altgeld's most important innovation was the harnessing of reform energy to the office of the governor and his party organization. In Altgeld's America, considerable distance separated progressive ideals of the public interest and the politico-governmental apparatus through which the public interest was to be served.

The dynamism of the progressive mind and imagination promised more. In Chicago the creative ferment of the Progressive Era produced intellectual and artistic achievements of lasting consequence. The fledgling University of Chicago produced an American school of philosophy—pragmatism—and a philosophy for American schools—child-centered progressive education—that deeply influenced American thought. Chicago provided a seedbed for the settlement house movement from which the concerns and methods of Hull House, Chicago Commons, and the University of Chicago Settlement spread across the nation. Clarence Darrow helped push the law in new directions. Powerful expressions of a new American architecture conceived by Sullivan, Burnham, and Wright took shape in Chicago as well, and in the city's social cauldron, Theodore Dreiser and Upton Sinclair found the inspiration that transformed American literature and journalism. In diverse fields, pioneers such as Brand Whitlock, Eugene Debs, Florence Kelley, Harold Ickes, and Adolf Meyer cut their professional teeth and learned their lessons in progressive-era Illinois; from the schoolhouse of their Illinois experience, Whitlock went on to a life of art and politics as mayor of Toledo, Debs developed an indigenous radical response to industrialism, Kelley launched a public career defending the rights of children and consumers, Ickes helped oversee the growth of the bureaucratic national state, and Meyer became a major force in the creation of modern American psychiatry.

In the public arena of politics and governance, however, reformers influenced by the progressive ferment could not complete the rough work of translating ideas into action. The barriers to a democratic, efficient exercise of the public interest, which emerged so concretely in progressive-era Illinois, were as central to the developing public life of the nation as the cultural advances of Illinois progressives had been to its creative spirit; the shortcomings of the public interest in politics also shaped the contours of Altgeld's America. Notions of cooperative democratic citizenship and harmonious social relations harbored by civic reformers, settlement house activists, and political insurgents could not unite a society divided by race, ethnicity, class, region, and outlook. Divisions between large and small farmers, state and city public health officials, and regulatory agencies and the General Assembly hampered attempts to protect consumers from impure milk and milk-borne diseases. Progressive efforts to reduce class antagonisms by means of protective factory legislation crippled the independent power of organized labor and unintentionally accorded unequal influence to organized capital on the state industrial commissions. Ethnic conflict in Chicago stalled the bid by civic reformers to win fiscal and administrative independence for the city with a new charter. Disputes involving class, gender, neighborhood, and political rivalries became obstacles to the peaceful, efficient, and democratic management of public schools and transportation in Chicago. The structure of politics and government that progressives desired to rebuild in the service of the public interest incorporated specific reform initiatives without moving off its partisan foundations.

Progressive political visions of democracy and harmonious compromise not only encountered resistance in public-policy debates, but they sometimes were made to appear altogether superfluous by the realities of conflict and interest. The ideas of John Dewey quickly became peripheral in the battle over control of Chicago schools, while the Illinois Manufacturers' Association and Charles Deneen's Republican faction smoothly steered the public-spirited suggestions of Jane Addams and Graham Taylor toward their own partisan purposes. Democratic ideals gradually buckled under the weight of legislative and bureaucratic impediments. Some progressives such as Darrow abandoned politics after short, disillusioning encounters and invested their energies in more specialized pursuits. When Whitlock departed the Altgeld administration for Ohio and Meyer left the state hospital at Kankakee, each man took along the recognition that the "foul and heavy" influence of politics in Illinois intractably seeped into every public enterprise.[2]

The enduring strength of partisan political organizations in public affairs is the central conclusion this study can offer to the historical treatment of progressive-era politics. Historians have indisputably established that popular electoral participation and party identification declined significantly at the turn of the century, but changes in voter turnout and new prominence for highly organized interest groups in the policy-making process did not signal a decline in the significance of political organizations. Indeed, it has been the argument of this study that party organizations become more streamlined, more closely controlled by officeholders, and more flexible in choosing and manipulating public issues than ever before.

Unable to harness contentious democracy to the selfless ideals of the public interest, Illinois political progressives after 1912 relied on state government to protect the public interest through administrative expertise. They were not alone. Across the United States, in staggered regional patterns dating back in some cases to the 1890s, access to public power through the channels of democratic participation shrank during the Progressive Era. In the name of social peace, racial solidarity, and partisan advantage, southern states disfranchised blacks and rebellious whites by means of restrictive voter registration laws that were cemented in place by new state constitutions. Initiatives to "purify" public life and combat political organizations, including the Australian ballot, tightened registration procedures, and more stringent naturalization requirements for voting, culled immigrant, marginal, or "suspect" Americans from the

electorate in the north. Reforms such as the short ballot, at-large elections, and commission and city manager government trimmed the power
of ethnic enclaves in many cities and removed some public questions from
the direct influence of voters. In some locales, restrictive measures coincided with the introduction of democratic innovations such as the direct
primary; direct election of United States senators; the initiative, referendum, and recall; and women's suffrage. These ballot laws were linked by
the progressive quest for a responsible polity that would check the power
of partisan politicians and advance the public interest.[3]

The progressive tendency to gravitate toward the responsible concentration of power achieved its preeminent expression in Herbert Croly's
Promise of American Life. Croly's 1909 treatise strongly influenced Theodore Roosevelt's vision of the New Nationalism and the Progressive party
revolt against conservative Republicanism, but it also laid bare the progressive generation's inability to fuse democracy with efficiency or escape
its own partisan proclivities. Croly proposed that to be effective and responsive to public needs, American government must outmaneuver professional politicians and sidestep the fragmented, bickering electorate.
First, American democracy should be "organized" by a core group of public-spirited citizens free from selfish motives. Next, strong executive
power should be developed so that the concerns of "organized democracy"
could be effectively addressed. On the national level, an assertive president would accomplish this purpose; in the states, a reshuffling of existing
governmental organization would be required. Such a procedure would
reduce legislative power, centralize authority in the office of the governor,
and turn many elective offices into appointive posts controlled by the
executive, thus creating a reform "boss" who would act as "the sworn
enemy of the unofficial 'Bosses' who now dominate local politics."[4] Croly
advised Americans to work through the mechanism of the Republican
party to effect such reforms. In its resemblance to the actual course of
progressive political activity in Illinois, Croly's prescription for advancing
the public interest took on the appearance of a blueprint for the Civil
Administrative Code.[5]

But *The Promise of American Life* also illustrated the separation of
democratic intentions from the structure of efficient administration. Although Croly's nationalistic vision invited the contributions of such organized interests as labor and business to public-policy counsels, little
space seemed to be reserved for average Americans. Indeed, the role of
everyday people in Croly's democratic vision, as it ultimately proved to
be in reality for progressive activists, crossed the boundaries of the im-
probable into the fantastic. "If a noble and civilized democracy is to sub-
sist," Croly concluded, "the common citizen must be something of a saint

and something of a hero."[6] This semimystical hope shared more in spirit with Henry Adams's conservative longing for the community of the high middle ages than it did with the remainder of Croly's nascent liberalism. His suggestions for governmental centralization certainly corresponded to practical political circumstances better than his formula for democratic participation operated in a society in which self-interest determined positions on pure milk and cultural allegiances influenced matters of municipal taxation. The democratic component of progressive political thinking had turned down a blind alley.

That is not to say that progressive thinkers and political activists were antidemocratic. Neither Dewey, Croly, Walter Lippmann, nor the settlement house workers turned their backs on democratic aspirations during the Progressive Era, but because the progressive understanding of democracy leaned so heavily on the ideal of the public interest, the search for responsible democratic forms led progressives away from the grassroots and into the corridors of bureaucratic expertise and executive leadership. James T. Kloppenberg points out that to American progressive thinkers, pragmatic democracy required a scientific "process of critical analysis and intelligent evaluation, not merely the notion of popular participation." Ultimately, they lodged their hopes in "regulatory agencies, which these thinkers envisioned as the political arm of science," capable of alerting the public to its duty and instructing elected officials as to the proper means of executing the public will. By trusting streamlined government institutions to carry the burden of democracy, however, progressives ensnared themselves in the contradictions between efficiency and democracy.[7]

Both theorists and more prosaic progressive activists believed that the driving force of the public interest could turn bureaucratic institutions into democratic institutions. Croly recognized the dangers of a powerful, insulated bureaucracy, but he remained confident that legislative checks would guard against abuses. The growing progressive faith in the public spirit of nonpartisan administrators was even more influential. As Kloppenberg reminds us, progressive thinkers stressed that "democratic government becomes simply an institutionalized scramble for private advantage through public legitimation" unless fortified by a virtuous commitment to the public interest.[8] Experience in public affairs taught reformers that few Americans exhibited that commitment; few, that is, outside the ranks of educated professionals. If expert members of regulatory commissions, appointive boards, and state agencies were not objective proponents of the public interest, then efficient democratic government could not be carried on. They had to be trusted.

A wave of regulatory enactments at the state and national level during the progressive period testified to the increasing American acceptance of state power as a means of restraining excessive private advantage. Reformers were particularly eager to break the ties between corporations and political parties that had hobbled the public interest. Between 1903 and 1908, forty-one state legislatures created or strengthened commissions to regulate railroads; within a short time, other public utilities also came under their purview. Additional measures chipped away at the layers of private influence that encrusted public service. Many states prohibited public officials from accepting free railroad passes, some restricted the access of lobbyists to state legislatures, and, in the legislative sessions of 1907–8, nineteen states took steps to ban corporate contributions to political campaigns. Progressive insurgencies against the entrenched inner circles of political parties also took regulatory expression as direct primary laws placed legal restraints on the process of nominating candidates for public office. By 1917, all but four states had direct primary laws, thirty-two of them mandatory statutes providing for the nomination of all elected state officials. Progressives had enlisted state government as an ally in the defense of the public interest.[9]

Goaded by state action, public opinion, and vigorous presidential leadership, the regulatory apparatus of the federal government underwent a pell-mell expansion during the Progressive Era. President Theodore Roosevelt's commitment to nationalism, much of which centered on the insistence that the selfish advantages of particular groups had to give way in the face of the nation's interest, spurred the growth of a government structure better attuned to the public consequences of uneven private power. The bluntest expression of presidential leadership in this regard came during the bitter coal strike of 1902. As the stalemate between miners and operators lengthened into autumn, fear that the public would be left without heating coal for the coming winter provoked calls for intervention into the dispute. Although unsure of his legal authority to do so, Roosevelt met with the contending sides and cajoled the obstinate mine owners to accept arbitration at the hands of a presidential commission. With similar vigor, Roosevelt undertook a small number of antitrust prosecutions to remind corporations of the primacy of the public interest, declared the public stake in conservation, reinforced the authority of the Interstate Commerce Commission, and pushed for the means to prevent the adulteration of drugs and foodstuffs and improve the quality of meat for American consumers.[10]

Roosevelt's departure from the White House in 1909 did not reverse the course of bureaucratic expansion. The scope and power of the ICC increased during the administrations of William Howard Taft and Woodrow Wilson. Despite Wilson's allegiance to traditional Democratic suspicions of concentrated power, he accepted the extension of federal controls over banking and, at the urging of Louis Brandeis, pushed Congress to create a Federal Trade Commission. As had Roosevelt, Wilson justified his policies as practical reflections of the public interest. "There is only one thing in this world, gentlemen, that binds men together," he announced in 1916. "That is unselfishness. Selfishness separates them. Selfishness divides them into camps." [11] The progressive quest for harmony and justice in large part had come to depend on the ability of government institutions to deflect base considerations of private aggrandizement from public-policy calculations.

As it turned out, private power exerted greater influence on regulatory government in the twentieth century than did the idealized public interest of the progressives. This outcome partly derived from the fact that regulators often were not experts or, if they were, could not be characterized as nonpartisan. Government boards and agencies charged with economic regulation of highly specialized industries frequently became dependent on industry sources for technical knowledge or else were staffed by personnel with close ties to regulated companies or their commercial rivals. Max Weber argued that even if regulatory agencies maintained their independence, "the superior expert knowledge of the interested groups" redirected specific measures to "unforeseen and unintended" consequences. The evolution of the "model" Railroad Commission of Wisconsin from a reform idea promising to bring down railroad rates in the interest of consumers and small producers to a working agency that cooperated closely with state carriers is symptomatic of the difficulties that hamstrung progressive administrative reform. [12]

The flaws in the progressive-era state, however, ran far deeper than the ability of some businesses to influence regulatory bodies. Despite images popular among some scholars of an efficient "corporate liberal" state controlled by business interests and their government allies, American public-policy formulation seems to have been entirely too fragmented to support such notions of cooperation and foresight, to say nothing of the many setbacks to business interests that have peppered the history of regulatory agencies from the Progressive Era into our own time. [13] Insistent demands by organized private interests may have acted as a wedge to split the ideal of the public interest away from the structure of American government, but the cornerstone of the progressive-era state was fatally cracked from the very start. A broad, clear vein of partisanship ran through the whole of the new government structure and ruined any chance that it could support the expectations progressives piled onto it. Executive officeholders who doubled as ambitious partisan leaders were given the responsibility of advancing the public interest. Even though the governors and presidents of the progressive years embraced many reform issues, they connected public-policy decisions to the pluralistic competition for influence and political success.

Progressive political insurgency did not undermine partisanship so much as it pushed it in new directions, away from the nineteenth-century pattern of party identification and toward the modern emphasis on particular leaders and policy packages. As progressive political sentiment grew into revolts against corrupt or hidebound party hierarchies, new political leaders who identified themselves with progressive causes were thrust into prominence. As the nineteenth-century system of informal party government, which traded favors for loyalty during a period of unregulated national expansion, was challenged in the Progressive Era, the formal structure of state power increased. Progressive political leaders became the architects of responsible state power. However, just as the old party system used government weakness to build partisan strength, newly powerful executives in the Progressive Era used state power to fashion coalitions of interest groups into personal political organizations. In the hands of powerful officeholders, party organizations retained a decisive influence over public affairs.

Progressive political movements sprang from partisan roots and produced partisan reform fruits. Most progressive state governors were veteran politicians who split from regular party organizations after factional struggles. Robert La Follette, Albert Cummins of Iowa, Theodore Roosevelt in New York, California's Hiram Johnson, and other political leaders of reform were aggrieved partisans rather than nonpartisans. Strong-willed, ambitious, and sometimes unpleasant men, they combined reform principles with keen attention to their own political fortunes. Popular reformers without political experience managed to lead progressive campaigns as mayors or legislators, but they seldom rose to successful careers in higher office. Most of the midwestern reform mayors of the late nineteenth century who initiated struggles against utility companies were not professional politicians. Samuel Jones of Toledo, Tom Johnson of Cleveland, and Hazen Pingree of Detroit were all businessmen, whereas Brand Whitlock was a novelist. Johnson, who had served in Congress, most resembled the successful state progressive leaders. He attracted the personal loyalty of a talented circle of advisers, gained control of the local Democratic party machinery, and made a bid for statewide influence in Ohio. Still, Johnson remained too much an outsider to prevail. Jones made no attempt to build a political organization and died in office without ever seeking to rise higher. Whitlock followed Jones as four-term mayor of Toledo, but he was equally indifferent to political organization and hungered only for time in which to write. Pingree alone moved on to become a governor, but his inability to dominate the legislature and the state Republican organization made his two terms as chief executive of Michigan something of an anticlimax. For the most part, practical politicians such as La Follette, Hiram Johnson, and Theodore Roosevelt carried the reform standard into higher offices.[14]

Personal political organizations and partisan reform policies—the political style practiced in Illinois by Altgeld and Deneen—were the common building blocks of power for progressive governors, senators, and presidents. La Follette and Hiram Johnson best combined personal organizations and reform. La Follette began with a Republican faction opposed to the dominant wing of the state party. He built that faction of frustrated office-seekers and offended interest groups into a popular movement by aligning himself with the growing urban revolt against powerful corporations and compliant political parties. Using newspapers and his own charismatic personal appeal, La Follette redirected political debate to suit his issues and his strengths. Once in office, he packed conventions with his followers, made fealty to his issues the test of partisan loyalty, and pushed for a direct primary bill tailored to his political style. Even more than did La Follette, Hiram Johnson of California intertwined the prospects of reform with his personal ambition. Johnson set up his own political organization outside the insurgent Lincoln-Roosevelt League, insisted on personal power as governor, and refused to support his successor after being elevated to the Senate. Theodore Roosevelt brought personalism and partisan reform to the White House. As president, Roosevelt intended "to establish himself as the pre-eminent figure in the Republican party, to elevate the executive as the dominant force in national government, and to make that government the most important single influence in national affairs."[15] Woodrow Wilson, who as a political amateur might have qualified as the great exception to the pattern of progressive politicians, quickly developed into a demanding and self-promoting party leader.[16]

Across the United States, the new structure of politics and governance erected by hopeful progressives abetted the growth of personal political organizations headed by powerful officeholders. In Nebraska, for instance, the appearance of independent regulatory commissions and direct primary elections encouraged a new careerist attitude toward public office and the cultivation by political leaders of stable personal organizations within the existing political parties. The darker side of personalism can be seen in the popularity of southern "demagogues" during the Progressive Era. Politicians such as Jeff Davis of Arkansas and James K. Vardaman of Mississippi mobilized the hostility many white rural and small-town southerners felt toward the "interests" into rebellions against conservative Democratic regimes. Some standard elements of progressive politics—demands for railroad regulation and institutional improvements, attention to public opinion, and the personal charisma of reform leaders—accompanied ugly appeals to white supremacy and regional chauvinism on the rostrums of these politicians.[17]

The politics of demagoguery was not a pinched variant of progressivism; it lacked the commitment to practical problem solving, the faith in government authority, and the hope of achieving harmony through fidelity to the public interest that informed progressive political action. Nevertheless, as a parallel response to the changing political structure of twentieth-century America, demagoguery casts a brutal light on the two central imperfections of the progressive polity. First, Davis, Vardaman, and their fellows confirmed that political movements based on principles of confrontation and competition still attracted enthusiastic popular support. It would be unwise to consider the eagerness of demagogues to pitch their appeal to discrete social groups as a regional or time-bound phenomenon. In less sensational and vulgar style, La Follette hedged his bets on the unselfish public spirit of Wisconsin by pressing the agendas of dairy farmers and Scandinavians. Self-interest still fueled American politics. Second, the new politics of personality and government structure of executive authority allowed powerful and charismatic figures to shape public issues. Executives who were also ambitious partisan leaders found it possible to campaign by means of public policy. Partisan reform and executive power could produce a Frankenstein's monster such as Huey Long. More often, public policy making became a means for officeholders to determine the strength of contending interest groups and fashion reform packages that produced favorable alliances for future elections. The public interest blended into marketplace pluralism, in which all social groups are afforded opportunity to influence public policy, but the best organized gain disproportionate rewards.

The course of progressive-era politics in Illinois not only reflected the realities of progressive political struggles elsewhere, but, as Daniel Rodgers has observed, was "part of a major, lasting shift in the rules of the political game" in the United States.[18] As government assumed greater responsibilities for promoting the public interest, powerful officeholders and coalitions of self-interested groups worked to bend it to their narrower ends. Those forces, not a dispassionate appraisal of the public interest, shape modern public policy. In the early years of this century, progressive reformers found that the ideals of democracy, efficiency, and unselfish harmony could not smother partisanship in public life. In their optimistic pursuit of the public interest, progressives miscalculated the willingness of people to forfeit their personal interest for the sake of community progress, exaggerated the probity and effectiveness of government institutions, and overlooked the extent to which progressive nonpartisanship was itself an expression of a discrete agenda. We of the late twentieth century have lost the optimism of the progressives, but the problems that vexed them remain. The pioneering contributions progressives made to the health, safety, and happiness of society have been improved on in subsequent decades, but the underlying harmony they longed for still eludes us.

Notes

Introduction

1. See William A. Link, "Privies, Progressivism, and Public Schools: Health Reform and Education in the Rural South, 1909–1920," *Journal of Southern History* 54 (November 1988): 625, and Daniel T. Rodgers, "In Search of Progressivism," *Reviews in American History* 10 (December 1982): 113–32. The work of Richard L. McCormick is at the center of the new approach to progressive-era politics. McCormick's most important articles are gathered in *The Party Period and Public Policy: American Politics from the Age of Jackson to the Progressive Era* (New York: Oxford University Press, 1986); see also his pathbreaking monograph, *From Realignment to Reform: Political Change in New York State, 1893–1910* (Ithaca: Cornell University Press, 1981). Other important studies include Carl V. Harris, *Political Power in Birmingham, 1871–1921* (Knoxville: University of Tennessee Press, 1977); David C. Hammack, *Power and Society: Greater New York at the Turn of the Century* (New York: Russell Sage Foundation, 1982; reprint, New York: Columbia University Press, 1987); and Stephen Skowronek, *Building a New American State: The Expansion of National Administrative Capacities, 1877–1920* (New York: Cambridge University Press, 1982).

2. To my mind, the best short recent evaluations of progressivism are Rodgers, "In Search of Progressivism," and Richard L. McCormick, "Progressivism: A Contemporary Reassessment," in *Party Period and Public Policy*, 263–88. Valuable book-length treatments include Arthur S. Link and Richard L. McCormick, *Progressivism* (Arlington Heights, Ill.: Harlan Davidson, 1983), and John D. Buenker, John C. Burnham, and Robert M. Crunden, *Progressivism* (Cambridge, Mass.: Schenkman, 1977). The latter volume is particularly useful for its presentation of clashing political, cultural, and ethnic interpretations of progressivism. For a provocative treatment of progressivism as a religious and cultural phenomenon, see Robert M. Crunden, *Ministers of Reform: The Progressives' Achievement in American Civilization, 1889–1920* (New York: Basic Books, 1982; reprint, Urbana: University of Illinois Press, 1985). For a short survey of intellectual and cultural trends, see David W. Noble, *The Progressive Mind, 1890–1917* (Chicago:

Rand McNally, 1970). For an example of inventive cultural history, see T. J. Jackson Lears, *No Place of Grace: Antimodernism and the Transformation of American Culture, 1880–1920* (New York: Pantheon, 1981).

3. Rodgers, "In Search of Progressivism," 127.

4. Richard L. McCormick, "The Party Period and Public Policy: An Exploratory Hypothesis," in *Party Period and Public Policy*, 197–227, figs. 222; Michael E. McGerr, *The Decline of Popular Politics: The American North, 1865–1928* (New York: Oxford University Press, 1986); Samuel P. Hays, "The New Organizational Society" and "Political Parties and the Community-Society Continuum," in *American Political History as Social Analysis: Essays by Samuel P. Hays* (Knoxville: University of Tennessee Press, 1980), 244–63, 293–325. For patterns of voter turnout, see Paul Kleppner, *Who Voted? The Dynamics of Electoral Turnout, 1870–1980* (New York: Praeger, 1982), especially 32, 57.

5. McCormick, for example, points out that progressive regulation "embedded parties more firmly in the legal machinery of the elections than they had ever been before" ("Progressivism: A Contemporary Reassessment," 278).

6. Peter Filene, "An Obituary for the 'Progressive Movement,'" *American Quarterly* 22 (1970): 20–34.

7. The intellectual and social ferment in Illinois received a classic portrayal in Ray Ginger, *Altgeld's America: The Lincoln Ideal versus Changing Realities* (New York: Funk & Wagnalls, 1958; reprint, New York: New Viewpoints, 1973). On the Chicago School, see Darnell Rucker, *The Chicago Pragmatists* (Minneapolis: University of Minnesota Press, 1969). Two books by Allen F. Davis, *Spearheads for Reform: The Social Settlements and the Progressive Movement, 1890–1914* (New York: Oxford University Press, 1967) and *American Heroine: The Life and Legend of Jane Addams* (New York: Oxford University Press, 1973), are the essential starting points for understanding the settlement house movement. New treatments of Hull House include Rivka Shpak Lissak, *Pluralism and Progressives: Hull House and the New Immigrants, 1890–1919* (Chicago: University of Chicago Press, 1989), and Mina Carson, *Settlement Folk: Social Thought and the American Settlement Movement, 1885–1930* (Chicago: University of Chicago Press, 1990). For women's suffrage, see Steven M. Buechler, *The Transformation of the Woman Suffrage Movement: The Case of Illinois, 1850–1920* (New Brunswick: Rutgers University Press, 1986). The Chicago Vice Commission is analyzed in Paul Boyer, *Urban Masses and Moral Order in America, 1820–1920* (Cambridge, Mass.: Harvard University Press, 1978), 194–218, and Mark Thomas Connelly, *The Response to Prostitution in the Progressive Era* (Chapel Hill: University of North Carolina Press, 1980), chap. 5. The best new treatment of the Great Migration in Illinois is James R. Grossman, *Land of Hope: Chicago, Black Southerners, and the Great Migration* (Chicago: University of Chicago Press, 1989).

Chapter 1

1. David P. Thelen, *The New Citizenship: Origins of Progressivism in Wisconsin, 1885–1900* (Columbia: University of Missouri Press, 1972), 308.

2. Russel B. Nye, *Midwestern Progressive Politics* (East Lansing: Michigan State University Press, 1959; reprint, New York: Harper and Row, 1965), 223. For a detailed (although dated) chronicle of political reform in a state that experienced much in common with Illinois, see Hoyt Landon Warner, *Progressivism in Ohio 1897–1917* (Columbus: Ohio State University Press, 1964).

3. Ernest Bogart and Charles Thompson, *The Industrial State, 1870–1893* (Springfield: Illinois Centennial Commission, 1920).

4. William Bayard Hale, "Chicago—Its Struggle and Its Dream," *World's Work* 19 (April 1910): 12792.

5. A general history of Chicago architecture is Carl W. Condit, *The Chicago School of Architecture: A History of Commercial and Public Building in the Chicago Area, 1875–1925* (Chicago: University of Chicago Press, 1964). For Sullivan and Wright, see Robert M. Crunden, *Ministers of Reform: The Progressives' Achievement in American Civilization, 1889–1920* (New York: Basic Books, 1982; reprint, Urbana: University of Illinois Press, 1985), 139–42, 158–59.

6. For differing treatments of meat packing, muckraking, and the Pure Food and Drug Act, see Crunden, *Ministers of Reform*, 163–99, and John Braeman, "The Square Deal in Action: A Case Study in the Growth of the 'National Police Power,'" in John Braeman, Robert H. Bremner, and Everett Walters, eds., *Change and Continuity in Twentieth-Century America* (Columbus: Ohio State University Press, 1964), 35–80. For more on Sinclair, see Christopher P. Wilson, *The Labor of Words: Literary Professionalism in the Progressive Era* (Athens: University of Georgia Press, 1985), 113–40.

7. James T. Kloppenberg, *Uncertain Victory: Social Democracy and Progressivism in European and American Thought, 1870–1920* (New York: Oxford University Press, 1986), 43–45, 373–77. For the ideas of Dewey and his colleagues at the University of Chicago, see Darnell Rucker, *The Chicago Pragmatists* (Minneapolis: University of Minnesota Press, 1969). For another example of the link between activism and ideal community, see Robert M. Barry, "A Man and a City: George Herbert Mead in Chicago," in Michael Novak, ed., *American Philosophy and the Future: Essays for a New Generation* (New York: Scribner's, 1968), 176–81.

8. Jane Addams, "A Function of the Social Settlement," *Annals of the American Academy of Political and Social Science* 13 (May 16, 1899): 36.

9. For activism as citizenship, see Jane Addams, *Philanthropy and Social Progress* (New York: Crowell, 1893; reprint, Freeport, N.Y.: Books for Libraries Press, 1969), 55–56, 1, 4. For Dewey and Hull House, see Crunden, *Ministers of Reform*, 58–59.

10. For the impact of the settlement house movement on progressive activity, see Allen F. Davis, *Spearheads for Reform: The Social Settlements and the Progressive Movement, 1890–1914* (New York: Oxford University Press, 1967). Raymond Robins is profiled in "Raymond Robins," *The Public* 10 (September 21, 1907): 579–85; for Margaret, see Elizabeth Anne Payne, *Reform, Labor, and Feminism: Margaret Dreier Robins and the Women's Trade Union League* (Urbana: University of Illinois Press, 1988). For Kelley and Lathrop, see Allen Davis, *American Hero-*

ine: The Life and Legend of Jane Addams (New York: Oxford University Press, 1976), 75–77. Mead is treated in Rucker, *Chicago Pragmatists*, 20–22. For the activities of University of Chicago professors and members of civic clubs, see Steven J. Diner, *A City and Its Universities: Public Policy in Chicago, 1892–1919* (Chapel Hill: University of North Carolina Press, 1980).

11. Mead quoted in Rucker, *Chicago Pragmatists*, 47–48.

12. Addams, *Philanthropy and Social Progress*, 29, 30–31.

13. Jane Addams, *Democracy and Social Ethics* (New York: Macmillan, 1907), 257.

14. Addams, *Democracy and Social Ethics*, 254. For Addams's observations and conclusions about bosses and politics, see ibid., 224–77. An account of the Hull House campaign against Powers is presented in Davis, *Spearheads*, 152–62.

15. For a classic statement of the political hostility between urban centers and state government during the Progressive Era, see William L. Riordon, *Plunkitt of Tammany Hall* (New York: E. P. Dutton, 1963), 21–24, 65–68, 84–87. For an interpretation that downplays urban-rural conflict in midwestern state legislatures in the decades before 1900, see Ballard C. Campbell, *Representative Democracy: Public Policy and Midwestern Legislatures in the Late Nineteenth Century* (Cambridge, Mass.: Harvard University Press, 1980).

16. Morton Keller, "The Politics of State Constitutional Revision, 1820–1930," in Harold M. Hyman, *et al.*, eds., *The Constitutional Convention as an Amending Device* (Washington, D.C.: American Historical Association, 1981), 76.

17. Bogart and Thompson, *Industrial State*, 1–2. For national trends in the reduction of state and local governmental authority after the Civil War, see Morton Keller, *Affairs of State: Public Life in Late Nineteenth Century America* (Cambridge, Mass.: Harvard University Press, 1977), 110–14.

18. For state regulatory agencies, see William R. Brock, *Investigation and Responsibility: Public Responsibility in the United States, 1865–1900* (Cambridge: Cambridge University Press, 1984), especially table, 255–56. For growth of national state power, see Stephen Skowronek, *Building a New American State: The Expansion of National Administrative Capacities, 1877–1920* (New York: Cambridge University Press, 1982).

19. Statement of "The 29th Ward Woman's Civic League—Mary E. McDowell Chairman," March 1914, Mary E. McDowell Papers, Chicago Historical Society.

20. For examples of the democratic cost of efficiency and the erosion of administrative initiatives by political organizations and ethnic division in a number of American municipalities, see the essays in Michael H. Ebner and Eugene M. Tobin, eds., *The Age of Urban Reform: New Perspectives on the Progressive Era* (Port Washington, N.Y.: Kennikat Press, 1977).

21. The insights of Seymour J. Mandelbaum in *Boss Tweed's New York* (New York: John Wiley, 1965) remain germane in this regard.

22. Joseph F. Tripp, "An Instance of Labor and Business Cooperation: Workmen's Compensation in Washington State (1911)," *Labor History* 17 (Fall 1976):

530–50; Roy Lubove, "Workmen's Compensation and the Prerogatives of Voluntarism," *Labor History* 8 (Fall 1967): 258–59; Melvin I. Urofsky, "State Courts and Protective Legislation during the Progressive Era: A Reevaluation," *Journal of American History* 72 (June 1985): 83–91; James Weinstein, *The Corporate Ideal in the Liberal State, 1900–1918* (Boston: Beacon Press, 1968), 51–61.

23. Louise C. Wade, *Graham Taylor: Pioneer for Social Justice, 1851–1938* (Chicago: University of Chicago Press, 1964), 205–6.

24. Graham Taylor, *Pioneering on Social Frontiers* (Chicago: University of Chicago Press, 1930), vii-viii.

25. Graham Taylor, *Chicago Commons* (Chicago: Chicago Commons Association, 1904), 3.

26. Davis, *American Heroine*, 110.

27. Graham Taylor, *Religion in Social Action* (New York: Dodd, Mead, 1913), 246. This work was Taylor's major literary contribution to the Social Gospel movement, which had inspired his commitment to an active life of social service. See Wade, *Taylor*, 106–16. For the reciprocal impact of the Social Gospel and municipal political reform, see the connections between minister George D. Herron, Toledo mayor Samuel M. Jones, and Columbus clergyman turned city councilman Washington Gladden sketched out in Warner, *Progressivism in Ohio*, 23–46, and Robert M. Crunden, *A Hero in Spite of Himself: Brand Whitlock in Art, Politics, and War* (New York: Knopf, 1969), 88–104. A recent institutional treatment of the Social Gospel in the Progressive Era can be found in Donald K. Gorrell, *The Age of Social Responsibility: The Social Gospel in the Progressive Era, 1900–1920* (Macon, Ga.: Mercer University Press, 1988).

28. Morgan's youthful confrontations are mentioned in Eugene Staley, *A History of the Illinois State Federation of Labor* (Chicago: University of Chicago Press, 1929), 94. For Taylor, Morgan, and the free floor, see Taylor, *Pioneering*, 318–19. For discussion groups elsewhere, see Addams, *Philanthropy and Social Progress*, 52–54.

29. Mina Carson, *Settlement Folk: Social Thought and the American Settlement Movement, 1885–1930* (Chicago: University of Chicago Press, 1990), 120–21. Carson portrays the spectrum of settlement house opinion by placing Addams at its most democratic end and Robert Woods of Boston's South End House at the opposite extreme of expert supervision. Woods accepted class differences and more frankly advocated controls on working-class and immigrant behavior by means of enlightened middle-class influence and restrictive legislation. See Rivka Shpak Lissak, *Pluralism and Progressives: Hull House and the New Immigrants, 1890–1919* (Chicago: University of Chicago Press, 1989) for Hull House and immigrants.

30. Untitled, undated (1911?) draft of speech, 6–7, Ernst Freund Papers, Special Collections, University of Chicago Library.

31. Walter L. Lippmann, *Drift and Mastery: An Attempt to Diagnose the Current Unrest* (New York: Mitchell Kennerly, 1914; reprint, Englewood Cliffs, N.J.: Prentice-Hall, 1961), 115.

32. Richard L. McCormick, "The Party Period and Public Policy: An Ex-

ploratory Hypothesis," in McCormick, *The Party Period and Public Policy: American Politics from the Age of Jackson to the Progressive Era* (New York: Oxford University Press, 1986), 197–227. The major themes of the emerging "organizational society" treated in this paragraph are developed at length in Robert H. Wiebe, *The Search for Order: 1877–1920* (New York: Hill and Wang, 1967), and Burton J. Bledstein, *The Culture of Professionalism: The Middle Class and the Development of Higher Education in America* (New York: Norton, 1976), and analyzed acutely in Samuel P. Hays, "The New Organizational Society," in *American Political History as Social Analysis: Essays by Samuel P. Hays* (Knoxville: University of Tennessee Press, 1980), 244–63.

33. Daniel T. Rodgers, "In Search of Progressivism," *Reviews in American History* 10 (December 1982): 116.

34. Thelen, *The New Citizenship*, 225–89. The program of the municipal reformers was not uniformly successful. Wisconsin's cities failed to obtain municipal home rule during the progressive period (Thelen, 306).

35. Richard L. McCormick, "The Discovery that Business Corrupts Politics: A Reappraisal of the Origins of Progressivism," in *Party Period and Public Policy*, 311–56. McCormick extensively analyzes the case of New York in *From Realignment to Reform: Political Change in New York State, 1893–1910* (Ithaca: Cornell University Press, 1981).

36. Reform in Wisconsin is treated in Thelen, *The New Citizenship*, 225–49, 290–91, 302–8. For Pingree, see Melvin G. Holli, *Reform in Detroit: Hazen S. Pingree and Urban Politics* (New York: Oxford University Press, 1969), 61–124, 185–210. Ohio reform is covered in Warner, *Progressivism in Ohio*, 33, 54–79, 119–66. For more on Jones and Whitlock, see Crunden, *A Hero in Spite of Himself*, 127–29, 210–23. Johnson's campaigns are recounted by an admiring lieutenant in Frederic C. Howe, *The Confessions of a Reformer* (New York: Scribner's, 1925), 100–181.

37. Lincoln Steffens, *The Shame of the Cities* (New York: McClure, Phillips, 1904; reprint, New York: Hill and Wang, 1957), 3.

38. An overall picture of the reform campaigns appears in McCormick, "The Discovery that Business Corrupts Politics," 332–39. For the Armstrong investigation, see Morton Keller, *The Life Insurance Enterprise, 1885–1910: A Study in the Limits of Corporate Power* (Cambridge, Mass.: Harvard University Press, 1963), 245–59. Hughes's role in the investigation is presented in Robert F. Wesser, *Charles Evans Hughes: Politics and Reform in New York, 1905–1910* (Ithaca: Cornell University Press, 1967), 40–48. For Hiram Johnson, railroads, and California politics, see George E. Mowry, *The California Progressives* (Berkeley: University of California Press, 1951; reprint, New York: Quadrangle, 1963), 1–85; Spencer C. Olin, *California's Prodigal Sons: Hiram Johnson and the Progressives, 1911–1917* (Berkeley: University of California Press, 1968), 1–41; and R. Hal Williams, *The Democratic Party and California Politics, 1880–1896* (Stanford, Cal.: Stanford University Press, 1973), 206–32. For Alabama and Georgia, see Sheldon Hackney, *Populism to Progressivism in Alabama* (Princeton: Princeton University Press, 1969), 235–323, and Dewey W. Grantham, *Hoke Smith and the*

Politics of the New South (Baton Rouge: Louisiana State University Press, 1958), 131–55.

39. Steffens, *Shame of the Cities*, 162.

40. Graham Taylor, "Lincoln's Soul Goes Marching on in Illinois," *Survey* 24 (September 3, 1910): 754.

41. For a similar situation in California, see Martin J. Schiesl, "Politicians in Disguise: The Changing Role of Public Administrators in Los Angeles, 1900–1920," in Ebner and Tobin, *The Age of Urban Reform*, 102–16.

42. For an argument that the Democratic party was a receptacle for progressive values, see David Sarasohn, *The Party of Reform: Democrats in the Progressive Era* (Jackson: University Press of Mississippi, 1989).

43. David P. Thelen, *Robert La Follette and the Insurgent Spirit* (Boston: Little, Brown, 1976), 99–124.

44. Lippmann, *Drift and Mastery*, 96.

45. Crunden, *Ministers of Reform*, x.

46. For leading interpretations of the "new middle class" see Samuel P. Hays, *The Response to Industrialism: 1885–1914* (Chicago: University of Chicago Press, 1957), and Wiebe, *The Search for Order*. For the influence of businesspeople see Gabriel Kolko, *The Triumph of Conservatism* (New York: Free Press, 1963); Wiebe, *Businessmen and Reform* (Cambridge, Mass.: Harvard University Press, 1962); Weinstein, *Corporate Ideal in the Liberal State*; Mansel G. Blackford, *The Politics of Business in California, 1890–1920* (Columbus: Ohio State University Press, 1977); and Martin J. Sklar, *The Corporate Reconstruction of American Capitalism, 1890–1916: The Market, the Law, and Politics* (New York: Cambridge University Press, 1988).

47. Diner, *A City and Its Universities*, 52–75.

48. Diner, *A City and Its Universities*, 43–44, 138–47, 158, 165; Ernst Freund to Edgar A. Bancroft, December 18, 1918, Freund Papers; Freund to Efficiency and Economy Committee of the 49th General Assembly, July 3, 1914, Freund Papers; James Whittaker (secretary to Governor Charles Deneen) to Freund, December 19, 1912, Freund Papers. See also Oscar Kraines, *The World and Ideas of Ernst Freund* (Tuscaloosa: University of Alabama Press, 1974).

49. Untitled, undated (1911?) draft of speech, 5, Ernst Freund Papers.

50. Lippmann, *Drift and Mastery*, 135.

51. Taylor, *Religion in Social Action*, viii.

52. Raymond Robins to Margaret Dreier Robins, May 19, 1910, Raymond Robins Papers, State Historical Society of Wisconsin, Madison.

53. Barry D. Karl, *Charles E. Merriam and the Study of Politics* (Chicago: University of Chicago Press, 1974), 16. For an interpretation that stresses the Victorian background of progressives, see David B. Danbom, *"The World of Hope": Progressives and the Struggle for an Ethical Public Life* (Philadelphia: Temple University Press, 1987).

54. Draft of speech (1911?), Ernst Freund Papers.

55. John W. Chambers II, *The Tyranny of Change: America in the Progressive Era, 1900–1917* (New York: St. Martin's Press, 1980), 107–9, 119–25.

56. For a few examples, see John D. Buenker, *Urban Liberalism and Progressive Reform* (New York: Scribner's, 1973); Roy Rosenzweig, *Eight Hours for What We Will: Workers and Leisure in an Industrial City, 1870–1920* (New York: Cambridge University Press, 1983), 127–52; Payne, *Reform, Labor, and Feminism*.

57. David Paul Nord, *Newspapers and New Politics: Midwestern Municipal Reform, 1890–1900* (Ann Arbor: UMI Research Press, 1981).

58. For a detailed examination of this theme, see Keller, *Affairs of State*.

59. Charles McCarthy, *The Wisconsin Idea* (New York: Macmillan, 1912), 16.

60. Detailed studies have questioned the success of progressive initiatives in Wisconsin. See Stanley P. Caine, *The Myth of a Progressive Reform: Railroad Regulation in Wisconsin, 1903–1910* (Madison: State Historical Society of Wisconsin, 1970), and Elliot W. Brownlee, Jr., *Progressivism and Economic Growth: The Wisconsin Income Tax, 1911–1929* (Port Washington, N.Y.: Kennikat, 1974).

Chapter 2

1. Richard Hofstadter, *The Age of Reform: From Bryan to FDR* (New York: Vintage Books, 1955), 94–130; See also Fred A. Shannon, *The Farmer's Last Frontier: Agriculture, 1860–1897* (New York: Holt, Rinehart and Winston, 1945), 356–59. For a sympathetic treatment of the producer mentality among southern Populists, see Bruce Palmer, *"Man Over Money": The Southern Populist Critique of American Capitalism* (Chapel Hill: University of North Carolina Press, 1980).

2. For an early example of the agricultural modernization thesis, see H. E. Hoagland, "The Movement of Rural Population in Illinois," *Journal of Political Economy* 20 (November 1912): 913–27. Support for agricultural modernization can be found in Orville M. Kile, *The Farm Bureau through Three Decades* (Baltimore, Md.: Waverly Press, 1948), and Lex Renda, "The Advent of Agricultural Progressivism in Virginia," *The Virginia Magazine of History and Biography* 96 (January 1988): 55–82. Negative assessments appear in Grant McConnell, *The Decline of Agrarian Democracy* (Berkeley: University of California Press, 1953), and David B. Danbom, *The Resisted Revolution: Urban America and the Industrialization of Agriculture, 1900–1930* (Ames: Iowa State University Press, 1979). Danbom's stimulating suggestion that the Country Life Movement (which flourished for the first two decades of the twentieth century) attempted to bend rural America to urban ends should be balanced by the more sympathetic treatment in William L. Bowers, *The Country Life Movement in America, 1900–1920* (Port Washington, N.Y.: Kennikat Press, 1974).

3. Melvyn Hammarberg, *The Indiana Voter: The Historical Dynamics of Party Allegiance during the 1870s* (Chicago: University of Chicago Press, 1977), 127.

4. Ballard C. Campbell, *Representative Democracy: Public Policy and Midwestern Legislatures in the Late Nineteenth Century* (Cambridge, Mass.: Harvard University Press, 1980), 149.

5. For a comparison of Illinois agriculture with that of the northern Plains

and a breakdown of agricultural regions within the state, see Roy V. Scott, *The Agrarian Movement in Illinois, 1880–1896* (Urbana: University of Illinois Press, 1962), 6–13. For figures on agricultural production and farm tenantry, see United States, Department of Commerce, Bureau of the Census, *Tenth Census of the United States, 1880: Agriculture*, 44–47, 149–50, 185–86, and idem., *Thirteenth Census of the United States, 1910: Agriculture*, 6: 426–55.

6. For the standard treatment of the Granger movement (and the political timidity of the Grange), see Solon J. Buck, *The Granger Movement: A Study of Agricultural Organization and Its Political, Economic, and Social Manifestations, 1870–1880* (Cambridge, Mass.: Harvard University Press, 1913; reprint, Lincoln: University of Nebraska Press, 1963). For an interesting challenge to Buck that stresses the radical tendencies of the Grange (until 1873) and its founder, Oliver Kelley, see Thomas A. Woods, *Knights of the Plow: Oliver H. Kelley and the Origins of the Grange in Republican Ideology* (Ames: Iowa State University Press, 1991), especially 94–164.

7. Buck, *Granger Movement*, 74.

8. Quoted in Jonathan Periam, *The Groundswell: A History of the Origin, Aims, and Progress of the Farmers' Movement* (Chicago: Hannaford & Thompson, 1874), 227.

9. Buck, *Granger Movement*, 127–28.

10. Periam, *Groundswell*, 230.

11. Ernest L. Bogart and Charles M. Thompson, *The Industrial State 1870–1893* (Springfield: Illinois Centennial Commission, 1920), 3–4, 19; George M. Miller, *Railroads and the Granger Laws* (Madison: University of Wisconsin Press, 1971), 75–79.

12. Bogart and Thompson, *The Industrial State*, 90; *Chicago Tribune*, March 11, 18, 1871; Miller, *Railroads and the Granger Laws*, 83–86.

13. Periam, *Groundswell*, 296–97; for a representative case, see *Chicago Tribune*, March 21, 1873.

14. *Chicago Tribune*, January 16, 1873. Periam (*Groundswell*, 250) gave the number of delegates as 275, but the *Tribune* reported 800.

15. For the Bloomington convention, see *Chicago Tribune*, January 17, 18, 1873 (quotation is from January 17). For the Kewanee convention, see Periam, *Groundswell*, 232–41.

16. For the leaders of the Farmers' Association, see Periam, *Groundswell*, 233–34, 251–57, *Chicago Tribune*, January 10, 1873, and Miller, *Railroads and the Granger Laws*, 75. Details on Flagg are from Periam, *Groundswell*, 383–88, and Paul W. Gates, "Large-Scale Farming in Illinois, 1850 to 1870," *Agricultural History* 6 (January 1932): 24. Prime's land transactions are recounted in Chester M. Destler, "Agricultural Readjustment and Agrarian Unrest in Illinois, 1880–1896," *Agricultural History* 21 (April 1947): 110. For the vote rejecting the name Illinois State Farmers' and Mechanics Association, see *Chicago Tribune*, January 17, 1873.

17. *Chicago Tribune*, January 13, 1873.

18. Support for the farmers' movement can be found in the *Chicago Tribune*,

January 20, February 25, April 1, 2, 1873; for county farmer meetings, see *Chicago Tribune*, March 6, 12, 22, 1873; for Savage and the Will County meeting, see *Chicago Tribune*, February 20, 1873.

19. *Chicago Tribune*, April 3, 1873.

20. For the campaign to strengthen the Railroad and Warehouse Commission, see *Chicago Tribune*, January 18, 1873, and Buck, *Granger Movement*, 83–84, 145–49. The text of the altered law can be found in Periam, *Groundswell*, 302–9. For the appointment of commission members, see *Journal of the Senate of the 30th General Assembly of the State of Illinois* (Springfield: Illinois State Journal, 1873), 154, 226, 323, 325.

21. Miller, *Railroads and the Granger Laws*, 92–93; Edward F. Dunne, *Illinois* (Chicago: Lewis, 1933), 2: 128–29; for divisions in the Illinois State Farmers' Association, see *Chicago Tribune*, April 4, 1873.

22. Miller, *Railroads and the Granger Laws*, 89–90. For the decision, see *Chicago & Alton Railroad v. People ex rel. Koerner*, 67 Ill. 11 (1873).

23. *Chicago Tribune*, March 22, 1873.

24. Buck, *Granger Movement*, 85.

25. Hooton's remarks are reported in *Chicago Tribune*, April 16, 1873. For criticism of the Princeton convention, see *Chicago Tribune*, May 2, 1873; for a disputatious farmers' convention in the Twenty-third Judicial District, see *Chicago Tribune*, May 12, 1873. The farmer conventions and the election are covered in Periam, *Groundswell*, 312–15, and Buck, *Granger Movement*, 84–85.

26. *Chicago Tribune*, June 3, 1873. For election results, see *Chicago Tribune*, November 19, 1873.

27. For the third-party platform of the Farmers' Association, see Illinois Department of Agriculture, *Transactions 1873* (Springfield: State Journal, 1874), 200–201. Declining membership figures and fading support for third-party adventures can be traced in *Chicago Tribune*, April 3, 1873, and Buck, *Granger Movement*, 76, 89. For the drift of farmer organizations from the Anti-Monopoly to the Greenback party, see ibid., 98, and Paul Kleppner, *The Third Electoral System, 1853–1892: Parties, Voters, and Political Cultures* (Chapel Hill: University of North Carolina Press), 262–67.

28. The key agricultural organizations in Illinois were the Farmers' Mutual Benefit Association, the National Farmers' Alliance and Industrial Union (Southern Farmers' Alliance), the National Farmers' Alliance (Northern Farmers' Alliance), the Patrons of Husbandry (Grange), and the Patrons of Industry.

29. For the Southern Farmers' Alliance, see Robert C. McMath, Jr., *Populist Vanguard: A History of the Southern Farmers' Alliance* (Chapel Hill: University of North Carolina Press, 1975). Southern Populism is treated as a radical democratic social movement in Lawrence Goodwyn, *The Populist Moment: A Short History of the Agrarian Revolt in America* (New York: Oxford University Press, 1978). The fortunes of the People's party can best be followed in John Hicks, *The Populist Revolt: A History of the Farmers' Alliance and the People's Party* (Minneapolis: University of Minnesota Press, 1931; reprint, Lincoln: University of Ne-

braska Press, 1961). For an excellent account of the problems that beset Populist politics at the state level, see Barton C. Shaw, *The Wool-Hat Boys: Georgia's Populist Party* (Baton Rouge: Louisiana State University Press, 1984).

30. Scott, *Agrarian Movement*, 37–61.

31. Ibid., 63–68.

32. Ibid., 86–88.

33. Chester M. Destler, "The People's Party in Illinois, 1888–1896; A Phase of the Populist Revolt" (Ph.D. diss., University of Chicago, 1932), 54–59.

34. Scott, *Agrarian Movement*, 84.

35. *Effingham Republican,* May 30, 1890, clipping in Walter C. Headen Papers, Illinois Historical Survey, University of Illinois Library, Urbana.

36. Destler, "People's Party in Illinois," 58–61; Scott, *Agrarian Movement,* 93–95, 100–101.

37. For the Democratic and Alliance platforms, see *Appletons' Annual Cyclopedia* (New York: D. Appleton, 1891), 428–29; Scott, *Agrarian Movement,* 98–101; Bogart and Thompson, *The Industrial State,* 179.

38. *Chicago Times,* January 12, 1891, clipping in Headen Papers.

39. *Rockford Register-Gazette,* March 25, 1891.

40. *Rockford Register-Gazette,* February 12, March 11, 1891; Scott, *Agrarian Movement,* 105–17.

41. Scott, *Agrarian Movement,* 118–24.

42. For the faction-ridden history of the Illinois People's party, see Chester M. Destler, *American Radicalism, 1865–1901* (New London: Connecticut College, 1946), 162–211.

43. For the rise of the commercial butter industry, see Bogart and Thompson, *The Industrial State,* 252–53; on country butter, see Shannon, *Farmer's Last Frontier,* 256–58. For complaints against oleomargarine and the movement to regulate it, see *Chicago Produce* 2 (January 18, 1896): 24; *Chicago Produce* 3 (April 3, 1897): 10; James Harvey Young, *Pure Food: Securing the Federal Food and Drugs Act of 1906* (Princeton, N.J.: Princeton University Press, 1989), 71–94; and Morton Keller, *Affairs of State: Public Life in Late Nineteenth Century America* (Cambridge, Mass.: Harvard University Press, 1977), 413. On the oleomargarine industry, see Johannes H. van Stuijvenberg, ed., *Margarine: An Economic, Social and Scientific History* (Toronto: University of Toronto Press, 1969).

44. *Chicago Produce* 2 (January 25, 1896): 2.

45. Charles Y. Knight to Lawrence Y. Sherman, May 10, 1897, Lawrence Y. Sherman Papers, Illinois State Historical Library, Springfield; *Chicago Produce* 3 (February 20, 1897): 8; ibid. (March 20, 1897): 18; ibid. (March 27, 1897): 10–11.

46. See, for example, *Chicago Produce* 3 (April 10, 1897): 2; ibid. (April 24, 1897): 2, 14; ibid. (May 8, 1897): 12; ibid. (May 22, 1897): 2.

47. Undated (probably 1898) draft of speech, Sherman Papers. Knight pursued Sherman into the next election, sending circulars into his district requesting the local farmers to turn him out of office; see Illinois Dairy Union circular dated

April 21, 1898, Sherman Papers. The ploy failed, and the two mended fences in the next legislative session; see Knight to Sherman, March 31, 1899, Sherman Papers.

48. *Chicago Produce* 3 (April 24, 1897): 1; ibid. (May 29, 1897): 1; *Chicago Produce* 4 (June 5, 1897): 1.

49. Illinois State Dairymen's Association, *Annual Report 1900*, 39.

50. Dairymen's Association, *Annual Report 1908*, 156–57.

51. Dairymen's Association, *Annual Report 1900*, 151.

52. Ibid., 189.

53. *Farmers' Voice*, January 20, 1900, 5; Dairymen's Association, *Annual Report 1900*, 35–39, 150–51.

54. The Illinois Bankers' Association, Chicago Board of Trade, and such corporations as International Harvester and Sears helped bankroll the county agent system that made possible the organization of the Illinois Agricultural Association. See McConnell, *Decline of Agrarian Democracy*, 30; Bowers, *Country Life Movement*, 20; Theodore Saloutos and John D. Hicks, *Agricultural Discontent in the Middle West 1900–1939* (Madison: University of Wisconsin Press, 1951), 263–64; William B. Storm, "An Analysis of the Illinois Agricultural Association as a Pressure Group for Farmers," (Ph.D. diss., University of Chicago, 1951), chap. 2, p. 10.

55. Following the Civil War, the first American campaigns against adulterated food focused on milk, "the most basic food item." See Mitchell Okun, *Fair Play in the Marketplace: The First Battle for Pure Food and Drugs* (De Kalb: Northern Illinois University Press, 1986). For earlier battles against "swill" milk, see Young, *Pure Food*, 35–39. The latest study of children's health reform is Richard A. Meckel, *Save the Babies: American Public Health Reform and the Prevention of Infant Mortality, 1850–1929* (Baltimore: Johns Hopkins University Press, 1990). On the campaign for clean milk in Milwaukee, see Judith W. Leavitt, *The Healthiest City: Milwaukee and the Politics of Health Reform* (Princeton, N.J.: Princeton University Press, 1982), 156–89. For New York, see John E. Sayles, "Clean Milk for New York City," *Survey* 17 (January 12, 1907): 677–84; Ernst J. Lederle, "The Sanitary Control of New York's Milk Supply," *Survey* 27 (October 21, 1911): 1034–37; *Survey* 28 (April 13, 1912): 90–91. For Baltimore, see Harlean James, "How a Civic League Secured a Clean Milk Supply," *Survey* 33 (January 16, 1915): 421–22.

56. For the agricultural service-state, see Elliot W. Brownlee, Jr., *Progressivism and Economic Growth: The Wisconsin Income Tax, 1911–1929* (Port Washington, N.Y.: Kennikat Press, 1974), 72–73. Examples of progressive dairying can be found in Keach Johnson, "Iowa Dairying at the Turn of the Century: The New Agriculture and Progressivism," *Agricultural History* 45 (April 1971): 95–110; for Virginia, Renda, "Advent of Agricultural Progressivism," 74–77; and, for Wisconsin, Eric E. Lampard, *The Rise of the Dairy Industry in Wisconsin* (Madison: University of Wisconsin Press, 1963). For La Follette and dairy farmers, see David P. Thelen, *The New Citizenship: Origins of Progressivism in Wisconsin, 1885–1900* (Columbia: University of Missouri Press, 1972), 299.

57. Okun, *Fair Play*, 185–87.

58. *Chicago Tribune*, February 2, 1911.

59. Dairymen's Association, *Annual Report 1915*, 14.

60. Dairymen's Association, *Annual Report 1918*, 12. The association campaigned ardently against oleomargarine, but on the grounds that the new product was fraudulently marketed as butter. It was not therefore a public health question.

61. Dairymen's Association, *Annual Report 1906*, 156; Ernest L. Bogart and John M. Mathews, *The Modern Commonwealth 1893–1918* (Springfield: Illinois Centennial Commission, 1920), 431.

62. Dairymen's Association, *Annual Report 1910*, 15–16. For efficiency guidelines, see *Report of the State Food Commissioner of Illinois 1910*, 10, and *Food Commissioner Report 1901*, 23. Comparisons of dairy cattle to factory machinery were fairly common in the association's *Annual Report*, as was the constant exhortation that farmers keep careful records and adopt businesslike attitudes toward dairying. Such strictures also appeared in the popular agricultural press. See *Farmers' Voice*, February 10, 1900, 177, and July 15, 1908, 3; *Prairie Farmer* 72 (November 10, 1900): 5 and 78 (November 15, 1906): 6.

63. Dairymen's Association, *Annual Report 1907*, 37.

64. Dairymen's Association, *Annual Report 1901*, 134.

65. *Chicago Tribune*, September 23, 1892. Inspectors from the newly created State Food Commission reported similar conditions in 1899 (*Food Commissioner Report 1899–1900*, 25–27). For similar conditions in mid-nineteenth-century New York, see Okun, *Fair Play*, 18–20.

66. *Chicago Tribune*, January 19, 1902.

67. Dairymen's Association, *Annual Report 1903*, 57.

68. Dairymen's Association, *Annual Report 1904*, 17.

69. Dairymen's Association, *Annual Report 1901*, 56, 273–78.

70. Dairymen's Association, *Annual Report 1910*, 140–41.

71. For the text of the law, see Dairymen's Association, *Annual Report 1901*, 283–92, quotation on 284; see also *Food Commissioner Report 1899–1900*, 2–3; *Farmers' Voice*, June 9, 1900, 698–99. For the anti-oleomargarine National Dairy Union's support of the bill, see Charles Y. Knight to Lawrence Y. Sherman, March 31, 1899, Sherman Papers.

72. *Chicago Tribune*, February 7, 1906. With a greenhorn's enthusiasm, Patterson insisted on personally milking one of the cows undergoing a state test. The technical personnel conducting the test indulged the assistant commissioner then discreetly excluded his pail from the analysis (*Food Commissioner Report 1903*, 66).

73. Dairymen's Association, *Annual Report 1905*, 128–31. For a similar attempt by Yates to use the Illinois Farmers' Institute for political advantage, see *Farmers' Voice*, April 19, 1902, 3.

74. *Farmers' Voice*, January 18, 1902, 7; Dairymen's Association, *Annual Report 1902*, 165, 169–71. There were 100,000 dairies in the state by 1912 (*Food Commissioner Report 1912*, 24).

75. Dairymen's Association, *Annual Report 1905*, 242–43; *Annual Report 1906*, 342.

76. The mayor of Marengo, Illinois, located nearly thirty miles from Chicago, testified that "most of our farmers have dairies and the majority of them produce milk for the Chicago market" (Dairymen's Association, *Annual Report 1908*, 11).

77. Inspection figures are from *Report and Handbook of the Department of Health of the City of Chicago for the Years 1911 to 1918 Inclusive* (Chicago, 1919), 857. For dirt in milk, see Dairymen's Association, *Annual Report 1906*, 180; for milk production in the Chicago region and the need for tighter standards of cleanliness, see idem., *Annual Report 1904*, 98–99. See also *Food Commissioner Report 1909*, 174.

78. Dairymen's Association, *Annual Report 1907*, 126–28.

79. Ibid., 132.

80. Dairymen's Association, *Annual Report 1907*, 128.

81. Ibid., 129.

82. Ibid., 127–33. Schuknecht's successor reported in 1911 that the campaign of publicity and prosecutions greatly reduced the adulteration of milk with formaldehyde (*Food Commissioner Report 1911*, 200).

83. *City Club Bulletin* 1 (May 1, 1907): 129.

84. Chicago Department of Health, *Report 1911–18*, 855.

85. Dairymen's Association, *Annual Report 1908*, 163.

86. *Chicago Tribune*, May 9, 1907. For the federal law, see John Braeman, "The Square Deal in Action: A Case Study in the Growth of the 'National Police Power,'" in John Braeman, Robert H. Bremner, and Everett Walters, eds., *Change and Continuity in Twentieth-Century America* (Columbus: Ohio State University Press, 1964), 35–80.

87. *Chicago Tribune*, April 24, 1907.

88. *Chicago Tribune*, April 20, 23, 1907. Health Commissioner Evans of Chicago noted that the original draft of the bill "was introduced in rather an immature form and admittedly required a good deal of amendment." He apparently had no objection to the alterations proposed by the Elgin Board of Trade (*City Club Bulletin* 1 [May 1907]: 128). An outbreak of scarlet fever in Chicago, traced to tainted milk shipped from Wisconsin, increased public clamor for stricter supervision of milk (*Prairie Farmer* 79 [February 7, 1907]: 10).

89. Dairymen's Association, *Annual Report 1905*, 191; Danbom, *Resisted Revolution*, 84–85. Association member and Assistant Food Commissioner John E. Newman lamented in 1911 that "if the farmers would only attend the dairy meetings, convention and farmers' institutes and profit by the valuable lectures given to them free gratis at these meetings, the benefits to them would be manifest within two years" (*Food Commissioner Report 1911*, 27).

90. *Farmers' Voice*, January 17, 1903, 6; Dairymen's Association, *Annual Report 1919*, 19.

91. *Farmers' Voice*, March 15, 1912, 14. See also Dairymen's Association, *Annual Report 1913*, 52; *Annual Report 1910*, 34.

92. *Farmers' Voice*, January 1916, 357; Dairymen's Association, *Annual Report 1906*, 180–81; *Annual Report 1915*, 95–96.

93. *Farmers' Voice*, October 1, 1908, 5.

94. Dairymen's Association, *Annual Report 1908*, 163; *Annual Report 1907*, 128.

95. Dairymen's Association, *Annual Report 1907*, 45.

96. *Prairie Farmer* 79 (May 16, 1907): 1; for Shurtleff's actions, see *Chicago Tribune*, April 20, 22, 1907.

97. *Chicago Tribune*, April 22, 1907. See also *Prairie Farmer* 79 (May 16, 1907): 1.

98. *Chicago Tribune*, April 23, 24, May 1, 1907.

99. *City Club Bulletin* 1 (May 1, 1907): 130.

100. Dairymen's Association, *Annual Report 1908*, 79.

101. Dairymen's Association, *Annual Report 1910*, 120. With only two inspectors devoting their full attention to dairy matters, Newman complained that his "entire force" could be kept "more than busy in either the North, South or West Side of the city of Chicago alone" (*Food Commissioner Report 1910*, 22; for the number of inspectors, see *Food Commissioner Report 1909*, 23).

102. *Chicago Tribune*, April 2, 1911.

103. Chicago Department of Health, *Report 1911–1918*, 858; *City Club Bulletin* 2 (May 13, 1909): 447; Sherman C. Kingsley, "On the Trail of the White Hearse," *Survey* 22 (August 14, 1909): 685–87.

104. Dairymen's Association, *Annual Report 1910*, 37. For the nature of tuberculosis (in all its forms) and the effort to eradicate the disease, see J. Arthur Myers, *Man's Greatest Victory over Tuberculosis* (Springfield: Charles C. Thomas, 1940) and Michael E. Teller, *The Tuberculosis Movement: A Public Health Campaign in the Progressive Era* (Westport, Conn.: Greenwood Press, 1988).

105. *Farmers' Voice*, August 15, 1908, 7; ibid., May 15, 1912, 7; Dairymen's Association, *Annual Report 1911*, 187–88, 206; *Prairie Farmer* 79 (January 24, 1907): 10.

106. *Prairie Farmer* 75 (May 7, 1903): 1.

107. The appraised value of slaughtered animals averaged $40 per head; compensation averaged $17 per head (*Chicago Tribune*, January 9, 1901; for the proclamation, see *Chicago Tribune*, June 14, 1899). By 1901, eighteen states required tuberculin tests before dairy or breeding cattle could be imported. In 1894, Massachusetts paid full appraised value (up to $60) for slaughtered tubercular cows but stopped the practice because of a nearly 50 percent reactor rate. Many Massachusetts farmers apparently took advantage of the tuberculosis bounty to rid themselves of ailing or unproductive (but uninfected) cattle at state expense (Myers, *Victory*, 272–74; Teller, *Tuberculosis Movement*, 19).

108. Dairymen's Association, *Annual Report 1901*, 293. See also *Chicago Tribune*, January 1, 1901. For similar sentiments elsewhere in the nation, see Myers, *Victory*, 345–47.

109. *Farmers' Voice*, June 20, 1903, 2; *Report of Illinois Attorney General 1902*,

78; *Report of Illinois Attorney General 1904*, 76. For the decision, see *Pierce vs. Dillingham*, 203 Ill., 148.

110. Dairymen's Association, *Annual Report 1909*, 99–100.

111. Dairymen's Association, *Annual Report 1909*, 109.

112. *Farmers' Voice*, December 1, 1908, 9; ibid., February 15, 1913, 7; Dairymen's Association, *Annual Report 1911*, 191–96.

113. Dairymen's Association, *Annual Report 1909*, 104 (quotation), 107; *Annual Report 1911*, 214.

114. Dairymen's Association, *Annual Report 1909*, 103.

115. Dairymen's Association, *Annual Report 1909*, 180–81; *Annual Report 1910*, 119: *Annual Report 1916*, 220–21.

116. This particular term recurred frequently. See, for example, *Farmers' Voice*, April 15, 1912, 10.

117. Dairymen's Association, *Annual Report 1910*, 39–40; *Annual Report 1911*, 201; *Annual Report 1909*, 109. Some New England dairy farmers bribed veterinarians to certify untested cows (Myers, *Victory*, 345).

118. Dairymen's Association, *Annual Report 1909*, 20, 108. See also *Annual Report 1911*, 204.

119. *Journal of the Illinois House of Representatives 1911*, 153.

120. Dairymen's Association, *Annual Report 1911*, 213–14.

121. *City Club Bulletin* 2 (May 13, 1909): 435–36, 443–44; Chicago Department of Health, *Report 1911–18*, 853. The city council also passed ordinances applying the same standards to butter and cheese. The ordinances are printed in *Illinois House Journal 1907*, 138–39.

122. Chicago Department of Health, *Report 1911–18*, 855, 858, 901; *City Club Bulletin* 2 (May 13, 1909): 442, 444. See also *Survey* 24 (April 16, 1910): 100.

123. *City Club Bulletin* 2 (May 13, 1909): 437.

124. In 1918, only eight farms produced certified milk for Chicago (Chicago Department of Health, *Report 1911–18*, 908).

125. Ibid., 13–29, 203; *Farmers' Voice*, May 1907, 1–3; *Prairie Farmer* 78 (March 22, 1906): 6; *Chicago Tribune*, February 7, 1911. Three days before Durand claimed her ten cattle were condemned unfairly, Chicago health authorities had conducted a "showdown" slaughter of tuberculin test reactors before suspicious members of the Milk Producers' Association (*Chicago Tribune*, February 4, 1911).

126. Chicago Department of Health, *Report 1911–18*, 858.

127. *Chicago Tribune*, March 27, 1909.

128. *Illinois House Journal 1911*, 141, 152.

129. Ibid., 184.

130. Ibid., 183 and, more generally, 137–96. The committee reasoned that because Chicago had a 15 percent higher tuberculosis death rate than thirty-four smaller Illinois cities, milk could not be an important carrier of the disease because Chicagoans consumed less milk per capita than did the residents of the smaller, healthier cities (*House Journal 1911*, 182–83).

131. *Chicago Tribune,* January 19, 1911.

132. *Illinois House Journal 1911,* 190.

133. *Chicago Tribune,* January 20, 1911.

134. *Illinois House Journal 1911,* 616–17; William T. Hutchinson, *Lowden of Illinois* (Chicago: University of Chicago Press, 1957), 2: 498.

135. Steven J. Diner, *A City and Its Universities: Public Policy in Chicago, 1892–1919* (Chapel Hill: University of North Carolina Press, 1980), 136.

136. *Illinois House Journal 1911,* 183; Dairymen's Association, *Annual Report 1914,* 146; *Annual Report 1916,* 220–21; *Annual Report 1919,* 131–32; Illinois Agricultural Association, *The Story of the I.A.A. and Report for 1926,* 10. Even with government compensation, the "loss was heavy" for owners of condemned tubercular cows (Hutchinson, *Lowden of Illinois,* 2: 498).

137. Dairymen's Association, *Annual Report 1914,* 128.

138. *Survey* 28 (August 31, 1912): 680; Chicago Department of Health, *Report 1911–18,* 891–92; Citizens' Association of Chicago, *Annual Report, October, 1912,* 7; Dairymen's Association, *Annual Report 1915,* 184. See also Dairymen's Association, *Annual Report 1918,* 130–31.

139. Dairymen's Association, *Annual Report 1914,* 130.

140. Dairymen's Association, *Annual Report 1907,* 55.

141. Chicago Department of Health, *Report 1911–18,* 926–34; C. S. Duncan, "The Chicago Milk Inquiry," *Journal of Political Economy* 26 (April 1918): 322–42.

Chapter 3

1. Jane Addams, *Twenty Years at Hull-House* (New York: Macmillan, 1910; reprint, New York: Signet, 1960), 160–61.

2. Michael Kazin, *Barons of Labor: The San Francisco Building Trades and Union Power in the Progressive Era* (Urbana: University of Illinois Press, 1987), 285.

3. Elizabeth Anne Payne, *Reform, Labor, and Feminism: Margaret Dreier Robins and the Women's Trade Union League* (Urbana: University of Illinois Press, 1988), 120–21, 156–69. For similar ideas within the settlement house movement, see Rivka Shpak Lissak, *Pluralism and Progressives: Hull House and the New Immigrants, 1890–1919* (Chicago: University of Chicago Press, 1989), 23, and Mina Carson, *Settlement Folk: Social Thought and the American Settlement Movement, 1885–1930* (Chicago: University of Chicago Press, 1990), 81.

4. David Montgomery, *The Fall of the House of Labor: The Workplace, the State, and American Labor Activism, 1865–1925* (Cambridge: Cambridge University Press, 1987), 269.

5. John H. M. Laslett, *Labor and the Left: A Study of Socialist and Radical Influences in the American Labor Movement, 1881–1921* (New York: Basic Books, 1970), 205; Montgomery, *Fall,* 371. For community action among packing house

workers, see James R. Barrett, *Work and Community in the Jungle: Chicago's Pack-inghouse Workers, 1894–1922* (Urbana: University of Illinois Press, 1987).

6. Montgomery, *Fall,* 269–72; Barrett, *Jungle,* 176–82; Richard Oestreicher, "Urban Working-Class Political Behavior and Theories of American Electoral Politics, 1870–1940," *Journal of American History* 74 (March 1988): 1270–73.

7. David Brody, *Workers in Industrial America: Essays on the 20th Century Struggle* (New York: Oxford University Press, 1980), 27.

8. For Gompers and political participation, see Marc Karson, *American Labor Unions and Politics, 1900–1918* (Carbondale: Southern Illinois University Press, 1958), 29–41; a different interpretation is offered in Gwendolyn Mink, *Old Labor and New Immigrants in American Political Development: Union, Party, and State, 1875–1920* (Ithaca: Cornell University Press, 1986). For state-level labor lob-bies, see Gary M. Fink, *Labor's Search for Political Order: The Political Behavior of the Missouri Labor Movement, 1890–1940* (Columbia: University of Missouri Press, 1973), 1–23; Philip Taft, *Labor Politics American Style: The California State Federation of Labor* (Cambridge, Mass.: Harvard University Press, 1968), 10; and Irwin Yellowitz, *Labor and the Progressive Movement in New York State, 1897–1916* (Ithaca: Cornell University Press, 1965), 23–26. For San Francisco, see Kazin, *Barons of Labor,* 13–31, 177–202.

9. Fink, *Labor's Search,* 53. For the weakness of state labor federations, see Taft, *Labor Politics,* 3–4, and Yellowitz, *Labor and the Progressive Movement,* 26–39.

10. Charles E. Merriam, *Chicago: A More Intimate View of Urban Politics* (New York: Macmillan, 1929), 115.

11. Leon Fink, *Workingmen's Democracy: The Knights of Labor and American Politics* (Urbana: University of Illinois Press, 1983), 226.

12. Richard Schneirov, "Haymarket and the New Political History Reconsid-ered: Workers' Presence in Chicago's Municipal Politics, 1873–1894," unpub-lished paper presented at the annual meeting of the Organization of American Historians, April 13, 1986, New York City. See also Edward B. Mittelman, "Chi-cago Labor in Politics," *Journal of Political Economy* 28 (May 1920): 407–27.

13. Illinois State Federation of Labor, *Proceedings 1905,* 19.

14. For the ISFL's claim to be the largest state labor federation "in the world," see ISFL, *Proceedings 1911,* 10. Membership numbers for 1913 are taken from idem., *Proceedings 1918,* 38. The percentage of labor bills that focused on rail-roads and mining is based on lists of successful bills found in State of Illinois, Bureau of Labor Statistics, *Labor Legislation in the Forty-Sixth General Assembly of Illinois* (Springfield: Illinois State Journal, 1909), 200–202; ISFL, *Proceedings 1911,* 12, idem., *Proceedings 1913,* 29–30; idem., *Proceedings 1915,* 53; idem., *Proceedings 1917,* 78–79; and idem., *Proceedings 1919,* 101.

15. Eugene Staley, *A History of the Illinois State Federation of Labor* (Chicago: University of Chicago Press, 1929), 59–130.

16. Staley, *State Federation,* 193. The official quoted was Edwin Wright, ISFL president from 1906 to 1913.

17. Staley, *State Federation,* 131–39, 189–93.

18. For the weakness of ISFL legislative and electoral influence until 1907, see Staley, *State Federation*, 230, 234, and ISFL, *Proceedings 1905*, 18–19. The legislative scorecard can be found in idem., *Proceedings 1915*, 107–34. For the endorsement of candidates, see John H. Oltman to Victor Olander, July 29, 1916, Olander to John H. Walker, August 3, 1916, and Walker to Olander, August 8, 1916, John H. Walker Papers, Illinois Historical Survey, University of Illinois Library, Urbana.

19. In a 1916 address, IMA president Samuel M. Hastings emphasized the importance of unity: "Twelve or thirteen hundred firms standing together for a one hundred percent result have more strength than five thousand firms that will not march in the same column. You are like the Spartan six hundred, and while our membership may seem somewhat small when compared with the number of manufacturing concerns in Illinois, it is much better that we should remain as we are than to have a larger membership with a divided effort" (Illinois Manufacturers' Association, *Proceedings of the Annual Meeting* [Chicago, 1916], 62 [hereafter designated *Annual Report*]).

20. Mansel G. Blackford, *The Politics of Business in California, 1890–1920* (Columbus: Ohio State University Press, 1977). For the appearance of anti-labor business trade associations, see Isaac F. Marcosson, "The Fight for the 'Open Shop,'" *World's Work* 11 (December 1905): 6955; Ray Stannard Baker, "Organized Capital Challenges Organized Labor," *McClure's* 23 (July 1904): 279–92; and William F. Willoughby, "Employers' Associations for Dealing with Labor in the United States," *Quarterly Journal of Economics* 20 (November 1905): 110–50. For the evolution of these organizations, see Robert H. Wiebe, *Businessmen and Reform: A Study of the Progressive Movement* (Cambridge, Mass.: Harvard University Press, 1962; reprint, Chicago: Quadrangle, 1968), 18–23.

21. For the activities of the National Association of Manufacturers and its relationship with the IMA, see Clarence E. Bonnett, *Employers' Associations in the United States* (New York: Macmillan, 1922), 291–92, 296–301. IMA membership figures can be found in George E. Stephens, "The IMA—A National Institution," *Manufacturers' News* 16 (December 14, 1922): 30; IMA, *Annual Report 1910*, 43–44; and idem., *Annual Report 1915*, 29. For commercial rivalries, see ibid., 66.

22. For the development of mining regulation in Illinois prior to Altgeld's election, see Earl R. Beckner, *Labor Legislation in Illinois* (Chicago: University of Chicago Press, 1929), 290–93. For progressive-era mining regulation in general, see William Graebner, *Coal-Mining Safety in the Progressive Period* (Lexington: University Press of Kentucky, 1976). The creation of the Illinois Railroad and Warehouse Commission is covered in George H. Miller, *Railroads and the Granger Laws* (Madison: University of Wisconsin Press, 1971), 86–87. On Altgeld and his lieutenants, see Harvey Wish, "The Administration of Governor John Peter Altgeld of Illinois, 1893–1897" (Ph.D. diss., Northwestern University, 1936), 24–28.

23. For Florence Kelley and the origins of the sweatshop act, see Kathryn Kish Sklar, "Hull House in the 1890s: A Community of Women Reformers,"

Signs 10 (Summer 1985): 665–71; Florence Kelley, "I Go to Work," *Survey* 58 (June 1, 1927): 272; Addams, *Hull-House*, 150–52; and Wish, "Altgeld," 232–36. For the enforcement of the law, see Illinois State Factory Inspector, *First Annual Report of the Factory Inspectors of Illinois for the Year Ending December 15, 1893*. The sweatshop act provided for twelve factory inspectors and authorized the granting of $14,000 to the new department (Factory Inspector, *Annual Report 1895*, 125).

24. Illinois Manufacturers' Association Board of Directors Minutes, August 24, 1893, February 14, 1894, IMA Papers, Chicago Historical Society; Stephens, "National Institution," 27; *Constitution and By-Laws of the Illinois Manufacturers' Association* (Chicago, 1896), 5–6, IMA Papers; J. E. Tilt to Manufacturers of Illinois, 1894, IMA Papers.

25. Beckner, *Labor Legislation*, 188–89. The IMA resolution to pay the attorneys' fees for member firms is in IMA Minutes, April 19, 1894, IMA Papers. For Kelley's reports, briefs filed in the case, and the decision, see Factory Inspector, *Annual Report 1894*, 58–59, 73–99; idem., *Annual Report 1895*, 5–7, 128–38; and *Ritchie v. People*, 155 Ill. 98 (1895).

26. In 1901 IMA president Martin Madden said of Glenn: "To him, more than to any other man is due the credit of the influence wielded by the Association (IMA, *Annual Report 1901*, 2); *Who Was Who in America*, vol. 1, 1897–1942 (Chicago: A. N. Marquis, 1943), 461; Alfred H. Kelly, "A History of the Illinois Manufacturers' Association" (Ph.D. diss., University of Chicago, 1938), 20–23, 82 n. 13.

27. IMA pamphlet, "Power is in Acting Together," January 1900, 5, IMA Papers.

28. For the activities of the membership committee, see Auxiliary Membership Committee to Pontiac Stove Mnfg. Co., November 10, 1908, IMA Papers, and IMA circular, "Gentlemen of the Membership Committee," 1909, IMA Papers. Increases in IMA membership can be charted in Glenn to T. C. Louche & Co., June 29, 1909, IMA Papers; untitled IMA pamphlet, October 21, 1909, IMA Papers; Samuel M. Hastings to Benjamin Barron, June 30, 1911, IMA Papers; IMA pamphlet, "The Reason Why," IMA Papers; and IMA *Annual Report 1917*, 38. For the number of manufacturers in Illinois, see United States Department of Commerce and Labor, Bureau of the Census, *Thirteenth Census of the United States, 1910: Manufacturers*, 9: 254; for East St. Louis, see the list of firms in East St. Louis Commercial Club, *Messenger* (February 1914): 18. The IMA was sensitive to the charge of concentrating too much on Chicago concerns and tried to demonstrate the statewide implications of Chicago affairs ("Power is in Acting Together," January 1900, 7–8, IMA Papers).

29. The standard wisdom on employers' associations is reflected in Wiebe, *Businessmen and Reform*, 20. Information on important IMA firms and leaders comes from IMA pamphlet, "To Manufacturers," 1899, IMA Papers; *Illinois Steel Company* (Cleveland: Cleveland Ptg. & Pub., 1897), 3–4; Daniel Nelson, *Managers and Workers: Origins of the New Factory System in the United States, 1880–1920* (Madison: University of Wisconsin Press, 1975), 7, table 3; Mont-

gomery, *House of Labor*, 231–32 (on Link-Belt); William L. Downard, *Dictionary of the History of the American Brewing and Distilling Industries* (Westport, Conn.: Greenwood Press, 1980), 240 (on Seipp); Bessie Louise Pierce, *A History of Chicago* (Chicago: University of Chicago Press, 1957), 3: 108–91 (on Chicago dry goods, clothing, and publishing concerns); and, for influential IMA members, Kelly, "History of the IMA," 86.

30. Edgar W. Brent, *Martin B. Madden, Public Servant* (Chicago: Author, 1901), 33. For Madden as a "gray wolf," see Nick A. Komons, "Chicago, 1893–1907: The Politics of Reform" (Ph.D. diss., George Washington University, 1961), 120–21.

31. For information on Sullivan and his undertakings, see Harold Zink, *City Bosses in the United States* (Durham, N.C.: Duke University Press, 1930), 292–93; Paul M. Green, "The Chicago Democratic Party, 1840–1920" (Ph.D. diss., University of Chicago, 1975), 56–57; and IMA, *Annual Report 1911*, 45. For Upham, Meese, MacVeagh, and Hurley, see *Who Was Who, vol., 1*, 1265; William T. Hutchinson, *Lowden of Illinois* (Chicago: University of Chicago Press, 1957), 1: 172–73; Pierce, *Chicago*, 3: 184 n. 105; and IMA, *Annual Report 1915*, 33. The IMA claimed it never stooped to "questionable methods" or used "money or any wrongful influence" in pursuit of its goals, although Jane Addams reported that association officials attempted to bribe her during the sweatshop act struggle. For the association's claims see IMA circular, "Stop Double Taxation," April 28, 1905, IMA Papers, and IMA, *Annual Report 1911*, 41. For Addams's allegation, see *Hull-House*, 39–40.

32. Glenn to Manufacturers, July 19, 1904, IMA Papers; IMA, *Annual Report 1901*, 8; idem., *Annual Report 1904*, 7. For the notion of state building as patchwork, see Stephen Skowronek, *Building A New American State: The Expansion of National Administrative Capacities, 1877–1920* (New York: Cambridge University Press, 1982).

33. IMA, *Annual Report 1898*, 3–7; Glenn to Members, March 15, 1899, IMA Papers; IMA pamphlet, "To Manufacturers," 1899, IMA Papers. The 1897 fire escape law, supposedly passed at the insistence of insurance underwriters anxious to provide firemen safer access to fires in tall buildings, improved public safety but also was a private boondoggle. The bill, authored by Chicago assemblyman Gus Nohe, empowered state factory inspectors to supervise the construction of automatic fire escapes in buildings occupied above the second floor. The type of fire escapes specified closely resembled those manufactured by Nohe's own company, whose stock Nohe apparently had distributed among his fellow lawmakers. This episode earned Nohe the sobriquet "Fire Escape Gus" (Beckner, *Labor Legislation*, 225; Kelly, "History of the IMA," 17–18).

34. IMA activity during the Kellogg and Teamsters strikes is covered in Kelly, "History of the IMA," 33–42; Stephens, "National Institution," 30; Glenn to Members, May 20, 1905, IMA Papers; Glenn to Gentlemen, May 20, 1905, IMA Papers; IMA, *Annual Report 1905*, 14–15. On the Employers' Association, see Isaac F. Marcosson, "Labor Met by Its Own Methods," *World's Work* 7 (January 1904): 4309–14, and "The Fight for the 'Open Shop,'" *World's Work* 11 (Decem-

ber 1905): 6959–61. See also William English Walling, "Can Labor Unions Be Destroyed?" *World's Work* 8 (May 1904): 4755. The IMA exercised influence over the reform carrot as well as the open shop stick. One of its presidents, LaVerne Noyes, also headed the Civic Federation of Chicago.

35. Undated, (1912?) advertisement from *Manufacturers' News*, IMA Papers; IMA, *Annual Report 1911*, 34–35. In a brief and inglorious departure from the standard IMA position, Glenn made an unsuccessful play for the Republican gubernatorial nomination in 1911. This experiment, never to be repeated, stood in stark contrast to the normal and more effective practice of cultivating political influence without seeking office (*New York Times*, April 23, 1928).

36. IMA, *Annual Report 1901*, 7–10; idem., *Annual Report 1904*, 3–4; idem., *Annual Report 1916*, 60–61; Albro Martin, *Enterprise Denied: Origins of the Decline of American Railroads, 1897–1917* (New York: Columbia University Press, 1971), 202–4, 232–33.

37. IMA circular, "Remarks of Hon. C. P. Gardner," March 30, 1915, IMA Papers.

38. "Report Prepared by the Legislative Organization Committee of the Illinois Manufacturers' Association," 1911, IMA Papers. For similar advice, see IMA bulletin, "Know Thy Statesmen," October 23, 1911, IMA Papers; "Minutes of the Conference of the Legislative Committee of the Illinois Manufacturers' Association," January 6, 1913, IMA Papers; and E. C. Westman to Members, October 23, 1916, IMA Papers.

39. Occasional IMA pronouncements asked for more businessmen in the General Assembly, but given the accompanying plaintive advice not to ignore politics completely, the requests sound more wistful than insistent (IMA, *Annual Report 1915*, 61).

40. Richard L. McCormick, "The Discovery that Business Corrupts Politics: A Reappraisal of the Origins of Progressivism," in McCormick, *The Party Period and Public Policy: American Politics from the Age of Jackson to the Progressive Era* (New York: Oxford University Press, 1986), 311–56. For reform-group interest in the telephone franchise dispute, see *City Club Bulletin* 1 (September 25, 1907) and (November 13, 1907).

41. Glenn to Members, April 16, 1906, IMA Papers. The telephone controversy can be followed in Glenn to Telphone Subscribers, November 19, 1906, IMA Papers; IMA circular, "Telephone Facts," November 28, 1906, IMA Papers; *Chicago Tribune*, August 2, 1906; *City Club Bulletin* 1 (November 13, 1907): 237–44. The IMA formed a competing corporation, Manufacturers' Telephone Company, to force concessions from Chicago Telephone.

42. IMA circular, "What Was Really Accomplished in Telephone Litigation," July 22, 1908, IMA Papers; "Chicago's New Telephone Franchise," *Outlook* 87 (November 30, 1907): 709–10. On the doubtfulness of municipal ownership, see *City Club Bulletin* 1 (September 25, 1907): 187, 190. The IMA also conducted investigations of Chicago water rates and the sanitary condition of the Union Stockyards (Stephens, "National Institution," 32; IMA circular, "A Four Cent Water Rate," December 12, 1906, IMA Papers; IMA pamphlet, "Report of

Investigating Committee," June 1906, IMA Papers; Glenn to Manufacturers, July 16, 1906, IMA Papers).

43. Nearly 150 women workers died in the Triangle Fire, prompting the creation of the New York State Factory Investigating Commission and a push for protective legislation (Yellowitz, *Labor and Progressive Movement*, 94, 155; Nancy Schrom Dye, *As Equals and As Sisters: Feminism, Unionism, and the Women's Trade Union League of New York* [Columbia: University of Missouri Press, 1980], 143–45).

44. Graham Taylor, "The Aftermath at the Cherry Mine," *Survey* 23 (December 11, 1909): 356. The Cherry mine disaster is reported in State of Illinois, Bureau of Labor Statistics, *Report on the Cherry Mine Disaster* (Springfield: Illinois State Journal, 1910); Graham Taylor, "A Mine Test of Civilization," *Survey* 23 (December 4, 1909): 297–304; and Graham Taylor, *Pioneering on Social Frontiers* (Chicago: University of Chicago Press, 1930), 162–69.

45. Beckner, *Labor Legislation*, 440–41.

46. *Report of the Employers' Liability Commission of the State of Illinois* (Chicago: Stromberg, Allen, 1910), 183.

47. Ibid., 5–19, 167–82; IMA, *Annual Report 1910*, 3; Stephens, "National Institution," 34; Beckner, *Labor Legislation*, 441–48; Joseph L. Castrovinci, "Prelude to Welfare Capitalism: The Role of Business in the Enactment of Workmen's Compensation Legislation in Illinois, 1905–12," *Social Service Review* 50 (March 1976): 80–102. For IMA interest in participating on the commission, see Glenn to Charles E. Kimball, May 8, 1909, IMA Papers. Alfred Kelly erroneously reported that all six of the employers' representatives were prominent IMA members ("History of the IMA," 64). The members of the commission were Charles Piez, president of Link-Belt Company; I. G. Rawn (died), president of Monon Railroad; Mason B. Starring, president of Northwestern Elevated Railroad; Robert E. Conway, general manager of Armour Packing Company; E. T. Bent, secretary of the Illinois Coal Operators' Association; P. A. Peterson, president of Union Furniture Company; W. J. Jackson, vice-president and general manager of Chicago and Eastern Illinois Railroad (succeeded Rawn); Edwin R. Wright, president of the Illinois State Federation of Labor; George Golden, president of the Packing House Teamsters; Patrick Carr of the United Mine Workers of America; M. J. Boyle of the Switchmen's Union of North America; Daniel J. Gorman, president of the Amalgamated Association of Street Railway Employees; and John Flora of the Chicago Federation of Labor (*Employers' Liability Commission Report*, 15).

48. *Employers' Liability Commission Report*, 11.

49. Ibid., 10.

50. Graham Taylor, "The Aftermath at the Cherry Mine," *Survey* 23 (December 11, 1909): 356; *Employers' Liability Commission Report*, 12–13.

51. Ibid., 20–38; Beckner, *Labor Legislation*, 449–51; Eugene Staley, *History of the Illinois State Federation of Labor*, 251–53.

52. Staley, *State Federation*, 253.

53. Illinois State Federation of Labor, *Proceedings 1911*, 14; IMA, "Legisla-

tive Bulletin no. 5," February 18, 1911, 3, IMA Papers; IMA, *Annual Report 1911*, 37–38; IMA, "Legislative Bulletin no. 11," April 8, 1911, IMA Papers; IMA, "Legislative Bulletin no. 12," April 15, 1911, IMA Papers; IMA circular, "Act Quick," 1911, IMA Papers; IMA circular, "Compensation—Will the Cure Kill the Patient?" May 20, 1911, IMA Papers.

54. IMA circular, "Unite in Securing a Veto of the Compensation Act," May 23, 1911, IMA Papers.

55. IMA circular, "Compensation or Confiscation," May 24, 1911, IMA Papers; Beckner, *Labor Legislation*, 452–53.

56. Illinois State Federation of Labor, *Proceedings 1911*, 113–17, 140–41; Staley, *State Federation*, 232; ISFL, *Proceedings 1915*, 48–49.

57. IMA circular, "Compensation—Will the Cure Kill the Patient?" IMA Papers.

58. Beckner, *Labor Legislation*, 454–55; IMA, *Annual Report 1911*, 37–38.

59. IMA circular, "Workmen's Compensation," December 1911, IMA Papers.

60. Staley, *State Federation*, 231.

61. Illinois State Federation of Labor, *Proceedings 1905*, 9–10; Staley, *State Federation*, 180, 191.

62. LaVerne W. Noyes to Montgomery Ward, April 8, 1909, IMA Papers. See also IMA circular, "Report Prepared by the Legislative Organization Committee," 1911, IMA Papers.

63. *Chicago Tribune*, May 6, 1907.

64. *Mendon Dispatch*, May 22, 1907.

65. IMA, "Legislative Bulletin no. 1," February 12, 1907, IMA Papers; IMA, *Annual Report 1915*, 31; IMA circular, "Legislative Bulletin Service," 1913, IMA circulars, "Special Legislative Announcements," May 16, 1913, and May 23, 1913, IMA Papers; IMA, "Legislative Bulletin," March 10, 1915, IMA Papers; IMA, "The Pink Sheet," 1917, IMA Papers; S. M. Hastings to Sir, January 22, 1916, IMA Papers; IMA circular, "Special Offer," February 8, 1917, IMA Papers. *Manufacturers' News* also carried regular reports on the legislative programs of labor and the IMA at Springfield.

66. For the legislative organization committee and its subcommittees, see IMA, *Annual Report 1911*, 38–42, and idem., *Annual Report 1912*, 17–18. For the completion of organization and the Leland Hotel headquarters, see idem., *Annual Report 1915*, 60, and IMA circular, "Springfield Headquarters," May 6, 1913, IMA Papers.

67. IMA, *Annual Report 1915*, 60–61. For national trends, see William Graebner, "Federalism in the Progressive Era: A Structural Interpretation of Reform," *Journal of American History* 64 (September 1977): 331–57; J. Roffe Wike, *The Pennsylvania Manufacturers' Association* (Philadelphia: University of Pennsylvania Press, 1960); and Don D. Lescohier and Elizabeth Brandeis, *History of Labor in the United States, 1896–1932* (New York: Macmillan, 1935), 3: 399–610.

68. State of Illinois, Bureau of Labor Statistics, *Labor Legislation in the Forty-Sixth General Assembly of Illinois*.

69. *City Club Bulletin* 1 (April 17, 1907): 116.

70. Ibid., 106. Illinois was the slowest of the northern industrial states in passing factory health and safety laws (Nelson, *Managers and Workers*, 123–24). Laws already on the books were difficult to enforce. See Edgar T. Davies, "The Difficulties of a Factory Inspector," *Annals of the American Academy of Political and Social Science* 29 (January 1907): 125–31.

71. Glenn to Employers of Illinois, April 30, 1907, IMA Papers. Reference to "czarlike" power is from IMA, "Legislative Bulletin no. 3," April 15, 1907, IMA Papers.

72. *City Club Bulletin* 1 (April 17, 1907): 106–9; Beckner, *Labor Legislation*, 228–29; IMA circular, "Act Quick on Factory Inspection Bill," April 27, 1907, IMA Papers; IMA circular, "Factory Inspection Law," April 15, 1907, IMA Papers; IMA circular, "Senate Bill No. 500," May 2, 1907, IMA Papers; *City Club Bulletin* 1 (June 6, 1907): 145–46.

73. Glenn to W. W. Kimball, May 8, 1909, IMA Papers. The members of the Industrial Commission were chairman Edwin R. Wright, president of the Illinois State Federation of Labor; Samuel A. Harper, attorney; Charles Piez, president of Link-Belt Company; Emerit E. Baker, president of Kewanee Boiler Company; P. A. Peterson, president of Union Furniture Company; Dr. Henry B. Favill, president of the Tuberculosis Institute; Graham Taylor, president of Chicago Commons; David Ross, secretary of the State Bureau of Labor Statistics; Peter W. Collins, secretary of the International Brotherhood of Electrical Workers; and William Rossell of the legislative committee of the Chicago Federation of Labor (Illinois Bureau of Labor Statistics, *Labor Legislation in the Forty-Sixth General Assembly*, 183); Beckner, *Labor Legislation*, 231–40.

74. IMA circular, "The Reason Why," 1911, IMA Papers. For the report of the commission, see *Labor Legislation in the Forty-Sixth General Assembly*, 173–77; Graham Taylor, "Illinois Bill to Protect Employees," *Survey* 22 (April 3, 1909): 77–78; and Taylor, "Making Peace to do Justice," *Survey* 22 (July 3, 1909): 523–26.

75. For the history of the ten hour bill, see the report of Anna Willard, Elizabeth Maloney, Agnes Nestor, and Lulu Holly taken from the *Union Labor Advocate* of July 1909 and reprinted in *Labor Legislation in the Forty-Sixth General Assembly*, 15–21. See also Beckner, *Labor Legislation*, 190–206; Mary E. McDowell, "The Girls' Bill," *Survey* 22 (July 3, 1909): 509–13; LaVerne W. Noyes to Montgomery Ward, April 8, 1909, IMA Papers; Glenn to Liquor Dealers' Assoc., Rochelle, Illinois, April 24, 1909, IMA Papers; Graham Taylor, "Ten-Hour Law Held Up in Illinois," *Survey* 22 (September 18, 1909): 841–43; IMA circular, "Ten Hour Injunction Proceedings," September 10, 1909, IMA Papers; Ernst Freund, *Constitutional Aspects of the Ten Hour Law Enacted by the Forty-Sixth General Assembly of Illinois* (Springfield: Illinois State Journal, 1909); Graham Taylor, "Illinois Ten-Hour Law," *Survey* 23 (November 6, 1909): 205–6; Louis D. Brandeis and Josephine C. Goldmark, *W. C. Ritchie and Company Et Als. Appellees, Vs. John E. W. Wayman and Edgar T. Davies, Appellants, Brief and Arguments for Appellants in the Supreme Court of the State of Illinois, December Term, A. D. 1909* (Chicago? 1909).

76. IMA, *The Closed Shop: The Labor Trust Scored by the Appellate Court of Cook County* (Chicago, 1904), 16; IMA pamphlet, "The Best Methods of Securing Better Representation in the State Legislatures and in Congress," June 15, 1918, 14–15, IMA Papers.

77. IMA circular, "Factory Inspection Legislation," March 21, 1908, IMA Papers; *Manufacturers' News* 8 (January 27, 1916): 5; Oscar Beckman, "Reign of Terror in Two Illinois Towns," *Manufacturers' News* 11 (March 22, 1917): 11, 30; "Why Courts Issue Injunctions against Strikers," *Manufacturers' News* 11 (April 19, 1917): 15, 29: "Fight against the Extortion by Labor Leaders," *Manufacturers' News* 11 (March 8, 1917): 7, 10.

78. IMA circular, "Injunction or No Injunction," March 9, 1917, IMA Papers; Glenn to Liquor Dealers' Assoc., Rochelle, Illinois, April 24, 1909, IMA Papers.

79. "Social Uplifters and the Workingman," *Manufacturers' News* 14 (July 11, 1918): 9.

80. *City Club Bulletin* 2 (February 17, 1909): 283.

81. Graham Taylor, "State's Shame on National Exhibit," *Survey* 23 (March 5, 1910): 896–97.

82. See comments of George J. McGowan in IMA pamphlet, "Minutes of Conference Legislative Committee," January 6, 1913, IMA Papers; IMA circular, "Remarks of Hon. C. P. Gardner," March 30, 1915, IMA Papers.

Chapter 4

1. Frederic C. Howe, *The City: The Hope of Democracy* (New York: Scribner's, 1905), 163–67, 300.

2. Graham Taylor, *Religion in Social Action* (New York: Dodd, Mead, 1913), 216–23.

3. For examples of home rule as a reformist consolidation movement, see Michael Kazin, *Barons of Labor: The San Francisco Building Trades and Union Power in the Progressive Era* (Urbana: University of Illinois Press, 1987), 40–42, and Samuel P. Hays, "The Politics of Reform in Municipal Government in the Progressive Era," in Hays, *American Political History as Social Analysis* (Knoxville: University of Tennessee Press, 1980), 205–32. Examples of labor and business participation in home-rule campaigns can be found in Ernest S. Griffith, *A History of American City Government: The Progressive Years and Their Aftermath* (New York: Praeger, 1974), 241, and Judith Sealander, *Grand Plans: Business Progressivism and Social Change in Ohio's Miami Valley, 1890–1929* (Lexington: University Press of Kentucky, 1988), 92–128. For greater New York, see David C. Hammack, *Power and Society: Greater New York at the Turn of the Century* (New York: Russell Sage Foundation, 1982; reprint, New York: Columbia University Press, 1987), 185–229.

4. For a treatment of the working-class saloon as the hub of an alternative culture, see Roy Rosenzwieg, *Eight Hours for What We Will: Workers and Leisure*

in an Industrial City, 1870–1920 (New York: Cambridge University Press, 1983), 35–64.

5. Untitled draft of address (1916?), Charles E. Merriam Papers, Special Collections, University of Chicago Library. On young professionals in Chicago civic reform, see Michael P. McCarthy, "Businessmen and Professionals in Municipal Reform: The Chicago Experience, 1877–1920" (Ph.D. diss., Northwestern University, 1970), especially i-v, 26, 36–39.

6. Donald David Marks, "Polishing the Gem of the Prairie: The Evolution of Civic Reform Consciousness in Chicago, 1874–1900" (Ph.D. diss., University of Wisconsin, 1974), 58–84; Jon C. Teaford, *The Unheralded Triumph: City Government in America, 1870–1900* (Baltimore, Md.: Johns Hopkins University Press, 1984), 201–2.

7. On the founding of the Civic Federation, see Graham Taylor, *Pioneering on Social Frontiers* (Chicago: University of Chicago Press, 1930), 27–39. For the central role of businesspeople and professionals, see Albion Small, "The Civic Federation of Chicago," *American Journal of Sociology* 1 (July 1895): 101–2. See also Marks, "Gem of the Prairie," 89–138, and Daniel Levine, *Varieties of Reform Thought* (Madison: State Historical Society of Wisconsin, 1964), 57–61.

8. Lincoln Steffens, *The Shame of the Cities* (New York: McClure, Phillips, 1904; reprint, New York: Hill and Wang, 1957), 194. For the MVL campaign, see Michael P. McCarthy, "The New Metropolis: Chicago, the Annexation Movement, and Progressive Reform," in Michael H. Ebner and Eugene M. Tobin, eds., *The Age of Urban Reform: New Perspectives on the Progressive Era* (Port Washington, N.Y.: Kennikat Press, 1977), 43–54, and Edwin Burritt Smith, "The Municipal Voters' League of Chicago," *Atlantic Monthly* 85 (June 1900): 835–37.

9. Milton J. Foreman, "The Chicago New Charter Movement—Its Relation to Municipal Ownership," *Annals of the American Academy of Political and Social Science* 31 (May 1908): 106. For the constitutional background, see Charles E. Merriam, "The Chicago Charter Convention," *American Political Science Review* 2 (November 1907): 1.

10. Chicago's governmental and electoral complexity is laid out in Merriam, "Chicago Charter Convention," 4; McCarthy, "Businessmen and Professionals," 48; and Joel A. Tarr, *A Study in Boss Politics: William Lorimer of Chicago* (Urbana: University of Illinois Press, 1971), 16. If minor government bodies are included, Chicago's political Balkanization is more striking. Douglas Sutherland counted sixteen separate administrations in Chicago; the number later grew to twenty-seven (Douglas Sutherland, *Fifty Years on the Civic Front* [Chicago: Civic Federation of Chicago, 1943], 19).

11. *City Club Bulletin* 1 (June 26, 1907): 159; Maureen Anne Flanagan, *Charter Reform in Chicago* (Carbondale: Southern Illinois University Press, 1987), 24–25; Bennett S. Stark, "The Political Economy of State Public Finance" (Ph.D. diss., University of Wisconsin, 1982), 77, 93. For township assessors, see McCarthy, "Businessmen and Professionals," 48–49.

12. For property tax assessment in general, see Clifton K. Yearley, *The Money*

Machines: The Breakdown and Reform of Governmental and Party Finance in the North, 1860–1920 (Albany: State University of New York Press, 1970). Comparative percentages are from Stark, "State Public Finance," 62, 77–79.

13. Stark, "State Public Finance," 78, 131; *City Club Bulletin* 1 (June 26, 1907): 158–59; Augustus R. Hatton, *Digest of City Charters* (Chicago: Chicago Charter Convention, 1906), 132–33. For a comparative (and more hopeful) discussion of municipal finance, based mostly on nineteenth-century examples, see Eric H. Monkkonen, *America Becomes Urban: The Development of U.S. Cities and Towns, 1780–1980* (Berkeley: University of California Press, 1988), 131–57.

14. *City Club Bulletin* 1 (June 26, 1907): 159–60. This procedure allowed the clerk to adjust the levies according to the dictates of political favoritism (Hugo S. Grosser, "Municipal Problems of Chicago," *Annals of the American Academy of Political and Social Science* 23 [March 1904]: 89–90).

15. *City Club Bulletin* 1 (June 26, 1907): 160. The General Assembly evaded the legal proscription against special acts by framing bills "general in their terms but special and local in their application" (ibid.).

16. Merriam, "Chicago Charter Convention," 8. Chicago's debt had risen little since 1870.

17. *City Club Bulletin* 1 (June 26, 1907): 157–58; Grosser, "Municipal Problems of Chicago," 90–91; Foreman, "Chicago New Charter Movement," 107.

18. The efforts of the Citizens' Association and the creation of the Chicago Sanitary District can be traced in Citizens' Association of Chicago, *Annual Report 1884*, 9–11; idem., *Annual Report 1885*, 12–14; idem., *Annual Report 1886*, 7; idem., *Annual Report 1887*, 23–24; and Marks, "Gem of the Prairie," 71–83. For the relationship between Chicago and the sanitary district, see McCarthy, "Businessmen and Professionals," 47.

19. McCarthy, "Businessmen and Professionals," 95. For restrictions on city revenue and dependence on saloon licenses, see *City Club Bulletin* 1 (June 26, 1907): 158–60, and Perry Duis, *The Saloon: Public Drinking in Chicago and Boston, 1880–1920* (Urbana: University of Illinois Press, 1983), 115–16, 259.

20. Martin J. Schiesl, *The Politics of Efficiency: Municipal Administration in America, 1880–1920* (Berkeley: University of California Press, 1977), 3, 51–54, 91–92; Tom L. Johnson, *My Story* (New York, 1911; reprint, New York: AMS Press, 1970), 148–49.

21. Marks, "Gem of the Prairie," 76–77; Flanagan, *Charter Reform*, 49. The enabling amendment vote was statewide, but only Chicagoans participated in the charter ratification election. For proposals to pass, a majority of voters in the election had to cast favorable ballots, not simply those voting on the charter question.

22. Teaford, *Unheralded Triumph*, 92.

23. Walter S. Rundle to Lawrence Y. Sherman, April 5, 1897, Lawrence Y. Sherman Papers, Illinois State Historical Library, Springfield. On reapportionment, see William Booth Philip, "Chicago and the Downstate: A Study of their Conflicts, 1870–1934" (Ph.D. diss., University of Chicago, 1940), 36–41, 51–54.

24. *Chicago Tribune*, May 3, 1907.

25. Merriam was a delegate to the charter convention; University of Chicago law professor Freund served as charter draftsman (Chicago Charter Convention, *Proceedings*, March 1, 1907, 1198).

26. Schiesl, *Politics of Efficiency*, 4.

27. City of Chicago Department of Finance, *Forty-fourth Annual Statement of Finances of the City of Chicago* (1900), 40–41; Schiesl, *Politics of Efficiency*, 93–94.

28. The power of the Chicago city council is discussed in Charles E. Merriam, *Chicago: A More Intimate View of Urban Politics* (New York: Macmillan, 1929), 222–23. For comparisons of council powers in Chicago and other cities, see Teaford, *Unheralded Triumph*, 17–25, and Hatton, *Digest of City Charters*. For the sentiment of the Charter Convention, see Chicago Charter Convention, *Proceedings*, December 10, 1906, 209–10.

29. Sutherland, *Fifty Years*, 23; Flanagan, *Charter Reform*, 49–50.

30. *Chicago Tribune*, October 28, 1902. For an evaluation of the Civic Federation as representative of Chicago's varying interests, see Albion Small, "The Civic Federation of Chicago," *American Journal of Sociology* 1 (July 1895): 96–99.

31. *Chicago Tribune*, October 29, 1902.

32. *Chicago Tribune*, December 8, 1902; Sutherland, *Fifty Years*, 23; Flanagan, *Charter Reform*, 50–52.

33. *Chicago Tribune*, December 19, 1902.

34. Foreman, "Chicago New Charter Movement," 108; Sutherland, *Fifty Years*, 24; Flanagan, *Charter Reform*, 54–56. Out of 1,089,458 voters participating in the statewide election, 678,393 endorsed the charter amendment and only 94,038 opposed it. Chicago voters approved the amendment ten to one.

35. Flanagan, *Charter Reform*, 59–61; Merriam, "Chicago Charter Convention," 2.

36. The three CFL delegates included organizer John J. Fitzpatrick (who attended no charter meetings), James Linehan, and George Thompson.

37. For Robins's critical assessment of the convention's personnel and accomplishments, see *Public Policy League Bulletin* 1 (September 1907): 2, and *City Club Bulletin* 1 (October 23, 1907): 217; a more favorable judgment appears in Sutherland, *Fifty Years*, 24–25. For reform of the "justice shops," see McCarthy, "Businessmen and Professionals," 54–56. All the listed measures were subject to voter approval.

38. Chicago Charter Convention, *Proceedings*, March 1, 1907, 1201.

39. For the referendum, see Chicago Federation of Labor to Milton J. Foreman, December 20, 1906, copy in Chicago Teachers' Federation Papers, Chicago Historical Society; Chicago Charter Convention, *Proceedings*, December 15, 1906, 378–80, December 17, 424, and March 1, 1907, 1159–60. For the primary and women suffrage, see Chicago Charter Convention, *Proceedings*, February 23, 1907, 1037–38; Foreman, "Chicago New Charter Movement," 110–11; Merriam, "Chicago Charter Convention," 9; *City Club Bulletin* 1 (July 10,

1907): 165–66; Charles E. Merriam and Louise Overacker, *Primary Elections* (Chicago: University of Chicago Press, 1928), 64–65; *Outlook* 88 (February 15, 1908): 343–44; and Flanagan, *Charter Reform*, 84–86.

40. Chicago Charter Convention, *Proceedings*, December 20, 1906, 561, December 21, 622–23.

41. Chicago Charter Convention, *Proceedings*, December 20, 1906, 565–66, December 21, 614. The convention's temperate stance was carried on by the Civic Federation, whose president, Joseph E. Otis, urged in 1913 that the federation adopt the role of the "honest conservative" to prevent the triumph of "extremes in either direction" (Civic Federation of Chicago, *Bulletin No. 9: The Civic Federation of Chicago—Its Achievements and Its Function* [1913], 3).

42. Chicago Charter Convention, *Proceedings*, December 13, 1906, 292.

43. *City Club Bulletin* 1 (June 19, 1907): 152.

44. See Paul Kleppner, *The Cross of Culture: A Social Analysis of Midwestern Politics, 1850–1900* (New York: Free Press, 1970); Kleppner, *The Third Electoral System, 1853–1892: Parties, Voters, and Political Cultures* (Chapel Hill: University of North Carolina Press, 1979); Richard J. Jensen, *The Winning of the Midwest: Social and Political Conflict, 1888–1896* (Chicago: University of Chicago Press, 1971); and Samuel T. McSeveney, *The Politics of Depression: Political Behavior in the Northeast, 1893–1896* (New York: Oxford University Press, 1972).

45. Duis, *The Saloon*, 233–34; *City Club Bulletin* 1 (December 27, 1907): 321.

46. *Abendpost*, June 15, 1894, translation from Chicago Foreign Language Press Survey (CFLPS), Special Collections, University of Chicago Library. See also *Abendpost*, October 14, 1890, February 4, 1896, February 10, 1908, November 11, 1910, November 1, 1918; *Denni Hlasatel*, March 30, 1915; and *Dziennik Zwiarkowy*, February 19, 1908, CFLPS.

47. Jensen, *Winning of the Midwest*, 134–35.

48. *Illinois Staats-Zeitung*, June 17, 1892, CFLPS.

49. For the saloon and vice, see Norman H. Clark, *Deliver Us from Evil: An Interpretation of American Prohibition* (New York: Norton, 1976), and Paul Boyer, *Urban Masses and Moral Order in America, 1820–1920* (Cambridge, Mass.: Harvard University Press, 1978), 191–219. For Kenna, Coughlin, and the levee, see Lloyd Wendt and Herman Kogan, *Lords of the Levee* (Indianapolis, Ind.: Bobbs-Merrill, 1943). On blind pigs, see Duis, *The Saloon*, 61–64. For pressure on city government, see Chicago Commission on the Liquor Problem, *Preliminary Report*, (1916), 17. The Anti-Saloon League of Illinois is profiled in Thomas R. Pegram, "The Dry Machine: The Formation of the Anti-Saloon League of Illinois," *Illinois Historical Journal* 83 (Autumn, 1990), 173–86. The official historian of the Illinois Anti-Saloon League characterized the saloon as "the acme of evil, the climax of iniquity, the mother of abominations, and the sum of villainies" (W. A. Smith, *A History of the Anti-Saloon League of Illinois* [Chicago: Anti-Saloon League of Illinois, 1925], 8).

50. See Duis, *The Saloon*, passim. For the place of the saloon in Chicago's working-class and immigrant communities, see Jon M. Kingsdale, "The 'Poor

Man's Club': Social Functions of the Urban Working-Class Saloon," in Elizabeth H. Pleck and Joseph H. Pleck, eds., *The American Man* (Englewood Cliffs, N.J.: Prentice-Hall, 1980), 258, 263–64; Rudolph J. Vecoli, "Chicago's Italians prior to World War I: A Study of Their Social and Economic Adjustment" (Ph.D. diss., University of Wisconsin, 1962), 299–300; and Royal L. Melendy, "The Saloon in Chicago," *American Journal of Sociology* 6 (November 1900): 289–306.

51. *Chicago Tribune*, February 12, 1906. See also Louise De Koven Bowen, *The Public Dance Halls of Chicago* (Chicago: Juvenile Protective Association of Chicago, 1917).

52. *Champion of Fair Play*, September 23, 1905; *American Issue* 15 (January 25, 1907): 11; *City Club Bulletin* 1 (April 1, 1908): 62–63; Bowen, *Public Dance Halls*, 8; Duis, *The Saloon*, 253–54, 262.

53. Maureen Anne Flanagan, "The Ethnic Entry into Chicago Politics: The United Societies for Local Self-Government and the Chicago Reform Charter of 1907," *Journal of the Illinois State Historical Society* 75 (Spring 1982): 2; Duis, *The Saloon*, 259; *Outlook* 82 (March 17, 1906): 587–88; *City Club Bulletin* 1 (April 1, 1908): 64.

54. *Abendpost*, March 16, 1906, CFLPS.

55. *Abendpost*, March 10, 13, 17, 1906, CFLPS. Quotation is from March 13.

56. *Abendpost*, March 26, 1906, CFLPS; *Champion of Fair Play*, March 24, 1906.

57. *Abendpost*, May 24, 1906, CFLPS; *Champion of Fair Play*, June 9, 1906; *City Club Bulletin* 1 (April 1, 1908): 64.

58. For diverse ethnic representation in the United Societies see, Flanagan, "Ethnic Entry," 3. For tension between Irish and Germans in Chicago, see Duis, *The Saloon*, 156–57, and Paul M. Green, "The Chicago Democratic Party, 1840–1920: From Factionalism to Political Organization" (Ph.D. diss., University of Chicago, 1975), 51–52. On the role of Cermak, see *Abendpost*, November 1, 1918, CFLPS, and Alex Gottfried, *Boss Cermak of Chicago* (Seattle: University of Washington Press, 1962), 51–54. Chicago's Irish and Germans had battled earlier in politics and saloonkeepers' organizations (*Abendpost*, March 18, 1891; *Illinos Staats-Zeitung*, March 27, 1891, CFLPS; Duis, *The Saloon*, 81–82). See also *Denni Hlasatel*, April 2, 1914, CFLPS, for an example of Bohemian political antagonism toward the Irish. For German prejudice against Italians, see Rudolph J. Vecoli, "Chicago's Italians prior to World War I," 218–19.

59. *Dziennik Chicagoski*, March 30, 1895, November 6, 1905, CFLPS; Edward R. Kantowicz, *Polish-American Politics in Chicago, 1888–1940* (Chicago: University of Chicago Press, 1975). Sabath did support his Polish constituents.

60. *City Club Bulletin* 1 (April 1, 1908): 68–69.

61. *Champion of Fair Play*, March 24, 1906. For Anti-Saloon League charges and liquor industry representation in the United Societies, see Anti-Saloon League of America, *Proceedings 1909*, 10; idem., *Proceedings 1916*, 190; *American Issue* 15 (October 18, 1907): 2; *American Issue* 16 (April 4, 1908): 11; and Flanagan, "Ethnic Entry," 3.

62. Gottfried, *Boss Cermak*, 54–55; United States Senate, *Senator from Illi-*

nois: Proceedings before a Committee of the United States Senate, pts. 1 & 4 (62d Congress, First Session, 1911), 206–10, 1119–23, 1127–30; Tarr, *Boss Politics*, 190; *Champion of Fair Play*, September 30, 1905.

63. *Champion of Fair Play*, March 9, 1907; *Abendpost*, May 24, 1909, CFLPS.

64. *Champion of Fair Play*, April 7, 1906.

65. Robert McCurdy to Raymond Robins, December 3, 1906, Raymond Robins Papers, State Historical Society of Wisconsin, Madison. For an example of persistent nativism in rural Illinois, see *Sheffield Times*, November 19, 1915.

66. Chicago Charter Convention, *Proceedings*, December 6, 1906, 189–90.

67. Chicago Charter Convention, *Proceedings*, December 26, 1906, 712.

68. Ibid.

69. Flanagan, *Charter Reform*, 88; *Union Labor Advocate* 7 (January 1907): 12; Chicago Charter Convention, *Proceedings*, February 16, 1907, 914–16.

70. Milton J. Foreman, "Chicago New Charter Movement," 114.

71. Chicago Charter Convention, *Proceedings*, December 27, 1906, 791. For the entire debate, see 785–94.

72. Ibid., 788–89.

73. Ibid., 790.

74. *Champion of Fair Play*, February 23, March 9, 1907. For the strategy of the Anti-Saloon League, see William H. Anderson, *The Church in Action against the Saloon* (Anti-Saloon League of America, 1906), and Pegram, "The Dry Machine," 179–85.

75. *Chicago Tribune*, May 2, 1907.

76. *Chicago Tribune*, May 3, 1907.

77. Chicago Charter Convention, *Proceedings*, March 1, 1907, 1195; Merriam, "Chicago Charter Convention," 11–12; *City Club Bulletin* 1 (June 19, 1907): 153.

78. *Champion of Fair Play*, May 11, 1907. For the maneuvers leading to passage of the charter and local option bills, see Merriam, "Chicago Charter Convention," 11; William B. Philip, "Chicago and the Downstate," 268; *City Club Bulletin* 1 (April 24, 1907): 124–25; Flanagan, *Charter Reform*, 106; Sutherland, *Fifty Years*, 25–26; Smith, *Anti-Saloon League of Illinois*, 15–16; and *Illinois House Journal 1907*, 812–13. The charter bill passed by a 93–47 vote. The local option bill passed by an 83–65 vote—eighteen Cook County representatives provided the margin of victory. For the local option law, see *The Illinois Local Option Law* (Chicago: Anti-Saloon League of Illinois, 1907), copy in William H. Anderson Papers, Special Collections, University of Chicago Library.

79. *City Club Bulletin* 1 (July 19, 1907): 152.

80. Ibid., 147; see also *Outlook* 86 (June 8, 1907): 269–70.

81. *City Club Bulletin* 1 (July 10, 1907): 172.

82. *Public Policy League Bulletin* 1 (September 1907): 7. See also John E. Owens to Raymond Robins, June 26, 1907, Robins Papers; *City Club Bulletin* 1 (October 23, 1907): 216; McCarthy, "Businessmen and Professionals," 74–78; Civic Federation of Chicago, "The New Chicago Charter: Why It Should be Adopted at

the Special Election, September 17, 1907," pamphlet in Charles E. Merriam Papers, Special Collections, University of Chicago Library; Merriam, "Chicago Charter Convention," 13–14.

83. *Union Labor Advocate* 7 (August 1907): 12; Democratic Central Committee of Cook County, "Reasons Why the Proposed Charter Should be Defeated," 1907 pamphlet in Merriam Papers.

84. A United Societies' pamphlet complained that the charter "makes civil service reform a farce, increases very materially the burden of the small taxpayer, endangers the efficiency of the public schools, . . [and] reduces the people's representation in the city council, thereby making it easier for privilege-seeking corporations to attain their ends," but it laid greatest stress on the General Assembly's rejection of its liquor regulation proposals and the tyranny of state control over local customs (United Societies for Local Self-Government, "Seven Reasons Why the Proposed New Charter To Be Voted upon September 17th, 1907, Should Be Defeated," pamphlet in Merriam Papers).

85. *Dziennik Chicagoski,* April 3, 1896; *Denni Hlasatel,* November 14, 1909, CFLPS. For Democrats and the Independence League, see Flanagan, "Ethnic Entry," 11, and Theodore Nelson to Raymond Robins, July 19 and August 21, 1907, Robins Papers. The United Societies refused to define its opposition to the charter as part of a struggle against the Republican party. See *Abendpost,* September 19, 1907, CFLPS.

86. Flanagan, "Ethnic Entry," 10.

87. *City Club Bulletin* 1 (June 19, 1907): 152–56; (October 23, 1907): 215–17; Kantowicz, *Polish-American Politics in Chicago,* 89–92; *Narod Polski,* November 2, 1898; *Dziennik Zwiazkowy,* April 4, 1910, March 30, 1918; *Abendpost,* August 26, 1910; *Denni Hlasatel,* May 5, 1911, CFLPS. See also McCarthy, "Businessmen and Professionals," 72.

88. Harold L. Ickes, *Autobiography of a Curmudgeon* (New York: Reynal and Hitchcock, 1943), 110.

89. McCarthy, "Businessmen and Professionals," 72–73; *Abendpost,* March 28, 1907, CFLPS; George Sikes, "Chicago's New Mayor," *Review of Reviews* 35 (May 1907): 586; *Champion of Fair Play,* September 14, 1907; Flanagan, *Charter Reform,* 132–33.

90. *Abendpost,* September 16, 1907, CFLPS.

91. *Abendpost,* September 19, 1907, CFLPS. For other opponents of the charter, see Merriam, "Chicago Charter Convention," 14.

92. Merriam, "Chicago Charter Convention," 13–14; *City Club Bulletin* 1 (October 23, 1907): 219.

93. For advocacy of a constitutional convention, see George E. Cole to Dear Sir, June 14, 1913, Citizens' Association and Municipal Voters' League Papers, Chicago Historical Society, and draft of speech by Charles E. Merriam, 2–3, Merriam Papers. For the Civic Federation, see Sutherland, *Fifty Years,* 29–31, 36–48. The other charter attempts are covered in Flanagan, *Charter Reform,* 141–46. See *City Club Bulletin* 2 (May 19, 1909): 451–63, for a campaign to

enroll the Union League Club, the Hamilton Club, and the Association of Commerce in active support of the 1909 charter. This charter took the form of eleven
separate bills.

94. *Abendpost,* May 24, 1909, CFLPS. For Cermak and the continuing battle
over Chicago saloons, see Duis, *The Saloon,* 282, and *Outlook* 94 (April 2, 1910):
738. For Sunday closing under Thompson, see *Survey* 35 (October 23, 1915):
80–81. For Cermak's 1931 election as mayor, see John M. Allswang, *A House
for All Peoples: Ethnic Politics in Chicago, 1890–1936* (Lexington: University Press
of Kentucky, 1971), 156–60, and Gottfried, *Boss Cermak,* 344–45. Some progressives, such as Fletcher Dobyns, painted Cermak and the United Societies as
representatives of the "underworld in politics" who seized control of the Chicago
Democratic machine. Dobyns characterized the United Societies' adherents as
"Chicago's dregs" and insisted the marchers in a 1915 parade protesting Sunday
closing consisted of "saloon keepers, bartenders, beer drivers, and ex-convicts"
(Fletcher Dobyns, *The Underworld of American Politics* [New York: Author, 1932],
37, 147).

Chapter 5

1. Charles E. Merriam, *Chicago: A More Intimate View of Urban Politics* (New
York: Macmillan, 1929), 24–28.

2. Lincoln Steffens, *The Autobiography of Lincoln Steffens* (New York: Harcourt, Brace, 1931), 450–51; Melvin G. Holli, *Reform in Detroit: Hazen S. Pingree and Urban Politics* (New York: Oxford University Press, 1969), 28; David B.
Tyack, *The One Best System: A History of American Urban Education* (Cambridge,
Mass.: Harvard University Press, 1974), 101.

3. Tyack, *Best System,* 88.

4. For Philadelphia, see Lincoln Steffens, *The Shame of the Cities* (New York:
McClure, Phillips, 1904; reprint, New York: Hill and Wang, 1957), 155; see also
David John Hogan, *Class and Reform: School and Society in Chicago, 1880–1930*
(Philadelphia: University of Pennsylvania Press, 1985), 198–99 for placement
procedures. On Rice, see Tyack, *Best System,* 82–83.

5. *Chicago Tribune,* November 2, 1902. See also *Report of the Educational
Commission of the City of Chicago* (Chicago: University of Chicago Press, 1900),
55–56.

6. Joseph M. Rice, "The Public Schools of Chicago and St. Paul," *Forum* 15
(April 1893): 202. For a general history of Chicago public schools, see Mary J.
Herrick, *The Chicago Schools: A Social and Political History* (Beverly Hills, Cal.:
Sage, 1971).

7. Tyack, *Best System,* 127; Cherry Wedgwood Collins, "Schoolmen, Schoolma'ams, and School Boards" (Ed.D. diss., Harvard University, 1976), 86–152.
For the centralization movement in New York, see Diane Ravitch, *The Great
School Wars: New York City, 1805–1973* (New York: Basic Books, 1974), 107–
58. The history of American public education in this period has taken some

querulous turns. The encyclopedic, celebratory standard set by Lawrence A. Cremin, most notably in *The Transformation of the School: Progressivism in American Education, 1876–1957* (New York: Vintage, 1961), has been effectively challenged by revisionist scholars. Michael B. Katz, the most subtle of the revisionists, argues in *The Irony of Early School Reform: Educational Innovation in Mid-Nineteenth Century Massachusetts* (Cambridge, Mass.: Harvard University Press, 1968) that halfway through the nineteenth century, an educational bureaucracy committed to social control over working-class aspirations had been cemented into place. Finally, Ravitch has assaulted the revisionist view as overly deterministic in "The Revisionists Revised," *Proceedings of the National Academy of Education* 4 (1977): 1–84.

8. Tyack, *Best System*, 127, 94; Hogan, *Class and Reform*, 198. Katz has argued that class bias was embedded in the bureaucratic structure of school reform (Michael B. Katz, *Class, Bureaucracy, and Schools: The Illusion of Educational Change in America* [New York: Praeger, 1971]).

9. Cremin, *Transformation of the School*, 168.

10. On Harper, see Stephen J. Diner, *A City and Its Universities: Public Policy in Chicago, 1892–1919* (Chapel Hill: University of North Carolina Press, 1980), 11–18, 81–82.

11. Ibid., 82–83.

12. *Report of Educational Commission*, 241–42. The report cites the need for "the rugged and forceful personality of men" in the schools (79).

13. For a positive evaluation of the Harper report, see Herrick, *Chicago Schools*, 81–87.

14. Young quoted in David Tyack and Elisabeth Hansot, *Managers of Virtue: Public School Leadership in America, 1820–1980* (New York: Basic Books, 1982), 181; for sketch of Young's career, see 194–201. For Young as Dewey's "wisest" student, see George Dykhuizen, *The Life and Mind of John Dewey* (Carbondale: Southern Illinois University Press, 1973), 87. John Dewey, *The School and Society* (Chicago: University of Chicago, 1899) contains the kernel of Dewey's educational ideas. For a revisionist view of Dewey as a servant of the corporate liberal state, see Clarence J. Karier, ed., *Roots of Crisis: American Education in the Twentieth Century* (Chicago: Rand McNally, 1973), 95–104.

15. Tyack, *Best System*, 178; Marjorie Murphy, "From Artisan to Semi-Professional: White Collar Unionism among Chicago Public School Teachers, 1870–1930" (Ph.D. diss., University of California-Davis, 1981), 160.

16. Arvilla C. De Luce, "Brief Account of the Pension Movement," undated manuscript, Chicago Teachers' Federation Papers, Chicago Historical Society; Robert L. Reid, ed., *Battleground: The Autobiography of Margaret A. Haley* (Urbana: University of Illinois Press, 1982), 33–34; Collins, "Schoolmen," 157–59. Annual contracts were still signed after 1895, but renewal was reasonably certain. For a general treatment of teachers' pensions, see William Graebner, "Retirement in Education: The Economic and Social Functions of the Teachers' Pension," *History of Education Quarterly* 18 (Winter 1978): 397–417.

17. De Luce, "Pension Movement"; "The Chicago Teachers' Federation,"

November 3, 1906, typescript, CTF Papers; Reid, *Battleground*, 34; Collins, "Schoolmen," 157–58.

18. "The Chicago Teachers' Federation," undated (1905?) typescript, CTF Papers.

19. "Chicago Teachers' Federation," November 3, 1906, CTF Papers.

20. *Chicago Tribune*, March 16, 1899.

21. "Report, Showing Results of Fifteen Years of Organization, to the Teachers of Chicago," December 1, 1908, 4, 9, 11, CTF Papers; Reid, *Battleground*, 34; E. Benjamin Andrews, "The Public School System of Chicago," *Education* 20 (January 1900): 264–65; *Chicago Tribune*, March 15, 1899.

22. Reid, *Battleground*, 35.

23. Ibid., 39.

24. Collins, "Schoolmen," 162.

25. "Mass Meeting of Grade Teachers," February 18, 1899, CTF Papers; Collins, "Schoolmen," 162–63.

26. Reid, *Battleground*, xx.

27. Collins, "Schoolmen," 163; *Chicago Teachers' Federation Bulletin* 1 (June 13, 1902): 2.

28. Reid, *Battleground*, 3–27; *Union Labor Advocate* 7 (October 1906): 6. For an example of Haley's frenetic lobbying at Springfield, see Margaret A. Haley to Catherine Goggin, November 13, 1900, CTF Papers.

29. Reid, *Battleground*, 33, 176–77; Collins, "Schoolmen," 158–59.

30. *Chicago Tribune*, March 26, 1899.

31. *Chicago Tribune*, March 24, 1899.

32. Reid, *Battleground*, 40 and, more generally, 37–38; *Chicago Tribune*, March 25, 1899.

33. *Chicago Tribune*, November 7, 1902.

34. *Chicago Tribune*, November 16, 1902.

35. *Chicago Tribune*, November 14, 1902; see also November 8, 9, 13.

36. *Chicago Teachers' Federation Bulletin* 4 (December 2, 1904): 5; Haley to Goggin, undated (probably 1900), CTF Papers; "To the Newspapers of Illinois," October 1900, CTF Papers; Reid, *Battleground*, 65–66.

37. *The Dial* 26 (April 16, 1899): 262–63.

38. *The Dial* 27 (July 1, 1899): 10.

39. Julia Wrigley, *Class Politics and Public Schools* (New Brunswick, N.J.: Rutgers University Press, 1982), 102–3. For Haley's claims, see *CTF Bulletin* 2 (January 16, 1903): 1–2; ibid., (January 23, 1903): 1–2; and ibid., (January 30, 1903): 1–2. For support of the Cooley school bill, see "Proposed Legislation for Chicago," *Educational Review* 25 (February 1903): 214–16. For CTF hostility to the proposed Chicago charter, see *CTF Bulletin* 7 (September 17, 1907): 4.

40. *Chicago Tribune*, November 11, 1902. For Cooley and reorganization, see Truman A. DeWeese, "Two Years' Progress in the Chicago Public Schools," *Educational Review* 24 (November 1902): 325–37; Collins, "Schoolmen," 197–98; Murphy, "From Artisan to Semi-Professional," 54–61.

41. John Dewey, "Democracy in Education," *Elementary School Teacher* 4 (1903): 195. On Cooley's new contract, see DeWeese, "Progress," 328, and Hogan, *Class and Reform*, 200–201. For the merit system and CTF opposition to it, see *CTF Bulletin* 1 (September 19, 1902): 1; Margaret A. Haley to the Editor, 1904, CTF Papers; "Fifteen Years of Organization," 1908, 13, CTF Papers; Reid, *Battleground*, 86–87; and George H. Mead, "The Educational Situation in the Chicago Public Schools," *City Club Bulletin* 1 (May 8, 1907): 134. For the end of advisory teachers' councils, see Reid, *Battleground*, 114.

42. Don T. Davis, "The Chicago Teachers' Federation and the School Board," February 1917, 2, typescript, CTF Papers; *CTF Bulletin* 1 (November 15, 1901): 1–2; Carter H. Harrison to Helen B. Eastman, March 8, 1900, CTF Papers; Reid, *Battleground*, 43–50.

43. Graham H. Harris to Catherine Goggin, January 2, 1900, CTF Papers; CTF Minutes, January 20, 1900, CTF Papers; Haley to Goggin, November 13, 1900, CTF Papers; Robert L. Reid, "The Professionalization of Public School Teachers: The Chicago Experience, 1895–1920" (Ph.D. diss., Northwestern University, 1968), 62–63.

44. "Mass Meeting of the Teachers' Federation at Central Music Hall," October 29, 1900, transcript, CTF Papers; Reid, *Battleground*, 50–67; "Victory for the Teachers," *The School Weekly* 7 (May 3, 1901); "A Tax Reform Victory," *Outlook* 69 (November 2, 1901): 527–28.

45. Reid, *Battleground*, 72. The *CTF Bulletin* followed the tax fight from November 15, 1901 to its conclusion; see volume 1 (1901–2). See also Reid, "Professionalization of Teachers," 63–64; Marjorie Murphy, "Taxation and Social Conflict: Teacher Unionism and Public School Finance in Chicago, 1898–1934," *Journal of the Illinois State Historical Society* 74 (Winter 1981): 248; and *Margaret A. Haley's Bulletin* 1 (October 21, 1915): 4. For the pension, see Graham H. Harris to Governor Richard Yates, May 7, 1901, CTF Papers.

46. "Fifteen Years of Organization," 10, CTF Papers; *CTF Bulletin* 1 (September 19, 1902): 1; *CTF Bulletin* 3 (September 9, 1904): 1–5.

47. *CTF Bulletin* 2 (November 14, 1902): 1.

48. *Chicago Tribune*, November 12, 1902.

49. *Chicago Tribune*, November 23, 1902.

50. For the CFL election, see *CTF Bulletin* 2 (January 23, 1903): 6–8; Reid, *Battleground*, 91–93; and Eugene Staley, *A History of the Illinois State Federation of Labor* (Chicago: University of Chicago Press, 1929), 190. For Haley's political activities in Springfield and Chicago, see *CTF Bulletin* 1 (June 6, 1902): 1–2; idem., (October 24, 1902): 1–3, 6; *CTF Bulletin* 2 (March 13, 1903): 1; idem., (April 24, 1903): 4; and Reid, "Professionalization of Teachers," 88–90. For use of children, see "Address of Miss Margaret A. Haley, before Public Ownership League of the Chicago Federation of Labor," August 29, 1914, CTF Papers. The nonbinding public ownership measures passed without difficulty in the 1902 Chicago election (*Chicago Tribune*, April 2, 1902).

51. National Educational Association, *Proceedings 1904*, 146.

52. Ibid., 146, 150.

53. City of Chicago, *Proceedings of the Board of Education, City of Chicago, 1904–1905*, June 21, 1905, 785, 814.

54. "School Question in Chicago," *Elementary School Teacher* 7 (February 1907): 365.

55. Reid, "Professionalization of Teachers," 101; *Chicago Tribune*, November 7–12, 1902; "The Chicago Teachers' Federation," November 13, 1906, CTF Papers. The CTF never went on strike during its affiliation with organized labor. For criticism of the union affiliation, see "Struggle in the School System of Chicago," *School Review* 15 (February 1907): 160–65, and "Teachers and the Federation of Labor," *Scribner's* 33 (June 1903): 763–64. For qualified support, see "Teachers' Federation and Labor Unionism," *Elementary School Teacher* 5 (March 1905): 439–46.

56. Steffens, *Shame of the Cities*. For the development of public transit in all its forms in three major cities, see Charles W. Cheape, *Moving the Masses: Urban Public Transit in New York, Boston, and Philadelphia, 1880–1912* (Cambridge, Mass.: Harvard University Press, 1980).

57. Civic Federation of Chicago, *The Street Railways of Chicago* (Chicago: Civic Federation of Chicago, 1901), 7–8; Edward F. Dunne, *Illinois: The Heart of the Nation* (Chicago: Lewis Publishing, 1933), 2: 196–202.

58. For Yerkes and his streetcar lines, see Civic Federation of Chicago, *Street Railways*, 38–45; Harvey Wish, "The Administration of Governor John Peter Altgeld of Illinois, 1893–1897" (Ph.D. diss., Northwestern University, 1936), 270–71; Clarence S. Darrow, "The Chicago Traction Question," *International Quarterly* 12 (October 1905): 16–18; and Ray Ginger, *Altgeld's America: The Lincoln Ideal versus Changing Realities* (New York: Funk & Wagnalls, 1958; reprint, New York: New Viewpoints, 1973), 107–8. For a modest defense of Yerkes, see Forrest McDonald, *Insull* (Chicago: University of Chicago Press, 1962), 85. For Harrison and Yerkes, see Carter H. Harrison, *Stormy Years: The Autobiography of Carter H. Harrison* (Indianapolis, Ind.: Bobbs-Merrill, 1935), 147.

59. For Altgeld's veto, see Wish, "Altgeld," 282–87. For the Allen bill and the opposition it provoked in Chicago, see Harrison, *Stormy Years*, 136–75. For Yerkes's departure, see "The Story of the Street Car Companies of Chicago," in William L. Sullivan, ed., *Dunne: Judge, Mayor, Governor* (Chicago: Windermere Press, 1916), 216–17.

60. For Grosscup, see "Street Car Companies of Chicago," 217. Support for municipal ownership and the passage of the Mueller bill are covered in Dunne, *Illinois*, 2: 224–26, and Ginger, *Altgeld's America*, 270–77. For the municipal-ownership coalition, see Chester M. Destler, *Henry Demarest Lloyd and the Empire of Reform* (Philadelphia: University of Pennsylvania Press, 1963), 515–16. For an account of the General Assembly melee, see *Chicago Chronicle*, April 24, 1903.

61. Harrison, *Stormy Years*, 245–50.

62. Destler, *Henry Demarest Lloyd*, 515–23 (Lloyd died at the height of the campaign); Tuley's letter can be found in Sullivan, *Dunne*, 170–75.

63. *Chicago Tribune*, April 7, 1904.

64. Haley to Owen P. Thompson, May 2, 1911, CTF Papers. For appointments to the school board, see *CTF Bulletin* 3 (April 8, 1904): 3.

65. *Chicago Tribune*, April 5, 1904.

66. *Chicago Tribune*, April 6, 7, 1904; Richard Becker, "Edward Dunne, Reform Mayor of Chicago, 1905–1907" (Ph.D. diss., University of Chicago, 1971), 98–99. In 1904, 230,777 voters cast ballots for aldermen and 171,637 voted on the IMO proposition.

67. *Chicago Tribune*, April 6, 1904.

68. Becker, "Dunne," 43–44; Dunne, *Illinois*, 2: 502.

69. Becker, "Dunne," 31–40, 177–79.

70. For arrests, see *Union Labor Advocate* 6 (October 1905): 24. For the failure of the Commission of Inquiry and the collapse of the strike, see Graham Taylor, *Pioneering on Social Frontiers* (Chicago: University of Chicago Press, 1930), 138–40, and Becker, "Dunne," 69–72.

71. *Union Labor Advocate* 6 (September 1905): 18.

72. Dunne, *Illinois*, 2: 268.

73. Becker, "Dunne," 99–102; Ginger, *Altgeld's America*, 297; Dunne, *Illinois*, 2: 268–73, quotation on 276.

74. *Chicago Tribune*, February 9, 10, 1906; Ginger, *Altgeld's America*, 299–300.

75. Becker, "Dunne," 122–26; Harrison, *Stormy Years*, 244–45; Ginger, *Altgeld's America*, 300; Dunne, *Illinois*, 2: 277–78. In the 1906 election, the ordinance issuing Mueller certificates received 110,225 favorable votes and 106,859 negative ones. The municipal operation ordinance received inadequate approval by a vote of 121,916 to 110,323. In mid-April 1907, the Illinois Supreme Court ruled that the Mueller certificates exceeded Chicago's legal debt limitation and therefore were unconstitutional (Ginger, *Altgeld's America*, 302).

76. "The Chicago Election and the City's Traction Outlook," *Review of Reviews* 35 (May 1907): 581–85; Becker, "Dunne," 130–33.

77. *Union Labor Advocate* 7 (January 1907): 26.

78. Ibid., 26–28; Dunne, *Illinois*, 2: 279–88; "The Chicago Election and the City's Traction Outlook," 581.

79. McDonald, *Insull*, 127–28, 156–58.

80. For Addams and De Bey, see *CTF Bulletin* 4 (September 15, 1905): 4–5, and Reid, *Battleground*, 102–3. For the other appointees, see Dominic Candeloro, "The Chicago School Board Crisis of 1907," *Journal of the Illinois State Historical Society* 68 (November 1975): 397–98; Collins, "Schoolmen," 219–21; and "The Public Schools of Chicago," 1907, 2–4, pamphlet, CTF Papers.

81. "Report of the Sub-Committee of the School Management Committee of the Board of Education of the City of Chicago on the Secret Marking System and its Salary Promotional Features in use with Reference to Teachers in the Chicago Public School Service," 1906, typescript, CTF Papers; Collins, "Schoolmen," 221–26; Reid, "Professionalization of Teachers," 120–28; Candeloro, "Chicago School Board Crisis," 398–401; Reid, *Battleground*, 106–7; Hogan, *Class and Reform*, 204–6.

82. For opposition to the Post plan, see Candeloro, "Chicago School Board Crisis," 399. Addams's viewpoint is presented in Jane Addams, *Twenty Years at Hull-House* (New York: Macmillan, 1910; reprint, New York: Signet, 1960), 231–36. On tax fight proceeds, see "Struggle in the School System of Chicago," *School Review* 15 (February 1907): 160. Haley criticizes Addams in Reid, *Battleground*, 103 (quotation), 113. For a defense of Haley, see Murphy, "From Artisan to Semi-Professional," 121–26.

83. George S. Counts, *School and Society in Chicago* (New York: Harcourt, Brace, 1928), 58–59; "School Report of 1895," mimeograph, CTF Papers; "The Truth of the *Tribune's* 'Lease,'" CFL Circular, CTF Papers; Reid, *Battleground*, 114–20; Candeloro, "Chicago School Board Crisis," 401.

84. *Chicago Tribune*, October 10, 1906.

85. Quotations from *Educational Review* 33 (May 1907): 538, and "School Question in Chicago," *Elementary School Teacher* 7 (February 1907): 362. See also Collins, "Schoolmen," 226–27, and Reid, "Professionalization of Teachers," 128–30.

86. On Busse and the final stage of the school board crisis, see George C. Sikes, "Chicago's New Mayor," *Review of Reviews* 35 (May 1907): 585–88, and Candeloro, "Chicago School Board Crisis," 401–6. Busse captured 164,702 votes, Dunne received 151,779, and some 13,000 went to the Socialist candidate (Candeloro, "Chicago School Board Crisis," 401).

87. Counts, *School and Society in Chicago*, 136–44, 166–67; Reid, "Professionalization of Teachers," 147–57; Reid, *Battleground*, 162–63; Diner, *A City and Its Universities*, 94–96.

88. Reid, *Battleground*, 179. For the decision, see *The People vs. City of Chicago*, 278, Ill. 313 (1917).

89. "Resolution Adopted by the Board of Education of the City of Chicago," April 16, 1913, CTF Papers; "The Business Man in Office," *New Republic* 7 (July 15, 1916): 267–68; Reid, *Battleground*, 166; *Margaret A. Haley's Bulletin* 1 (September-December 1915); Transcript of Chicago Board of Education meeting, June 27, 1916, CTF Papers; *Chicago Tribune*, June 28, 1916; Illinois State Federation of Labor, "Report of the Committee on Schools," October 16, 1916, 6, CTF Papers; CFL, "Report Recommending the Withdrawal of the Chicago Teachers' Federation," May 20, 1917, CTF Papers; *School and Society* 5 (April 28, 1917): 492.

90. Reid, *Battleground*, 189.

91. Tyack, *Best System*, 171–72.

Chapter 6

1. *City Club Bulletin* 5 (March 6, 1912): 33.

2. Quoted in Morton Keller, *Affairs of State: Public Life in Late Nineteenth Century America* (Cambridge, Mass.: Harvard University Press, 1977), 251.

3. W. H. Powell to Joseph Fifer, February 29, 1892, Joseph Fifer Papers, Illi-

nois State Historical Library, Springfield; Lafayette Funk to Fifer, February 10, 1891, Fifer Papers.

4. *Jonesboro Gazette*, May 14, 1892.

5. *Chicago Journal*, February 20, 1892, clipping in Fifer Papers.

6. James J. Walsh to Lawrence Y. Sherman, December 30, 1896, Lawrence Y. Sherman Papers, Illinois State Historical Library, Springfield.

7. Roy O. West to Lawrence Y. Sherman, January 7, 1899, Sherman Papers; Bloomington Republican City Central Committee, Minutes, 1896–1909, entries for April 17, 1896, March 22, 27, and April 3, 7, 15, 1897, Illinois State Historical Library, Springfield; *Blue Book of the State of Illinois 1907* (Springfield: Phillips Brothers, 1908), 468.

8. *Chicago Times* quoted in *Jonesboro Gazette*, April 15, 1893; Ballard C. Campbell, *Representative Democracy: Public Policy and Midwestern Legislatures in the Late Nineteenth Century* (Cambridge, Mass.: Harvard University Press, 1980), 45–47.

9. *Peoria Herald*, April 1, 1899.

10. *Jonesboro Gazette*, March 25, 1893.

11. *Rockford Register-Gazette*, February 25, 1891, October 17, 1892.

12. John R. Tanner, Speech at Golconda, Illinois, September 15, 1898, Sherman Papers.

13. F. Walton to Sherman, March 8, 1897, Sherman Papers; Sherman to H. S. Lewis, March 15, 1897, Sherman Papers.

14. Roy O. West to Sherman, March 26, 1897, Sherman Papers. For German Lutheran antagonism toward the Republican party, see Lutheran School Committee, "To the Friends of Liberty of Conscience and Religion," 1892, Waldo R. Browne Papers, Illinois State Historical Library, Springfield; *Chicago Tribune*, May 29, 1890; *Effingham Democrat*, May 16, 23, 1890, clippings in Walter C. Headen Papers, Illinois Historical Survey, University of Illinois Library, Urbana; and *Illinois State Journal*, April 13, 1892, clipping in Fifer Papers. For ethnocultural conflict in the Midwest, see Paul Kleppner, *The Cross of Culture: A Social Analysis of Midwestern Politics, 1850–1900* (New York: Free Press, 1970), and Richard J. Jensen, *The Winning of the Midwest: Social and Political Conflict, 1888–1896* (Chicago: University of Chicago Press, 1971).

15. Richard L. McCormick, "The Party Period and Public Policy: An Exploratory Hypothesis," in McCormick, *The Party Period and Public Policy: American Politics from the Age of Jackson to the Progressive Era* (New York: Oxford University Press, 1986), 197–227. For an approach to the decline of parties that emphasizes shifts in the style of political campaigns, see Michael E. McGerr, *The Decline of Popular Politics: The American North, 1865–1928* (New York: Oxford University Press, 1986).

16. Cary A. Vaughan to Fifer, June 28, 1892, Fifer Papers.

17. Robert W. Cherny, *Populism, Progressivism, and the Transformation of Nebraska Politics, 1885–1915* (Lincoln: University of Nebraska Press, 1981), 147; Jensen, *Winning of Midwest*, 154–77; *Sheffield Times*, March 8, 1912. For a cautionary note describing the unintended consequences of ballot reforms in New

York and New Jersey, see John F. Reynolds and Richard L. McCormick, "Outlawing 'Treachery': Split Tickets and Ballot Laws in New York and New Jersey, 1880–1910," *Journal of American History* 72 (March 1986): 835–58.

18. Richard L. McCormick, *From Realignment to Reform: Political Change in New York State, 1893–1910* (Ithaca: Cornell University Press, 1981).

19. Campbell, *Representative Democracy,* 31–32, 228. Campbell determined that between 1886 and 1895, 68 percent of the members serving in the lower house of the Illinois General Assembly were freshmen legislators, only 5 percent of them had three consecutive terms in office, and only 25 percent of the legislators were reelected to the next session. In contrast, 52 percent of the lower house members at the 1907 session of the General Assembly were freshmen, 15 percent of the members had served three consecutive terms, and 56 percent of the representatives were reelected to the 1909 session (*Blue Book,* 242–93).

20. William Chaplin to Len Small, March 1912, Len Small Papers, Illinois State Historical Library, Springfield.

21. J. F. Montague to Len Small, March 29, 1912, Small Papers. See also the following documents, all in Small Papers: James Lee Greenville to Small, March 28, 1912; A. Holman to Small, March 23, 1912; Frank Heilman to Small, March 30, 1912; Andrew Glover to Small, March 21, 1912; R. C. Rains to Small, April 4, 1912; H. M. Redding to Small, March 26, 1912; G. W. Crider to Small, April 1, 1912.

22. See Harry Barnard, *Eagle Forgotten: The Life of John Peter Altgeld* (Indianapolis, Ind.: Bobbs-Merrill, 1938); Ray Ginger, *Altgeld's America: The Lincoln Ideal versus Changing Realities* (New York: Funk & Wagnalls, 1958; reprint, New York: New Viewpoints, 1973); Kleppner, *Cross of Culture,* 242–43.

23. *Rockford Register-Gazette,* May 12, 13, 1892.

24. W. T. Hodson to Fifer, September 24, 1892, Fifer Papers; *Rockford Register-Gazette,* September 24, 1892.

25. Joseph Medill to Fifer, 1892, Fifer Papers.

26. Ethel L. Dewey, ed., *Recollections of Richard Dewey* (Chicago: University of Chicago Press, 1936), 147–52; Barnard, *Eagle Forgotten,* 169; Ginger, *Altgeld's America,* 75; William R. Brock, *Investigation and Responsibility: Public Responsibility in the United States, 1865–1900* (Cambridge: Cambridge University Press, 1984), 100.

27. For the history of the board, see Board of State Commissioners of Public Charities of the State of Illinois, *12th Biennial Report* [1892] (Springfield: H. W. Rokker, 1893), 88–107. On Wines, see Brock, *Investigation and Responsibility,* 99–102. For Kankakee, see Henry M. Hurd, ed., *The Institutional Care of the Insane in the United States and Canada* (Baltimore, Md.: Johns Hopkins University Press, 1917), 4: 531–34; Gerald N. Grob, *Mental Illness and American Society, 1875–1940* (Princeton, N.J.: Princeton University Press, 1983), 99–102. Meyer's tenure there is chronicled in Eunice E. Winters, "Adolf Meyer's Two and a Half Years at Kankakee May 1, 1893-November 1, 1895," *Bulletin of the History of Medicine* 40 (September-October 1966): 441–58. For a stinging critique of state institutions in the Progressive Era (and beyond), see David J. Rothman,

Conscience and Convenience: The Asylum and its Alternatives in Progressive America (Boston: Little, Brown, 1980). The experiences of Meyer, who drew on the pragmatism of Charles Peirce, John Dewey, and William James in developing his approach to "pluralism" in mental illness and decried the interference of Altgeld into hospital affairs, illustrate the gap between progressive intellectual ferment and political reform. For critical appraisals of Meyer, see Grob, *Mental Illness,* 112–18, and Rothman, *Conscience and Convenience,* 302–20. For Meyer's work, see Eunice E. Winters, ed., *The Collected Papers of Adolf Meyer,* 4 vols. (Baltimore, Md.: Johns Hopkins University Press, 1950–2).

28. Board of Public Charities, *Report 1892,* 91, 100; E. L. Merritt to Altgeld, October 15, 1902, Waldo R. Browne Papers.

29. Board of Public Charities, *Report 1888,* 194. For examples of political activity in state institutions, see E. J. Murphy to J. B. Messick, January 19, 1892, Fifer Papers; Fifer to Henry D. Dement, February 22, 1892, Fifer Papers; and Walter S. Rundle to Lawrence Y. Sherman, April 5, 1897, Sherman Papers.

30. Lucy L. Flower, "The Merit System in Public Institutions," *National Conference of Charities and Correction Proceedings* 23 (1896), 388–91, quotation on 390. For an anecdotal account of appalling conditions at the Cook County Asylum in the 1880s, see Victor Robinson, *The Don Quixote of Psychiatry* (New York: Historico-Medical Press, 1919), 72–97.

31. Board of Public Charities, *Report 1890,* 81–100, quotations on 87.

32. Board of Public Charities, *Report 1892,* 60.

33. Board of Public Charities, *Report 1894,* 44; idem., *Report 1892,* 162 (quotation). Brock makes this point for public charity boards across the United States (*Investigation and Responsibility,* 90–91).

34. Frederick H. Wines, "Ideal Public Charity," *National Conference of Charities and Correction Proceedings* 22 (1895): 35. See also Henry Smith Williams, "Politics and the Insane," *North American Review* 161 (October 1895): 394–404.

35. Altgeld speech at Sterling, Illinois, September, 1892, Browne Papers.

36. *Chicago Tribune,* September 14, 1892: *Weekly Illinois State Register,* September 22, 1892; W. P. Callon to Altgeld, September 28, 1892, Browne Papers.

37. For Fifer's denial, see *Chicago Tribune,* September 21, 1892. The political relationship between Fifer, Cullom, and Tanner is analyzed in James W. Fullinwider, "The Governor and the Senator: Executive Power and the Structure of the Illinois Republican Party, 1880–1917" (Ph.D. diss., Washington University, 1974), 21, 23–29. For Fifer's appointees, see E. J. Murphy to J. B. Messick, January 19, 1892, Fifer Papers; Fifer to Henry D. Dement, February 22, 1892, Fifer Papers; A. T. Barnes to Fifer, November 3, 1892, Fifer Papers; and J. H. Clark to Fifer, November 19, 1892, Fifer Papers.

38. 1892 clipping from *Sparta Plaindealer* in scrapbook, Fifer Papers; *Fifteenth Biennial Report of the Illinois Northern Hospital for the Insane* (Springfield: Phillipps Brothers, 1898).

39. E. L. Merritt to Altgeld, October 15, 1892, Browne Papers.

40. *Chicago Tribune,* January 20, 1893.

41. Luther L. Hiatt to Altgeld, January 18, 1893, John P. Altgeld, Official

Gubernatorial Correspondence, Illinois State Archives, Springfield. See also W. R. Newton to William Dose, January 17, 1893, and C. W. Marsh to Altgeld, January 16, 1893, Altgeld Correspondence.

42. *Chicago Tribune*, January 16, 1893; Hurd, *Institutional Care of the Insane*, 2: 256–57.

43. Wish, "Administration of Altgeld," 50–51.

44. Grob, *Mental Illness and American Society*, 64–65; Dewey, *Recollections*, 149–52; Winters, "Meyer's Years at Kankakee," 442–43. For Clevenger's point of view, see Robinson, *Don Quixote of Psychiatry*, 110–22.

45. For Cleveland appointment, see Illinois Central Hospital for the Insane, Jacksonville, *24th Biennial Report* (Springfield: Hartmann, 1894), 6. For Mc-Claughry, see Chairman Democratic Central Committee to Altgeld, February 8, 1894, Altgeld Correspondence, Illinois State Archives; R. W. McClaughry to Altgeld, May 7, 1894, Altgeld Correspondence; McClaughry to Altgeld, January 7, 1896, Altgeld Correspondence; and *Chicago Tribune*, September 9, 1892, January 24, 1893. For appointment of women and rejection of nepotism, see Wish, "Administration of Altgeld," 53–54. Republican critics had predicted that Altgeld's partisan design would exclude women appointees, because "only voters will be tolerated on the payrolls" (see *Chicago Tribune*, November 19, 1892).

46. For Altgeld's interest in penal reform, see John Peter Altgeld, *Live Questions: Including Our Penal Machinery and Its Victims* (Chicago: Donahue, Henneberry, 1890); for the abolition of striped prison uniforms, see Wish, "Administration of Altgeld," 314. For competitive bidding and detailed records in state hospitals, see Northern Hospital for the Insane, *14th Biennial Report, 1896*, 7, 86–91, and Central Hospital for the Insane, *24th Biennial Report, 1894*, 5–6. For overcrowding, see Board of Public Charities, *Report 1894*, 32–33. On Altgeld's veto and push for new hospitals, see Wish, "Administration of Altgeld," 318, and Waldo R. Browne, *Altgeld of Illinois* (New York: B. W. Huebsch, 1924), 228–29. See also the report to Altgeld from Adolf Meyer reproduced in Winters, *Collected Papers of Adolf Meyer*, 2: 37–49.

47. Browne, *Altgeld of Illinois*, 225.

48. Board of Public Charities, *Report 1894*, 33–37; idem., *Report 1896*, 43–47; *National Conference of Charities and Correction Proceedings* 22 (1895): 343; *National Conference of Charities and Correction Proceedings* 23 (1896): 36; Adolf Meyer to G. Stanley Hall, December 7, 1895, in Gerald N. Grob, *The Inner World of American Psychiatry, 1890–1940* (New Brunswick, N.J.: Rutgers University Press, 1985), 60–61; Barnard, *Eagle Forgotten*, 171.

49. W. G. Eggleston to Altgeld, November 8, 1895, Altgeld Correspondence. For Altgeld's devotion to the University of Illinois, see Altgeld to Lambert Tree, May 11, 1897, Browne Papers, and, for his policies and appointments, Browne, *Altgeld of Illinois*, 210–18. For Schilling's report, see *Eighth Biennial Report of the Bureau of Labor Statistics of Illinois* (1894).

50. Barnard, *Eagle Forgotten*, 177; Niels H. Debel, "The Veto Power of the Governor of Illinois," *University of Illinois Studies in the Social Sciences* 6 (June 1917): 87.

51. For detailed treatments of these themes among the party leadership, see

Fullinwider, "The Governor and the Senator," and Joel A. Tarr, *A Study in Boss Politics: William Lorimer of Chicago* (Urbana: University of Illinois Press, 1971), 89–114.

52. G. H. Lane to S. B. Roach, September 15, 1911, Small Papers; Lane to C. E. Robinson, November 1, 1911, Small Papers. See also Robert L. Reid, ed., *Battleground: The Autobiography of Margaret A. Haley* (Urbana: University of Illinois Press, 1982), 64.

53. Board of Public Charities, *Report 1906*, 190.

54. Northern Hospital for the Insane, *15th Biennial Report 1898*.

55. *Charities* 9 (September 6, 1902): 211.

56. Fullinwider, "Governor and Senator," 82–87.

57. Francis A. Riddle to Lawrence Y. Sherman, March 18, 1901, Sherman Papers. For Tanner, see "Politics and the Public Charities of Illinois," *Charities* 8 (June 7, 1902): 532–37. For resignations, see Board of Public Charities, *Report 1910*, 318.

58. *Charities* 9 (September 6, 1902): 210–11. See also Board of Public Charities, *Report 1902*, 9, and Board of Public Charities, *Report 1910*, 319.

59. *Charities* 9 (August 2, 1902): 97 (quotation); Board of Public Charities, *Report 1910*, 230–31; Fullinwider, "Governor and Senator," 131.

60. *Charities* 9 (October 25, 1902): 389–90; ibid., (November 1, 1902): 423; *Charities* 10 (January 17, 1903): 64–65; Board of Public Charities, *Report 1902*, 319–23; unidentified newspaper clipping, 1903, Sherman Papers; Fullinwider, "Governor and Senator," 125–30.

61. Roy O. West and William C. Walton, "Charles S. Deneen 1863–1940," *Journal of the Illinois State Historical Society* 34 (March 1941): 7–9, quotation on 9.

62. William T. Hutchinson, *Lowden of Illinois* (Chicago: University of Chicago Press, 1957), 1: 123.

63. Charles E. Merriam, *Chicago: A More Intimate View of Urban Politics* (New York: Macmillan, 1929), 181; Tarr, *Boss Politics*, 127.

64. Charles E. Merriam and Louise Overacker, *Primary Elections* (Chicago: University of Chicago Press, 1928), 61–62; Fullinwider, "Governor and Senator," 159–160; *City Club Bulletin* 1 (February 19, 1908): 384.

65. Walter Clyde Jones, "The Direct Primary in Illinois," *Annals of the American Political Science Association* 7 (1910): 140–42; Fullinwider, "Governor and Senator," 162–64.

66. Edward Pierson to John G. Oglesby, March 26, 1908, John G. Oglesby Papers, Illinois State Historical Library, Springfield.

67. "The Administration of Charles S. Deneen, 1905–1912," campaign pamphlet, 26–27, Charles S. Deneen Papers, Illinois State Historical Library, Springfield; Edward D. Shurtleff to Oglesby, January 7, 1908, Oglesby Papers; *City Club Bulletin* 1 (February 19, 1908): 383–92; Fullinwider, "Governor and Senator," 185–90.

68. Len Small to J. E. N. Edwards, April 26, 1912, Small Papers.

69. *Charities and the Commons* 17 (April 26, 1907): 932 (quotation); Board of Public Charities, *Report 1910*, 127–28; idem., *Report 1906*, 143–245.

70. Hutchinson, *Lowden of Illinois*, 1: 123.

71. Ernest L. Bogart and John M. Mathews, *The Modern Commonwealth, 1893–1918* (Springfield: Illinois Centennial Commission, 1920), 278; Fullinwider, "Governor and Senator," 172–73.

72. 45th General Assembly, *House Journal 1908*, 1171–72.

73. Board of Public Charities, *Report 1906*, 194.

74. Shurtleff to Oglesby, February 7, 1908, Oglesby Papers.

75. *House Journal 1908*, 1716–72.

76. *Charities and the Commons* 19 (March 7, 1908): 1657–59; *Charities and the Commons* 20 (May 30, 1908): 284–85; William C. Graves, "The Problem of State Supervision in Illinois," *National Conference of Charities and Correction Proceedings* 36 (1909): 430–39.

77. O. L. Mann to Frank O. Lowden, June 10, 1908, Frank O. Lowden Papers, Special Collections, University of Chicago Library.

78. Harry B. Ward to Lowden, April 11, 1906, Lowden Papers; Tarr, *Boss Politics*, 190–94; United States Senate, *Senator from Illinois: Proceedings before a Committee of the United States Senate* (62d Congress, First Session, 1911), 4: 1109–11.

79. B. Y. Shaw to Lowden, April 17, 1908, Lowden Papers.

80. Tarr, *Boss Politics*, 190–91.

81. Fullinwider, "Governor and Senator," 187, n. 69.

82. Tarr, *Boss Politics*, 188; Ralph A. Straetz, "The Progressive Movement in Illinois, 1910–1916" (Ph.D. diss., University of Illinois, 1951), 3.

83. W. E. Taylor to Len Small, February 2, 1912, Small Papers.

84. *Senator from Illinois*, 4: 1180–90; Straetz, "Progressive Movement in Illinois," 53; Fullinwider, "Governor and Senator," 197–98.

85. On Rock Island County, see A. E. Williams to Len Small, October 17, 1911, Small Papers, and Gust Falk to C. R. Miller, (April?) 1912, Small Papers. On Danville, see F. D. Knox to Small, February 13, 1912, Small Papers.

86. George N. Kreider to Small, March 20, 1912, Small Papers.

87. A. D. Warner to Len Small, March 22, 1912, Small Papers. For Rockford newspapers, see Warner to Small, January 26, 1912, Small Papers, and Thomas Ferguson to Small, April 5, 1912, Small Papers.

88. Tarr, *Boss Politics*, 202–4; *City Club Bulletin* 2 (December 16, 1908): 207–13.

89. The narrative of the deadlock and the ensuing Lorimer scandal is from the detailed account in Tarr, *Boss Politics*, 199 ff.

90. Harry B. Ward to Frank O. Lowden, September 6, 1909, Lowden Papers. For background on Lorimer, see Tarr, *Boss Politics*, 5–12.

91. *Senator from Illinois*, 4: 1121–29.

92. *City Club Bulletin* 3 (October 19, 1910): 364.

93. "Resolutions Adopted by Conference at Peoria, Illinois, June 28, 1910," Raymond Robins Papers, State Historical Society of Wisconsin, Madison.

94. Committee of Seven circular, "Representative Government at Stake," August 10, 1910, Robins Papers; Straetz, "Progressive Movement in Illinois," 34–38.

95. Graham Taylor, "Lincoln's Soul Goes Marching on in Illinois," *Survey* 24 (September 3, 1910): 750–55; "Citizens' Campaign Waged in Illinois," *Survey* 25 (October 1, 1910): 5–6; C. O. Gardner, "The Working of the State-Wide Referendum in Illinois," *American Political Science Review* 5 (August 1911): 417.

96. *City Club Bulletin* 3 (October 19, 1910): 368.

97. Fletcher Dobyns to Charles S. Deneen, September 3, 1912, Robins Papers. See also *Chicago Inter-Ocean*, July 16, 1910, clipping in Charles E. Merriam Papers, Special Collections, University of Chicago Library. For Deneen and Cannon, see Straetz, "Progressive Movement in Illinois," 30.

98. *City Club Bulletin* 4 (August 14, 1911): 188.

99. Harold Ickes, *The Autobiography of a Curmudgeon* (New York: Reynal and Hitchcock, 1943), 142. For Merriam's commission, see Michael P. McCarthy, "Businessmen and Professionals in Municipal Reform" (Ph.D. diss., Northwestern University, 1970), 145–50. The 1911 campaign is recounted in Straetz, "Progressive Movement in Illinois," 79–88.

100. Deneen to Raymond Robins, May 11, 1912, Robins Papers; Robins to Deneen, May 8, 1911, Robins Papers; Fullinwider, "Governor and Senator," 250–51.

101. Straetz, "Progressive Movement in Illinois," 115–17, 179–80; Fullinwider, "Governor and Senator," 251–52.

102. Tarr, *Boss Politics*, 286–90; Fullinwider, "Governor and Senator," 262. Deneen received 152,997 votes, Small 88,829, and Jones 22,491.

103. Straetz, "Progressive Movement in Illinois," 309, 325–27.

104. Local Good Government League campaign letter, October 26, 1912, Deneen Papers.

105. Dunne received 443,120 votes, Deneen 318,469, and Funk 303,401. Fullinwider, "Governor and Senator," 270.

106. Fletcher Dobyns to Deneen, September 3, 1912, Robins Papers.

107. Medill McCormick to Chauncey Dewey, November 19, 1912, Robins Papers.

108. Straetz, "Progressive Movement in Illinois," 452–54, 462–63; Ickes to Robins, December 24, 1912, Robins Papers; Ickes, *Curmudgeon*, 166–68.

109. John M. Mathews, "The New Role of the Governor," *American Political Science Review* 6 (May 1912): 226.

Chapter 7

1. *City Club Bulletin* 3 (November 5, 1910): 379.

2. *City Club Bulletin* 3 (September 14, 1910): 336, 338–39.

3. *City Club Bulletin* 3 (November 5, 1910): 382–83.

4. *City Club Bulletin* 3 (September 14, 1910): 342. On cumulative voting, see George S. Blair, "The Adoption of Cumulative Voting in Illinois," *Journal of the Illinois State Historical Society* 47 (Winter 1954): 373–84.

5. *City Club Bulletin* 5 (March 6, 1912): 40.

6. Arthur S. Link and Richard L. McCormick, *Progressivism* (Arlington Heights, Illinois: Harlan Davidson, 1983), 62.

7. For Merriam's analysis, see Charles E. Merriam, "Investigation as a Means of Securing Administrative Efficiency," *Annals of the American Academy of Political and Social Science* 41 (May 1912): 281–303. For the shale scam and Busse's associates, see William Bayard Hale, "Chicago—Its Struggle and Its Dream," *World's Work* 19 (April 1910): 12800–801. See also *Outlook* 94 (March 5, 1910): 509–11. Resignations and indictments are treated in Michael P. McCarthy, "Businessmen and Professionals in Municipal Reform: The Chicago Experience, 1887–1920" (Ph.D. diss., Northwestern University, 1970), 149–50.

8. *City Club Bulletin* 3 (June 8, 1910): 315–17. See Martin J. Schiesl, *The Politics of Efficiency: Municipal Administration and Reform in America, 1880–1920* (Berkeley: University of California Press, 1977) for an account of fiscal reform in a number of cities, including Chicago (99–108) and for an analysis of the New York Bureau of Municipal Research and its national influence (112–26).

9. Chicago Bureau of Public Efficiency, *Unification of Local Governments in Chicago* (January 1917), 17.

10. Chicago Bureau of Public Efficiency, *The Nineteen Local Governments of Chicago* (December 1913), 5–11; idem., *Consolidation of Local Governments in Chicago* (January 1920).

11. William T. Hutchinson, *Lowden of Illinois* (Chicago: University of Chicago Press, 1957), 1: 244.

12. Hutchinson, *Lowden of Illinois*, 1: 311.

13. *Clayton Enterprise*, February 27, 1913.

14. Edward F. Dunne, *Illinois: The Heart of the Nation* (Chicago: Lewis, 1933), 2: 424–26.

15. John D. Buenker, "Edward F. Dunne: The Urban New Stock Democrat as Progressive," *Mid-America* 50 (January 1968): 3–21; Buenker, *Urban Liberalism and Progressive Reform* (New York: Scribner's, 1973).

16. Dunne, *Illinois*, 2: 346–47.

17. *Clayton Enterprise*, July 3, 1913. For two accounts of the legislative session, see Dunne, *Illinois*, 2: 318–27, 347–48, and John A. Fairlie, "The Illinois Legislature of 1913," *Journal of Political Economy* 21 (December 1913): 931–37.

18. *City Club Bulletin* 1 (June 6, 1907): 139.

19. Ernest L. Bogart and John M. Mathews, *The Modern Commonwealth, 1893–1918* (Springfield: Illinois Centennial Commission, 1920), 315.

20. *Report of the Efficiency and Economy Committee Created under the Authority of the Forty-eighth General Assembly* (Chicago: Windermere Press, 1915), 7–11; Bogart and Mathews, *Modern Commonwealth*, 316.

21. Dunne, *Illinois*, 2: 339–40; *Report of the Efficiency and Economy Committee*, 24.

22. *Clayton Enterprise*, May 1, 1913.

23. *City Club Bulletin* 2 (December 9, 1908): 195–96. For the legislative reference bureau, see Charles McCarthy, *The Wisconsin Idea* (New York: Macmillan, 1912), 207–18.

24. *City Club Bulletin* 2 (December 9, 1908): 202.

25. Ibid., 203–5.

26. For the creation of the Illinois Reference Bureau and its functions, see Dunne, *Illinois*, 2: 338–39, and Walter F. Dodd and Sue H. Dodd, *Government in Illinois* (Chicago: University of Chicago Press, 1923), 158–89. On the need for a budget system (and the shortcomings of the bureau), see *Efficiency and Economy Report*, 22, and Bogart and Mathews, *Modern Commonwealth*, 317.

27. Most of the material in this and the following two paragraphs is taken from the *Efficiency and Economy Report*. See also Dunne, *Illinois* 2: 338.

28. *Efficiency and Economy Report*, 18.

29. Ibid., 32.

30. Dunne, *Illinois*, 2: 338.

31. Frank L. Smith press release, December 29, 1915, Frank O. Lowden Papers, Special Collections, University of Chicago Library. For criticism of Dunne, see *Sheffield Times*, August 25, 1916.

32. Frank O. Lowden, draft of speech, January 21, 1915, Lowden Papers.

33. James W. Gordon to William H. Stead, December 16, 1915, Lowden Papers; Cairo A. Trimble to Lowden, September 17, 1915, Lowden Papers. In return for Thompson's aid, Lowden apparently pledged to help the mayor gain the Illinois seat on the Republican national committee (Hutchinson, *Lowden*, 1: 264).

34. Stead to James W. Gordon, December 21, 1915, Lowden Papers.

35. Stead to Lowden, April 8, 1916, Lowden Papers; E. E. Wheeler to Lowden, December 7, 1914, Lowden Papers; Hutchinson, *Lowden*, 1: 266, 277.

36. Lowden to Medill McCormick, undated (April 1916?), Lowden Papers.

37. Stead to James R. Cowley, December 6, 1915, Lowden Papers; Hutchinson, *Lowden*, 1: 273; *Rockford Star*, May 14, 1916, clipping in Lowden Papers. Lowden's campaign had to fight off Anti-Saloon League charges that the candidate was backed by Illinois liquor interests and went to great trouble to dispel damaging rumors that he had made drunken public appearances, suffered from delirium tremens, and otherwise exhibited the degrading effects of personal intemperance. See the following documents in the Lowden Papers: F. Scott McBride to Illinois Supreme Court Justice James H. Cartwright, July 22, 1915; Harry B. Ward to Lowden, July 16, 1915; Theodore S. McCoy to Stead, July 20, 1915; Emery C. Graves to Cowley, August 12, 1916. See also Hutchinson, *Lowden*, 1: 270.

38. W. M. Mercer to Lowden, September 8, 1915, Lowden Papers; Resolutions of the Executive Committee, Progressive-Republican League of Peoria County, August 12, 1916, Lowden Papers; Hutchinson, *Lowden*, 1: 282–91.

39. Frank O. Lowden, "Reorganization in Illinois and Its Results," *Annals of the American Academy of Political and Social Science* 113 (May 1924): 158.

40. Frank O. Lowden, "Executive Responsibility in Illinois," *Proceedings of the Academy of Political Science* 8 (July 1918): 3.

41. Charles E. Woodward, "The Illinois Civil Administrative Code," *Proceedings of the Academy of Political Science* 8 (July 1918): 10.

42. Woodward, "The Illinois Civil Administrative Code," 13.

43. Frank O. Lowden, "Problems of Civil Administration," *North American Review* 210 (August 1919): 188.

44. Lowden, "Reorganization in Illinois and Its Results," 160.

45. Lowden to John L. Dwight, January 25, 1917, Lowden Papers.

46. Hutchinson, *Lowden*, 1: 301.

47. Hutchinson, *Lowden*, 1: 310, n. 33.

48. Theodore Roosevelt to Lowden, February 7, 1917, Lowden Papers; Lowden to Roosevelt, February 15, 1917, Lowden Papers; Walter F. Dodd, "Reorganizing State Government," *Annals of the American Academy of Political and Social Science* 113 (May 1924): 165.

49. Francis W. Shepardson, "The Civil Administrative Code in Operation," *Blue Book of the State of Illinois, 1919–1920*, 8. For spending and the code, see *First Administrative Report of the Directors of Departments under the Civil Administrative Code*, (1918), 17, and Hutchinson, *Lowden*, 1: 313.

50. John H. Walker to William Carter, October 6, 1916, John H. Walker Papers, Illinois Historical Survey, University of Illinois Library, Urbana.

51. Walker to Edward A. Wieck, June 20, 1917, Walker Papers; John H. Walker, "Labor and the War," *Blue Book, 1919–1920*, 111; Illinois State Federation of Labor, *Proceedings 1918*, 169.

52. Samuel Insull, "Civilian Achievements of Illinois in the War," *Blue Book, 1919–1920*, 97–103, quotations on 100, 97. For open shops, see Walker, "Labor and the War," 112. See also Marguerite E. Jenison, *The War-Time Organization of Illinois* (Springfield: Illinois State Historical Library, 1923), 29–34, and *City Club Bulletin* 11 (May 13, 1918): 163–64, 166.

53. Frederick C. Luebke, *Bonds of Loyalty: German-Americans and World War I* (De Kalb: Northern Illinois University Press, 1974), 3–24; Victor Hemphill to John G. Oglesby, March 25, 1918, and Evangelical Lutheran St. Mark's Congregation of Steeleville to Frank O. Lowden, April 7, 1918, both in Lowden Papers.

54. For black Illinoisans and white attitudes, see Allan H. Spear, *Black Chicago: The Making of a Negro Ghetto, 1890–1920* (Chicago: University of Chicago Press, 1967), 12; James R. Grossman, *Land of Hope: Chicago, Black Southerners, and the Great Migration* (Chicago: University of Chicago Press, 1989), 168–75, 218–19; and Thomas Lee Philpott, *The Slum and the Ghetto: Neighborhood Deterioration and Middle-Class Reform, Chicago, 1880–1930* (New York: Oxford University Press, 1978), 293–301. For the East St. Louis riot, see Elliott Rudwick, *Race Riot at East St. Louis, July 2, 1917* (Carbondale: Southern Illinois University Press, 1964; reprint, New York: Atheneum, 1972). The Chicago riot is analyzed in The Chicago Commission on Race Relations, *The Negro in Chicago: A Study of Race Relations and a Race Riot in 1919* (Chicago: University of Chicago Press, 1922), and William M. Tuttle, Jr., *Race Riot: Chicago in the Red Summer of 1919* (New York: Atheneum, 1971).

55. For the frequency of strikes in Chicago, see Tuttle, *Race Riot*, 139. For the development of the Illinois Labor party and Walker's gubernatorial bid on the Farmer-Labor ticket, see Eugene Staley, *A History of the Illinois State Federation of Labor* (Chicago: University of Chicago Press, 1929), 361–73, and John H.

Keiser, "John H. Walker, Labor Leader from Illinois," in Donald F. Tingley, ed., *Essays in Illinois History* (Carbondale: Southern Illinois University Press, 1968), 91–92. Insull's hope is recorded in Insull, "Civilian Achievements," 103.

56. John M. Allswang, *Bosses, Machines, and Urban Voters* (Baltimore, Md.: Johns Hopkins University Press, 1986), 96–110; Tuttle, *Race Riot*, 200–207; Hutchinson, *Lowden*, 1: 378–80.

57. For the special legislative session and senatorial campaign, see William Hale Thompson to Lowden, February 9, 1918, Lowden Papers; Lowden to Thompson, February 16, 1918, Lowden Papers; and Clarence F. Buck to Lowden, August 29, 1918, Lowden Papers. A breezy account of Thompson's mayoral re-election campaign is provided in Lloyd Wendt and Herman Kogan, *Big Bill of Chicago* (Indianapolis, Ind.: Bobbs-Merrill, 1953), 161–71. For the streetcar strike and the public utilities commission, see Hutchinson, *Lowden*, 2: 400–404.

58. Undated statement, (August 1920), Lowden Papers.

59. Campaign letter signed by Thompson, September 10, 1920, John G. Oglesby Papers, Illinois State Historical Library, Springfield; Hutchinson, *Lowden*, 2: 453, 472–73.

60. *Peoria Transcript*, September 17, 1920, quoted in Hutchinson, *Lowden*, 2: 477.

61. L. H. Weldon to John G. Oglesby, October 17, 1920, Oglesby Papers.

62. Hutchinson, *Lowden*, 2: 476, 481; Franklin County Republican Central Committee to Lowden, October 2, 1920, Lowden Papers; Lawrence MacIntyre to Oglesby, October 16, 1920, Oglesby Papers.

63. Carroll H. Wooddy, *The Case of Frank L. Smith* (Chicago: University of Chicago Press, 1931; reprint, New York: Arno Press, 1974), 159.

64. *Chicago Daily News*, March 11, 1921; Gordon A. Ramsey to Lowden, March 17, 1921, Lowden Papers.

65. *Illinois: Progress, 1921–1928* (Springfield: State of Illinois, 1928), 8, 259; Wooddy, *The Case of Frank L. Smith*, 161.

66. "Illinois's Indicted Governor," *Literary Digest* 70 (August 6, 1921): 15; Wooddy, *Frank L. Smith*, 160–61 and passim.

67. For Small's interest-group appeals, see Wooddy, *Frank L. Smith*, 162. For good roads, see Conrad Rockel to Lawrence Y. Sherman, undated (1899), Lawrence Y. Sherman Papers, Illinois State Historical Library, Springfield, and *Farmers' Voice*, December 1, 1900. Bond issues and construction are discussed in *City Club Bulletin* 11 (October 7, 1918): 260–61, and *Progress*, 5, 105. See also Dunne, *Illinois*, 2: 330–31, and William G. Edens to Lowden, November 2, 1918, Lowden Papers. For a discussion of road building that places political decisions over technological innovations as the critical causative factor, see Eric H. Monkkonen, *America Becomes Urban: The Development of U.S. Cities and Towns, 1780–1980* (Berkeley: University of California Press, 1988), 164–76.

68. Edward S. Baker to Len Small, August 3, 1922, Len Small Papers, Illinois State Historical Library, Springfield.

69. *Progress*, 105–39.

70. Morton Keller, "The Politics of State Constitutional Revision,

1820–1930," in Harold M. Hyman, et al., eds., *The Constitutional Convention as an Amending Device* (Washington, D.C.: American Historical Association, 1981), 82.

71. For supporters of the convention, see Janet Cornelius, *Constitution Making in Illinois, 1818–1970* (Urbana: University of Illinois Press, 1972), 96. For the proposals, see Charles Woodward, "Constitutional Convention," *Blue Book, 1919–1920,* 306–8, and *City Club Bulletin* 13 (March 15, 1920): 65.

72. *City Club Bulletin* 11 (November 11, 1918): 285; Cornelius, *Constitution Making,* 98, 101; Janet M. Clark, "Constitution Making in Illinois: A Comparison of Two Conventions, 1920 and 1970" (Ph.D. diss., University of Illinois, 1973), 63.

73. Citizens' Association of Chicago to the Members of the Constitutional Convention of Illinois, June 23, 1920, Citizens' Association of Chicago Papers, Chicago Historical Society. City Club members are listed in *City Club Bulletin* 12 (November 10, 1919): 220. For the judiciary proposal, see *City Club Bulletin* 15 (October 16, 1922): 111. For limitation on Chicago representation, see *City Club Bulletin* 13 (June 28, 1920): 141.

74. *City Club Bulletin* 13 (December 13, 1920): 241.

75. Section 21 of "The Proposed New Constitution of Illinois," *Blue Book, 1923–24,* 294. For support of the initiative and referendum, see ibid., 349; *City Club Bulletin* 13 (March 15, 1920): 55–58, and Cornelius, *Constitution Making,* 104. Outrage at the rejection of the intitiative and referendum appears in Willis J. Spaulding, "Proposed Constitution Would Make Initiative and Referendum Forever Impossible in Illinois," *Illinois State Federation of Labor Weekly News Letter* 8 (November 4, 1922): 1, 3, copy in Victor A. Olander Papers, University of Illinois, Chicago. For Lowden's doubts, see Charles E. Woodward to Lowden, June 2, 1922, Lowden Papers.

76. Cornelius, *Constitution Making,* 103–16. Labor's objections are presented in *Illinois State Federation of Labor Weekly News Letter* 8 (October 7, 1922): 1–2, Olander Papers; ibid., (December 9, 1922): 1–4, Olander Papers; and John H. Walker to Alexander Howat, December 11, 1922, Walker Papers. For separate submission of articles, see *City Club Bulletin* 15 (June 5, 1922): 89–90, and Hutchinson, *Lowden,* 1: 322.

77. Straw poll in *City Club Bulletin* 15 (December 4, 1922): 137. For Small's opposition, see Cornelius, *Constitution Making,* 114, and "A Threat to All Liberties," unidentified newspaper clipping, Small Papers. For People's Protective League, see Dunne, *Illinois,* 2: 427–54. Returns by county are in *Blue Book, 1923–1924,* 791. For a modest endorsement of the constitution, see Ernst Freund, "A New Constitution for Illinois," *New Republic* 33 (December 13, 1922): 67–69.

78. Allswang, *Bosses, Machines, and Urban Voters,* 91–147. See also Harold F. Gosnell, *Machine Politics Chicago Model,* 2d ed., (Chicago: University of Chicago Press, 1968); Roger Biles, *Big City Boss in Depression and War: Mayor Edward J. Kelly of Chicago* (De Kalb: Northern Illinois University Press, 1984).

79. *State Journal-Register,* November 25, 1984. For a critique of pluralism, see

Dianne M. Pinderhughes, *Race and Ethnicity in Chicago Politics: A Reexamination of Pluralist Theory* (Urbana: University of Illinois Press, 1987).

80. Otis L. Graham, Jr., *An Encore for Reform: The Old Progressives and the New Deal* (New York: Oxford University Press, 1967), 180–81.

Chapter 8

1. Ray Ginger, *Altgeld's America: The Lincoln Ideal versus Changing Realities* (New York: Funk and Wagnalls, 1958; reprint, New York: New Viewpoints, 1973), 2.

2. Brand Whitlock, *Forty Years of It* (New York: D. Appleton, 1914; reprint, Cleveland, Ohio: Press of Case Western Reserve University, 1970), 95.

3. Important works on suffrage and reform include J. Morgan Kousser, *The Shaping of Southern Politics: Suffrage Restriction and the Establishment of the One-Party South, 1880–1910* (New Haven, Conn.: Yale University Press, 1974); Martin J. Schiesl, *The Politics of Efficiency: Municipal Administration and Reform in America: 1880–1920* (Berkeley: University of California Press, 1977); Bradley R. Rice, *Progressive Cities: The Commission Government Movement in America, 1901–1920* (Austin: University of Texas Press, 1977); Paul Kleppner and Stephen C. Baker, "The Impact of Voter Registration Requirements on Electoral Turnout, 1900–1916," *Journal of Political and Military Sociology* 8 (1980): 205–26; John F. Reynolds and Richard L. McCormick, "Outlawing 'Treachery': Split Tickets and Ballot Laws in New York and New Jersey, 1880–1910," *Journal of American History* 72 (March 1986): 835–58.

4. Herbert Croly, *The Promise of American Life* (New York: Macmillan, 1909; reprint, New York: E. P. Dutton, 1963), 340.

5. This treatment of Croly is drawn from Charles Forcey, *The Crossroads of Liberalism: Croly, Weyl, Lippmann and the Progressive Era, 1900–1925* (New York: Oxford University Press, 1961), especially 38–44.

6. Croly, *The Promise of American Life*, 454.

7. James T. Kloppenberg, *Uncertain Victory: Social Democracy and Progressivism in European and American Thought, 1870–1920* (New York: Oxford University Press, 1986), 384.

8. Ibid. See 383–85 for a discussion of Croly's *Progressive Democracy* and the perils of bureaucratic government.

9. Richard L. McCormick, "The Discovery that Business Corrupts Politics: A Reappraisal of the Origins of Progressivism," in Richard L. McCormick, *The Party Period and Public Policy: American Politics from the Age of Jackson to the Progressive Era* (New York: Oxford University Press, 1986), 342–46; Charles E. Merriam and Louise Overacker, *Primary Elections* (Chicago: University of Chicago Press, 1928), 60–66.

10. For a brief treatment of the coal strike, see George E. Mowry, *The Era of Theodore Roosevelt and the Birth of Modern America, 1900–1912* (New York: Harper and Row, 1958), 134–40. For the history of regulation, see Thomas K.

McCraw, ed., *Regulation in Perspective: Historical Essays* (Cambridge, Mass.: Harvard University Press, 1981), and Thomas K. McCraw, *Prophets of Regulation: Charles Francis Adams, Louis D. Brandeis, James M. Landis, and Alfred E. Kahn* (Cambridge, Mass.: Harvard University Press, 1984).

11. Wilson quoted in John Milton Cooper, *The Warrior and the Priest: Woodrow Wilson and Theodore Roosevelt* (Cambridge, Mass.: Harvard University Press, 1983), 254. For more on the Federal Reserve Act and the Federal Trade Commission, see Cooper, 233–35, and Arthur S. Link, *Woodrow Wilson and the Progressive Era, 1910–1917* (New York: Harper and Row, 1954), 45–53, 68–75.

12. Weber quoted in Kloppenberg, *Uncertain Victory*, 385. For the Railroad Commission of Wisconsin, see Stanley P. Caine, *The Myth of a Progressive Reform: Railroad Regulation in Wisconsin, 1903–1910* (Madison: State Historical Society of Wisconsin, 1970). Members of government boards and commissions were not the only public officials who drew on the expertise of interested parties. As Robert Wiebe has aptly commented, harried legislators ill equipped to untangle complex points at issue learned that "the reliable lobbyist had become an indispensable intermediary in representative government" (Robert H. Wiebe, *The Search for Order, 1877–1920* [New York: Hill and Wang, 1967], 184).

13. For disagreement over "corporate liberal" interpretations of railroad regulation, compare Gabriel Kolko, *Railroads and Regulation, 1877–1916* (Princeton, N.J.: Princeton University Press, 1965), and Albro Martin, *Enterprise Denied: Origins of the Decline of American Railroads, 1897–1917* (New York: Columbia University Press, 1971). The political sources of regulation are explored in Samuel P. Hays, "Political Choice in Regulatory Administration," in McCraw, ed., *Regulation in Perspective*, 124–54.

14. La Follette, Cummins, and progressive leaders from Minnesota, South Dakota, Nebraska, and Kansas are profiled in Russel B. Nye, *Midwestern Progressive Politics: A Historical Study of Its Origins and Development, 1870–1958* (East Lansing: Michigan State University Press, 1959; reprint, New York: Harper and Row, 1965), 190–224. For progressive leaders as politicians, see Wiebe, *Search for Order*, 178–79. For Jones and Johnson, see Hoyt Landon Warner, *Progressivism in Ohio, 1897–1917* (Columbus: Ohio State University Press, 1964), 22–41, 54–137. For Pingree as governor, see Melvin G. Holli, *Reform in Detroit: Hazen S. Pingree and Urban Politics* (New York: Oxford University Press, 1969), 185–218.

15. Wiebe, *Search for Order*, 190.

16. David P. Thelen, *Robert La Follette and the Insurgent Spirit* (Boston: Little, Brown, 1976), 19–41; Spencer C. Olin, *California's Prodigal Sons: Hiram Johnson and the Progressives, 1911–1917* (Berkeley: University of California Press, 1968), 25–26, 97, 101, 147, 170; George E. Mowry, *The California Progressives* (Berkeley: University of California Press, 1951; reprint, New York: Quadrangle, 1963), 136–38, 278–79.

17. For Nebraska, see Robert W. Cherny, *Populism, Progressivism, and the Transformation of Nebraska Politics, 1885–1915* (Lincoln: University of Nebraska Press, 1981), 146–48. For Davis and Vardaman, see Raymond Arsenault, *The*

Wild Ass of the Ozarks: Jeff Davis and the Social Bases of Southern Politics (Philadelphia: Temple University Press, 1984), and William F. Holmes, *The White Chief: James Kimble Vardaman* (Baton Rouge: Louisiana State University Press, 1970). Still useful on these matters is Albert D. Kirwan, *Revolt of the Rednecks: Mississippi Politics, 1876–1925* (Lexington: University of Kentucky Press, 1951).

18. Daniel T. Rodgers, "In Search of Progressivism," *Reviews in American History* 10 (December 1982): 116.

Selected Primary and Unpublished Sources

Manuscripts

CHICAGO HISTORICAL SOCIETY, CHICAGO

Chicago Teachers' Federation Papers.
Chicago Law and Order League Minutes and Reports.
Citizens' Association of Chicago and Municipal Voters' League Papers.
Walter F. Dodd Papers.
Illinois Manufacturers' Association Papers.
Mary E. McDowell Papers.
Agnes Nestor Papers.

ILLINOIS HISTORICAL SURVEY, UNIVERSITY OF ILLINOIS LIBRARY, URBANA

Cairo Democratic Central Committee Record Book.
Flagg Family Papers.
Walter C. Headen Papers.
Cyrus H. McCormick Papers.
John H. Walker Papers.
Woman's Christian Temperance Union, 10th Congressional District Records.
John Wesley Yantis Papers.

ILLINOIS STATE ARCHIVES, SPRINGFIELD

John P. Altgeld, Official Gubernatorial Correspondence.
John R. Tanner, Official Gubernatorial Correspondence.

ILLINOIS STATE HISTORICAL LIBRARY, SPRINGFIELD

Belleville Trades and Labor Assembly Records.
Bloomington Republican City Central Committee Minutes.

Waldo R. Browne Papers.
Charles S. Deneen Papers.
Joseph W. Fifer Papers.
Joseph Buckner Gill Papers.
Herman H. Kohlsaat Papers.
John G. Oglesby Papers.
Lawrence Y. Sherman Papers.
Len Small Papers.
Lawrence B. Stringer Papers.
John R. Tanner Papers.
Richard Yates, Jr. Papers.

STATE HISTORICAL SOCIETY OF WISCONSIN, MADISON

Raymond Robins Papers.

SPECIAL COLLECTIONS, UNIVERSITY OF CHICAGO LIBRARY, CHICAGO

William H. Anderson Papers.
Chicago Foreign Language Press Survey.
Ernst Freund Papers.
Frank O. Lowden Papers.
Charles E. Merriam Papers.

UNIVERSITY OF ILLINOIS-CHICAGO

Victor A. Olander Papers.

Newspapers

Camp Point Journal.
Champaign Daily Gazette.
Chicago Tribune.
Clayton Enterprise.
Illinois State Register.
Jonesboro Gazette.
Mendon Dispatch.
Peoria Daily Gazette.
Peoria Herald-Transcript.
Rockford Register-Gazette.
Sheffield Times.

CHICAGO FOREIGN LANGUAGE PRESS SURVEY

Abendpost.
Denni Hlasatel.

Dziennik Chicagoski.
Dziennik Zjednoczenia.
Dziennik Zwiazkowy.
Illinois Staats-Zeitung.
Narod Polski.
Polonia.
Svenska Amerikanaren.
Svenska Kuriren.
Svenska Tribunen-Nyheter.
Svornost.

Trade Journals, Proceedings, and Reports

American Issue.
Annals of the American Academy of Political and Social Science.
Annals of the American Political Science Association.
Anti-Saloon League of America. *Proceedings.*
Anti-Saloon League of Illinois. *Report.*
Anti-Saloon League Year Book.
Champion of Fair Play.
Charities.
Chicago Bureau of Public Efficiency. *Consolidation of Local Governments in Chicago.* January 1920.
Chicago Bureau of Public Efficiency. *The Nineteen Local Governments of Chicago.* December 1913.
Chicago Bureau of Public Efficiency. *Unification of Local Governments in Chicago.* January 1917.
Chicago Charter Convention. *Proceedings.*
Chicago Produce.
Chicago Teachers' Federation Bulletin.
Citizens' Association of Chicago. *Annual Report.*
City Club Bulletin.
Civic Federation of Chicago. *Bulletin.*
East St. Louis Commercial Club Messenger.
Education.
Educational Review.
Elementary School Teacher.
Farmers' Voice.
Illinois Agricultural Association. *Report.*
Illinois Manufacturers' Association. *Proceedings of the Annual Meeting.*
Illinois State Dairymen's Association. *Annual Report.*
Illinois State Federation of Labor. *Convention Proceedings.*
Illinois State Federation of Labor. *Weekly-News Letter.*
Manufacturers' News.

Margaret A. Haley's Bulletin.
National Conference on Charities and Correction. *Proceedings.*
Prairie Farmer.
Proceedings of the Academy of Political Science.
Proceedings of the National Municipal League.
Public Policy League Bulletin.
School Review.
The Survey.
Union Labor Advocate.

Government Documents

CHICAGO

Chicago Commission on the Liquor Problem. *Preliminary Report.* Chicago: December, 1916.
Report and Handbook of the Department of Health of the City of Chicago for the Years 1911 to 1918 Inclusive. Chicago: 1919.

ROCKFORD

Reports of the City Officers of the City of Rockford, Illinois, for the Fiscal Year 1895. Rockford: 1895.

ILLINOIS

Administrative Report of the Directors of Departments under the Civil Administrative Code.
Blue Book of the State of Illinois.
Board of State Commissioners of Public Charities. *Report.*
Bureau of Labor Statistics. *Labor Legislation in the 46th General Assembly of Illinois.* Springfield: 1909.
Bureau of Labor Statistics. *Report on the Cherry Mine Disaster.* Springfield: 1910.
Illinois Department of Agriculture. *Transactions.*
Illinois State Factory Inspector. *Report.*
Journal of the Illinois House of Representatives.
Journal of the Illinois Senate.
Proceedings of the Constitutional Convention of the State of Illinois Convened January 6, 1920. 5 vols. Springfield: 1920–22.
Report of the Bureau of Labor Statistics of Illinois.
Report of the Efficiency and Economy Committee Created under the Authority of the Forty-eighth General Assembly. Chicago: Windermere Press, 1915.
Report of the Employers' Liability Commission of the State of Illinois. Chicago: Stromberg, Allen, 1910.

Report of the Illinois Central Hospital for the Insane.
Report of the Illinois Northern Hospital for the Insane.
Report of the State Food Commissioner of Illinois. Springfield: 1911.

UNITED STATES

Department of Labor, Bureau of Labor Statistics. *Workmen's Compensation Laws of the United States and Foreign Countries.* Washington, D.C.: 1917.
Senate. *Election of William Lorimer: Hearings before a Committee of the Senate Pursuant to Senate Resolution No. 60 Directing a Committee of the Senate to Investigate Whether Corrupt Methods and Practices Were Used or Employed in the Election of William Lorimer as a Senator of the United States from the State of Illinois.* Senate Doc. 484. 62nd Cong., 2nd Sess. 9 vols. Washington, D.C.: 1912.

Unpublished Papers and Dissertations

Becker, Richard. "Edward Dunne, Reform Mayor of Chicago, 1905–1907." Ph.D. dissertation, University of Chicago, 1971.
Clark, Janet M. "Constitution Making in Illinois: A Comparison of Two Conventions, 1920 and 1970." Ph.D. dissertation, University of Illinois, 1973.
Collins, Cherry Wedgwood. "Schoolmen, Schoolma'ams and School Boards." Ed.D. dissertation, Harvard University, 1976.
Destler, Chester M. "The People's Party in Illinois, 1880–1896; A Phase of the Populist Revolt." Ph.D. dissertation, University of Chicago, 1932.
Dohn, Norman H. "The History of the Anti-Saloon League." Ph.D. dissertation, Ohio State University, 1959.
Duis, Perry. "The Saloon and the Public City, Chicago and Boston 1880–1920." Ph.D. dissertation, University of Chicago, 1975.
Fullinwider, James W. "The Governor and the Senator: Executive Power and the Structure of the Illinois Republican Party, 1880–1917." Ph.D. dissertation, Washington University, 1974.
Green, Paul M. "The Chicago Democratic Party, 1840–1920." Ph.D. dissertation, University of Chicago, 1975.
Keiser, John H. "John Fitzpatrick and Progressive Unionism 1915–1925." Ph.D. dissertation, Northwestern University, 1965.
Kelly, Alfred H. "A History of the Illinois Manufacturers' Association." Ph.D. dissertation, University of Chicago, 1938.
Komons, Nick A. "Chicago, 1893–1907: The Politics of Reform." Ph.D. dissertation, George Washington University, 1961.
McCarthy, Michael P. "Businessmen and Professionals in Municipal Reform: The Chicago Experience, 1877–1920." Ph.D. dissertation, Northwestern University, 1970.
Marks, Donald David. "Polishing the Gem of the Prairie: The Evolution of Civic

Reform Consciousness in Chicago, 1874–1900." Ph.D. dissertation, University of Wisconsin, 1974.

Murphy, Marjorie. "From Artisan to Semi-Professional: White Collar Unionism among Chicago Public School Teachers, 1870–1930." Ph.D. dissertation, University of California-Davis, 1981.

Philip, William Booth. "Chicago and the Downstate: A Study of Their Conflicts, 1870–1934." Ph.D. dissertation, University of Chicago, 1940.

Reid, Robert L. "The Professionalization of Public School Teachers: The Chicago Experience, 1895–1920." Ph.D. dissertation, Northwestern University, 1968.

Schneirov, Richard. "Haymarket and the New Political History Reconsidered: Workers' Class Presence in Chicago's Municipal Politics, 1873–1894." Paper delivered at the Organization of American Historians conference, New York, April 13, 1986.

Stark, Bennett S. "The Political Economy of State Public Finance." Ph.D. dissertation, University of Wisconsin, 1982.

Storm, William B. "An Analysis of the Illinois Agricultural Association as a Pressure Group for Farmers." Ph.D. dissertation, University of Chicago, 1951.

Straetz, Ralph A. "The Progressive Movement in Illinois, 1910–1916." Ph.D. dissertation, University of Illinois, 1951.

Tingley, Ralph R. "From Carter Harrison II to Fred Busse: A Study of Chicago Political Parties and Personages from 1896 to 1907." Ph.D. dissertation, University of Chicago, 1950.

Vecoli, Rudolph J. "Chicago's Italians prior to World War I: A Study of their Social and Economic Adjustment." Ph.D. dissertation, University of Wisconsin, 1962.

Wish, Harvey. "The Administration of Governor John Peter Altgeld of Illinois, 1893–1899." Ph.D. dissertation, Northwestern University, 1936.

Index

A Note on the Author

Thomas R. Pegram received a Ph.D. in 1988 from Brandeis University. He has taught at the Ohio State University and Suffolk University and is currently assistant professor of history at Loyola College in Maryland.